J
E
S

D0436591

NN

OTHER BOOKS BY AMITAI ETZIONI

From Empire to Community: A New Approach to International Relations
(New York: Palgrave Macmillan, 2004)

Political Unification Revisited: On Building Supernational Communities
(Lexington Books, 2001)

Winning Without War (Garden City, N.Y.: Doubleday, 1964)

How Patriotic Is the Patriotic Act? (New York: Routledge, 2004)

The Common Good (Cambridge, Mass.: Polity Press, 2004)

My Brothers Keeper: A Memoir and a Message (Lanham, Md.: Rowman
and Littlefield, 2003)

The Limits of Privacy (New York: Basic Books, 1999)

The New Golden Rule: Community and Morality in a Democratic Society
(New York: Basic Books, 1997)

The Moral Dimension: Toward a New Economics (New York: The Free
Press, 1988)

The Active Society: A Theory of Societal and Political Processes (New York:
The Free Press, 1968)

Comparative Analysis of Complex Organizations (New York: The Free
Press, revised edition, 1975)

SECURITY FIRST

AMITAI ETZIONI

Security First

FOR A MUSCULAR, MORAL FOREIGN POLICY

YALE UNIVERSITY PRESS   NEW HAVEN & LONDON

Copyright © 2007 by Amitai Etzioni.
All rights reserved.
This book may not be reproduced, in whole or in part, including illustrations, in any form
(beyond that copying permitted by Sections 107 and 108 of the U.S. Copyright Law and
except by reviewers for the public press), without written permission from the publishers.

Set in Scala and Scala Sans by Keystone Typesetting, Inc.
Printed in the United States of America.

Library of Congress Cataloging-in-Publication Data
Etzioni, Amitai.
Security first : for a muscular, moral foreign policy / Amitai Etzioni.
p. cm.
Includes bibliographical references and index.
ISBN 978-0-300-10857-6 (hardcover : alk. paper)
1. Security, International. 2. United States—Foreign relations. I. Title.
JZ5588.E86 2007
355′.033073—dc22
2007003748

A catalogue record for this book is available from the British Library.

The paper in this book meets the guidelines for permanence and durability of the
Committee on Production Guidelines for Book Longevity of the Council on Library
Resources.

10 9 8 7 6 5 4 3 2 1

SECURITY FIRST

OTHER BOOKS BY AMITAI ETZIONI

From Empire to Community: A New Approach to International Relations
(New York: Palgrave Macmillan, 2004)

Political Unification Revisited: On Building Supernational Communities
(Lexington Books, 2001)

Winning Without War (Garden City, N.Y.: Doubleday, 1964)

How Patriotic Is the Patriotic Act? (New York: Routledge, 2004)

The Common Good (Cambridge, Mass.: Polity Press, 2004)

My Brothers Keeper: A Memoir and a Message (Lanham, Md.: Rowman
and Littlefield, 2003)

The Limits of Privacy (New York: Basic Books, 1999)

The New Golden Rule: Community and Morality in a Democratic Society
(New York: Basic Books, 1997)

The Moral Dimension: Toward a New Economics (New York: The Free
Press, 1988)

The Active Society: A Theory of Societal and Political Processes (New York:
The Free Press, 1968)

A Comparative Analysis of Complex Organizations (New York: The Free
Press, revised edition, 1975)

AMITAI ETZIONI

Security
First

FOR A MUSCULAR, MORAL

FOREIGN POLICY

YALE UNIVERSITY PRESS   NEW HAVEN & LONDON

Copyright © 2007 by Amitai Etzioni.

All rights reserved.

This book may not be reproduced, in whole or in part, including illustrations, in any form (beyond that copying permitted by Sections 107 and 108 of the U.S. Copyright Law and except by reviewers for the public press), without written permission from the publishers.

Set in Scala and Scala Sans by Keystone Typesetting, Inc.

Printed in the United States of America.

Library of Congress Cataloging-in-Publication Data

Etzioni, Amitai.

Security first : for a muscular, moral foreign policy / Amitai Etzioni.

p. cm.

Includes bibliographical references and index.

ISBN 978-0-300-10857-6 (hardcover : alk. paper)

1. Security, International. 2. United States—Foreign relations. I. Title.

JZ5588.E86 2007

355'.033073—dc22

2007003748

A catalogue record for this book is available from the British Library.

The paper in this book meets the guidelines for permanence and durability of the Committee on Production Guidelines for Book Longevity of the Council on Library Resources.

10 9 8 7 6 5 4 3 2 1

For my son Michael Etzioni (1967–2006), his wife, Lainie,
their son Max (b. February 2005), and their daughter Maya Michal
(b. February 2007).

No father could have asked for a better son;
no son could have hoped for a better father;
no wife—for a more devoted husband;
no friend—for a more loyal other.

CONTENTS

PREFACE   ix

PART I: SECURITY FIRST: FOR US, THEM, AND THE WORLD   1

   A. A Principled, Realistic Approach   2

   B. Policy Implications   8

   C. Implications for Failing States   14

   D. Implications for Newly Liberated Nations   19

PART II: THE LIMITS OF SOCIAL ENGINEERING   37

   A. A Primitive Art   37

   B. The Lessons of Democratization   42

   C. The Lessons of Reconstruction and Economic Development   58

   D. The Lessons of Nation-Building   76

PART III: THE TRUE FAULT LINE: WARRIORS VS. PREACHERS   85

   A. Fewer Enemies, More (Potential) Allies: The Global Importance of Illiberal Moderates   85

   B. Violent vs. Persuasive Beliefs in Three Religious Belief Systems   103

C. Violent and Persuasive Beliefs in Secular Theories of Social Change   127

D. Violent and Persuasive Beliefs in Islam   134

E. Illiberal Moderate Muslims: The Global Swing Vote   140

PART IV: THE IMPORTANCE OF MORAL CULTURE   152

A. The Soft Underbelly of Security   152

B. Religion's Key Role in U.S. Foreign Policy   173

PART V: GROUNDS FOR INTERVENTION   193

A. Whose Security? The Responsibility to Protect   193

B. Responsibility as an International Communitarian Principle   199

C. A Second Duty: To Prevent?   204

PART VI: SECURITY REQUIRES A NEW GLOBAL ARCHITECTURE   208

A. The Third Ought to Be First   209

B. Who Will Attack?   220

C. A Strategic Shift: From Controlled Maintenance to Deproliferation   234

D. Muscular, Moral Power   243

NOTES   249
ACKNOWLEDGMENTS   295
INDEX   297

Rarely have more profound changes in American foreign policy been called for than today. Democratization as the rallying cry of America's mission in the world has essentially failed, and global respect for American power has dwindled. This book, however, is not one more lengthy criticism of past policies—whether those of the Bush administration or of its predecessors, or of the conflicting Democratic agendas. I file here a brief for the future, about that which must next be done on the international front.

My argument is that there are strong principled *and* pragmatic reasons to turn U.S. foreign policy 180 degrees: instead of assuming that democratizing nations such as Iraq and Afghanistan will turn them into guardians of the peace and reliable friends, we must aim first to ensure *basic* security, both for its own sake and for the sake of the democracy that might gradually grow in these faraway places. Moreover, I show that not only in these two nations, but also in many other parts of the world, security drives democracy, while democracy does not beget security.

Instead of threatening nations such as North Korea and Iran with "regime change," we must understand that rogue states will not surrender their nuclear weapons and the means to produce them—until we pledge not to topple their governments. Leverage used against Russia and China to pressure them to democratize should instead first be deployed to encourage them to contain the spread of nuclear weapons and related technologies. And instead of taking us into nations such as Grenada, Panama, or Haiti, the "Security First" approach to foreign policy would have taken us into Rwanda and Darfur—where millions of lives were and still are threatened.

I appreciate that my thesis according security priority over democratization challenges a long-established foundation of U.S. foreign policy. After all, America has pursued democratization at least since Woodrow Wilson's presidency, if not earlier. Both liberals and neo-conservatives—whatever the differences in the practical means they have advocated—have shared this fundamental goal. John F. Kennedy's administration, for instance, promised $20 billion over a decade to Latin American countries that implemented democratic elections as well as land reform and fairer taxation policies.[1]

To be clear, I am not suggesting that the United States go back to its Cold War policy of installing pro-Western dictatorships. But at the same time it must be acknowledged that liberal democracy cannot be imposed at gunpoint, most assuredly not on societies with little history that would prepare them for it, nations without the tradition of a free press and civil liberties, and without the institutions of a flourishing civil society. Before these prerequisites to liberal democracy can be established, there must be basic security, a measure of social peace, and a stable government. This often means that, in working with those whose political and religious beliefs diverge sharply from our own, what matters most is that they condemn violence (as, for instance, Grand Ayatollah Ali al-Sistani did in Iraq). I call these voices and those who heed them "Illiberal Moderates." Their ranks include many millions of people—arguably most of the world's population—who are opposed to the use of force abroad and at home but do not necessarily favor our liberal-democratic form of government. They may well become our allies in bringing about, first and foremost, a world order free from terrorism and nuclear threats; one in which broadly more democratic forms of governments can gradually take shape. I cannot stress this point sufficiently; if we seek to democratize the world, at least initially most of the world will resist or not cooperate—if we aim to provide security for one and all, the majority of the nations and the citizens of the world will share this goal. (Details follow in Part III.)

I can practically hear critics chastising me for being "anti-democracy" and opposing human rights. Actually I merely hold that democratization cannot lead; it must follow the establishment of basic security. Such a realization in no way diminishes the respect for and the merit of liberal democratic regimes. Similarly, I will show that democracy cannot be rushed, must be largely homegrown, and is best promoted by nonlethal means. Listing these prerequisites is not to diminish the value of democratization, but to point to ways in which it actually can be promoted rather than merely paraded as a lofty goal.

Some may argue that the fundamental change of foreign policy I call for is already occurring. More and more, observers recognize that the governments of Iraq and Afghanistan are unable to take root despite the fact that they are the products of free elections; that basic security must first be provided. However, bringing democracy to those who lack it continues to be the lead argument employed to justify the policies pursued overseas by the Bush administration, many of its allies, and even its critics. Thus, for instance, addressing midshipmen at the Naval Academy in Annapolis in September 2006, President Bush continued to maintain, "Advancing the cause of freedom and democracy in the Middle East begins with ensuring the success of a free Iraq. Freedom's victory in that country will inspire democratic reformers from Damascus to Tehran, and spread hope across a troubled region."[2] Similarly, during a September 2006 speech at the United Nations, Bush addressed the Iranian people directly, stating: "You deserve an opportunity to determine your own future. The greatest obstacle to this future is that your rulers have chosen to deny you liberty."[3] In December 2006 Bush stated: "The only way to secure a lasting peace for our children and grandchildren is to defeat the extremist ideologies and help the ideology of hope, democracy, prevail."[4] The same sentiment was repeatedly echoed by British Prime Minister Tony Blair. Daniel J. Mahoney, a friendly critic of President Bush, notes, "The administration's official rhetoric continues to be marred by a tendency to treat modern democracy as a self-evident desideratum, even as the regime 'according to nature.' "[5] John Kerry, less friendly to the president, makes a related criticism: "Our valiant soldiers can't bring democracy to Iraq if Iraq's leaders are unwilling themselves to make the compromises that democracy requires."[6]

When Francis Fukuyama departed from the Neo-Con camp in his 2006 book and critiqued the ideology of the global march to democracy which he had done so much to formulate and foster, he called for different means to promote democracy but refused to give up democratization in favor of an alternative rationale for U.S. foreign policy.[7] The change proposed amounts to not much more than playing the same tune—on a different instrument.

To the extent that providing security overseas has been elevated as an American foreign policy priority, this reprioritization is considered a limited, pragmatic adjustment—for instance, taking into account that one cannot conduct elections without some modicum of security—rather than a matter of principle. And while the need to provide security has, on pragmatic grounds, become obvious in Iraq and Afghanistan, it has not been used to guide the ways in which the United States deals with Iran, North Korea, Russia, and weak and failing states that have nuclear bombs (or the materials from which these can be made) and that terrorists could obtain. In the following pages I spell out the deep and numerous changes in foreign policy that follow, once the central importance of security overseas truly is recognized and embraced.

There are those who argue that democratization is not competing with security, which should constitute the dominant U.S. foreign policy goal, but, on the contrary, that democratization is the shortest and surest way to security; that democracies do not fight one another; and that security cannot be provided without democratic political settlements. Much of Part I is devoted to responding to these claims. For now I just note that if Iraq and Afghanistan, Iran and North Korea could be turned into peaceful liberal democracies, this would indeed greatly enhance global security —but this does not mean that these and other nations *can* be democratized in the foreseeable future. For the nations at issue, it matters little if the democracy-peace theory is a valid one; it is simply irrelevant or at least inapplicable. Hence other avenues must be found to advance security from terrorism, rogue and failing states, and, above all, nuclear arms.

The basic policy change I advocate, focusing on security instead of on democratization, is not only in the best interest of the United States and its allies, but is also in the interest of most if not all other peoples. The moral precept I draw on to justify a Security First approach—the Primacy of Life— calls for securing the lives not just of Americans, Britons, Italians, or Poles, but also of the citizens of other nations, whether they are rich or poor, south or north, allies or not. Of course I do not assume that America can provide the same level of security to a child living in Djibouti as to a child in Dallas. However, U.S. decisions and actions in the international forum best show that it has a higher purpose than merely serving American interests; that the United States seeks to promote peace, or global security. Service to the common good of the global community is one major way to turn a pragmatic and realistic foreign policy into one that is also principled and legitimate. (Others have focused on obeying international laws and working via established international institutions, especially the United Nations.) Acting legitimately, we shall see, is both morally appropriate (allowing us to face ourselves at the end of the day, and justifying ourselves to our children and all others) and an essential element of a successful foreign policy. It is effective *and* right, pragmatic *and* principled.[8]

In societies long subject to tyranny, the moral culture that provides an essential source of social order is often severely damaged or absent. The sudden removal of the police state in such nations—whether in the former U.S.S.R., in post-Taliban Afghanistan, or in post-Saddam Iraq— tends to bring with it an explosive growth of antisocial behavior, in the form of murders, drug abuse, rape, and kidnapping. Hence basic security must be established. But in the longer run, security forces alone cannot maintain order; newly liberated societies require citizens with a strong set of shared ethics and moderate political opinions to legitimate the new, hopefully better order. Hence, beyond providing security, America has a role to play in helping such societies to reform and renew their moral cultures, rather than merely to liberalize their governments (the subject of Part IV).

Readers often want to know whether a book is liberal or conservative. This one is neither. I was among the sixty intellectuals who signed "A Letter from America" shortly after September 11, 2001, which justified a forceful response to terrorism. That letter was derided by a large number of German intellectuals from the left and elicited a well-reasoned response from a still larger group of Saudi professors and writers.[9] Several of those who signed the original "Letter from America" later issued a second letter supporting the invasion of Iraq. I was not on that list. And in a book I completed in 2003, *From Empire to Community*, I warned, drawing on my sociological studies and on having lived in the Middle East for twenty-one years, that Iraq would turn into another sort of Vietnam. I mention this to reiterate that I am not siding with one ideological camp or the other; rather I try to be guided by empirical evidence and moral reflection.

The book has a subplot: an examination of the psychological factors that deeply affect the ways many Americans view and deal with the world. Evidence presented in the following pages indicates that American foreign policy suffers from a "Multiple Realism Deficiency Disorder" (MRDD), or a "realism deficiency," for short.

America's realism deficiency is most manifest in the assumptions, whether stated or unstated, that we are omnipotent, that our society has achieved the final form of political organization and realized the conditions for human happiness, that we are more powerful than we actually are, especially when it comes to engineering desired changes in faraway nations. Whether the United States sets out to liberalize the Middle East or to convert scores of nations to prosperous market economies, we often appear to assume that we have the right and ability to remake the world in our own image. The level which that *un*realism has reached among many Neo-Cons and their followers in the White House and on the Hill was highlighted when Charles Krauthammer gently chastised his allies for overreaching in their rush to democratize the world. He argued that although "democratic globalism" should be "the ends and means of American foreign policy," it must be "targeted, focused, and limited." By this he meant that the United States can only "come ashore" in order to democratize "that Islamic crescent stretching from North Africa to Afghanistan."[10] As I see it, this scaled-back mission is still highly unrealistic.

The illusion that the United States can reengineer nation after nation is not limited to democratization; we have also repeatedly committed ourselves to "reconstruct" numerous nations, including some like Afghanistan, which were never "constructed" in the first place. We have pledged our resources to attempt to build peaceful, multiethnic, pluralistic societies in places such as Kosovo and Bosnia, and to curtail corruption in scores of developing nations, among other worthy but utopian goals. In the following pages, I show that these excessive ambitions are not only impossible to realize, but that their wanton pursuit actually undermines the more practical work, of that which could be accomplished.

MRDD is also manifested in the ways the United States and its allies view and characterize the enemy. To call them *mildly paranoid* is to use strong language. Nevertheless it seems to be the proper diagnosis, as there is a widely held belief that the West is engaged in an epic "clash of civilizations." The 9/11 attacks on our homeland are still viewed by all too many as having confirmed this thesis, first advanced by Bernard Lewis and Samuel Huntington. Others have attempted, not always with great success, to reduce the scope of the enemy we must confront, variously defining it as fundamentalism, Islamism, radical or extreme Islam, or—a bit vaguely—the "evil-doers." I will show in the following pages that the ranks of those we must fight are actually much smaller.

Realism deficiency is further manifested in the tendency to break the world down into starkly opposing sides, the simplistic notion that "if you are not with us—you are against us." Such a point of view lumps all those—and there are many—who do not care much for either side, with the opposition. Indeed, U.S. foreign policy has too often tended to treat all those opposed to human rights and liberal democracy, all believers in faiths other than our own political creed, as irrational and as a mortal threat. I will show that many of those who are today "nonaligned" in the Muslim world are in fact potential allies. There are legions upon legions of them—in all civilizations.

In short, *while we are much less powerful than we believe; we are also much less beleaguered than we assume.*

I use the term "realism" primarily in the psychological sense, pertaining to those who face facts and the world as it is rather than as they might like it to be—and not in the ways it is used in international relations theory.[11] U.S. reality-testing—our ability to approach the world as we find it and not on the basis of overblown fears or vain desires—needs to be much augmented. I do not mean that the United States ought to pursue a strategy based on assessments of military might, economic assets, control of oil, and other such "real" factors. Such factors have their place but this kind of realism, ironically, is an unrealistic guide to foreign policy. That is the case because it ignores the increasingly important role played by moral culture and religion within societies and in international relations. (When the French foreign minister, Pierre Laval, suggested that Stalin stop repressing Eastern European Catholics, the Soviet leader replied, "The Pope? How many divisions has he got?"[12] Well, the Pope's "divisions" turned out to be more powerful than Stalin's regime.)

Many who grant that morals have a role to play in domestic affairs—

attending to questions such as which tax policies are fair and what do we owe the poor and sick—will nevertheless doubt that they have any place in international relations. This seems a curious opinion. Suffice it to point to one recent change in international relations to show that moral precepts *do* have a major role to play in global affairs, and that this change has major bearings on our security. For centuries, nation-states agreed—and many of their citizens accepted as a guiding principle—that one government must not interfere in the internal affairs of another; the rights of national sovereignty must be respected. However, this principle is now being recast—in order to provide more security (for us and for the rest of the world). Morally speaking, *the bar for intervention in a nation's internal affairs has been set much lower.*

How low the bar for intervention should be set is a critical question for the evolving, post–Cold War global architecture. Are armed interventions now to be undertaken routinely in places like the Sudan, the Congo, and many others, to prevent genocides and ethnic cleansing? Are they also to be considered legitimate when they are initiated to prevent a nuclear attack or preempt support for terrorism? Are they allowed if, for instance, allies of the Taliban were to take over the government of Pakistan, and gain control of its nuclear arsenal? Are such armed interventions legitimate if they seek to promote liberal democracy in general and liberate nations still dominated by tyrants? (See Part V.)

My contention—that an emphasis on basic security is not merely a pragmatic argument but also a principled one—is part of a much more encompassing assertion that politics can pass both tests: what we ought to do and what it is in our interest to do, tend to converge. Many assume that these considerations are antagonistic. They have an image of a nation that *either* follows its self-interest, securing its borders and going to war, for instance, to ensure the flow of oil, or alternatively of a nation that seeks to serve international causes such as stopping the spread of HIV infection and starvation in Africa. Yet legitimate acts—those seen to conform to international law and to universally binding moral principles—are, as a rule, much more effective and less costly than those without the backing of this "soft power."[13] Consider when the United States and its allies rolled Saddam's troops out of Kuwait in 1991: this military intervention enjoyed broad approval, other nations (including Muslim ones) readily sent their troops to help and paid most of the costs. The contrast with the 2003 invasion could not be clearer. In short, there is room for the voices of "principled realists" who are also "pragmatic idealists."[14] Count mine among them.

My argument is certainly not that the tension between what is and what ought to be can be eliminated once and for all. I'm merely making the case that in the present day, in which more and more people follow international affairs, travel, participate in nongovernment organizations (NGOs), and study overseas, unreasonable laws and policies generate considerable resistance, i.e., have "real" consequences. In other words, the gap between the principled and the pragmatic is diminishing. Consequently it is as pragmatically necessary now, and perhaps more so than it ever has been, that a nation's foreign policy be a legitimate one.

THE PARTS OF THIS BOOK

Part I spells out the main thesis of the book in pragmatic and moral terms, namely that the Security First thesis is both realistic and principled. It then uses several short case studies to show what happened when this approach was ignored in Iraq and Afghanistan, and the reasons Security First would have served us and the people involved better in these newly liberated nations.

A case study of the development in Libya—as the poster child of deproliferation—suggests a Security First way of dealing with Iran and North Korea. A study of U.S.-Russian relations highlights the same basic thesis: we should not lead with demands for democratization, but for security. The same holds, we shall see, with regards to other failed and failing states, such as Pakistan, Nigeria, and the Congo.

Part II draws lessons from the grave limitations of the dubious art of social engineering, which is the basis of regime change. What are the foreign policy lessons that follow if many regimes cannot be democratized, in short order, especially not by foreign powers? The same key question—what are the foreign policy implications of the precarious state of social engineering?—is raised with regard to two other major realms: economic development and nation-building (in the sense of keeping disparate tribes and communities as members of one nation). Part II uses a case study of recent developments in Kosovo to support the conclusions reached—namely that our social engineering policies suffer from a high degree of realism deficiency.

Most importantly, Part II finds a course between the unrealistic course of democratization and the unethical one of supporting oppressive regimes. It entails a return to a once-popular theory of stages of development, drawing on the lessons of the short-lived, ill-fated Weimar Republic.

Part III builds on the observation that there is a global conflict about "values" or "culture" similar to the one we lived through during the Cold War—and not merely a clash of interests in oil, territories, or some other such "real" factors. However, it shows that by far the most important divide on the international level is not between our civilization and others, but between all those who legitimate violence and all those who renounce it. To illustrate this divide, Christian, Judaic, and Hindu beliefs are studied, as well as two secular belief systems. The analysis shows that on this essential point *Islam is no different*. Moreover, this line of analysis finds many more potential allies in other parts of the world than does the quest for liberal democrats. Illiberal Moderates, it turns out, hold the global swing vote. The same line of analysis also urges the United States to work more with religious groups and movements of the moderate kind.

Part IV shows that security rests not merely on guns and cops but also on a shared moral culture, one that makes most people behave most of the time (to follow the laws of the land) because they believe this is what they ought to do. We see that, when and where such a culture is absent, it must be recast in nations as different as former communist states and former theocracies of the Taliban's ilk. Part IV asks how this can be done.

Part V focuses on a major moral development in international relations of great importance for two key security issues: the prevention of attacks on our homelands and the prevention of genocide and ethnic cleansing. It shows that the principles under which military action and humanitarian intervention are justified have changed profoundly, and how they ought to be further recast.

Part VI takes it for granted that the provision of basic security is the paramount human good, upon which all other political goods depend, and draws out the implications of this observation for foreign policy. One major question arises: If we realize that we are much less powerful than we tend to assume, which threats deserve the most urgent attention?

SECURITY FIRST

PART I

Security First: For Us, Them, and the World

The next leaders of our nation—the next president, Congress, and opposition leaders—will have to come to terms with the demise of democratization as a rationale for U.S. foreign policy. Now is the time to determine which leitmotif can legitimate the U.S. role in the world. It is becoming ever more evident that democracy cannot be fostered by force of arms, especially not in poorly prepared nations; however, it is much less clear which overarching rationale could replace democratization as a justification for the foreign policy of the United States, more generally the West, and its various allies in the East.

I suggest that Security First foreign policy, drawing on the principle of the Primacy of Life, is both principled and pragmatic. At its core is the recognition that all people have an interest in and right to security, understood to include freedom from deadly violence, maiming, and torture. I argue in the following pages that this right is more fundamental than all the others, including legal-political and socioeconomic rights. It ought to be treated as a class unto itself.[1]

The preceding statements should not be taken to mean that I hold that the United States or other nations in the free world would be safer if their citizens gave up their various rights. These nations have effective police forces, domestic and foreign intelligence services, and powerful armies to protect themselves. True, in some limited matters even these states may need to be accorded some additional powers. However, this is called for only if there is compelling evidence that these powers are truly needed, and only if they are carefully monitored, with those who wield them being held accountable for any abuses.[2] The places where basic security is most lacking are in the Middle East, in failing states, and in newly liberated states. Hence in the following pages I outline the implications of a Primacy of Life–based foreign policy not just for establishing security in Iraq and Afghanistan, but also for conflicts with rogue states (especially North Korea and Iran); for dealing with failing states (especially Russia); and for assessing under what conditions armed humanitarian interventions are appropriate.

One central point runs through all these applications of the core Primacy of Life rationale: instead of assuming that democratization will provide a political process for resolving various inter- and intragroup conflicts—and the terrorism they help to foment—in places such as Iraq and Afghanistan, a Security First foreign policy is centered on precisely the opposite assumption, that democratization first requires security. Rather than assuming that democratizing rogue states will exorcise their aggressive inclinations, the United States and its allies should promise to forego coercive regime changes, and largely let internal forces lead domestic political progress.

All of these points require elaboration. However, I must note that when I refer to "security," I mean *basic* security, the conditions under which most people, most of the time, are able to go about their lives, venture onto the street, work, study, and participate in public life (politics included), without acute fear of being killed or injured—without being terrorized. To seek full-fledged security, to obviate all threats, to end fear, puts us on the slippery slope at the bottom of which is a police state. Often "basic" will have to do.[3]

CHAPTER A. A PRINCIPLED, REALISTIC APPROACH

Tragic Choices and the Role of Values

Neo-Con as well as liberal conceptions of the international reality share one key flaw: they greatly overestimate the extent to which one nation, even a superpower and even if accorded the full blessings of the United Nations, can reengineer the regimes of other nations. Neo-Cons believe that forced democratization is possible, as has been attempted in Iraq and Afghanistan, and before that in numerous places such as Haiti and the Congo. Liberals believe in the transformative power of foreign aid, debt relief, trade concessions, and support for reformers, peaceful regime changes that have been attempted in scores of nations. The tragic fact of the international reality is that both approaches to long-distance, large-scale social engineering have failed in most places.[4] Liberal democracy is a delicate plant that grows only slowly under favorable conditions; it needs to be cultivated carefully by those who aim to live under it rather than by those who wish it for them.[5]

Moreover, we cannot hide from the fact that painful and costly sacrifices must be made to achieve "merely" basic security. Ethnic cleansing often cannot be stopped without bringing home body bags (as the Dutch found out in Srebrenica). Enticing nations to give up nuclear arms or ambitions and cease supporting terrorism often entails tolerating illiberal or undemocratic regimes for the time being, provided that they do not engage in genocide, ethnic cleansing, or other atrocities.[6] More generally, utopian goals of the sort pursued in Iraq and Afghanistan are best avoided, and promises and expectations are best moderated. It must be assumed that, whatever the pursued international project, it is bound to be tough sledding all the way.

To put the same crucial point somewhat differently, the brutal international reality often requires following what might be called a "second-worse" course, in order to avoid having to negotiate the worst one—a long way from the notion that our choices are between the best and the second-best. In short, ask not what international order you desire—but which you can hope to help achieve.

The preceding point is essential to all that follows. It is often ignored by politicians who make grand promises that cannot be realized, and by many individuals—especially can-do, positive-thinking, optimistic Americans—who shy away from hard choices. To highlight this point here are the results of an informal survey I conducted. When I asked fellow Americans for their reaction to a news item that someone was in a car accident, his leg was pinned down, and it had to be amputated so that he could be evacuated, the first response of practically all those I queried was, "Was there no way to save the leg?!" This was said often with considerable anger or dismay. I grant that this is a decent, humane response. One empathizes with the victim and wishes him, well, a leg. However, if such sentiments cause one to delay making the tough choices, causing the victim to bleed out, what has started as a well-meaning, good-hearted reluctance to act turns into a death sentence. It is my thesis that this is approximately what is happening in most places when foreign powers seek to impose regime change in the name of spreading their own, arguably preferable, political institutions and corollary values.

Facing the fact that international reality requires making very difficult, even tragic, choices, and accepting very imperfect outcomes, is not to deny that our ideals play a key role in this realm, similar to the one they play in domestic affairs.[7] It is typically assumed that realism is the opposite of idealism, in that it is not encumbered by extensive moral deliberations. In fact, the kind of principled but realistic foreign policy I advocate (as distinct both from a policy of Realpolitik and from naïve idealism) has moral foundations all its own. It avoids squandering many thousands of lives and scarce resources in the pursuit of elusive or illusionary goals; it avoids delays in coping with conflicts that result from pursuing such goals; it avoids making promises that cannot be met, thus avoiding the loss of credibility abroad and at home—credibility that is essential for a successful foreign policy; and it avoids the hubris implicit in attempting to deliver more than one is capable of delivering, however sincere the effort may be. Thus a principled, realistic foreign policy might accept, for instance, a unilateral withdrawal by Israel from Gaza, even though a withdrawal following a negotiated agreement with the Palestinians was preferable. More importantly, such a policy would accept that bad regimes can improve their behavior in one area or another, especially in the foregoing of nuclear ambitions, without regime change—however desirable such a change might be.

The importance of a principled foreign policy, one that is morally legitimate and is widely perceived as such, has increased over recent decades and will continue to increase in the foreseeable future. Public opinion, whose support is often essential for a successful policy, is influenced by moral perceptions. Since at least World War II, the proportion of the public that is educated and involved in public affairs has grown steadily in free societies. In recent decades citizens have been entering politics in many parts of the world where they had previously been largely excluded. Globalization, the spread of worldwide communications (from CNN to al-

Jazeera), the Internet, and NGOs are among the forces that lead people to think and act "globally." In this sense, one can now speak of a "global public opinion" that helps to determine which policies enjoy legitimacy.[8]

A nation can choose to disregard global public opinion. However, such disregard will have real costs, as the U.S. government discovered during and after the 2003 invasion of Iraq. While the United States paid for only about 20 percent of the 1991 war that forced Saddam out of Kuwait, it has been obliged to cover nearly all of the vastly higher costs of the 2003 invasion. South Korea, an important U.S. ally, turned from being supportive to being neutral, and Turkey refused the use of its land as a springboard for the invasion. Thus, for pragmatic as well as principled reasons, acting legitimately has become an ever-more-important component of an effective foreign policy. "Realism" and "idealism" are converging—a trend that in some ways renders the conduct of foreign policy more challenging. But hence the special importance of careful deliberations about what should be our first priority.

Moral Grounds for the Security First Approach

Security commands moral preeminence. There is a tendency to view advancing security as antithetical to civil liberties and individual rights, and to warn that in the quest for security a nation might become a police state. These are indeed valid concerns; every society must constantly give heed to the extent to which the protection of life can be advanced without undermining rights. However, one should not overlook the primacy of the right to security. Not to be killed, maimed, or tortured is the most basic of human rights. Significantly, life *precedes* both liberty and the pursuit of happiness in the Declaration of Independence's lineup of the purposes for which government is instituted.

The idea that all rights and privileges need not be lumped together and that they can be ranked hierarchically is a common one. The most widely followed distinction is between legal-political rights (such as the right to vote and freedom of speech) and socioeconomic rights (such as the right to education, housing, and health care). Security is usually considered a legal-political right, but I draw an additional distinction here between it and all the other legal-political rights. This step is necessary to enable me to formulate the proposition that on both principled and pragmatic grounds, the right to security is of the highest order, and its successful provision is more urgent than advancing other rights—in chaotic, failing states, in dealing with rogue states, or in situations where genocide or ethnic cleansing is being committed. It is widely agreed that the first duty of the state is to provide security—on the domestic front. With the international reality being even more brutal than the internal conditions of many nation-states, this dictum applies with special force to the priority that must be accorded to forming a stable global order.

Much of ethics deals with the question of which good deed is to trump the other when two good deeds potentially conflict, rather than with determining which deed is good and which is not. Saving life and limb on the one hand, and advancing the full panoply of legal-political and socioeconomic rights on the other, are both goods. One is naturally inclined to refuse to choose between them and to insist that both can be served. But the question remains: what is to be done if both cannot be served well simultaneously?

In such all-too-common situations, from the streets of Moscow in the early 1990s to those of Baghdad from 2004 on, the main reason that the right to security takes precedence over all others is that all the others are contingent on the protection of life—*whereas the right to security is not similarly contingent on any other rights*. It sounds simplistic to state that dead people cannot exercise their rights, whereas those who are living securely at least have the possibility of exercising more rights in the future. However, it is still an essential truth: when and where the right to security is violated, all other rights are violated as well. (I refer here, of course, to true threats to life, not to drummed-up or manufactured threats or to antiterrorist demagoguery.) The Security First principle does not favor curtailing well-established freedoms for marginal gains in security in London, Paris, or New York. But it does command first priority in places where people cannot walk the streets, work, study, or worship without fear of being bombed or kidnapped, tortured or maimed.

The claim that we ought to rank the right to security above all other rights is also supported by the observation that in the criminal codes of all decent societies, the penalties for murder, maiming, and torture are much greater than those for petty theft, discrimination, and other crimes. Such codes reflect the hierarchy of values which societies have developed through the course of history. These hierarchies reflect the heritage of a society's public philosophy, its judicial precedents, religious and secular ethical precepts, and, in more recent, democratic ages, the dialogues of its citizens with their representatives, and the findings of social scientists. This is also the reason that the prevention of genocide is now considered a much more legitimate reason for intervening in the internal affairs of another nation,[9] than is, say, democratization.

The Empirical Case for a Security First Policy

The better that life is protected, the stronger the support is for nonsecurity rights—and not the other way around, as has been suggested by many supporters of the drive for global democratization, as well as by those who argue that regime change is required to make nations into peaceful members of the international community.

A review of public opinion polls concerning attitudes toward civil liberties following 9/11 indicates that shortly after al-Qaeda's attack on America, nearly 70 percent of the public was strongly inclined to give up various constitutionally protected rights in order to prevent further attacks. However, as no new attacks occurred on American territory and a sense of security gradually was restored, as revealed by the return of passengers to air traffic, support for rights increased. By 2004–05, about 70 percent of Americans were more concerned with protecting civil rights than with enhancing security. (Granted, the polls are not fully comparable.)[10]

Along the same lines, if an American city were wiped out tomorrow in a nuclear terrorist attack, rights would surely be suspended on a large scale (as the writ of *habeas corpus* was suspended in the United Kingdom at the height of the Nazi attacks, and in the United States during the Civil War). In short, this evidence, too, shows that the better that security is protected, the more secure are our other rights.

The same relationship between the right to security and all other rights was evident during the period in which violent crime rates were very high in major American cities. For instance, when Los Angeles police chief Daryl Gates suggested that the riots following the Rodney King verdict might have been stopped had police officers "gone down there and shot a few people," many sympathized with his viewpoint.[11] In recent years, as violent crime has significantly declined in American cities, a police chief who favored a policy that disregarded rights in such a summary way would likely be dismissed before the day was over. The safer that people are, the more concerned they will be for their other rights.

Finally, evidence shows that liberal-democratic regimes have been undermined primarily by their failure to provide for basic public needs, such as security, and not by the gradual erosion of legal-political rights, as is so often assumed. The main case in point is the Weimar Republic. From the extensive literature written on the question of what caused the fall of the Weimar Republic and the rise of the Third Reich, it is reasonable to conclude that liberal democracy lost legitimacy because it failed to address peoples' need for physical and economic security.[12]

Another example is post-Soviet Russia. Although Russia has never met the standards of a liberal democracy, a good part of what was achieved under Mikhail Gorbachev and Boris Yeltsin has gradually been eroded as Russians responded to their alarmingly high levels of crime. President Vladimir Putin, who has been moving his government in a strongly authoritarian direction, is widely regarded in Russia not as too powerful but as not powerful *enough,* because many still believe, and believe correctly, that basic security is lacking.

In short, moral arguments and empirical evidence support the same proposition: in circumstances under which a full spectrum of rights cannot be advanced simultaneously—a common situation—basic security must lead.

CHAPTER B. POLICY IMPLICATIONS

The proliferation of nuclear weapons, it is widely recognized, constitutes a grave threat to our security and to global peace. If Iran and North Korea continue to develop their nuclear programs, as well as long-range missiles, they will endanger our allies (from Saudi Arabia and Israel to South Korea and Japan) and, in the longer run, American and European homelands as well. Moreover such proliferation will push other nations to develop nuclear weapons, increasing the chances that states eventually will confront one another in the deadliest fashion imaginable. And the more that such weapons are available, the more likely they are to end up in the hands of terrorists.[13]

Although few doubt that deproliferation serves basic security well, the question remains: is the best way to achieve deproliferation through regime change, or by granting those nations that seek nuclear weapons iron-clad security guarantees? I examine this issue by first reviewing one of the great successes of diplomacy, the deproliferation of Libya, and its implications for democratization. I then apply the lesson of Libya to other rogue states, including North Korea and Iran.

The Libya Lesson

In 2003, the United Nations lifted the economic sanctions previously imposed on Libya following its agreement to accept responsibility for the Pan Am Flight 103 bombing and to pay $2.7 billion in damages.[14] Toward the end of the year, Libyan leader Muammar Qaddafi dramatically announced that his nation was voluntarily dismantling its nascent nuclear program and other weapons of mass destruction (WMD) programs, as well as committing Libya to fight international terror. Indeed, Libya's centrifuges and mustard gas tanks, as well as some SCUD missiles, were loaded onto a U.S. ship and removed. Sensitive designs of nuclear warheads were transported on a chartered 747 to the United States. Thirteen kilograms of highly enriched uranium were moved to Russia (America has no blending-down facilities for uranium), and chemical weapons shells were destroyed. Tripoli has been credited with helping the United States to shut down a global black market for nuclear weapons technology run by the Pakistani scientist A. Q. Khan. In short, major contributions to international security were made on two most important fronts: nuclear disarmament and prevention of terrorism.

If Libya may be said to have earned an A in deproliferation, it earned at best a D in advancing human rights. It remains a crime to criticize the government or "the Leader," and Law 71 forbids opposing the Revolution, the September 1969 uprising in which Qaddafi seized power. Although the infamous People's Court and the People's Prisons were abolished in 2005, this amounts largely to window dressing, as the People's Prisons inmates were shipped to other prisons. Torture is outlawed, but several allegations of torture remain unresolved, including those concerning a 1996 uprising at the Abu Salim prison. In another troubling case, five Bulgarian nurses and a Palestinian doctor, charged with infecting 426 children with HIV, were tortured until they confessed, and were then sentenced to death.[15] Freedom House, a U.S.-based group, continued to list Libya as one of the five worst nations in stemming the flow of free information. For all these reasons, rather than rewarding Libya for its contributions to global security, human-rights groups demand that the international community continue to limit Libya's access to the world's markets and to put off normalizing relations.[16]

How the international community responds to Libya's nuclear disarmament and cessation of support for terrorism—without a shot being fired—is of considerable importance, given that most analysts strongly agree that the world would be much more secure if other nations would follow the same course, especially Iran and North Korea. By recognizing that Libya has met international *security* standards, other rogue nations will note that if they move in the same direction, efforts to bring down their authoritarian regimes will cease. They will be given full access to various international institutions, all sanctions will be lifted, and investment will be encouraged, although promotion of democratization by non-lethal (educational and cultural) means will continue. That is, if a threatening nation meets the security standards set by the United States and its allies and largely supported by other parts of the international community, without necessarily meeting human-rights standards, it would reap substantial rewards. By contrast, if these rogue nations are told that they will be restored to good standing as members of the international community only if they also replace or drastically alter the form of their regimes, they will be much less likely to consider abandoning their programs of developing weapons of mass destruction and their support for terrorism. The first strategy is in line with the Security First approach; the second—with the Neo-Con notion that democratization drives security.

Unfortunately, from the Security First viewpoint advanced in this volume, it took three years after Libya chose to change course for the United States to restore full diplomatic relations with the Qaddafi government, to remove it from the list of nations that sponsor terrorism, and to lift the sanctions imposed on nations on that list. When I wrote in 2003 that Libya should be treated as the poster child of deproliferation and a model for other rogue states,[17] I was widely criticized. However, in 2006 Secretary of State Condoleezza Rice stated that Libya served as an "important model" for the way the disputes with North Korea and Iran could be resolved.[18] Better late than never.

Some argue that there was much less to the Libyan program of WMD than meets the eye, or at least as it had been built up by the press. Hence, they argue, Libya does not deserve much of a reward or recognition for giving up whatever programs it had. Even if this were the case, much is to be gained by nations giving up their mere ambitions to launch such programs. In the case of Libya, however, its WMD program was far from trivial.

Libyan scientists at the Rabta facility made, in a ten-year period ending in 1990, about twenty-five tons of sulfur mustard gas, a chemical weapons agent. Libya imported two types of centrifuges from A. Q. Khan's global nuclear black market, the aluminum P-1s (Pakistan-1), and the more advanced P-2s. In fact, these and other items Libya purchased from the Khan network would have sufficed to produce ten-kiloton bombs. Experts figured that "Libya could have produced enough fuel to make as many as 10 nuclear warheads a year."[19]

Among the terrorist groups Libya sponsored in one way or another were the IRA, the ETA Basque separatist group in Spain, and the Abu Nidal Organization. However, as of 2003 Libya had not only withdrawn all such support, but closely collaborated with the U.S. war against terrorism.

Still, the United States dragged its feet. Libyan officials expected, after such a radical change in their conduct, that Washington would generously reward them. To their disappointment, only a small U.S. liaison office was established in Tripoli. In fact, some now believe that "Washington's temporizing toward Libya has undermined its nonproliferation victory and has reinforced rogue-state conviction that disarmament will not get one far with Washington. . . . Giving up WMD alone should have been enough to warrant normalization of relations with the U.S."[20] Several former diplomats stated that "the Bush administration risked losing the terrorism list as a useful diplomatic tool if it didn't illustrate ways countries and organizations could successfully remove themselves."[21] Above all, the U.S. delay in rewarding Libya, and setting it up as a model for the world, occurred largely because the commitment to democratization has continued to be a U.S. foreign policy leitmotif, and Libya was making rather little progress on this front. Although the United States continues—and should continue—to foster respect for human rights in Libya by persuasive means, it did move in the right direction when it finally recognized and rewarded the grand contribution of Qaddafi's rejection of WMD and terrorism to our security and to world peace.[22]

Applying the Libya Lesson to Iran and North Korea

As of mid-2006, the United States has continued openly seeking regime change in both Iran and North Korea.[23] The United States continued to condemn the government of the mullahs in Iran, barely acknowledged Iran's contributions to curbing al-Qaeda, and increased funds for Iranian groups seeking to undermine the mullahs' regime. Meanwhile, in the case of North Korea, U.S. opposition to communist forms of government has a long pedigree. Cold War, anticommunist precepts are now applied in current condemnations of North Korea's violation of human rights. In dealing with both nations, the military option for disposing of the regimes has repeatedly and often been discussed within and around the Bush administration. All this fits the democratization-drives-security assumption.

What would a change of strategy, to Security First, entail? Both Iran and North Korea are reported to have sought nonaggression treaties or security guarantees from the West as part of a deproliferation deal. If these deals could be struck and faithfully carried out, they would in effect entail "trading" deproliferation, verified by vigorous inspections and by denying these nations their own weapons-grade fuel production, in exchange for leaving their authoritarian regimes in place.

The fact that Iran and North Korea have sought out such deals is not widely known and hence deserves some documentation. Selig Harrison of the Woodrow Wilson International Center for Scholars reported that Iran, during 2004 negotiations with the "European Three," offered guarantees that its nuclear program was "exclusively for peaceful purposes," in exchange for an understanding that the West would provide "firm commitments on security issues."[24] Similarly, North Korea has repeatedly put security guarantees on the table as one of its conditions for halting nuclear-weapons programs.[25]

There is no way to determine a priori whether Iran and North Korea made these offers in good faith or merely to gain time in order to further expand their nuclear programs. From their viewpoint, however, one can readily see the reasons these regimes might seek such a deal. Both nations are facing military bases belonging to the United States and its allies close to their borders. If the United States and its allies were willing to remove those bases and provide assurances that they would neither attack directly—nor indirectly subvert these harshly authoritarian regimes, one can see why their governments might be willing to give up their nuclear weapons programs. The only way to find out if this analysis is valid is to offer a deal.[26]

One thing, however, is clear on the face of it: one can hardly expect these governments to consider seriously a deal that would remove from power the very same people who must agree to the deal—which is exactly what regime change entails. It would be like demanding that Bush turn over the reins to Al Gore, or replacing the U.S. Constitution with the Islamic *shariah!*

The deal I suggest—if you deproliferate and cease supporting terrorism (the Libya formula), I will leave your regime intact—is less bitter than it might initially seem to some. It would not mean that the West must engage in some kind of Faustian bargain and give up its liberal soul to purchase security. Regime change is coming on its own in Iran soon enough, and has already come in some form in most communist states— North Korea, granted, is an exception. In Iran, many reporters have found that the majority of the population rejects the mullahs' strict theocratic rule and would prefer modern political and economic life along Western lines (from consuming alcohol to sporting popular consumer brands).[27] In spite of the mullahs' bellicose foreign policy pronouncements, their authority is waning. And there is much more conflict among various factions of mullahs than is commonly acknowledged in the Western media. Furthermore, Iran has started to liberalize its economy, which in the longer run tends to undermine politically authoritarian regimes. Also note that aggressive U.S. posturing damages the reformers' credibility. Iranian reformers have made it clear that U.S. announcements supporting liberal democracy in Iran discredit their efforts and even threaten their lives. (The United States declared in 2006 that it had set aside $85 million to help dissidents bring about regime change.)[28] Akbar Ganji, an Iranian journalist who was arrested after returning home from a conference in Berlin in 2000, wrote shortly after his release:

> For six years, I had been behind bars on account of investigative articles I had written about the assassinations of dissident intellectuals. On numerous occasions, my interrogators accused me, and the entire opposition to clerical rule, of being dependent on the United States. They even claimed that CIA agents with suitcases full of dollars routinely came to Tehran to distribute cash to members of the opposition, including reformists who supported the former president, Mohammad Khatami. Some of the interrogators took these propaganda claims seriously and asked

prisoners about the location of these dollar-filled suitcases. . . .
[W]e have . . . learned that we have to gain our freedom ourselves, and that only we can nourish that freedom and create a
political system that can sustain it.[29]

Indeed, when the CIA tried to undermine the Islamists in Somalia in the
struggle for Mogadishu in early 2006, the Islamists won.[30]

Finally, we must face the fact that no matter how much money and
effort the United States and its allies expend, they cannot make such
nations into liberal democracies. As we have seen time and time again,
the West can easily topple Saddam or the Taliban, but it cannot easily
found a liberal-democratic regime in their place. Hence, there is little to
be lost and much to be gained by providing security guarantees and other
rewards in exchange for vigorous and verified deproliferation, and an end
to harboring, financing, and equipping terrorists.

CHAPTER C. IMPLICATIONS FOR FAILING STATES

The most important change in the way we understand international relations since the 2001 attack on the U.S. homeland, and following the
attacks on the Madrid train station and the London buses and Underground, is that security is threatened by what political scientists like to call
"non-state actors," many of which are terrorists. The term "non-state
actors" helps to signal that we have been used to thinking about international security in terms of nations concluding treaties with each other,
developing international institutions such as the United Nations, "balancing" various powers, and so on—arrangements all based on relationships
between self-interested, sovereign states. In effect, even after 9/11, much
more attention has been paid to the threats posed by Afghanistan, Iraq,
Iran, and North Korea, than by the terrorists themselves.[31]

Unlike non-state actors, states have governments with which other
states can negotiate or, if all else fail, that they can be threatened militarily.
States are presumed to be able to enforce agreements and control their
own borders and citizens. In contrast, terrorists have no clear address,
symbolized by the fact that they wear no uniforms. Al-Qaeda maintains a
loose network of groups in places as different as the Afghan-Pakistani
border, Indonesia, the Philippines, Somalia, and the United Kingdom. In
short, ensuring security when contending with non-state actors requires

major changes in strategy. Some entail the introduction of new *domestic* security measures, which I have explored elsewhere.[32] Some do concern the ways we deal with other nations—but many of these states are not in fact the kind that traditional international relations theory envisions. Today many of the nations we must contend with are failed or failing states, in which the government cannot compel obedience from its citizens, states in which dangerous non-state actors can run amok. Such states are ideal havens for terrorists and, as we shall see, are also often major sources of nuclear bombs and the materials from which they can be made. Regime change here entails nation-building of the highest order, turning failing governments into viable, effective ones. As I show in Part II, most of these efforts have failed, as is all too evident in the post-invasion situations of Iraq and Afghanistan, which were turned from authoritarian regimes into failed ones. Security calls for a different approach to failing states.

Russia: The Wrong Priority

The Security First policy indicates that our first, second, and third interest in Russia is ensuring that loose nuclear arms and materials do not fall into the wrong hands. Before I show that this is the exact opposite of the policy which the United States has been and is still pursuing, I briefly list the reasons why Russia is considered, by practically all the leading experts on nuclear terrorism, far and away the gravest threat to international security. The threat is not that Russia itself will attack the United States or that its government will arm terrorists, but that Russia, as a failing state, will be unable to prevent inadvertent nuclear proliferation or the arming of terrorists.[33]

The Russian federal government is consistently unable to implement its policies. Corruption is widespread, as are alcoholism and drug abuse, while individual entrepreneurs, "oligarchs," mafiosi, and military officers —a whole plethora of non-state actors—wheel and deal in an atmosphere reminiscent of the Wild West.

Securing Russia's numerous and sizable nuclear facilities is the mission of the Interior Ministry, whose troops are drawn from the pool of people rejected for service in the army, which has very low standards to begin with. Chechen terrorists were able to bribe Interior Ministry border guards so they could get, fully armed, into the school in Beslan, leading to the massacre of 344 people, including many children. Two Chechen widows, wearing suicide belts, bribed their way onto Russian airliners and blew themselves up. It is only a matter of time before someone bribes his way into the poorly guarded facilities in which material needed to make nuclear bombs is stored.

As if this were not troubling enough, many of Russia's ten thousand or so tactical nuclear weapons are reported to be positioned close to Russia's southern borders, shared with several unstable, predominantly Muslim nations. Moreover, these arms are under the control of unreliable local commanders.[34]

In spite of all these threats, the United States in its dealings with Russia has put much more emphasis on democratization and promoting human rights than on securing or blending down nuclear materials and safeguarding or dismantling nuclear arms. U.S. officials have kept up a steady drumbeat, at the highest level, on the liberal-democracy theme, and have struck but few notes on nuclear security. For instance, Vice President Cheney declared at the Vilnius conference in May 2006: "America and all of Europe also want to see Russia in the category of healthy, vibrant democracies. Yet in Russia today, opponents of reform are seeking to reverse the gains of the last decade. In many areas of civil society—from religion and the news media, to advocacy groups and political parties—the government has unfairly and improperly restricted the rights of her people."[35]

In March 2006 President Bush said, "Recent trends [in Russia] regrettably point toward a diminishing commitment" to democratic freedoms and institutions.[36] A press report that followed the speech stated, "Bush made clear he has differences with President Vladimir Putin on his increasingly authoritarian stand on issues such as political, religious, and press freedoms and the emergence of democracies on Russia's borders."[37] And Condoleezza Rice said in February 2006, "We are very concerned, particularly about some of the elements of democratization that seem to be going in the wrong direction."[38]

John V. Hanford III, U.S. Ambassador-at-Large for International Religious Freedom, stated that U.S. strategy in Russia is "to promote awareness of and respect for the entire range of human rights, including freedom of religion." He also said, "Although the majority of Russians feel free to worship, many religious minorities have encountered restrictions and harassment, including some of those that are registered [in accord with Russia's 1997 law on Freedom of Conscience and On Religious Associations]."[39]

Barry F. Lowenkron, U.S. Assistant Secretary for Democracy, Human Rights, and Labor, denounced Russia's new laws regarding NGOs: "The experience of nations worldwide has shown that a flourishing civil society —especially the activism of NGOs—is essential to reaching democratic goals. The Bush administration shares the concerns of this Commission that civil society in Russia is under increasing pressure. Recent months have seen raids on NGO offices, registration problems, visa problems for foreign NGOs, and intimidation of NGO leaders and staff. These measures have disrupted the work of key NGOs and have had a chilling effect on Russian civil society."[40]

The State Department's 2004 human-rights report asserts: "In Russia changes in parliamentary election laws and a shift to the appointment, instead of election, of regional governors further strengthened the power of the executive branch. . . . Greater restrictions on the media, a compliant Duma, shortcomings in recent national elections, law enforcement corruption, and political pressure on the judiciary also raised concerns about the erosion of government accountability."[41]

And Senator Richard Lugar, chairman of the Senate Foreign Relations Committee, stated in February 2005: "In recent months, the Kremlin has taken action to stifle public dissent and political opposition. Rival political parties have been suppressed, the election of regional governors was cancelled and most of the media has been brought under state control. This pattern of behavior has spilled into the Russian government's handling of the economy."[42] Numerous other similar statements by U.S. officials could be cited.

In contrast to the extent to which Russian democratization has been promoted, issues concerning nuclear security have been raised only rarely and in a low-key manner. This is in spite of the fact that Russian cooperation is vital to prevent terrorists from getting their hands on nuclear arms and materials.

One of the few occasions on which this issue was raised on a high level was during negotiations leading to the February 2005 U.S.-Russia conference in Bratislava, in which presidents Bush and Putin participated. During these negotiations the United States sought to include the conversion of civilian reactors in Russia that use weapons-grade uranium (WGU) to low-grade uranium (LGU), from which bombs cannot be made. When Russia demurred, this crucial item was omitted. Even this occasion was used to berate Russia about human-rights violations rather than pressure it to safeguard its tactical nuclear weapons and fissile materials or blend them down.

Two senators made sure that no one misunderstood what the leading U.S. priority was for the Bratislava summit. Senator Sam Brownback (R-KS) and Rep. Christopher H. Smith (R-NJ) wrote: "The Bush-Putin summit comes at a time when the Kremlin is on the offensive. It is moving to contain the burgeoning democracy in the former Soviet Union. . . . We must not ignore the fact that human rights, civil and religious liberties and media freedom have been gravely undermined on Mr. Putin's watch. The deteriorating human-rights trends give cause for serious concern. . . . The Bratislava summit will provide a timely opportunity for the president to underscore this point face to face with his Russian counterpart."[43] Most devastating, the Nunn-Lugar program, which is dedicated to deproliferation, has basically not been increased compared to what it was before 9/11. It continues to be one of the smallest U.S. security programs. (For discussion of details see Part VI.)

As I see it, Putin might be willing to agree to much tighter controls on Russia's nuclear materials and arms if the proper incentives were offered; such controls add to his own security and have only small political costs. He is extremely unlikely, on the other hand, to reverse the numerous undemocratic measures he has introduced. The reason is elementary: if he moves significantly in this direction, he endangers his own power and the small amount of stability he has managed to secure for his country. Here we see another major example of the ways wanton pursuit of democratization undermines security. The opposite ranking of priorities should be followed.

In Part VI, I return to Russia, the main source of nuclear materials and of the small nuclear arms terrorists may use, when I discuss which security measures should take priority over others. Here I have merely shown that regime change has been given much higher priority in dealing with Russia than has promoting security directly.

Russia is not the only failing state that poses a nuclear threat. There are major concerns about nuclear weapons in Pakistan, a nation whose government might be overthrown by violent Islamists overnight. Also, materials from which nuclear bombs can be made, both weapons-grade uranium and plutonium, have been found in places such as Nigeria and Egypt. In fact, much of this material was provided by the United States (and the U.S.S.R.) and most recently by China.[44] However, the reason these threats have not been properly tackled is not only the wanton quest for democratization, but also the improper priorities in security matters. Hence I return to this issue in Part VI.

A typical American response at this point would be, "Why not do both? Why not deproliferate *and* democratize?" The fact is that even superpowers have limited leverage over failing states, and hence priorities must be set. Such prioritization calls for according much higher standing to measures that directly lead to nuclear security than possibly getting there at some unknown future date via democratization. (Democracies do not exactly rush to up the nuclear arsenal.)

CHAPTER D. IMPLICATIONS FOR NEWLY LIBERATED NATIONS

As late as 2004, it was still widely agreed that liberal democracy was on the march and that the United States could and should lead this historical trend. The trend was said to favor the West and world peace because democracies do not attack other democracies.[45] Moreover, providing newly liberated nations such as Iraq and Afghanistan with liberal-democratic institutions was held to be an effective means of providing security, because conflicts would henceforth be resolved politically, rather than violently in the streets.

By the end of 2005, however, it became increasingly clear, though not yet incorporated into the main elements of American foreign policy, that "the world" is not democratizing. Democratic-peace theory may hold for truly liberal democracies, but does not do so for societies which are democratizing—often a violent and unstable process.[46] Moreover, liberal forces have been slipping in Russia, Latin America, parts of Africa, and elsewhere. It also has become increasingly clear that there is in fact little the United States can do to rush democratization along. Also, Iraq has taught us that the provision of basic security is essential to the development of liberal-democratic institutions, not the other way around; postwar Germany, Japan, and Italy all followed this sequence, as did Turkey and Mali, although these latter nations still have a considerable way to go before they conform to Western standards.

The Lessons of Afghanistan and Iraq

From the viewpoint of advocates of democratization, the United States has been moving both Iraq and Afghanistan in the right direction.[47] In both countries U.S. military offensives quickly toppled authoritarian, oppressive governments. In Afghanistan, an assembly composed of prominent Afghans selected one of their own, Hamid Karzai, as president, a choice subsequently validated by free and open elections. Despite some accusations of fraud, his election, as well as the 2005 parliamentary elections, were verified by the United Nations as fair and equitable. It is estimated that as many as three quarters of Afghanistan's ten million eligible voters participated, a much higher proportion than those who regularly participate in American elections. Also in 2004, a constitution was drafted and ratified.

Continuous efforts have been made in Afghanistan to overcome rule by domineering warlords and replace them with local elected officials, or to co-opt them into the new national government. In that spirit, for instance, Ismael Khan was moved from his position as a regional warlord in Herat to Kabul, to become a minister in the national government. In Iraq, the United States worked hard to incorporate regional militias, linked to specific ethno-religious groups such as the Shias and the Kurds, into a single national army.

In line with the democratization script, shortly after overthrowing Saddam in 2003, the U.S. military turned over the reins of control to an American civilian. L. Paul Bremer served as the head of the Coalition Provisional Authority (CPA) for approximately one year, after which he was succeeded by an Iraqi, the interim prime minister, Iyad Allawi. In April of 2005, following Iraq's first post-Saddam elections, Ibrahim al-Jaafari and his Islamic Dawa Party assumed control of Iraq's government. Much like in Afghanistan, the threat of insurgent disruption did little to deter Iraqi voters. Even the disaffected Sunni population had a high turnout. In December of 2005, al-Jaafari's coalition again won in national elections. Thus in mid-2006 the democratic scenario had in theory made considerable progress: liberated Iraq had a ratified constitution, a freely elected parliament, and a national government that gained the approval of the parliament.

In the process, the United States succeeded in getting the nascent governments of Iraq and Afghanistan to enshrine in their constitutions several Western, liberal principles (alongside several Islamic ones). The foremost of these was a broad respect for human equality. Article 14 of Iraq's constitution states, "Iraqis are equal before the law without discrimination because of sex, ethnicity, nationality, origin, colour, religion, sect, belief, opinion or social or economic status." The freedoms and rights section of the Iraqi constitution resembles a Western bill of rights. The same is true of the Afghan constitution: in its protection of equal rights, freedom of speech, religion, and assembly, it is a document that could not fail to please many a Western liberal. In just a few short years, Afghanistan had moved from the rule of the Taliban to a constitutional rule, under which, according to the constitution's Article 44, "The state shall devise and implement effective programs for balancing and promoting of education for women, improving of education of nomads and elimination of illiteracy in the country." Article 83 mandates that two women from each province serve in Afghanistan's lower house of parliament. (Article 47 of the Iraqi constitution states: "The elections law aims to achieve a percentage of women representation not less than one-quarter of the Council of Representatives members.") In a sense, women's rights are better protected in these nations than in the United States, where no such requirements exist and the proportion of women in Congress is lower than those required in Afghanistan and Iraq.

The United States and its allies also worked hard in both countries to develop various elements of a civil society: training journalists in the ways of a free press, helping the formation of literally hundreds of NGOs, providing new textbooks for newly constructed schools, and so on.[48] Thus, as has often been claimed by Neo-Cons and the Bush administration, these nations were well on their way toward democratization, which in turn was to end the insurrections as political outlets were provided to resolve sectarian and other conflicts.

The same developments read dramatically differently from a Security First viewpoint. Democratization, such as it was, has not ensured security, and much of it was disingenuous to boot. The violent insurgency that broke out after President Bush optimistically proclaimed the end of major combat operations in Iraq on May 1, 2003, while standing in front of a banner reading "Mission Accomplished," has, by the end of 2006, claimed almost three thousand American lives and tens of thousands of Iraqi lives. Many more have been severely wounded. Not only has the insurgency raged undiminished since 2003, it has seen *increasing* sectarian violence, even in previously calm areas such as Basra. With each announcement of "progress" on the political front, a secure Iraq seems like an ever-more distant goal. In short, the democratization-drives-security scenario has not panned out, to put it mildly.

To digress briefly: prior to Israeli independence in 1948, the Jewish community in British Palestine was engaged in a war of national liberation. Its diplomatic representatives and underground forces sought to make the British cede control of the area to the Jewish community, and thus accord it an opportunity to invest the Jewish people, as an ethno-religious community, in a state. The underground forces were politically divided. One, called the Palmach, in which I served, was close to the social-democratic labor party, Mapai, to which David Ben-Gurion and Golda Meier belonged. The other, Irgun, was close to the right-wing Heruit, predecessor to Likud. The Palmach's strategy was to destroy the bridges and police stations and other assets that the British used, but often only after they were warned to leave. The Irgun, on the other hand, directly attacked British personnel; in one of its major operations it blew up part of the King David Hotel in Jerusalem, which served as a British headquarters.

Soon after the founding of the State of Israel, Ben-Gurion feared that these political factions would follow their own agendas. He therefore decided—in the midst of a war against seven invading Arab armies, during which casualties were very high and the survival of Israel was far from assured—to send my unit to surround the main contingent of the Irgun, demanding that they disarm and join the newly formed Israeli Defense Force. The Irgun very reluctantly disbanded. Next the Palmach was dissolved, leaving only one Israeli armed force—one loyal to the national, democratically elected, government.

All the conditions that made this kind of nation-building possible in Israel are lacking in Iraq and Afghanistan. The members of the different political factions in Israel had a strong, shared commitment to Israeli nationhood, and they saw the danger of the invading Arab armies as vastly exceeding in importance their domestic rivalries. Ben-Gurion was a highly charismatic and effective statesman; no one claimed that he was a puppet manipulated by a foreign government or that foreign influence was shaping the institutions of the new Israeli state. In short, both the Irgun and the Palmach were hard-pressed to find legitimate reasons to refuse to disband. The United States probably expected similar developments in the wake of the fall of Saddam and the Taliban, but by all indications such national unity remains very elusive. Here the Ben-Gurion strategy, of rapid nation-building under fire, cannot be followed.

By disbanding the Iraqi army and purging all Ba'ath Party officials from the government (two national forces already in place), and by attempting to suppress regional loyalties of the ethnic militias, the United States has generated a power vacuum in Iraq that is inimical to both security *and* democratization. During his first days in office, L. Paul Bremer ordered the total dismantling of the Ba'ath Party apparatus, which entailed the removal and permanent ban from public life of everyone who had held one of four party ranks. One hundred and twenty thousand Iraqis, including thousands of doctors, teachers, and numerous local leaders, were cast out of a job.[49] Bremer also dismissed four hundred thousand Iraqi soldiers, disregarding U.S. military advice.[50] Many of those purged actively opposed the U.S.-sponsored transitional government. Ostensibly modeled on de-Nazification, "de-Ba'athification" failed to take into account that the Allies left many low-level Nazis in power in order to avoid precisely the sort of power vacuum that has occurred in Iraq. And that the German military was defeated decisively, whereas the Iraqi military was merely disbanded—many taking their arms with them. The lack of manpower, of "boots on the ground," has repeatedly been identified as a postwar failure that led to the breakdown of security. In an often-used example, the Iraq National Museum was looted in April 2003. Undermanned and unable to secure any U.S. troops to assist in guarding the facility, the museum staff was powerless to prevent it.

The new Iraqi army and police force ran into severe difficulties. These included extensive penetration by insurgents; massive desertion when under fire or when deployed in parts of Iraq beyond the soldiers' home region; the use of national units as sectarian death squads; pervasive corruption and gross incompetence. True, here and there some progress has been made, but by the end of 2006 these new forces could not provide even elementary security.

The violence and chaos which have followed have undermined confidence in democratic institution-building. They have also driven many middle-class families out of the country, thus removing one of the major facilitating factors of democratization.[51]

In Afghanistan security too has been poor and declining. The U.S. State Department's Bureau for International Narcotics and Law Enforcement Affairs (INL) was charged with the task of building a new Afghan police force. INL was able to train a large number of police officers quickly in a handful of regional training centers, but at the price of not training them thoroughly—and without sustained support they fell back into old bad habits.[52] As in Iraq, expectations for the Afghan police have fallen short of what has been accomplished: "Five years after the fall of the Taliban, a joint report by the Pentagon and the State Department found that the American-trained police force in Afghanistan is largely incapable of carrying out routine law enforcement work, and that managers of the $1.1 billion training program cannot say how many officers are actually on duty or where thousands of trucks and other equipment issued to police units have gone."[53] By the end of 2006 Karzai was often referred to as the "mayor of Kabul." He rarely dared to venture outside the national capital, and within it he traveled only when surrounded by heavily armed American bodyguards. In effect much of the nation is ruled by warlords. An Indian reporter puts it well: "In theory, democracy has been restored and reconstruction has begun after two decades of civil war. In practice, the country remains in a mess. The bad news is that the reach of the government is feeble, and it cannot control thousands of bandits raiding travellers, or powerful warlords (many of whom are provincial governors). . . . Max Weber defined the state as an entity that has a legal monopoly on the use of force. That is, the state can legally tax, jail and execute people, but nobody else can. By that definition, Afghanistan has a multitude of states in the form of warlords."[54]

The warlords have huge militias that hold an estimated one hundred thousand soldiers. The poorly equipped Afghan National Army by contrast numbers only thirty-seven thousand. The militias are used by warlords not just for control of their territories but also to exact revenue. The biggest source of legal revenue in Afghanistan is customs duties. All the main import customs points, including those in Herat, Kandahar, Mazar, and Jalalabad, are controlled by local warlords. As a result, the national government has been pathetically dependent on foreign aid to run the country and to pay salaries. The Indian reporter concludes: "For most Afghans, peace and security is the top priority. Large sections of the west and south, especially the areas bordering Pakistan, are ruled by the guns of warring factions, including the Taliban. People cannot move safely on highways for fear of gunmen. Half a dozen provinces are out of bounds to U.N. staff, so dangerous are conditions. No economic development can take place without security, and Afghans need this above all."[55]

Attempts to replace, marginalize, or co-opt the regional warlords have often backfired. To return to Ismael Khan, his successor resigned within a year when he could not provide the same services Khan had provided the people of the region. Sectarian riots broke out between Shias and Sunnis, which Khan had formerly been able to prevent. Although Westerners thought his rule repressive, he was nevertheless popular in Herat for his ability to maintain order and security and bring in revenue.[56]

At each step in the development of the new regimes—at each election, the approval of both constitutions, the first meeting of the parliaments, the approval of the governments—the United States viewed the step as a crucial "turning point" or "critical juncture," assuming that once the various conflicting interests enjoyed a political forum in which to work through their differences, the violence would subside. This has hardly proved to be the case. Three reasons stand out. Security did not precede democratization but was meant to be driven by it; the U.S.-promoted institutions were not well designed for the Iraqi and Afghan peoples; and these institutions were far too unitary, national (as opposed to federal or decentralized) in character.

In both countries, much of the democratization was disingenuous; details follow. One may hence argue that if genuine democratization would have taken place, security would have followed. It is difficult to disprove hypotheticals. However, even in those areas in which Iraqis and Afghans were left to follow their own lights, they hardly laid the foundations for secure democracy.

The main thrust of democratization followed these contours: America placed leaders in charge or in positions of power who were widely viewed as puppets. In Iraq, the first major politician the United States promoted was Ahmad Chalabi, whom many distrusted as a stooge and an expatriate seeking to capitalize on Saddam's expulsion. American "advisers" were appointed to shadow the various Iraqi ministers, and these advisers controlled the funds provided by the United States and its allies, the main source of revenue of these ministries. Thus they in effect had veto power on many decisions by the elected government. The increasing application of "tough love in Baghdad"—what the *Wall Street Journal* termed America's blunt intrusion into Iraqi politics—shows the extent to which U.S. political leaders were unsatisfied with leaving political choices to the Iraqis.[57] As in Afghanistan, United States Ambassador to Iraq Zalmay Khalilzad has worked diligently to impose America's vision of Iraq's future government on Prime Minister Nouri Kamel al-Maliki and other top officials. Indeed, on several occasions Maliki tried to maintain his standing by claiming that he was not America's man in Iraq and by demanding the various raids by the Iraqi and American forces be first cleared by him. But to little avail.

In Kabul, where Khalilzad served as ambassador until his June 2005 transfer to Iraq, he incurred the enmity of local politicians through what was seen as excessive micromanagement of Karzai's policies. In 2005 Karzai publicly clashed with President Bush, when Bush demanded greater efforts in the eradication of poppies, the source of much of the world's heroin. After initially demurring, saying that he preferred an "Afghan solution" to the problem, Karzai acquiesced. And when he appointed the religious conservative Faisal Ahmad Shinwari to head the Afghan Supreme Court in April 2006, Western diplomats objected on the grounds that he had insufficient respect for or knowledge of international law.[58]

The constitutions which the United States has promoted in both countries do not adequately reflect the beliefs and habits of large segments of both societies. Thus Article 7 of the Afghan constitution binds the country to observe the Universal Declaration of Human Rights, many of whose tenets flatly contradict the precepts of traditional Afghan laws. For instance, although women in most parts of Afghanistan have been at best second-class citizens since time immemorial, the constitution asserted their inalienable equality with men and positively mandates their participation in politics.

In the early days of Bremer's administration, he frequently vetoed Iraqi requests for an elected constituent assembly and for local elections. Rebuffing calls from Grand Ayatollah Ali al-Sistani, Bremer instead turned to an "opaque, convoluted process"[59] whereby the constitution would be written by a handpicked group of Iraqis, the Coalition's "Iraqi

Governing Council," rather than by an elected body, which might well have composed a constitution significantly less to American liking—and less liberal. Moreover, as the Council did work to craft a constitution, its progress was often slowed by Bremer himself, who objected to language that elevated Islam as the source of legislation and established Iraq as an Islamic state.[60]

American micromanagement of Iraqi politics has continued unabated. Under American pressure to resign, then–Prime Minister Jaafari called on the United States to cease its interference in Iraqi politics. More importantly, he defended his alliance with the powerful Shia cleric Muqtada al-Sadr, whose political ambitions and militia he called "a fact of life."[61] The United States worked to replace him, and succeeded: in May 2006 Nouri al-Maliki took his place. U.S. Ambassador Khalilzad has come under fire from both Sunnis and Shias for attempting to shape policy around U.S. interests.

Last but far from least, security was severely hampered by America's extremely ambitious social engineering attempts. One can argue whether these ideas were good or bad, but there is very little room for doubt that they were a major cause for diminishing security. The United States sought to build a highly unitary state in Iraq instead of a highly federated one. Its reasons included the concern that if various regionally concentrated, ethno-religious groups maintained their own security forces or militias, it could lead to the breakup of the country, to the formation of a pro-Iran Shia region in the south and, in the north, an independent Kurdistan, threatening to draw Kurds to break away from Turkey—which would have greatly distressed this U.S. ally and NATO member. Accordingly America tried to "nationalize" the Shia and Kurdish militias, disband them or incorporate them into the national security forces—and to place Sunni units in Shia areas and Kurdish units in Sunni areas.

Ignored was the fact that Iraq was, from its inception in the 1920s, a country artificially cobbled together by the European colonial powers. Although some sense of Iraqi nationhood did develop over the decades, the primary loyalties of most Iraqis are still to their respective ethno-religious group or tribe. Moreover, the fact that the Sunni minority savaged the other two main groups during Saddam's long rule is very much on the mind of those who suffered.

Also, despite the long history of Kurdish pseudo-autonomy within

Iraq and long-standing claims to the northern city of Kirkuk, in January 2004 Bremer demanded that the Kurds disband the *peshmerga*, their assembly, withdraw their claims to Kirkuk's oil, and accept the authority of the central Iraqi state.[62] Similarly in the south, British forces and administrators labored to limit attempts to install local political leaders who originated in the Basra area without ties to the national government.

The opposite track would have relied, initially, on maintaining security in the south and north by the respective Shia and Kurdish militias. This would have allowed the United States and its allies to focus on pacifying the mixed areas. Here, too, security could have been organized by neighborhoods that are often ethnically monolithic, such as in Baghdad. Indeed, wherever the United States and its allies have enjoyed small successes in imposing security, it has been through the cooperation (surprising to some) of the local tribal authorities: for instance in the southern city of Amara, capital of Maysan province, an alliance of fourteen tribes has been instrumental in keeping Islamists under control.[63] A particularly telling case in point occurred in 2006 when, during a prolonged battle between NATO forces and Taliban fighters, the tribal elders in Helmand Province of Afghanistan struck a deal with both sides. Both agreed to withdraw and leave the locals be. "The accord, reached with virtually no public consultation and mediated by the local governor, has brought some welcome peace for residents of the district, Musa Qala," reported the *New York Times*. The newspaper reporters added that the deal was being widely debated. "Some say the agreement points the way forward in bringing peace to war-torn parts of the country. Others warn that it sets a dangerous precedent and represents a capitulation to the Taliban and a potential reversal of five years of *American* policy to build a strong central government. They say the accord gives up too much power to local leaders, who initiated it and are helping to enforce it."[64]

Security would also have benefited if the United States had accorded a high measure of regional autonomy to all of Iraq's eighteen provinces. After all, America once had "dry" states; why not allow the Shias to ban the sale of alcohol in Basra? And the United States has dress codes that vary from state to state; why not allow some regions of the south to demand that women cover themselves, so long as violence or terrorism is not employed to enforce the rules? The same is true for regional forces in

Afghanistan. All this could be changed gradually as new national security forces formed.[65]

One may argue that although regime change did not provide domestic security in Iraq, it enhanced national security back in the United States. However, Iraq has turned into a training ground for terrorists; a 2006 National Intelligence Estimate established that the conflict in Iraq has created many more terrorists than it has eliminated.[66] Many thousands of Iraqis and Muslims from other countries are making ever-more-sophisticated bombs, importing equipment from neighboring Iran, fashioning secure communications, and organizing cell networks difficult to penetrate. Given that Saddam did not possess WMD[67] and did not link up with al-Qaeda,[68] removing him seems to have provided no net gain from the standpoint of American security, however fortunate it may have been for the Iraqi people. In addition, the continued failure to secure both nations has resulted in U.S. conventional forces being stretched thin and exhausted, to the point that taking on a challenge in another area (without using nuclear arms) does not seem possible—one major reason that Iran and North Korea have been emboldened.

U.S. military credibility suffered a great deal, as did its political reputation, in large parts of the world.[69] If America folds in Iraq and withdraws after establishing a nominally "democratic" state that is, in reality, chaotic and lawless, U.S. credibility as a superpower will be further undercut.

The situation in Afghanistan is more complex. It used to be a safe haven for terrorists. Now they are largely limited to some areas near the border with Pakistan, although the Taliban have been making something of a comeback since 2006, which may well grow in scope and power. In addition, the United States has succeeded, at least for now, in internationalizing the security of the area by turning it over to NATO. If, however, the Taliban insurgency in Afghanistan spreads, many of the U.S. gains in the country are likely to be reversed.[70]

Starting from Scratch

Under a Security First scenario, occupying forces must make the "second-worst" decision to leave many elements of the old regime in place, and then slowly work to convert them, while allowing considerable time for new and more liberal forces to grow. If the foreign powers occupying newly liberated states are to provide basic security, they must make the bitter choice of working initially within the existing power structures (albeit not with those persons directly involved with the previous regimes' atrocities) and the established tribal, ethnic, or religious communities, rather than presuming that national identities can take precedence over such group loyalties. (The fact matters little that many of these identities are neither "natural" nor "organic" but have been altered or intensified in earlier generations by colonial powers. These group loyalties now command power over the members.)

The occupying powers must initially tolerate illiberal ideological or religious regimes, as long as the leadership in place helps maintain basic security, which includes not imposing a strict interpretation of the *shariah* code through the use of force. As basic security is established, the United States and its allies may either seek to move these regimes toward liberal democracy—as long as they realize that this is a slow, costly, and imperfect process, especially in nations largely unprepared for such developments— or leave this transformation to be undertaken by the citizens of the involved nations.

This is the course the United States and its allies followed after occupying Nazi Germany at the end of World War II. In Afghanistan this would have meant working with the warlords and the heads of the main ethnic groups and leaving them with extensive leeway as long as they maintained security within their territories and did not engage in civil war with one another. They would then have had to be won over to whatever national agenda could be implemented.

In Iraq this would have meant giving much greater leeway on local issues to Kurdish and Shia leaders in their areas of the country, and leaving some of the Ba'athists in power in the Sunni areas. In mixed areas, especially Baghdad, neighborhoods would have had to be segregated as they were in Belfast, Beirut, and Jerusalem, until a more effective national government could have taken hold. This would have entailed allowing local militias to remain intact but confined to "their" areas, rather than deliberately placing them in others' territory or trying to blend them together. The U.S. role would have been to minimize militia clashes and prevent the imposition of religious codes by violent, extralegal means. Thus, the leaders of Basra, for instance, would have been free to pass regulations that ban the sale of alcohol and fine those who did not obey, and even to enact dress codes for women, but not to assassinate Sunnis or bomb liquor stores.

According greater respect to particularistic communities that the Security First approach builds on is supported by the global trend toward greater local and regional autonomy from national governments. In contrast, forced nation-building, in the name of democratization, bucks current historical trends and the preferences of overwhelming majorities of the people involved.

Implications for Humanitarian Interventions

A Security First approach also provides guidance on conditions under which armed humanitarian interventions are justified. The Primacy of Life principle indicates that the international community has a responsibility to intervene wherever populations suffer from genocide, defined in 1948 by the United Nations as widespread violence "committed with intent to destroy, in whole or in part, a national, ethnical, racial or religious group." The same principle also justifies peacekeeping operations when the contenders involved request it to enforce a settlement. However, armed interventions are not justified to protect a regime from internal challenges of the kind faced by Haiti in 1994, when President Clinton sent twenty thousand troops to reinstate ousted leader Jean-Bertrand Aristide. Such challenges are common, and even a superpower cannot realistically expect to deal with all or most of them. Hence, decisions about when to intervene become inconsistent and difficult to justify, aside from raising false expectations in the populations involved. One of the tragic features of the international reality is that these matters must often be left for the people involved to sort out themselves; they are the painful domestic struggles that are a part of the growing pains of incipient democracies.

Moreover, interventions are best limited to help provide basic security rather than to bring about regime change, using the occupying forces only to advance this mission. Troops should not be used for nation-building or reconstruction. It is an odd notion that when one nation intervenes in another to stop a genocide, the nation that came to the rescue also "owes" the nation it saved an array of liberal-democratic institutions and a modern economy. It is like saying that because you gave shelter to a motorist whose car broke down during a snowstorm, you owe him a newer, better car.

Indeed, the entanglements that followed large-scale, life-saving interventions in Kosovo and Bosnia have contributed to the reluctance of many nations to act to stop genocides in places like Rwanda and Sudan. A Primacy of Life foreign policy avoids this pitfall. It narrows the mission and thus makes it more tolerable. Its application to humanitarian interventions is but one more—albeit a key—example of a policy that has less lofty goals, but delivers more than those that promise democratization as a side-benefit to ending genocide and end up delivering neither.

The preceding conclusion presumes that foreign powers *cannot* democratize and modernize a nation like Afghanistan in the foreseeable future. This fact constitutes a fatal flaw in the theory that democratization drives security, which I further highlight in Part II. For now I just note that refraining from seductive illusions does not mean that one cannot or should not expand humanitarian aid—as long as one does not justify it on the grounds of attempting the impossible.

A question may be raised by those who basically accept the practical consequences of Security First as a basis for foreign policy, but who take exception to its core moral criterion—saving life. They may well hold—in what might be called a neo-realist mode—that a nation indeed ought to be concerned first and foremost about its own security and even that of its allies, but not that of other peoples. Thus, for instance, armed U.S. interventions in Somalia and Kosovo, insofar as they did not serve any obvious American or allied security interest, might be said not to have been called for. More generally, some may say, humanitarian interventions should not be included in our foreign policy, unless they happen to serve a more immediate national security interest, such as limiting immigration from Haiti.

This issue more than most allows me to highlight the key differences between a realistic but principled foreign policy, one that is idealistic (or utopian), and one that is realistic but amoral—"realistic" in the sense of a policy that is focused on narrow self-interest and that views ethical considerations as a pretext employed by weaker powers to tie down stronger powers. Hence big powers—it is said—should either ignore morality altogether or pay lip service to it with the purpose of merely appearing (though not of actually being) moral.

But a nation that accepts the importance of limiting itself by moral judgments, and that adopts the Primacy of Life as the mainspring of legitimacy for its foreign policy, will be unable to maintain this justification successfully if it is applied only to securing the lives of its own citizens and not those of others. For a principle to be legitimate it has to be capable of being applied universally, that is, heeded when and where the conditions are identical or close to identical. Thus when the United States pressures some nations to give up their nuclear arms but looks the other way at the nuclear arms programs of others, much less helps some countries to enrich theirs, the legitimacy of its claims are greatly diminished. The same is true about the promotion of human rights. American presidents have been asked for decades how they justify the active promotion of human rights in some states (e.g., Russia) but not in others (e.g., Saudi Arabia). The challenge is a valid one; tragically the answer is that consistent application of the principles entailed in deproliferation as well as the full spectrum of human rights is so taxing that the United States is doomed to be unable to live up to the commitments involved, even if some leader had the courage to try to adhere to the precepts required. Hence the widely held accusation that U.S. foreign policy is hypocritical, hence the lack of legitimacy of several key U.S. foreign policies.

A Security First foreign policy is much more modest, much less demanding, and the conflicts between its ideals and the vital interests of the various nations involved are much more limited. It is one thing to claim that the United States and company are out to democratize the world, and quite another to claim that they are out to provide basic security to one and all. I am not saying that such a policy is cost-free, but rather that it can be adhered to much more readily than can a policy of worldwide democratization.

Hence when genocide or ethnic cleansing is unfolding, armed intervention to stop it is both morally right and a price worth paying to maintain the legitimacy of Security First. I need not rehash here the well-made arguments about the merits of soft power and the role legitimacy plays in commanding such power, but only reiterate that narrow realism has considerable costs of its own.[71] It costs us allies, it stokes the fervor of those who oppose us, and it undermines support at home, aside from failing our own moral tests.

Hence when all is said and done, we are better off—and better human beings—if we follow a policy whose goals are legitimate, rather than either a policy whose goals are utopian or whose goals barely conceal naked self-interest. A principled but pragmatic foreign policy will gain more traction as well as allow us to look into the mirror—and justify ourselves to our children and others, and justify the preservation of our regime.

A realist may counter here that there is no public support for extensive armed humanitarian interventions. This is true—under current conditions. However, public intellectuals and political leaders were often able to convince the same public to make enormous sacrifices in order to contain the spread of communism in far-flung corners of the globe. Humanitarian interventions are likely to find more support if they are similarly "sold," especially if they are an integral part of a new global foreign policy, one based on the Primacy of Life, and couched as a response to the devastation of 9/11.

Moreover, such a consistent policy of humanitarian intervention would benefit from two considerations. First, calls for armed humanitarian interventions would be met with less resistance because they would no longer be undertaken or expected for the futile purpose of democracy promotion in places such as Haiti. Second, each intervention would make the threat of future ones more credible, that is, each would have a deterrent effect. Indeed, there have been several reports that before Serbians unleashed their forces in Bosnia and elsewhere, they "checked" with Germany and, indirectly, the United States. When they did not receive any reaction, they interpreted this to mean that they had a green light to proceed.[72] A number of other historical examples have followed a similar pattern. The United Nations and other international bodies received multiple warnings of an impending massacre of Tutsis.[73] In March 1994, "The officer in charge of intelligence for the Rwandan army told a group including some Belgian military advisers that 'if Arusha [Accords] were implemented, they were ready to liquidate the Tutsi.' "[74] On April 4, 1994, "[Col. Théoneste] Bagosora told people that 'the only plausible solution for Rwanda would be the elimination of the Tutsi.' "[75] Numerous U.N. and Western diplomats were present for Bagosora's warning. Moreover, "France certainly knew about the preparations for killing Tutsi and opponents of Hutu Power," well in advance of April 1994.[76] None of these warnings, however, precipitated a Western reaction.

A consistently implemented humanitarian interventions policy would have given a red light to such genocidal drives.[77]

The Security First approach in no way precludes the advancement of democratization by nonlethal means. To reiterate, the more that basic security is achieved, the better the ground will be prepared for developing the other elements necessary for democratization by peaceful means, mainly by the local people involved.

In effect, the United States already has a huge array of public and private programs that aim to foster liberal democracy through nonlethal means. These include programs that are directly focused on democratization, such as training people in the skills needed to run for office or to maintain fair and open elections. Others aim to advance the institutions necessary to sustain a liberal political order, for instance by training journalists. Still other programs help to prepare the ground through exchanges in which young leaders from newly liberated nations are invited to spend time in America, and Americans are sent to serve in democratizing nations. A great deal of attention has been dedicated to "public diplomacy," which includes extensive broadcasts beamed to these nations with the intention of changing "hearts and minds."

Some of these programs are run by the United States Agency for International Development (USAID) and some by the National Endowment for Democracy and its affiliated institutions, including the International Republican Institute and the National Democratic Institute for International Affairs. Other programs are sponsored by American business associations and labor unions.

The effectiveness of each of these programs is difficult to evaluate, but in combination they may gradually move the political cultures of the beneficiary nations in the desired direction. All this suggests that to refrain from forcefully imposing a liberal-democratic regime—and to adhere to a Security First approach to foreign policy—does not mean giving up on democratization in the longer run or promoting it in the shorter run by peaceful means.

In Conclusion

It is true that there has been some backpedaling by the Bush administration on its democratization drive in places like Egypt and Syria, given the fear of increasing the power of Islamists in those countries. Democratization, however, has not been dethroned as the leitmotif of American foreign policy. It is time to relieve our foreign policy of this onerous and disappointing burden, and replace it with a worthy goal that can actually be accomplished and that others would wish to serve. To provide security is the first duty of a state, and the enjoyment of security is the right of all people. Securing the Primacy of Life is thus not merely of pragmatic worth; it is also a legitimate and ennobling pursuit. However, none of the preceding arguments will be acceptable unless one acknowledges that the international reality is brutal, and that even the capacity of superpowers to change it is surprisingly limited. At the same time, focusing first on security-building in newly liberated and failing states, and in dealing with rogues, in no way precludes helping democratization through nonlethal means, as long as one realizes that it cannot be rushed and must be largely homegrown.

PART II

The Limits of Social Engineering

CHAPTER A. A PRIMITIVE ART

I have argued thus far that security must be ranked as the first priority in the United States' engagement with troubled parts of the world. I mentioned in passing that leaving the advancement of democracy and human rights largely to the people of the nations involved—limiting foreign powers to the still formidable task of helping with the establishment of security—is much less of a loss than it initially seems; that according Security First does not entail selling our soul to an authoritarian devil in order to gain safety. I turn now to spell out the reasons for this central assertion.

At issue is the question: how difficult are "regime change" and post-conflict reconstruction, especially if carried out by foreign powers in nations that have limited preparation for the sought-after changes? If democratization were half as easy as Paul Wolfowitz (and other Neo-Cons) told the American people it was going to be, there would be little reason to ask whether some other goals ought to command a higher priority, and there would be little reason to delay changing boatloads of regimes around the world. When the United States invaded Iraq in 2003 the Bush administration expected that the American troops would be "greeted as liberators,"[1] met in the streets of Baghdad by cheering crowds, and showered with rose petals. The war and occupation were supposed to cost little.

White House Press Secretary Ari Fleischer claimed before the war that "Iraq, unlike Afghanistan, is a rather wealthy country. Iraq has tremendous resources that belong to the Iraqi people. And so there are a variety of means that Iraq has to be able to shoulder much of the burden for their own reconstruction."[2] Deputy Secretary of State Richard Armitage declared of Iraq, "This is not Afghanistan. . . . When we approach the question of Iraq, we realize here is a country which has a resource. And it's obvious, it's oil. And it can bring in and does bring in a certain amount of revenue each year . . . $10, $15, even $18 billion . . . this is not a broke country."[3] Similarly, Deputy Defense Secretary Paul Wolfowitz argued, "There's a lot of money to pay for this that doesn't have to be U.S. taxpayer money, and it starts with the assets of the Iraqi people . . . and on a rough recollection, the oil revenues of that country could bring between $50 and $100 billion over the course of the next two or three years. . . . We're dealing with a country that can really finance its own reconstruction, and relatively soon."[4]

On April 23, 2003, Andrew S. Natsios, head of the U.S. Agency for International Development (USAID), laid out in a televised interview the costs to taxpayers of rebuilding Iraq. "The American part of this will be $1.7 billion," he said. "We have no plans for any further-on funding for this." The administration asked Congress for another $20 billion for Iraq reconstruction five months after Natsios made his assertion.[5]

In addition to such claims about reconstruction, many argued that as Iraq rapidly democratized, it would flip the entire Middle East and turn it into a crescent of shining, prosperous democracies. "Iraqi democracy will succeed—and that success will send forth the news, from Damascus to Tehran—that freedom can be the future of every nation," the president said in November 2003.[6] "Change toward democratic regimes in Tehran and Baghdad would unleash a tsunami across the Islamic world," predicted Neo-Con scholar Joshua Muravchik.[7] This in turn was going to be a mere stop on a global forced march to the end of history, a liberal-democratic "better place." As Francis Fukuyama famously put it in his 1989 essay "The End of History?," "What we may be witnessing is not just the end of the Cold War, or the passing of a particular period of post-war history, but the end of history as such: that is the end point of mankind's ideological evolution and the universalization of Western liberal democracy as the final form of human government."[8]

What is this blessed end? Fukuyama argues that "the state that emerges at the end of history is liberal in so far as it recognizes and protects, through a system of laws, man's universal right to freedom, and democratic in so far as it exists only with the consent of the governed." And if that were not optimistic enough, we are also promised that "all prior contradictions are resolved and all human needs are satisfied. There is no struggle or conflict over large issues and consequently no need for generals or statesmen. What remains is primarily economic activity."[9]

Yesterday it was the ex-communist world that marched toward liberty. Today, the Muslim world. All the United States would have to do is join the victory parade; America could simply stand and be admired, as "a majority of Arabs will come to see America as the essential ally in progress toward liberty in their own lands."[10]

Similar grandiose claims have been made for other forms of social engineering, especially economic development. If a communist nation could within two years "jump" into a world of free markets and thriving capitalism (often considered an important corollary of democratization), as Jeffrey Sachs promised,[11] all the developed nations would have to do is uncork the champagne, bring flowers and chocolates, and join the celebration.

Actually, social engineering is an extremely primitive art that faces countless obstacles, especially in the short run, and especially when undertaken by foreign powers in lands that are poorly prepared for whatever grand changes are favored by those powers. Hence the questions of the proper allocation of resources and of political will (i.e., prioritization), the sequences in which one best proceeds, and the dangers of overpromising and of loss of credibility when one cannot deliver. It also follows that according Security First priority is not only essential for democratization to work, but also that democracy must be phased in gradually and is best done by the people directly concerned.

To support my case I proceed first to make a few general comments about the nature of social engineering (or, rather, its unnatural qualities). I then discuss the lessons of some attempts at democratization, reconstruction, and economic development more generally. I close by examining attempts to reengineer other elements of societies abroad, especially national community-building.

Social engineering is commonly defined as the art of introducing social changes broadly understood, including political and economic changes. Social engineering presumes a design and an agent, the one (or ones) who brings about the change. This is an important point because social change is occurring constantly around us, but most of it is organic or natural change, in the sense that it is not guided deliberately—not planned or controlled—by any specific government agency, although government may play some kind of a limited role in facilitating or allowing whatever changes that do occur. Millions of people change the habits of their hearts—and the institutions of their society—because of a complex combination of changes in a large variety of factors, such as the rise of new technologies and new means of communications, globalization, climate warming, immigration, and so on. They change under the influence of new social movements—such as national liberation campaigns or contemporary religious reawakenings—movements that typically arise without some social engineering master following carefully laid out plans.

Social engineering, by contrast, *is* planned and consciously carried out; some force, typically a government, commits resources to bring about an end state that it desires, one that otherwise would not perhaps arise. Just as there is no need for human engineering to make rivers flow downhill, but it is very much necessary if water is to flow uphill, so there is no need for social engineering if change is left to the ordinary operations of people's decisions and actions.

In short, social engineering by definition entails an intervention, and it must expect to encounter resistance by those forced to alter their course and who have had little or no say over the design of the planned changes. It is never completely voluntary, though if it is done well it may unleash powers that support the sought-after changes, powers that until then had been hidden or in abeyance.

The Neo-Cons originally rose in reaction to America's grand liberal experiments in social engineering in the 1960s. Their defining theme and great success were built around one central thesis: that social engineering in general, and by the U.S. federal government in particular, was bound to fail. Liberals could not deny that many of the scores upon scores of social programs introduced during the Kennedy and Johnson administrations did not deliver even a fraction of what they had promised. Liberals often argue that funding was insufficient or that additional design corrections had to be made. By and large, however, the Neo-Cons were convincing when they pointed out that social engineering by the government—no matter how much funding is allotted—often just does not work.

It was therefore particularly surprising when some of those same Neo-Cons, in the late 1990s, locked onto the idea that the U.S. government could reengineer (or introduce regime change in) scores of nations around the world, under conditions much less favorable than those at home. While they may have been excessively pessimistic about what could be done at home (although the great difficulties in the reconstruction of New Orleans hardly belie their main thesis), surely—I show next—their arguments regarding the limits of what can be accomplished by government-led social engineering hold many times over for the United States' endeavors abroad.

Long distance social engineering (LDSE), designed in Washington but applied overseas, has been attempted in numerous ways. The following discussion begins by focusing on democratization because it has been a major form of social engineering attempted over the last decade (although it was far from unknown in previous decades). I then examine reconstruction because the case has been made that the United States is obligated to rebuild the nations in which it has intervened, from Afghanistan to Kosovo and from Iraq to Haiti. Reconstruction is often closely linked to economic development in a much broader sense. Hence some comments about foreign attempts to bring about general economic development in faraway lands follow. And because America at the height of its social engineering pursuits has also decided to reengineer social relations in nations overseas, including relations among various ethnic, religious, and tribal groups, the discussion closes by reviewing those endeavors, with special attention to the lessons of Kosovo.

I cannot stress enough that in all these areas my focus is on LDSE—on social engineering promoted by one or more foreign powers with little familiarity or experience in dealing with the local cultures and conditions. These powers often project their preferences on other people and use force to impose change. Such forced LDSE is radically different from relying on persuasive means to inspire change among those concerned, in which education, expert knowledge, and some economic incentives are employed. Often when an argument is made in favor of or in opposition to social engineering abroad, particularly in reference to democratization, this distinction between force and persuasion is not observed. Hence I cannot stress enough that *democratization by foreign powers faces great difficulties, both because security must first be established—and because attempts to forcefully hurry it along tend to backfire*. In short, I refer to coerced democratization, not to advancing it through nonlethal, persuasive means.

CHAPTER B. THE LESSONS OF DEMOCRATIZATION

What Democracy Makes

Imported and forced democratization has been tried in Iraq and Afghanistan in recent years, but earlier attempts were made to plant it in scores of other nations, from Haiti to the Congo.[12] To assess the success of these efforts, a brief discussion of what democracy entails follows. Although there is no full agreement as to what constitutes a democracy, there are thorough and extensive studies of the subject by scholars such as Archie Brown,[13] Thomas Carothers,[14] Robert A. Dahl,[15] Adeed and Karen Dawisha,[16] and S. M. Lipset.[17] In addition there is the work and publications of the National Endowment of Democracy, headed by Carl Gershman, which includes a journal devoted to the subject, the *Journal of Democracy*, co-edited by Marc F. Plattner and Larry Diamond.

Some scholars insist, in the tradition of the area studies school, that each situation is unique and that only by immersing oneself in the particular history and culture of a country can a course of action be established. In contrast, I stand with those who think that a general theory of democracy formation is possible. One can draw up a checklist of the factors required to make a democracy. The list is best divided into *facilitating* factors and *constituting* factors. Facilitating factors are the conditions that ease or hinder the formation of democracy, the "democratic infrastructure." These factors are not all or even each prerequisites, because substitutes might be found, but their presence significantly improves the probability that a democracy will take shape and be sustainable. The constituting factors are the requisite building blocks for democracy to take hold. Both lists can be used to indicate a country's preparedness to democratize and what may be missing.

Two methodological comments are called for. The lists provided here are far from complete and are merely intended as an approximation. In addition, there are interactive effects among the various factors: namely, if one factor is present, it eases the formation of the others, but if one factor is maximized while all the others are grossly neglected, the absence of these other factors is likely to retard democratization. More or less even developments are superior to tilted ones.

Drawing on the scholarship already cited, as well as other studies and my own observations, the facilitating and constituting factors include:

Facilitating factors:
- law and order, pacification;
- literacy, general education, civic education;
- economic development, separation of economic power from political power, leveling of economic differences;
- a sizable, developed middle class;
- the rule of law, independent judges, respect for law enforcement authorities; and
- civil society, voluntary associations, communities.

Constituting factors:
- the unencumbered ability of parties to compete for support and votes;
- the determination of criteria regarding eligibility for public office;
- the assurance of free and fair elections;
- formulation of a constitutional order and process that ensures power sharing as well as separation of powers, essential for checks and balances among the executive, legislative, and judicial branches;
- a low level of corruption (and high level of transparency);
- protection of minority rights;
- freedom of association;
- freedom of the press; and
- enumeration of rights people have with respect to the government.

To reiterate, these lists are but a preliminary attempt to outline the factors needed to form a true and sustainable liberal democracy. *Even a cursory examination of most of these factors suffices to suggest that developing them is a slow process and well-nigh impossible for outsiders to direct.* Cultivating respect for the rule of law where little has existed historically, building a middle class in highly socially stratified societies, and reducing corruption where it is rampant and even culturally accepted and expected, are all overwhelmingly difficult tasks. It took Britain and America many decades, by some measures several generations or centuries, to develop solidly liberal-democratic regimes, under conditions fundamentally much more favorable than are found in many other parts of the world. Other nations will have to undergo a similar journey, although they may benefit to some extent from the experience and help of established liberal democracies—if it is truly offered as help rather than as forced regime change.

The Record

The great difficulties and ultimate disappointments that the United States and its allies have encountered in democratizing Afghanistan and Iraq are but new entries in a long list of failures. In an often cited 2003 policy brief titled "Lessons from the Past: The American Record on Nation Building," prepared for the Carnegie Endowment for International Peace, Minxin Pei and Sara Kasper examine U.S. attempts at forced democratization during the twentieth century.[18] They distinguish these military operations from America's other wars and armed interventions by the explicit adoption of the goal of regime change or of protecting and reforming a friendly but vulnerable regime; by U.S. deployment of significant numbers of troops to the nation in question for a sustained period of time; and by the crucial U.S. role in choosing the political leadership for the nation in question. By these measures, Pei and Kasper identify the following sixteen attempts at nation-building: in Cuba (1898–1902); in Panama (1903–36); in Cuba a second time (1906–09); Nicaragua (1909–33); Haiti (1915–34); Cuba a third time (1917–22); the Dominican Republic (1916–24); West Germany (1945–49); Japan (1945–52); the Dominican Republic a second time (1965–66); Cambodia (1970–73); South Vietnam (1964–73); Grenada (1983); Panama a second time (1989); Haiti a second time (1994–96); and Afghanistan (2001–present).

Of these efforts, eleven flatly failed to establish a functioning democracy, while Afghanistan is said to remain inconclusive and problematic. Only four of sixteen succeeded: West Germany, Japan, Grenada, and Panama. Grenada, however, is a very small island, and the population of Panama is under three million. West Germany and Japan thus constitute the only major examples of successful democratization by the United States in large, complex societies. In the case of Germany and Japan important factors were present which made successful democratization there possible, factors not available in the other nations under study—

including a high level of education, a sizable middle class, a relatively high per capita income, and ethnic homogeneity, among others.

Perhaps the most notorious among the failures were the American withdrawal from Cambodia, after which the genocidal Khmer Rouge gained power; and the withdrawal from South Vietnam, leading to the fall of the South Vietnamese government. More generally, as Thomas Carothers, author of *Aiding Democracy Abroad,* puts it, "The idea that there's a small democracy inside every society waiting to be released just isn't true."[19] And F. Gregory Gause III writes in his article "Can Democracy Stop Terrorism?" that the "confidence that Washington has in its ability to predict, and even direct, the course of politics in other countries . . . [is] . . . unjustified."[20]

Germany and Japan: Exceptions That Prove the Rule

The successful reconstruction and democratization of Germany and Japan after World War II rested on many conditions that are unlikely to be reproduced elsewhere. First of all, they had both surrendered after defeat in a war and fully submitted to occupation. The occupations lasted much longer than many assume. For Japan, it lasted nearly seven years, and for Germany, while the occupation itself lasted four years, full control over foreign relations, trade, industrial production, and military security was not turned over to the Germans until 1955, ten years after the end of the war.

Many facilitating factors also were much more established in these two nations than they were in other countries in which LDSE has been attempted. There was no danger that Japan or Germany would break up due to a civil war among ethnic groups, as is the case in Afghanistan and Iraq. No effort had to be expended on national unity-building. On the contrary, strong national unity was a major reason change could be introduced with relative ease. Other favorable factors included competent government personnel and a low level of corruption.[21] Some cite "technical and financial expertise, relatively highly institutionalized political parties, skillful and visionary politicians, well-educated populations, [and] strong national identifications" as factors that all contributed to democratization.[22] And, crucially, there was a strong culture of self-restraint present in both Japan and Germany.

Not only were the conditions in Japan and Germany different from what prevails today in Afghanistan and Iraq, but conditions in the United States were different as well. As John W. Dower has argued about the difference between the American occupation of Japan and that of Iraq, "We do not have the moral legitimacy we had then, nor do we have the other thing that was present when we occupied Japan—the vision of the American public that we would engage in serious and genuinely democratic nation-building and that we would do this in the context of an international order."[23] The commitment level of the United States to reconstruction after World War II was also significantly higher than the current U.S. commitment to foreign aid. In 1948, the first year of the Marshall Plan, aid to the sixteen European countries under the Plan totaled 13 percent of the entire U.S. budget, without counting funds spent in Japan and the costs of occupying Germany.[24] In comparison, the United States currently spends less than 1 percent of its budget on foreign aid and not all of that amount is dedicated to economic development.

Absence of facilitating and constituting factors of the kind that existed in Germany and Japan, and the drastically lower levels of foreign aid that the United States and its allies and partners have been willing to commit, have made other democratizing missions since World War II almost uniformly unsuccessful.

Yet despite the long history of America's failed attempts at democratizations, the Neo-Cons have made democratization a cornerstone of U.S. foreign policy, and the Bush administration has offered it as the number one, post hoc rationale for the invasion of Iraq, and to a lesser extent of Afghanistan. There are those who say that the Bush administration and the Neo-Con ideologues within and around it knew quite well that such democratization was impossible but merely used it as a fig leaf to cover their naked drive for power and oil, and as a demonstration to the world that, despite 9/11, "we are tough."[25] I do not share this view. Having repeatedly met with leading Neo-Cons and several members of the Bush White House staff and cabinet, including Karl Rove, I believe that they are sincere in their stated beliefs, although their foreign policy has also been out to serve other goals. After all, from their viewpoint, one could democratize a nation, display military strength, and grasp control of Iraqi oil fields from the Russians and the French, all on the run—all at the same time.

The Rise of the Faux Democracies

As democratization not only failed in Iraq and Afghanistan but also regressed in Russia, Latin America, Africa, and elsewhere, the U.S. government, an assortment of NGOs in the business of democratization, and select public intellectuals have engaged in what the late Senator Daniel Patrick Moynihan called "defining deviancy down." Moynihan used the term to describe the practice of considering forms of behavior as legitimate or legal which were previously considered illegitimate or illegal. One effect of this practice is that public authorities can vastly improve their achievements—without doing anything new or additional! Thus crime statistics plunge when whole categories of crimes are no longer deemed criminal. The public of course is hardly better off; in effect it suffers the indignity of being taken for a fool.

A similarly damaging tendency is now unfolding with regard to democratization. As it has turned out, though it may be very difficult to export or even domestically build a liberal-democratic polity, various public policymakers have kept the triumphant march of global democratization going by declaring "mission accomplished" for one nation after another. Often these nations have at best developed some elements of what one day might make for a democracy. Various euphemisms that are being applied to these "faux democracies" gild over the fact that they are no more democratic than a person who jogs five kilometers once every few months is a marathon runner. Employing these labels suggests that those who affix them to various corrupt, semiauthoritarian regimes or failing states realize that they are dealing with anything but the real thing. Thus, in its 2005 "Freedom in the World" survey, Freedom House counted some 119 "electoral democracies" around the globe.[26] These regimes are reported to have met certain minimal democratic standards, including open and competitive elections, secret balloting, and the absence of massive voter fraud. Civil rights in electoral democracies may, however, be curtailed heavily.[27] Among the nations so designated by Freedom House were such dubious democracies as Nigeria—subject to military government until 1999, its government deeply corrupt, and its people riven by sectarian disputes, with Muslims succeeding in imposing *shariah* law in the north; Namibia—where the revolutionary Marxist South-West Africa People's Organization won 90 percent of the vote for the upper house of parliament and 75 percent for the lower house in 2004; and Venezuela— whose popularly elected ruler, Hugo Chavez, has introduced a new constitution in which the parliament has been stripped of many of its powers.

Another popular euphemism has been "transitional democracies," used to describe nations which, it is hoped, are transitioning to democracy, but manifestly do not qualify as truly democratic. The "transitional democracy" paradigm has been applied to countries as different as postcommunist Russia and the Democratic Republic of the Congo.[28] "Oligarchical" and "restrictive" democracies have been used to describe regime types in Latin America.[29] James Q. Wilson identifies Kazakhstan, Pakistan, Ukraine, and Venezuela as "freedom-disdaining democracies," a prize-winning oxymoron.[30] Charles King comes much closer to the proper designation, when he referred to the "Potemkin democracy" of Edvard Shevardnadze's Georgia.[31]

Many of these labels—electoral, transitional, nascent, emerging—imply that that these regimes are or soon will be in fact democratic polities, but not quite yet full-grown. Actually, such stretching of the term democracy gives the real thing a bad reputation. We should call them what they are: faux democracies, knockoffs, de facto authoritarian regimes. They have democratic potential but are at least as likely to become more authoritarian over time (e.g., Russia) as to realize their democratic potential.[32]

Above all, these faux democracies should not have the rights and privileges due genuine liberal democracies. Seeing them for what they are will improve our collective reality-testing, and makes it more difficult to hide behind euphemisms that allow one to claim victory and continue to march on triumphantly, when in fact a major change in foreign policy is not only called for but long overdue.

Particularly popular, at least for a while, were the "color" or "flower" revolutions that supposedly turned authoritarian regimes into democracies, in a matter of a few days, following one grand, dramatic event. These are said to have occurred in Georgia (rose), Ukraine (orange), Kyrgyzstan (tulip), and Lebanon (cedar). They were typically depicted as a confrontation between "the people" and an authoritarian government that refused to yield to the majority's wishes. The ordinary citizens of these nations took to the streets and public squares and demonstrated peacefully, often for several days, until the authoritarian governments surrendered to what is called "people power."

You would indeed have to have a heart of stone and ice water flowing in your veins not to be moved by the sight of many thousands of citizens risking their lives as they challenge those in power. Indeed, on several of these occasions, it seemed as if there were going to be another Tiananmen Square, another massacre of protestors. However, when instead those in power gave in and gave up, the movements came to possess a seemingly irresistible magic. New democracies were said to have been born, practically overnight. You cannot but wipe away a tear of joy when you watch such "people power" at work on the evening news.

But then reality sets in. If the sociological elements needed for genuine democratization are not in place—and often they are not—the long, hard work of establishing a liberal-democratic regime merely starts in earnest at this point. For it to succeed, the color *moments* must be followed by *years* of taxing cultural, social, economic, and political changes. For these changes to take place it is essential that those laboring to transform these countries recognize that it will be a tough process, one that demands much more stamina and sacrifice than the color moments themselves. Without such efforts, these new regimes will in effect become faux democracies; regimes that have some of the trappings of democracy but that are actually just another version of the authoritarian regimes they sought to displace.[33]

Next to color moments, elections are an especially popular prop for sleight-of-hand democratizations, as voting greatly helps to create the illusion that a long-established authoritarian regime can be turned into a democracy in very short order and at relatively low cost. Many seem to hold that if a nation has had a fair and free election it is, on the face of it, a democracy. Actually, when the press is muzzled, when there are no competitive parties, when corruption is rampant, and when the people involved are inexperienced in the ways of a free society, elections by themselves are a sign of democratic yearnings, but little more.

George W. Bush—whether or not one agrees with the policies he has implemented—made this point well during a speech at the Summit of the Americas on April 21, 2001, in Quebec City. He stated: "Elections are the foundation of democracy, but nations need to build on this foundation with other building blocks, such as a strong judiciary, freedom to speak and write as you wish, efficient banking and social services, quality schools, secure ownership of land, the ability to start and own a business."[34]

Actually, his list provides a sound beginning but is far from complete. Especially regrettable is the fact that much of the time neither he nor various Neo-Con supporters of the administration paid much mind to what democracy-building entails, and they were too quick to declare that elections in places such as Iraq and Afghanistan ushered in a new age. Elections did open the door to democratization but left open the question of who and what will march in.

The "Democracy Backlash"

In reaction to the fact that the new, so-called democracies tend to be anti-Western, harm U.S. interests, oppressive at home, and often support terrorism in other nations, a "democracy backlash" has set in. That is, a growing number of observers have wondered if supporting free elections in places like Egypt and Saudi Arabia was truly in the best interest of the United States and its allies, as well as of regional and world peace.

Moreover, the marketing of faux democracy has major negative effects on the support for democratization at home and abroad. As Islamists win elections such as Hamas did in 2006 in the Palestinian National Authority legislative election or increased representation such as Hezbollah did in Lebanon, or political power (as the Muslim Brotherhood has done in Egypt and Jordan, and other Islamists have achieved in Morocco, Saudi Arabia, Yemen, Kuwait, and Bahrain), a growing chorus of public intellectuals, TV talking heads, and elected officials in the West have concluded that democratization is against U.S. interests. Several have hinted at, and others openly called for, a return to the long-established U.S. foreign policy of support for authoritarian regimes that support the United States. Such analysts prize stability, even if it means supporting autocrats.

Chris Zambelis, an independent Middle East analyst and consultant, holds: "Given the current circumstances, the advent of democracy in the Middle East will empower Islamists. For many reasons, Islamists represent the dominant form of political opposition in the Middle East. In general, the authoritarian regimes in question successfully rooted out secular-minded democratic opposition movements, often relying on repressive measures, including violence and torture, to maintain control."[35]

Events in Iraq have caused both Washington and the Arab public increasingly to conclude that while governments in the region badly need reform, anarchy can be even worse than authoritarianism. Now many argue that authoritarian rulers must constantly be pressured to reform, but not at the cost of dismantling the state or of giving rise to another form of authoritarianism.[36] A 2006 *Washington Post* editorial states: "The 'democracy backlash' is in full swing, largely because of the carnage in Iraq and the electoral success of the terrorist organization Hamas in the Palestinian Authority. In the past week our op-ed writers from right to left have expressed doubts about, or opposition to, the Bush administration's project of encouraging democracy in the Middle East. From their and others' arguments, three principles tend to emerge: You can't impose democracy by force. You shouldn't push for elections, or expect a democracy to develop, until a mature 'civil society' is in place. We are better off with dictators like Mubarak, Musharraf and the rest than with the alternative, which is anarchy, terrorism and religious fundamentalism."[37]

It should come as no surprise that when authoritarian regimes hold elections after persecuting opposition groups for years, often for decades, the only groups left standing are those with radical and violent tendencies. They thrive on oppression. *Elections under such circumstances, however, amount to little more than being part of the façades that make for Potemkin democracies.* The rise of elected Islamists in the Middle East and elsewhere is *not* an indication that democratization has failed, but only that elections do not provide a reliable gauge of the democratic quality of a state. They are, after all, only one of the nine constituting elements of a democracy listed above.

Granted, it was moving to see Iraqis and Afghans risking their lives to vote and the pride with which they displayed their inked fingers. However, if they are continually told that what they gained by voting is a democracy —rather than one step in that direction—they may soon become disillusioned with the entire concept.

Democracy for Democrats: For Selective and Staggered Opening

Several foreign policy analysts have suggested America ought nevertheless to support popularly elected Islamist governments, as there are no tolerable alternatives. For instance, former Secretary of State Madeleine Albright stated, "We should remember that the alternative to support for democracy is complicity in backing governments that lack the blessing of their own people. . . . If America values its standing with the Egyptian people—and it should—its support for democratic reform ought to be unwavering."[38]

The *Washington Post* editorialized: "So it's fair to oppose democracy promotion, but only if you're honest about the alternative. Throughout much of the Muslim world, that alternative is not a gentle flowering of civil society but the conditions that after September 11 were recognized as threatening: closed and stagnant economies that leave millions of young people unemployed; brutal secret police services that permeate society and stifle education and free thinking; corrupt rulers who nurture religious extremism to shield themselves at home and make trouble abroad."[39]

To push Francis Fukuyama's argument to its next logical (mis)step: we should allow Islamic regimes to rise because their domestic radicalism and fierce anti-Americanism are like childhood diseases that they must go through on their way to becoming friendly liberal democracies.[40]

The trouble is that Islamist theocracies tend to last, for example, as Iran has since 1979; they impose horrible sufferings on their people, as the Taliban did; the people of these nations are often unable to overthrow the regimes on their own. Nor is there any sign that as such regimes grow long in the tooth, they will mature to become more supportive of the interests of the free world.

In short, if the only alternatives for the United States and its allies were, on the one hand, to support elections in nations unprepared for such developments, and thus to suffer all the bitter, antidemocratic and de-stabilizing consequences—or, on the other hand, to support pro-Western autocrats—we would truly be between a rock and a hard place. I noted earlier that in dealing with the international reality we are often limited to choices between the worst and the second-worst, when more attractive courses of action elude us. In this case, through, it is hard to judge which is the worse; both outcomes are extremely damaging to us, the people directly involved, and the world.

There is, however, a third, viable alternative. The authoritarian governments currently in place should be encouraged, cajoled, helped, and pressured to lay the groundwork for the greater participation of moderate groups in the government—while keeping the Islamists at bay. As Gause puts it, "Rather than pushing for quick elections, the United States should focus its energy on encouraging the development of moderate, nationalist, and liberal political organizations that could compete on an equal footing with Islamist parties. Only by doing so can Washington help ensure that when elections do occur, the results are more in line with U.S. interests."[41]

It is often correctly stated that there are no liberal groups in these societies, or that the reformers are extremely weak. Hence elections end up as a contest between the old regime and the extremists. For true democratization eventually to take place, *a transition period is necessary that enables moderate groups to grow in strength and influence. Only then can they compete with extremists.*

To put it differently, we need to return to a sort of stages development theory. Not long ago such theory was all the rage (although it largely applied to economic development).[42] It was then—as often happens to popular theories—thoroughly debunked. It is time to return to a moderate version of such an approach. True, not all nations do or need to pass through the same stages of political development, and stages can overlap—but nations will be well served if they establish Security First. However, the term Security First must be taken literally. There are second and third phases. These are the ones in which reformers are encouraged while extremists, especially violent ones, are kept out of the political process. Once the reformers find their legs (and various elements of democratization are allowed to mature), political opening can be extended to include radical groups but not necessarily violent ones. It should be noted that elections—often viewed as the first step of democratization—are best deferred precisely because they are nonselective and constitute an opening to all comers, when the polity is not prepared for such a transformation. In the language of the staging theories, elections should be a lagging not a leading element.

No More Weimars

Before I outline how this might be done—and the reasons the current authoritarian rulers might well agree to such developments—I offer an argument based on democratic theory. When I ask political theorists if the Weimar Republic should have allowed the Nazi party, which was openly antidemocratic, to participate in elections and win seats in parliament, the near-unanimous response is in the affirmative. Political scientists stress, quite correctly, that liberal democracy is not simply a government by whoever has the current majority, as many tend to believe; the reason we have checks and balances is to prevent such takeovers. An independent judiciary exists to stand up for the basic rights of individuals, the constitution, and democratic institutions—even if an extremist party wins the elections.

My concern, however, is that the Weimar Republic *had* an independent judiciary. But it could not stand up to the Nazis. If, say, racist, far-right parties of the kind that in the last decades have sprung up in several E.U. nations, such as the British National Party in the United Kingdom and the National Democratic Party in Germany, were to win electoral majorities and take command of the military, police, and intelligence services—the courts would be unlikely to prevent such parties from enacting their platform. I can envision that the people, even if they initially voted for such a party, might possibly take to the streets to protect their constitution. This is to some extent what happened during the 1991 coup attempt by communist hard-liners in Moscow. Mikhail Gorbachev had agreed to grant significantly greater autonomy to the constituent republics of the Soviet Union, freeing them from Moscow's tight control. In response, on August 19, the Soviet vice president, prime minister, and KGB chairman placed Gorbachev under house arrest. Muscovites rallied to the help of the newly elected president of the Russian republic, Boris Yeltsin, who led the resistance efforts from in front of the parliament building, where he famously mounted a tank to denounce the coup. When the majority of the security forces in Moscow defected to Yeltsin's camp on August 21, the coup collapsed, Gorbachev was reinstated, and Yeltsin subsequently consolidated his position as Russia's new, reformist leader.

Such a course of events, however, cannot be relied upon to unfold in many nations, including Russia, in which the judiciary has limited or no independence, and in which democratic constitutions have been only recently introduced and enjoy only limited public support. (The point was illustrated in September 1993, when Yeltsin unconstitutionally dismissed the Congress of People's Deputies by decree, and after a two-week stand-off ordered the bombardment of the same parliament building which he had so recently defended.) Such nations do not have strong educational programs that cultivate in children a commitment to democratic virtues; nor do they have civic groups, a free press, or other vital institutions needed to protect democracy from forceful authoritarian challenges. Hence these institutions must be built up before conducting elections.

Moreover, during this fragile transitional period to democracy, Islamist and other extremist parties must be reined in. I agree here with Charles Krauthammer when he writes:

"A tolerant society has an obligation to be tolerant. Except to those so intolerant that they themselves would abolish tolerance. Call it situational libertarianism: Liberties should be as unlimited as possible—unless and until there arises a real threat to the open society. . . . Why curtail civil liberties to stop them? But when a real threat—such as jihadism—arises, a liberal democratic society must deploy every resource, including the repressive powers of the state, to deter and defeat those who would abolish liberal democracy."[43]

The great damage that faux democratization poses is that it confuses well-established liberal democracies, which can withstand the challenges of extremists, with those that are yet to pass through the needed transformation, and thus places too much of a burden on regimes that are just beginning to find their liberal legs.

Those who find such a claim difficult to accept should note that even well-established liberal democracies place various limits on antidemocratic groups. Germany has introduced a 5 percent minimum threshold in federal elections before a given party can be seated in the Bundestag—thus effectively keeping the neo-Nazi National Democratic Party out of the legislative body. In November 2004 Belgium's highest court found the Flemish nationalist party Vlaams Blok guilty of racism, cutting it off from receiving public election campaign funds and denying it television access. Many nations, including Canada, Britain, and France, impose limits on free speech when it is used to foster hate.

I see no reason why Islamists should be treated differently.

Ways and Means of Transitioning to Democracy

In nearly every nation in which Islamist parties have made political inroads, their success can be credited to three principal factors: they meet the demand for social services that the government is either unable or unwilling to provide; they are strongly religious and thus perceived as moral and trustworthy; and their fierce opposition to the government often leads to crackdowns and persecution, which increases their appeal among the populace.

Hamas's electoral victory in 2006 was due in large part to the extensive social services it provides and the perception that it is much less corrupt than Fatah—and not to its position advocating the destruction of

Israel. The fact that a vast majority of Palestinians continue to favor a peaceful solution to the conflict with Israel indicates that the space exists for an uncorrupt moderate party.

To succeed, any moderate alternative to the Islamist parties must incorporate some of these elements. Moderates must demonstrate that they too can provide services for the public efficiently and without corruption. On the question of religion, moderate parties need not preach secularism—in nations where nearly the entire population highly values public religiosity, secular parties fail. This does not mean that the new parties must take on the radical forms of Islam preached by Islamists. However, moderate Islamic groups pose the most effective political and moral challenge to extremists and, in contrast to what is often assumed, often serve the free world's interests. (Chapter and verse follow in Parts III and IV.)

In any nation ruled by a hated authoritarian regime, those who oppose and challenge the regime most stridently are often most cheered by the people. The Muslim Brotherhood has been persecuted in Egypt since 1954, yet it remains Egypt's most popular opposition group; the shah of Iran suppressed numerous Islamic groups until he was overthrown in a popular Islamist revolution; the Shia organizations in Iraq brutally persecuted by Saddam are now the most popular political parties. While I do not argue that moderate groups must get themselves arrested to win over the hearts of the people, it is essential that they demonstrate they are independent from the regime in power. The regimes, on the other hand, while tolerated by the West for a transition period, must be pressured to cease jailing and torturing anyone who is critical of their rule. Such steps would serve to moderate opposition groups and open up a political space for other than the violent and battle-hardened of leaders and parties.

One might well ask: why would regimes that have suppressed opposition for so long suddenly change course? In part, the answer is that they too see the writing on the wall and may prefer to share power—as the rulers of Bahrain, Qatar, and even Kuwait are *beginning* to do—than face removal from power, if not their own beheadings. Many rulers are also sensitive to their reputation in the eyes of the world, and would prefer to be perceived as tolerant and their nations as free rather than as breeding grounds for violent Islamists. These rulers know that the economic and diplomatic clout of their nations depends, in part, on their standing with the West. Thus in 2006 the emirate of Kuwait held parliamentary elections in which women were allowed for the first time to vote and to stand as candidates, and which yielded for the first time a potentially credible opposition bloc committed to electoral and constitutional reform.[44] And in 2005 Saudi Arabia conducted its first elections in forty years, for 178 municipal councils—yielding a strong victory for more moderate Islamists, who continue to oppose women's rights, but who are nevertheless willing to introduce some other reforms, for instance deleting inflammatory anti-non-Muslim language from school textbooks.[45] They are part of an important group of Illiberal Moderates, the focus of my discussion in the next part.

The United States and its allies have a major part to play in the gradual, partly top-down, transition of Arab and Muslim countries to democracy. The United States should especially pressure these regimes to lay the groundwork of a liberal political order by strengthening the independence of the judiciary, incorporating pro-democratic civic education in school curricula, and passing laws that guarantee freedom of the press and various civil rights. None of these changes amounts to anything like overthrowing the regime, or indiscriminately aligning with the opposition, or prematurely opening the door to elections for which primarily extremists are prepared.

In addition, the large amount of funds that Western nations and international institutions such as the World Bank provide Arab governments should be dedicated as much as possible to providing social services via moderate political groups. As noted already, the Palestinian Authority under Fatah was widely perceived as corrupt by those it was meant to serve; yet for years the United States and European Union provided billions of dollars in aid to the Palestinian Authority. In other nations, it has long been known that massive amounts of the foreign aid granted by Western nations ended up enriching rulers rather than helping their citizens. Yet for decades foreign powers and international institutions were extremely reluctant to provide funds directly to the civic groups in these nations, or insist on accountability and transparency in the government. Over recent years, the need for change in such policies has been increasingly recognized. It is now well known (though still too often not taken into account in designing actual programs) that a major way to help moderate groups compete with Islamists is providing services and demonstrating that it is possible to be moderate and uncorrupt.

The course here recommended, *reforming the autocracies so that mod-*

erate groups can become competitive, and more generally laying the ground-work for democratization beyond conducting elections, has several important precedents. David Brooks summarized these well when he wrote:

> In 1848 a democratic revolution swept across Europe, and then promptly collapsed. Thousands of protesters were killed in the streets. Authoritarian regimes were reestablished. Some called 1848 the turning point when Europe failed to turn.
>
> And yet that wasn't true. Anti-democratic regimes did regain power, but within decades they had enacted most of the reforms the revolutionaries of 1848 had asked for. Constitutions were written. Suffrage was expanded. Welfare systems were created.
>
> Conservative authoritarians enacted these reforms reluctantly, and with cynical motivations. But they knew they had to keep up with the times to retain their grip on power and to forestall more radical change. Democracy didn't move forward in a burst of glory, but in a long slog of gradual concessions made by reluctant conservative reformers.[46]

As the historical precedents indicate, one cannot sit back and expect the autocracies to reform themselves. For such a transformation to occur, they must be encouraged, rewarded, and pressured. No wonder Saudi Arabia and Egypt curtailed most of the limited reforms their autocracies introduced in the years leading to 2005, once the United States—as part of the backlash against democratization—softened its pressure for progress to continue. There is reason not to treat elections as a magic wand that can turn ugly authoritarian frogs into handsome liberal-democratic princes. This does not mean leaving the authoritarian rulers to follow their own course. Democratic transitions start best with reforming them and their regimes. As basic security is provided, democratization can begin in earnest, with elections as the lagging factor, and moderation—especially gradually opening the political channels of expression and network of building associations—the leading one.

CHAPTER C. THE LESSONS OF RECONSTRUCTION AND ECONOMIC DEVELOPMENT

Many of the same issues that arise with regard to democratization also pertain to postconflict reconstruction and, more generally, to economic development. There are those who believe that economic development drives security, i.e., that giving people jobs will get them off the streets, and that it can be promoted effectively on a large scale in scores of nations by the United States and its allies (working with international institutions such as the World Bank). I hold that (a) here, too, basic security must first be established; (b) economic development can be achieved, but it is a more gradual and taxing process than is often assumed; and (c) it is best undertaken primarily by the people directly concerned.

To illustrate the lack of realistic thinking and the unrealistic aspirations of those who keep calling for a Marshall Plan for this or that nation if not for a dozen of them, and who claim that America "owes" the nations we have liberated economic reconstruction, I draw on the experiences of the U.S. coalition in Iraq, adding some references to other situations. The British Chancellor of the Exchequer, Gordon Brown, did in fact call in 2002 for a Global Marshall Plan, and at the 2005 G-8 summit in Perthshire, Scotland, proposed raising total annual development aid to Third World nations from $50 billion to $100 billion by 2015.[47] My purpose is strictly illustrative; a full examination of the subject would require a hefty tome unto itself.

No Security, No Reconstruction

The fact that basic security first must be established if economic reconstruction is to proceed successfully seems so elementary that it is hardly worth mentioning. If contractors are regularly kidnapped, if the pipelines they lay are blown up, and if those who cooperate with them are kidnapped or shot, reconstruction will at best proceed with great difficulties and at huge costs. Yet before this lesson began to sink in, America made prolonged, vain attempts to proceed with reconstruction in areas of Iraq where basic security had been lacking.

By the end of 2006 the United States had spent over $25 billion of its own money and $40 billion of Iraq's to finance reconstruction.[48] Even by the most modest standards, the results have been dismal. Most glaringly, the critical areas of infrastructure—sewage, water, electricity, and oil—remain in poor condition. In March 2006, total oil production stood precariously at 2 million barrels per day—well under Saddam's 2.6 million average in 2003, and far below the U.S. goal for that date of 3 million.[49] In late 2006, electrical output was still woefully below demand.

A telling example of the ways in which lack of security is undermining reconstruction is the story of a $32-million trash dump, paid for by the United States, which sits idle at the outskirts of Baghdad. In 2005 an adjoining sewage plant's manager was killed. Since then, access roads to the dump have been considered too risky to use.[50] By the end of 2006 over four hundred contractors in Iraq had been killed. In areas where the fighting escalated, months of progress were undone in hours, such as in the aftermath of the 2004 Baghdad clash between American forces and those of Muqtada al-Sadr, during which militiamen destroyed public utilities, often stripping everything of value from electrical stations, waterworks, and sewage plants.[51] In several provinces this pattern is repeated. The obvious lesson, which was surprisingly long lost on the United States: to install and build and operate essential services, a U.S. military presence is required to defend the builders and to safeguard that which has been built.

These efforts are further limited by the lack of security of Americans trying to help reconstruction. The following few lines uttered by the former head of USAID say it all: "Americans are permitted to travel outside their working compounds—even inside the Green Zone—only if the trips are planned three days in advance, and then only with a security detail usually composed of a large contingent of retired commandos from Western militaries hired at great cost from private security contractors."[52]

Slowly the need to focus on Security First dawned on those involved in the planning of Iraq's reconstruction. After three years it became impossible to ignore that massive and ambitious reconstruction projects would not in and of themselves quell the insurgency or restore normalcy. By April 2006 the lack of progress was, in the words of Stuart Bowen Jr., the Special Inspector General for Iraq Reconstruction, "fundamentally due to unmet security needs driven by a lethal and persistent insurgency."[53] Andrew Natsios, the former director of USAID, acknowledged around the same time that without basic security, ambitious reconstruction projects were ill-advised, saying, "We set [them] up to fail."[54]

By the end of 2006 there was some recognition that without a Security First approach, reconstruction and economic development cannot proceed in an effective manner. Referring to the new approach, Carlos Pascual, the former head of the State Department's Office for Reconstruction and Stabilization, said, "If that is not done, then the society will unravel at some point."[55] After nearly three years of bloodshed and spasmodic progress, in April 2006 the State Department announced that in *future* wars it would focus on security and stability before reconstruction: "Under the new plan, the United States would first establish public security and order, and then encourage small-scale economic activity while promoting political reconciliation. . . . After that, banks, political parties and other institutions would be established, followed by news media, private aid organizations and civilian advocacy groups. Physical reconstruction would begin 'only when it seems to fit into the other priorities.' "[56]

Even at this point not everyone agrees that, without basic security, reconstruction will be very hard to achieve and, for that which is rebuilt, to remain standing. Thus Lt. Gen. Peter Chiarelli, who assumed command of the ground troops in January 2006, stated, "If you're saying you've got to get an area secure before you do any reconstruction, you'll never get any reconstruction done."[57] Echoing Chiarelli's statements, Lt. Col. Jeff Kenney mused, "Instead of kicking in doors, what we should have done was put in a water purification system on the Tigris River."[58] Kicking in doors may not be the best way to establish basic security. But neither are water purification plants. To reiterate, such plants are very difficult and costly to build and do not last if terrorism is not controlled; and, by themselves, they will do precious little to control it. I am all in favor of helping people obtain clean water. But they will not need it if they are killed, and the pumps help little if they are being blown up more quickly than they are installed. The case for basic Security First—for reconstruction and not just democratization—is that simple. Yet even as security remained elusive and casualties spiked in late 2006, the U.S. Joint Chiefs of Staff shied away from a Security First approach when they recommended a "shift" in focus from fighting insurgents to implementing "a much greater U.S. effort on political reconciliation and economic reconstruction, especially new jobs programs."[59]

Reconstruction or Economic Development?

Most scholars, public intellectuals, and those in the media who use the term *reconstruction* equate it with economic development, at least by implication. Some use it even more broadly to refer to general development, including democratization and the formation of civil society. I suggest that it is preferable to define reconstruction much more narrowly, as the restoration of the condition of the assets and infrastructure of an occupied nation or territory to the same or similar state prior to the outbreak of hostilities. The difference between these two definitions is akin to the distinction between restoring a burned-down house to its condition before the fire, versus turning a mud hut or old shack into a brand-new building with all the latest conveniences.

In the case of Iraq, in April 2003 the rarely used, narrow definition was applied by Carl Conetta, co-director of the Project on Defense Alternatives, who defined it as: "Repairing the residual damage to and accumulated disrepair of key infrastructure, industry, and services that resulted from 12 years of sanctions and the 1990–1991 Gulf war."[60]

The other, much broader and open-ended definition of reconstruction has been employed more often. In the months leading up to the war, Zalmay Khalilzad, who later became U.S. ambassador to Iraq, put forth his view of reconstruction:

> We believe that three sets of challenges will follow the liberation of Iraq. First will be political reconstruction. This will involve thorough reform of the Iraqi government. "De-Ba'athifying" Iraq means removing those elements used by Saddam to enforce his tyranny on the Iraqi people. Officials found guilty of crimes against humanity will be prosecuted. The larger issue of the transition to justice will be settled by Iraqis themselves. Second, the economy will need to be reformed to put Iraq on the path to prosperity. The United States is committed to ensuring that the Iraqi people's oil patrimony will be used to meet their own economic and reconstruction needs. Third, with regard to security reconstruction, Iraq's international borders will be protected and respected.[61]

Following the ouster of Saddam, John B. Taylor, U.S. Undersecretary of the Treasury for International Affairs, stated that with regard to reconstruction, the United States hoped to turn Iraq into a "well-functioning market economy that is growing, creating jobs, and is promising a future" for the Iraqi people.[62]

Writing about the task of postwar reconstruction, several scholars have similarly opted for the broader, open-ended definition. The reconstruction effort's goal in Iraq, according to Bathsheba Crocker, a senior associate at the Center for Strategic and International Studies, was "to transform a centralized economy into a market economy and to reconstruct a war-torn economy."[63] In their analysis of postwar reconstruction, Sultan Barakat and his associates, professors from the University of York's Post-war Reconstruction and Development Unit, define the five key areas of reconstruction as: "Security (I feel secure in my home and in my daily activities); Governance and participation (I have a say in how Iraq is run); Economic opportunity (I have a means of income); Services (I have access to basic services, such as power, water and sanitation); and Social well-being (my family and I have access to health care and education)."[64] One of the goals of the occupation and reconstruction was, according to Marc Grossman, Undersecretary of State for Political Affairs, "to begin the process of economic and political reconstruction, working to put Iraq on a path to become prosperous and free."[65]

Stephen Krasner, the Director of Policy Planning at the State Department, and Carlos Pascual, Coordinator from the Office of Reconstruction and Stabilization, wrote, "If we are going to ensure that countries are set on a sustainable path towards peace, democracy and a market economy, we need new, institutionalized foreign policy tools—tools that can influence the choices countries and people make about the nature of their economies, their political systems, their security, indeed, in some cases about the *very social fabric of a nation*."[66]

Furthermore, because failing or weak states are considered breeding grounds for terrorists, some have even called for a worldwide reconstruction and development of such states—dozens of them all told. In *Foreign Affairs,* former U.S. Undersecretary of State Stuart Eizenstat and his colleagues write:

> The United States needs a new, comprehensive strategy to reverse this trend and turn back the tide of violence, humanitarian crises, and social upheaval that is sweeping across developing countries *from Afghanistan to Zimbabwe*—and that could engulf the rest of the world. An effective strategy will embrace a four-pronged approach focused on crisis prevention, rapid response, centralized U.S. decision-making, and international cooperation. A plan of such scope must first recognize that the roots of the weak-state crisis, and any hope for a long-term solution, lie

in development: fostering stable, accountable institutions in struggling nations—institutions that meet the needs of the people, empowering them to improve their lives through lawful, not desperate, means. Washington must realize that weak and failed countries present a security challenge that cannot be met through security means alone; the United States simply cannot police every nation where danger might lurk. Thus, state building is not an act of simple charity but a smart investment in the United States' own safety and stability.[67]

In January 2007, President Bush unveiled his "New Way Forward" strategy for Iraq. One of the two key elements of the plan was a new commitment to reconstruction, but only $1.2 billion was set aside for this purpose. As I see it there is considerable merit in drawing a clear distinction between reconstruction and general economic development. First, such a distinction avoids unnecessary gaps between social science terminology and public vernacular. In the case at hand, the definitions used by the public clearly distinguish between the two processes. According to the Oxford English Dictionary, *reconstruction* is defined as "the rebuilding of an area devastated by war" and "the restoration of economic stability to such an area," whereas *development* is defined as "the economic advancement of a region or people, especially one currently under-developed."[68] Reconstruction occurred in Germany and Japan after World War II and is currently being attempted in Iraq and Afghanistan. Economic development has been achieved by nations acting on their own initiative, such as China, South Korea, Singapore, and Taiwan, and sustained efforts are being made to develop scores of other nations, especially in Africa.

Another merit of differentiating the terms is that reconstruction, in the narrow sense of the word, presumes an end at which reconstruction will be complete. At that point the foreign powers will have discharged their commitment to undo whatever harm their military intervention may have caused. Also, those on the receiving end will have a sense that a promise made to them has been honored, and that henceforth they will be expected to fend on their own. There is, of course, nothing to prevent foreign powers so inclined to set additional goals once reconstruction is completed or as it progresses, including laboring to gain other forms of development. Still, for reasons already indicated, it seems beneficial to be able to determine what reconstruction specifically entails as distinct from economic, social, and political development.

In contrast, equating reconstruction with economic development leaves the end state of the endeavors vague and indefinite at best. Economic development is in truth never complete. Indeed, as Singapore's per capita gross domestic product (GDP) was rapidly approaching that of the United States, former Prime Minister Lee Kuan Yew rationalized deferring further democratization on the grounds that, "[s]ince it was dire poverty that made for such low priority given to human life, all other things became secondary."[69] In short, reconstruction and economic development are best not conflated.

What Do We Owe?

There are those who hold that reconstruction is a moral obligation that occupying forces assume. For instance, the argument is made that because the United States invaded Iraq it is obligated to reconstruct the country. The same is said about other nations in which the United States has become involved, from Haiti to Afghanistan. Noah Feldman writes in his book, appropriately entitled *What We Owe Iraq*: "The Coalition's security obligation extends forward beyond just ending the insurgency, however. By its presence, even after the occupation formally ended, the Coalition was under a duty to guarantee that the country would not revert to anarchy. That means an obligation for American or international troops to remain until they can be replaced by Iraqi security forces under the command of the democratic state."[70] Once we have involved ourselves in this situation, he reasons, "The United States now has no *ethical* choice but to remain until an Iraqi security force, safely under the civilian control of the government of a legitimate, democratic state, can be brought into existence."[71]

In the face of a tenacious insurgency and the resulting damage to the nation, it is no longer enough for America to have Saddam deposed: "We owe it to Iraq to stay and try to make it work," argues Bill Wineke.[72] Since it was Saddam we overthrew, and not a foreign invader we repelled, Gerard Powers concludes that we assumed an obligation to engage in "institutional therapy" of Iraq.[73]

More generally it has been argued that the Pottery Barn motto applies to occupied countries. That motto, which author and *Washington Post* editor Bob Woodward records Secretary of State Colin Powell as invoking before the invasion of Iraq, and which presidential candidate John Kerry used in a presidential debate, is said to be, "If you broke it, you own it."[74] But Pottery Barn has no such rule, and thus one can hardly rely on it as an analogue to suggest that such a moral obligation exists toward nations.[75] Moreover it can be said that America did not *break* Iraq or Afghanistan, but liberated them from extremely oppressive regimes. True, the U.S. invasion may well have been propelled largely by more self-serving motives than the liberation of oppressed peoples. Also, several of the means used in Iraq, especially torture, are highly unethical. It follows that the United States is obligated to compensate the specific victims of such abuses. Yet whatever U.S. motives in invading the nations at issue, and the nature of some of subsequent U.S. practices, the people of Iraq and Afghanistan were, in the final analysis, delivered from tyranny. Hence a case can be made that these people owe America a vote of thanks—not a bill.

The situation is akin to someone who rescues a drowning person. Surely the lifeguard does not owe the person he saved a new swimming suit or swimming lessons. One can hold that those of means "owe" swimming lessons to everyone who needs them or to those of no means; but it does not follow that there is a moral duty to provide such lessons to the one person who happened to be saved. Thus, even if one accepts as morally binding an obligation to help develop the economies of poor nations, it does not follow that those nations that harbored terrorists, or that embraced authoritarian regimes for decades, have special claims over and above those of all other deprived nations.

One might argue that development ensures that the nation in question will not harbor terrorists or threaten its neighbors in the future. Such an argument, however, rests on a rightly disputed proposition, namely that developed nations do not provide havens for terrorists. Gause notes that "the academic literature on the relationship between terrorism and other sociopolitical indicators, such as democracy, is surprisingly scant."[76] What data there are, however, "certainly do not indicate that democracies are substantially less susceptible to terrorism than are other forms of government."[77] Other studies have reached similar conclusions. Not only is democracy not significantly correlated with reduced levels of terrorism, economic condition and education also fail to explain it. For instance, a study by Alan Krueger and Jitka Maleckova of the National Bureau of

Economic Research concludes, "The evidence we have assembled and reviewed suggests there is little direct connection between poverty, education and participation in terrorism and politically motivated violence."[78]

Arguments that hold that affluent nations owe less privileged nations help in economic development rest on rather different grounds. Most often cited among ethicists who hold that affluent nations owe such foreign aid is the controversial Princeton professor Peter Singer. He argues that there are duties we assume toward human beings whether or not they are members of our particular community: "Our obligation to help a stranger is as great as our obligation to help a neighbor's child."[79] Communitarians (among whom I count myself) need not necessarily object to this proposition; at least for this neo-communitarian, basic human rights and dignity are indeed universal. Particularistic communal responsibilities are not a substitute for universal claims. For example, the observation that we have some obligations to all children does not contradict the commonsense observation that we have additional ones to our own children.[80] Furthermore, there are those who argue that if we can help others without imposing great burdens on ourselves, we ought to do so.[81] Accordingly all human beings enjoy a fundamental dignity as potentially virtuous beings, which may be nurtured by economic development. Still others point out that our various religious traditions command us to be charitable. And still others consider socioeconomic rights just as sacred as legal-political rights.

On the other hand, some have raised a whole series of ethical concerns about the negative effects of economic development aid. One concern is the emergence of dependency, in which whole classes of people expect to be aided for extended periods of time and consequently curtail their own economic development efforts. Not only can foreign aid diminish the competitiveness of local economies, it is said that it can "support governments hostile to social justice or structural reforms," and prop up corrupt or unworthy leaders.[82] As a result, aid can function as a "poisoned gift" to Third World nations.[83] Still others hold that removal of Western barriers to exports of the products of poor nations should be preferred to ongoing aid payments. Yet another, not insignificant concern is with the intrinsic nature of economic development: that it is too materialistic and may irreparably undermine the spiritual and moral and civic roots of traditional societies.

The ways we treat the most heinous criminals—serial killers, terrorists, and child molesters—seem to me to provide an insight into what our moral intuition informs us about the subject at hand. Once these criminals are apprehended, all civilized societies provide them with three meals a day, shelter, and elementary medical care. Courts ensure that their living conditions are humane (e.g., not excessively crowded). I cannot see a reason why we should grant any person less. In other words, every human being, by virtue of being human, is entitled to a basic minimum standard of living, which increases as the "have" nations become more affluent.

We also have a moral obligation not to squander those resources available for economic aid. Whatever level these resources reach, even if all the "have" nations were to dedicate 1.7 percent or more of their GDP to foreign aid, there would still be numerous legitimate needs that remained unmet. Hence ensuring that these resources do not end up in the Swiss bank accounts of tyrants or wasted on poorly conceived and poorly managed projects is not merely a technical consideration, but also an ethical one.[84]

In toto, the ethical obligations of reconstruction (in the narrow sense) are far from fully established but nevertheless are much clearer than the obligations of ongoing development aid, about which there is much thoughtful and principled disagreement. Indeed, reconstruction obligations—unlike developmental ones—are ensconced in international law.

A Matter of Law

Obligations to provide for postwar reconstruction are laid out in the 1907 Hague Regulations and the 1949 Geneva Convention IV. Article 43 of the Hague Regulations states: "The authority of the legitimate power having in fact passed into the hands of the occupant, the latter shall take all measures in his power to restore and ensure, as far as possible, public order and [civil life], while respecting, unless absolutely prevented, the laws in force in the country."

Article 56 of Geneva IV states: "To the fullest extent of the means available to it, the public Occupying Power has the duty of ensuring and maintaining, with the cooperation of national and local authorities, the medical and hospital establishments and services, public health and hygiene in the occupied territory, with particular reference to the adoption and application of the prophylactic and preventive measures necessary to combat the spread of contagious diseases and epidemics. Medical personnel of all categories shall be allowed to carry out their duties." And Article 59 of the same document declares: "If the whole or part of the population of an occupied territory is inadequately supplied, the Occupying Power shall agree to relief schemes on behalf of the said population, and shall facilitate them by all the means at its disposal."

Eyal Benvenisti, writing in *The International Law of Occupation*, interprets the Hague article as the need to restore the status quo ante, but probably no further: "The need to 'restore' public order and civil life arises in the wake of hostilities that disrupt them. The restoration process includes immediate acts needed to bring daily life as far as possible back to the previous state of affairs. The occupant's discretion in this process is limited. At issue is the extent to which the occupant must adhere to the *status quo ante bellum*. This question becomes more pressing as the occupation is protracted."[85]

Writing in *The American Journal of International Law*, David Scheffer offers further support for the notion of preserving the status quo and questions the legal imperative to rebuild past that point: "Occupation law was not designed to transform society. It permits tinkering on the edges of societal reform, but it is not a license to transform. . . . The fundamental premise of occupation law has been to confine the occupying power to humanitarian objectives that essentially preserve the status quo, not to entitle the occupying power to transform the territory it holds (often illegally)."[86] Grant Harris, in *The Berkeley Journal of International Law*, concurs: "The law of occupation was meant to balance the security needs of the occupant against desired protections for the civilian population of the territory in an overall framework meant to preserve the *status quo ante* until ultimate sovereignty of the territory could be decided. To this end, the primary responsibilities of an occupying power according to the international law of occupation are to (1) temporarily preserve basic public order without prejudicing a final outcome and (2) preserve local institutions and law."[87]

Gary Bass, in *Philosophy and Public Affairs*, discusses the general question of *jus post bellum* and supports the notion that only the narrow definition of reconstruction is mandated after a conflict. Looking at the existing body of law that covers postconflict legal responsibilities and obligations, he sees as arguable that there is a duty to provide political or long-term aid, but recognizes a duty to restore a country to its original status:

Beyond the question of political reconstruction lies that of economic restoration: to what extent are the victors of a war obliged to assist in the restoration of a shattered economy and society to its prewar status, or at least to aid in pulling it out of the rubble? It is easier to argue for economic restoration—some obligation to restore wartime damage—than for transformative political reconstruction. Wartime damage inflicts a collective harm on the citizens of a country, including upon citizens who did not consent to the war or who played a trivial role in the decision to go to war that does not merit the kind of suffering they endured as a consequence of policies adopted in foreign ministries and cabinet meetings. The theologian Michael Shuck posits a "principle of restoration": at least cleaning up the battlefields, and at most helping to rebuild the country's infrastructure, as well as caring for innocent victims of the war.[88]

Bass further suggests that if we are to accept President Bush's original rationale for the invasions of Iraq and Afghanistan—just wars that are morally mandated—then it still places no obligation upon the United States to commit to a long-term reconstruction of the occupied nations, and no moral imperative to lift these countries up to our level: "In fact, the just war tradition originally only mandated a return to the *status quo ante*."[89]

The same is true about the fact that we owe all people a basic minimum. (Which, on the face of it, does not imply that we owe them aid until they possess economic equality with us.) Furthermore, there is a growing recognition that aid should be subject to certain conditions—that the receiving nations will use the resources in a legitimate and prudent manner. At the same time, affluent nations (and international institutions that are financed largely by these nations) should be expected to help less affluent ones to reform their institutions (e.g., to curb corruption) to a point that these nations will be able to benefit from foreign aid.

All said and done, there is a need for further deliberation about what the ethics of development entails, as there are rather disparate views on the issue. The moral (and legal) obligations of occupying forces to reconstruct the nations the war damaged are much less contested.

Triage vs. Scattergun Approaches to Reconstruction

The reconstruction difficulties in Iraq point to an issue that arises in all other such endeavors. It concerns the ways in which the resources that are dedicated to reconstruction are allocated, especially whether their allocation adheres to an established set of priorities, or whether those resources are dispersed widely, without any overarching sense of who is first on the list, who is second or third, or who may well have to fend on their own. In Iraq the United States and its allies set out not merely to rebuild the Iraqi infrastructure (itself a monumental task), but also to improve, modernize, and Americanize numerous other elements of Iraqi society. Hence the reconstruction effort has encompassed not only vital services such as water, irrigation canals, sewage, and electricity, but also a huge array of other services and structures—from schools and playgrounds to clinics and banks. In addition, programs were launched to retrain judges and civil servants, introduce prison reforms, and build a civil society. Furthermore, an ongoing USAID initiative since September 2004 focuses on the private sector. Among its goals are the establishment of an Iraqi stock exchange and an Iraqi securities commission, the provision of forty thousand hours of training in "international accounting standards, enabling businesses to secure loans and manage accounts," and the initiation of the process of joining the WTO.[90] The World Bank adds to the list of goals "establishing a social safety net," and strengthening the government.[91] To top it all, according to former USAID director Andrew Natsios, reconstruction and restoration "are not principally about building physical structures, but about building institutions, reforming policies, and transferring values."[92]

The mission statement of the U.S. Army Corp of Engineers Project and Contracting Office, which had discretion over the original $18.4 billion allocated to reconstruction, illustrates the scattergun approach and the wide range of activities and projects lumped under the term *reconstruction:*

Employment for hundreds of thousands of Iraqis, resulting in economic security, occupational training, and professional mastery of new skills . . .

Higher quality of life and enhanced internal security for Iraqis.

The building of the Iraqi industries required to sustain and further improve the basic infrastructure services required for a modern nation.[93]

In the "Facilities and Transportation" sector of reconstruction the Army Corps lists:

- Security Construction of 151 border forts, 10 points of entry, 90 fire stations and 583 police stations
- Justice Construction of two prisons, five new courts and renovation of 15 courts
- Military Construction of 38 projects at five military bases
- Health Renovation of 20 hospitals, construction of 150 primary healthcare centers and construction of up to seven extended healthcare centers
- Education Renovation of up to 800 schools
- Public Buildings Renovation of five Ministry buildings and a university facility
- Transportation Construction of 420 km of village roads, 200 km of expressways, five bridges, 107 railroad projects, five projects at Iraq's main port and seven projects at three airports
- Communications Construction of a national advanced first-responder emergency network, a wireless communications network for Iraqi Ministries in Baghdad and renovation of two communications buildings and 30 post offices
- Non-Construction Support equipment for prisons, health facilities and schools.[94]

All this may seem commendable until one takes into account that the resources available for reconstruction were—as they always are—limited, and that by scattering them so widely, few of the goals set were actually achieved. Moreover, vital services were neglected while resources were dedicated to initiate many projects that were worthy but less vital. "Resources" refers not merely to budgetary allocations but also to security personnel, army units, advisers, and reliable contractors and subcontractors and the attention span of leaders and top administrators, all of which are as a rule in short supply in view of what is called for.

In Iraq the scattergun approach to reconstruction meant that "this country is filled with projects that were never completed or were completed and have never been used," according to a U.S. official.[95] By June

2006 more than 75 percent of oil and gas reconstruction projects were unfinished; the same was true of 40 percent of water and sanitation projects.[96] Three years after the invasion, even basic services remained well below Saddam's prewar levels. In March 2006, total oil production stood well under Saddam's average in 2003, as we have already seen. Electrical output stood fully 2,000 megawatts below the U.S. goal of 6,000 (and 300 below what was generated in 2003), and the production of drinkable water was 1.4 million cubic meters less than the planned 2.5 million per day, and 1.9 million fewer than in 2003.[97] Access to reliable sewers has also fallen off noticeably since the invasion. In July 2006, Baghdad's residents received, on average, 7.6 hours of electricity per day. Under Saddam, they enjoyed anywhere from 16 to 24 hours.[98] In many other cities around the country it is not unusual to expect a mere four hours a day of power.

To add but one of many comparable examples: after two years and over $200 million spent, the American construction company Parsons, Inc., abandoned its efforts to build 150 primary health centers. It was ordered to build all the clinics simultaneously, and one year faster than its estimates dictated possible. Parsons exhausted the money allotted to it for the project—having finished just 20 and having left scores of unfinished buildings scattered throughout Iraq.[99] I am not arguing that nothing was accomplished. However, the effect of this hit-or-miss approach was that projects were started in numerous areas, but relatively little has been completed in the most important areas of reconstruction.

On top of failures in infrastructure reconstruction, planned market reforms in Iraq were not achieved, and welfare paternalism continued. The Special Inspector General for Reconstruction in Iraq, Stuart Bowen, testified before Congress late in 2005:

> While Iraq is sitting on an abundance of crude oil, it is a net im-
> porter of refined fuels, due to a lack of refining capacity. This
> costs the nation more than $300 million a month. As well, the
> Iraqi Transitional Government policy is to subsidize fuel prices.
> According to the IMF [International Monetary Fund], the gov-
> ernment paid more than $7 billion in 2004 to provide the con-
> sumer with gasoline and diesel at about a nickel a gallon. At this

price, demand is exaggerated, and smugglers have lucrative opportunities to deliver subsidized fuel to neighboring countries
where prices are 100 times greater. One third of Iraq's gasoline
and diesel fuel is stolen and sold over the border, costing the
country about $2 billion a year.[100]

The same was true with various endeavors to reform the country's civil
service. Although ample reconstruction funds were dedicated to this area
and to bring it in line with Western expectations, U.S. Comptroller General David M. Walker's report showed poor progress in this area as well:

According to the World Bank and U.N. specialized agency officials, public tendering is still an "alien concept" within Iraq Ministries. These officials reported several recent attempts by
Ministry officials to subvert the public procurement process. For
example, World Bank financing for two projects worth $40 mil-
lion each was cancelled after Iraqi ministry officials awarded
contracts to firms that were not included in the competitive bid-
ding process. U.S. officials also reported instances of corruption
related to the protection of essential infrastructure. According to
IRMO officials, the Ministry of Electricity contracts with tribal
chiefs, paying them about $60–$100 per kilometer to protect
transmission lines running through their areas. However,
IRMO officials reported that the protection system is flawed and
encourages corruption. According to U.S. and U.N. Development Program officials, some tribes that are paid to protect
transmission lines are also selling materials from downed lines
and extracting tariffs for access to repair the lines. IRMO officials stated that they want the Ministry of Electricity to change
the system so that tribes are only paid when the lines remain op-
erational for a reasonable period of time.[101]

Thus, while some substantial achievements were made (e.g., thousands of schools were built or refurbished, and the number of Iraqi Internet and cellular phone subscribers greatly increased), the shotgun approach meant that the most basic and fundamental services are still sorely
lacking. Furthermore, the credibility of the Western approach was severely undermined. As Col. Joseph Anderson, commander of the 2nd

Brigade, 101st Airborne Division, put it, "Money is our ammo. . . . We had many plans based on good faith, and people expect results. We are now having to explain why we can't follow through."[102]

Reconstruction would greatly benefit if the concept of triage were applied to it. Triage is employed when a disaster causes a large number of casualties and the responders lack sufficient numbers and resources to treat them simultaneously. Those who rush to assist must decide who is to be helped first, which victims can fend on their own at least for a while, and which sadly are most likely beyond hope. Not only is it unwise trying to help everyone at the same time, with the same level of intensity, but such a scattered approach also saves fewer lives and hence is morally defective compared to that of triage, however bitter its assumptions.

The lessons of triage are relevant to newly liberated nations. It is impossible to fix their oil wells, ports, roads, schools, hospitals, utilities, civil service, police, armed forces, markets, and so on as the United States has attempted. A progressive critic of this text suggested that basically what we need to do is to increase the funding available for reconstruction (or development). This may well be the case. However, there is *no* level of foreign aid at which all needs, indeed even all the major ones, could be properly covered—surely not in short order, and by short order I mean years as distinct from decades if not generations. Hence triage is essential; it cannot be obviated by increasing commitments of resources, however commendable such increases may be for other reasons.

The same critic further wondered if it might be possible to develop one part of a given society without the others, suggesting that the various elements are linked into a system and hence must be advanced simultaneously. This is true to some extent; if we fix only the roads but not corruption, the roads are likely to fare no better than the New Orleans levees. If we do not improve schooling, industries will lack human resources, and so on. However, the elements of the social system are not so tightly linked that it is impossible to proceed in some sectors, to a considerable extent, before building up the others. In effect there is considerable "play" among the linked elements. This is a fortunate feature of societies, as there is no way to develop all the elements in tandem. In this sense reconstruction triages differ from medical triages, because the latter usually deal with a one-time event, while in the case of the former, one can lay out a sequence of treatments, so that those elements first neglected can be picked up later.

If a triage approach had been applied from the beginning of the occupation of Iraq, the first priority would have been to establish basic security and the second to rebuild the crucial infrastructure. Given the limited resources available, most other projects might well have had to be left for the Iraqis to carry out themselves with little foreign aid or guidance, and still might have had to wait their turn. Such a triage approach would have taken into account that some developments have a strong multiplier effect (e.g., increasing the production and export of oil), whereas others do not (e.g., adding dump trucks). Some projects are quick to pay off (e.g., enhancing security), others very slow to deliver (e.g., improving primary education). The progress of some projects can be assessed readily and hence supervision and accountability are easier to come by (e.g., generating electricity); others are more ephemeral (e.g., retraining the civil service).

One may well provide different criteria to guide reconstruction triage; the record, however, strongly suggests that the scattergun approach is likely to fail, and there are serious doubts about its moral worth, given that it leads to the squandering of scarce resources and thus curtails the overall value of the help that is given. Triage is vital.

CHAPTER D. THE LESSONS OF NATION-BUILDING

Nation-building, another form of social engineering, is closely related to democratization and economic development. I use the term *nation* to mean, as most do, a community invested in a state. Hence the people involved are not merely citizens who hold the same passport, pay taxes to the same government, and elect its public officials, but who are also members of a community with which they have bonds of affinity and who share a core of moral commitments, a remembered past, and a destiny. When a nation is well formed it commands strong loyalty from its citizens; indeed, they are willing to die for it.

Nation-building as a term is often used loosely to refer to a large variety of endeavors, including political and economic development. Historically, however, nation-building meant establishing a nation in a territory that was previously encompassed within a multiethnic empire. This often meant enabling a previously stateless ethnic community to form its own state, even if that entailed the community breaking away from a larger state. Nation-building of this kind took place in the Balkans and Latin America and more recently, at the end of the colonial period, in Asia and Africa. In some other cases, one ethnic (or religious) group seceded from an established nation-state, the way Bangladesh did from Pakistan and Slovakia from Czechoslovakia.

A particular form of nation-building that is especially relevant to my examination of social engineering is when the national community labors to strengthen its communal bonds to discourage secession, much as Canada labored to discourage Quebec from seceding. It is this kind of anti-centrifugal nation-building that foreign powers have attempted to bring about in Iraq and Afghanistan, and especially in Kosovo and Bosnia.

Nation-building has been successful in earlier generations by working against—breaking away from—foreign colonial powers, rather than by being guided by their reengineering designs. The well-known wars of national liberation took place when scores of ethnic, religious, or other groups rebelled against colonial powers and won their independence. In other cases, nations were cobbled together from disparate fragments, but again only after prolonged wars that gave voice to a fledgling community, rather than by being engendered by an external power. Well-known examples include the formation of Bismarck's Germany, Cavour's Italy, and the consolidation of the United States as one nation during and after its civil war.

In many of those cases in which the foreign powers did engineer a state by arbitrarily combining various groups, the results have often not led to the formation of one solid national community, but instead to severe tensions among the groups that were forced to live together, as has been the case in India, Burundi, Nigeria—and Iraq and Afghanistan. These states have often only been held together under the thumb of a tyrant and have fallen apart soon after the central government weakened, such as when Yugoslavia disintegrated after the death of Marshal Tito. I am not suggesting that these engineered "nations" did not command some measure of loyalty from their citizens, especially when their country has been confronted by a foreign enemy. However, the *primary* loyalty of most citizens has remained to their particular ethnic, religious, or tribal group, such as the Pashtuns in Afghanistan, the Shia Arabs, Sunni Arabs, and Kurds in Iraq, and the Albanian Muslims and Orthodox Serbs in Kosovo.

When foreign powers interfere in the internal affairs of such nations —for whatever reason—they face the question of whether to pressure the members of the various groups to remain members of one political entity, one nation, or to allow them to break away along "natural" lines. Maintaining the states as one entity greatly increases the social engineering costs, hence several observers have strongly recommended allowing Iraq, for instance, to divide itself into three nations.[103] The likely result would be self-governing Shia and Kurdish states, leaving the United States and its allies to contend with the problems of a Sunni territory. Similar suggestions have been made with regard to Afghanistan and especially with regard to the secession of Kosovo from Serbia.

The foreign powers in these regions have thus far rejected such recommendations and have chosen to absorb the high social engineering costs generated by nation-building, that is, to encompass parties in one nation who do not wish to be so encompassed. These decisions suggest that the foreign powers involved believe that they can keep these nations together and are willing to pay the price for such ambitions. Often, though, they are unable to prevent a high level of interethnic tension and strife.

There is a middle course between allowing or even welcoming complete fragmentation and secession on the one hand, and undertaking yet one more onerous social engineering project on the other. A third option presents itself: "Hi-Devolution." This entails allowing maximum autonomy for the various provinces within a state (Iraq is divided into eighteen) to set their own regulations on scores of matters (the way American states do), rather than, for example, running education as one national program, in which the textbooks and curricula are all set by the national government. Similarly the Hi-Devolution State would allow for local militias to provide security in the provinces, rather than attempt to integrate them into a national police force. And variations in moral codes, those that determine what is considered "sinful" by the state, would also be tolerated—for instance, some provinces might ban the sale of alcohol while others would allow it. At the same time, several basic commitments to the nation as a whole would be maintained, such as honoring the constitution (including a bill of rights), participating in protecting the nation from external attacks, and voting for national legislative and executive bodies.[104]

One need not be a communitarian to note that the greater respect and latitude for particularistic groups on which the Hi-Devolution State builds in nations in danger of falling apart is supported by a global trend of regional groups gaining ever more autonomy from national governments. In contrast, forced nation-building, in the name of democratization, bucks current history and ignores people's legitimate preferences.[105]

A Security First approach calls for Hi-Devolution, leaving as much autonomy to local authorities as possible, so long as they refrain from violence in their regions and among each other. For instance, since Spain granted somewhat greater autonomy to the Catalonians and even began considering doing the same for the Basques, the threat of domestic terrorism there has subsided. In Canada, secession has been avoided by granting much more autonomy to Quebec. The United Kingdom has devolved increasing autonomy to Scotland and Wales. When this trend has been resisted, as in Russia's dealings with Chechnya, there has been a great deal of bloodshed. All these sociological experiences recommend Hi-Devolution in Afghanistan and Iraq. (An obvious way such devolution can be accomplished is by turning unitary states into federations, which by definition allow much more room for local variations. However, devolution can also be increased in unitary states, as the United Kingdom did under the Blair government. Hence Hi-Devolutions should not be equated with federalism.)

The Lessons of Kosovo

Development in Kosovo since 1999 illustrates the Hi-Devolution approach and the dire consequences of excessively ambitious social engineering and centralism in the name of nation-building and imported regime designs.[106] The most important fact about Kosovo is the split between the Serbs and the Albanians. The main failing of foreign forces has been their desire to foster, impose, or otherwise bring about a multiethnic society in Kosovo in which Serbs and Albanians would enjoy equal status. Five days before his assassination in March 2003, the reformist Serbian Prime Minister Zoran Djindjic put it this way: "Serbs and Albanians have never lived together in Kosovo and Metohija. They have always lived next to each other. A multiethnic Kosovo society is a great illusion. It has never existed. It has always been a society of ethnic co-existence."[107] Charles Kupchan of the Council on Foreign Relations echoed these sentiments: "In spirit as well as fact, multiethnic society is nowhere to be found. Pretending otherwise and denying or delaying independence risks a return to disorder and bloodshed."[108] Following another round of violence—the riots of March 2004—the president of the Kosovo Coordination Centre, Nebojsa Covic, told U.S. Undersecretary of Political Affairs Marc Grossman that "the concept of a multiethnic Kosmet (Kosovo-Metohija) has become an illusion,"[109] and even several Serbian officials have publicly voiced support for ethnic separation.

Despite their long residence in a province of Serbia, most Albanian Kosovars do not identify with Serbia, nor do they share a sense of loyalty to the Serbian state. Even before the beginning of Milosevic's 1998 campaign to kill or expel large numbers of Albanians from Kosovo, the Serbian government had instituted a policy of wide-ranging discrimination. Milosevic oversaw policies that sought to replace Albanian workers with Serbs, to close Albanian-run schools and universities, and to shut down Albanian-language television, radio, and newspapers. At the same time, the Albanian Kosovars hardly behaved as pacifists who turned the other cheek; the Kosovo Liberation Army engaged in terroristic brutalities of its own—mainly against Serbs, such as the massacre at a bar in Pec, but also against its own who got out of line. Hence, when the main armed conflict ended in 1999, the two groups remained extremely hostile to each other. It was into this climate of historical segregation and mutual hostility that the United States, its NATO allies, Russia, and the United Nations stepped in, following the war that saw many thousands of Albanian Kosovars killed, raped, terrorized, or evicted.

The exercise in nation-building in Kosovo began immediately after the end of the NATO bombing campaign, when the United Nations assumed governance of the province. The attempt at social engineering in Kosovo is of special interest because it resembles in many ways other unrealistic, pie-in-the-sky, grandiose plans crafted by superpowers to democratize and develop one nation after another. The plans for Kosovo were laid out in several documents that were endorsed by the United Nations, NATO, and Russia.

These documents, especially U.N. Security Council Resolution 1244 and the U.N. Mission in Kosovo's "Standards for Kosovo," call for the introduction of democratic institutions, a competitive market economy, and the rule of law and protection of minority rights, among other lofty goals. (One USAID official added that the United States is seeking to make Kosovo into a drug-free, gun-free society, without noting the irony that he was seeking to achieve overseas what the United States has been utterly unable to accomplish at home.)

The documents that lay out Kosovo's fate display an almost instinctive aversion to partitions and population exchanges on the part of the United States and its allies. Although they affirm a belief in pluralism, this is to be achieved only in the context of a single national community. They hence set out to form "a sustainable, multi-ethnic, democratic society, in which members of all communities can live in dignity and security."[110] America adamantly opposed suggestion of partition, cantonization, or ethnic separation. U.S. Undersecretary of State Nicholas Burns stated at one point, "It's a perilous exercise to begin drawing—for foreigners to begin to draw lines and redefine other people's reality, their borders."[111] He may not have noted that he was himself not exactly a native son of Kosovo and that he too was drawing borders—only those that suited the lofty goal of nation-building, which conflicts starkly with the assessments of those who truly know Kosovo and who are acquainted with the facts on the ground.

To this a critic might respond: "You could argue that any international effort to induce domestic change of any kind is by nature an attempt to 'disregard facts on the ground,' because the facts on the ground are deplorable. The reason for the international community's interest in state-building in Kosovo wasn't a response to a whim but, as you write above, a moral imperative to end ethnic cleansing—you can't fault the international community for seeming to 'disregard facts on the ground' when there is a moral imperative to change those facts." I readily grant that the U.S. and U.N. plans were not drafted on a whim, but they were nevertheless predicated on mistaken assumptions. Surely the ethnic cleansing had to be stopped; however, the plans for a sustainable, multiethnic, and democratic Kosovo were hatched for the most part *after* the ethnic cleansing had already been halted. No one is denying the extremely deplorable character of what transpired between Serbs and Albanians; but historical facts do not vanish because of our good intentions. Nor were all our intentions so clearly morally justified—for instance, trying to prevent Kosovo from breaking away from Serbia has much less of a moral imperative attached to it than does halting ethnic cleansing.

In accordance with the plans drawn up after the bombing ended, the foreign powers sought to impose their conception of nation-building on the province. I say "impose" because, as of 1999, United Nations Mission in Kosovo (UNMIK) has maintained de facto trusteeship of the province, with powers to shape the civil and political society of Kosovo as it deems fit. Established by the U.N. Security Council in the aftermath of the war, UNMIK styles itself as an interim civilian administration, with all the powers and authority due a normal government. The administrator of UNMIK, under whose authority Kosovo is run, acts as "proconsul of an imperial exercise in pacification and nation-building."[112] This arrogance is well captured in the following passage from a 2006 report by the International Crisis Group: "Although it will move the process closer to arbitration and imposition as the year deepens, the international community still risks *deciding* Kosovo by the wrong process. A negotiated settlement is the ideal, but by setting this as the target the international community implies that cutting a deal is a higher priority than ensuring lasting stability and development for Kosovo and the region. *Imposition* of an independence backing, if it should come to that, would be a better bet than attempting to finesse Pristina and Belgrade's differences."[113]

Bernard Kushner, the former head administrator in Kosovo, acted very much the part of the proconsul. To "create democracy where none has ever taken root before," he banned newspapers from printing divisive information, appointed specific judges to attain multiethnicity on judicial councils, and even declared the Deutsche mark the official Kosovo currency.[114] UNMIK tried to form an ethnically mixed Kosovo Police Service; the judiciary and criminal justice system were to be reconstituted similarly with a mix of ethnicities, and the United Nations has labored to appoint multiethnic municipal councils in mixed communities.

Six years later, the futility of seeking to impose such plans on people who suffered as much as the Albanian Kosovars did, and who yearn as strongly as they do for independence, and who are mostly of one ethnicity —stands out. Many Serbian civilians have also suffered greatly, to the point that they too have become more favorable to separation in one form or another. Serbs, who mainly live in their own segregated enclaves, often even fear to travel to other parts of Kosovo or non-Serbian areas of the cities in which they are concentrated. Interethnic crime remains high. Collaboration between the two groups in many matters ranges from minimal to nonexistent. Kosovo is now six years into the nation-building process. It is approaching the time for various foreign powers to scale down and finally remove their forces from the area. It is time to acknowledge that U.N. Security Council Resolution 1244, which lays out UNMIK's mission and role, is "political science fiction" written without regard to the realities of life and ethnic interactions in Kosovo.[115] Although written in regard to Bosnia, Michael Ignatieff's observations hold true for Kosovo, from the involvement of the United Nations to the supposed cooperation between ethnic leaders:

> Bosnia after Dayton offered laboratory conditions in which to ex-
> periment with nation-building. Now the money is almost spent,
> and Western governments are heading for the exits. The U.N.
> mission to train the police will be finishing up at the end of this
> year. "We are declaring victory and going home," one U.N. offi-
> cial told me sardonically. International disillusionment is palpa-
> ble. Instead of flowing towards reconstruction, much of the
> international money has ended up in the wrong pockets. The
> Jaguars, Audis and BMWs parked outside the Serbian govern-
> ment building in Banja Luka would do a New York nightclub
> parking lot proud. Throughout Bosnia, rule of law is next to
> non-existent, because there are still no independent prosecutors,
> judges or lawyers. Mostar is still ruled by people who rose to
> power during the years of war and madness. Leaders from both
> communities meet only for photo opportunities with visiting
> foreign dignitaries. Otherwise, they do not fraternize.[116]

Promoting a national unity design so far removed from reality has led to poor results. That Kosovo remained a part of Serbia essentially amounted to a technicality, as most forms of Serbian power and control were removed from the province. The United Nations kept pretending otherwise because it was reluctant to set a precedent that would encourage the right of self-determination to be realized through violent means especially in other parts of the Balkans such as Macedonia. In particular, Russia and Spain feared such a precedent would encourage breakaway communities within those states to intensify their violence in order to achieve their own state.

In contrast to the nation-building that has enjoyed such limited suc-cess in Kosovo, a Hi-Devolution approach would not only take into ac-count the history and current reality of the ethno-religious divide in Ko-sovo, but also largely replace U.S. and U.N. imposition from outside with decisions by the people of Kosovo themselves. A Hi-Devolution approach, which would have acknowledged both the facts on the ground as well as the limits of the foreign powers' agency, would have allowed the Albanian Kosovars to secede from Serbia. Most remaining Serbs after the conflict were concentrated in the north, in a region that abuts Serbia. That part could have been annexed to Serbia, or these Serbs could have traded places with a similar number of Albanian Kosovars who live in Serbia proper. For those few Serbs who would choose to remain to live in an independent Kosovo, such as those around Pristina and in other areas not adjacent to Serbia, their rights and privileges must be secured as part of the breakup agreement, and special protection must be given to Kosovo's medieval Orthodox Christian monuments.

Far from destabilizing the region, the 2006 secession of Montenegro from Serbia was effected peacefully, legitimately, and in accord with the wishes of the majority of the Montenegrin population. If Kosovo were to follow a similar path, there is no reason to expect that it would destabilize the Balkans any more than Montenegro has.

In Conclusion

The extent to which one nation or even a group of nations, superpowers included, can change the polity, economy, and community of other nations—the extent to which long-distance social engineering can succeed—is of major importance for all the issues at hand. If democratization, development, and nation-building could be accomplished with relative ease, the strategy of according security top priority would be moot. However, given that the opposite is true, one cannot rush regime change and hope it will lead to domestic law and order and contribute to international peace. Security must lead, to make it possible for the other developments slowly to follow.

The data are unmistakably clear. With rare exceptions, we find that democratization, economic development, and nation-building (in the sense of keeping disparate communities one) are likely to take much longer, cost much more, and are much more prone to failure than their advocates presume. Foreign policy is best built on the fact that basic security must be accorded first priority. The rest, if the proper efforts and investments are made, may follow.

PART III

The True Fault Line

WARRIORS VS. PREACHERS

The best lack all conviction, while the worst
Are full of passionate intensity.

—*William Butler Yeats, "The Second Coming"*

CHAPTER A. FEWER ENEMIES, MORE (POTENTIAL) ALLIES:
THE GLOBAL IMPORTANCE OF ILLIBERAL MODERATES

President Bush has repeatedly declared, "Either you are with us, or you are against us," or other words to the same effect.[1] This startlingly stripped-down conception of the international environment invites two basic but highly significant questions: first, who is on "the other side," who is the enemy with whom we must contend? Second, are all those who have not signed up with U.S.-orchestrated "coalitions of the willing" supporters of terrorists or rogue states? Or are there major segments of the world population that have not chosen sides, many millions of people who might be encouraged to stay out of the fray? Better yet, following appropriate adjustments in our foreign policy, might these millions lend us support in several key matters—especially those concerning security at home and peace overseas?

My response to these two questions revolves around a major thesis, namely that since 9/11 the U.S. government (and some influential public intellectuals, long before that pivotal date) *have grossly exaggerated the size of our opposition and mischaracterized its nature, and in the process they have come to view many potential allies as enemies.* It is as if during the Cold War the United States had viewed France and Italy as part of the Soviet empire, because they had large communist parties. To sort out who is "in," who is "out," and who is neither—so far—will take several steps.

First, I briefly review several belief systems (four religious and two secular) in order to show that the major fault line runs not *between* "us" and "them," but *through* each belief system; that each contains elements that can be employed to justify violence, as well as elements that can be employed to oppose violence; that in all these "civilizations" there are those who draw on extreme beliefs to justify their violent actions, to whom I refer as "Warriors," but also those who draw on moderate beliefs to justify their efforts at peaceful persuasion—"Preachers" in this book.

Second, I point out that *Islam is no different* in this respect from the other civilizations and belief systems reviewed herein. I draw on textual analysis, public opinion polls, and reports by observers to support this claim. Finally, I try to show that *major segments of the Muslim world are neither pro-liberal democracy nor pro-violence.* Call them "Illiberal Moderates." I ask about the major implications for our security in particular and foreign policy in general of this finding.

Illiberal Moderates are those who disavow violence (in most circumstances) but who do not necessarily favor a liberal-democratic regime or the full program of human rights. Both terms require brief elucidation. "Liberal" to many of us describes those who hold left-leaning opinions; but I use the term here in the way it is used in political theory: to designate those who support human rights and liberal democracy, in the Enlightenment tradition of regimes founded on reason. By "Moderate" I mean those who disavow violence; they may be strongly committed to whatever it is they believe. However, as long as they do not seek to impose their beliefs on others, they should be treated as akin to people who hold their political and religious opinions less fervently. You can be a fundamentalist or a true believer and still not favor coercion. In effect millions of fundamentalists and true believers of all religions and secular ideologies are keen for one and all to adopt their beliefs, but are unwilling to force them to do so. Mormons on mission, for instance. All these believers belong to the nonviolent camp, and by this crucial criterion are on the side of the angels.

Far from being treated as a part of the opposition, because they do not line up as liberals or as democrats, Illiberal Moderates are best treated as a kind of *global "swing vote."* They are the best group to be courted. The die-hard Warriors are most unlikely to be brought around to supporting our cause; liberal democrats are already on our side and need only to be nurtured and appreciated. Consequently, the most important group for our foreign policy, for the future of Islam, and for world peace, consists of those torn between their opposition to many Western "values" (or those they perceive as Western) and their rejection of violence—the Illiberal Moderates. After attending a conference of genuinely liberal and belea-guered Arab reformers at Doha, Qatar, in February 2006, David Brooks put the issue this way: "There is one old guy from a famous family in Egypt who doesn't fit either camp [i.e., he is neither a liberal nor a sup-porter of Hamas]. He spoke in Arabic. He went on at embarrassing length, about the evils of homosexuality, about how the only proper mean-ing of democracy is obedience to God's law. Everybody looked uncomfort-able as he droned on. He had unpolished conference manners. . . . *But this great contest of creeds—between democracy and orthodox Islam—will be re-solved in the breasts of people like him,* territory neither the reformers nor the Americans really understand."[2]

The Fault Line: Violence vs. Persuasion

It is empirically wrong, morally dubious, and politically unwise to hold that the major global confrontation is between "Western civilization" and all other "civilizations," especially Islam. I will demonstrate in the follow-ing pages that those who legitimate violence—whether they be called Crusaders, Jihadists, or simply terrorists—are found in all major civiliza-tions and belief systems, whether religious or secular. Moreover, I will demonstrate that in all these civilizations there are also those who seek to win the hearts and minds of people who have not yet seen the light by appealing to their opinions and concerns and by trying to convince them of the virtue of their respective values. That is, the true fault line in the world runs *through* civilizations, dividing each into two more or less dis-tinct camps—those who see and use violence as a principal tool by which to impose their conception of the good, whatever that may be, and those who regard the use of force for such purposes as abhorrent or at least problematic. In short, the fault line divides those of the sword from those of the word.

It is equally empirically invalid, ethically wrong, and politically dam-aging to treat all people of a given faith—these days Muslims—as if they

constituted a uniform, monolithic force, fated to take up arms as terrorists. This is the approach regrettably adopted by Samuel Huntington
when he wrote, "Some Westerners, including Bill Clinton, have argued
that the West does not have a problem with Islam but only with violent
Islamist extremists. Fourteen hundred years of history demonstrate otherwise. . . . The twentieth-century conflict between liberal democracy and
Marxist-Leninism is only a fleeting and superficial historical phenome-
non compared to the continuing and deeply conflictual relation between
Islam and Christianity."[3] Our conflict, in this view, is not with one interpretation of Islam, nor with radical Islamists, nor even simply with a
contemporary and particularly virulent manifestation of Islam—but simply with "Islam." Pope Benedict XVI felt a need to apologize repeatedly
after he quoted a fourteenth-century Byzantine emperor's characteriza-
tion of Islam as if it were all of one kind. To wit, "Show me just what
Muhammad brought that was new, and there you will find things only evil
and inhuman, such as his command to spread by the sword the faith he
preached."[4]

If it is a mistake, however, to reduce all of Islam to "its conflictual
relation" with the West or to an "evil and inhuman" essence, it is equally
mistaken to view all Muslims as essentially men and women of peace, as
George W. Bush suggested when he stated simply that "Islam is peace."[5] I
will show chapter and verse in the following pages that those who draw on
one belief system or another to justify their violence have not simply
"hijacked" their faith, as the former Norwegian Prime Minister Kjell
Magne Bondevik put it.[6] Warriors do not necessarily need to distort their
belief systems unreasonably; they can find in all major belief systems
deeply held interpretations that extol violence. It is hence necessary for
those who recognize nonviolent interpretations of their faiths, these days
especially in the Muslim world, to stand up and give stronger voice to
their persuasive beliefs. There is little to be gained, however, by claiming
that the violent camp has no text or leg to stand on. (True, Warriors will
make use of persuasion, and many Preachers may at some point be
driven to resort to violence. However, as we shall see, one can typically tell
them apart even if neither constitutes a "pure" type.) The full importance
of drawing the line in the way here suggested, in contrast to the often-
used opposition between extremists and liberals, will come into focus
shortly.

First, though, I should state up front, as someone who served as a commando (today it might well be called Special Forces), who killed and saw many killed long before reaching the age of twenty, from which camp I hail. I still pain for every life lost, whether it was one of "ours" or "theirs"; I deeply regret every death I helped cause, even though I was acting to defend those I loved from those who attacked us. Ever since I turned twenty, when I first sat at the feet of Martin Buber, I learned the value of rejecting violence and embracing persuasion.[7] I am not a pacifist but someone who holds that one is morally obligated truly to exhaust all other means possible before taking up arms, and that force should be applied only when there is a real, imminent, and severe danger. And that making a compelling case for one's cause is both morally right and much more effective in the long run than the violent alternatives. Thus I was a reluctant Warrior who turned into a realistic Preacher.

Needless to say, I am hardly alone. In effect, it is a thesis of the following pages that *Preachers greatly outnumber the Warriors in all major contemporary civilizations*. Most important, we ought to recognize that the Preachers of the world (and the many hundreds of millions of people who follow them) are the natural allies of anyone who rises up against the world of terror. Those on the persuasive side of the fault line today include (as distinct from earlier historical periods) the *majority* of Muslims (especially in nations such as Indonesia, Malaysia, Bangladesh, Morocco, and Turkey, despite some recent increases in radical Islam in these parts) as well as the majority of Hindus, Christians, Jews, and many other groups. *They are all potential allies to a power that promotes security, but not necessarily to one that insists that all embrace liberal-democratic regimes and the manners and mores that support them.*

Not—Extremists vs. Liberals

I cannot stress enough that *the* fault line this book points to divides the people of the world along a fundamentally different line than the one often drawn between supporters of democracy and human rights: the liberals, on the one hand, and extremists or fundamentalists on the other. Liberals are depicted as rational, deliberative, and typically secular, while extremists are depicted as impassioned, radical, and often fiercely religious. This division between liberals and extremists has been highlighted in the debate between those who hold that Islam cannot be rendered compatible with the prerequisites of a free and decent society and those who argue that Muslims are capable of becoming good citizens of liberal, democratic polities. It has raged between the likes of Bernard Lewis,[8] Samuel Huntington, Ayaan Hirsi Ali,[9] and Oriana Fallaci[10] on one side, and Edward Said,[11] John Esposito,[12] and Richard Bulliet[13] on the other. (Comparisons are often made to a similar debate that raged about Roman Catholics, who were also once said to be unable to become members of a modern or liberal-democratic society.)[14]

As a part of this debate, many attempts have been made to demonstrate that liberal, democratic Muslims do exist. Some prominent names that have been referenced include Irshad Manji,[15] Muqtedar Khan,[16] and Khaled Abou El-Fadl.[17] But those cited in this context are, unsurprisingly, found mainly to be living in the West. Liberal Muslim leaders and public intellectuals are found elsewhere but are relatively few and far between.

Above all, dividing the world between those who are pro-democracy and those opposed to it is central for the core Neo-Con thesis and to post-9/11 U.S. foreign policy: that only liberal democracies can be trusted allies of the West, support global peace, and refuse to harbor terrorists. All others must be converted "by all necessary means," extending to invasions and occupations. Good regimes produce good conduct, and the only ones that are naturally on the side of peace are democratic, Neo-Cons seem to claim.

In contrast, I hold that *one should not assume that because a Muslim, or an adherent of any other belief, is a true believer, and does not profess faith in modern liberal politics, and does not favor many of the rights enumerated in the Universal Declaration of Human Rights—he or she must therefore be an advocate of violence.* There is a world of difference between believing in some other form of government other than liberal democracy—say, tribal councils or adhering to the rulings of muftis or rabbis—and advocating violence. One can read the Bible or the Koran literally, closely follow numerous religious injunctions, and vehemently oppose modernization, democracy, and capitalism, and yet not believe in imposing one's beliefs on others by the use of force!

I readily grant that such true believers, whether religious or subscribing to a secular ideology, are, statistically speaking, *more likely* than those of little or no faith, religious or secular, to favor violence. *Some* true believers are so confident they have seen the light that they are willing to employ coercion on others in order to share their finding. Nevertheless, there are many millions of true believers who do not favor coercion. In effect, I suggest that if a survey were conducted of those with orthodox opinions in their respective belief systems, the majority across the board would oppose forcing their beliefs on others through the use of violence.

For example, there are about 55 million evangelical Christians in America, but few of them favor jailing homosexuals and adulterers. Most of the 5.5 million Mormons in America are strong believers; they go on missions to the four corners of the earth to spread their gospel, but hardly favor sending the Marines to convert people. There are over one billion Catholics worldwide, but most do not bomb abortion clinics, and most do not view the Inquisition as a tool they wish to employ in the future. There are hundreds of thousands of Orthodox Jews, but only a minority of them favors the use of force to foster compliance with the Law. And there have been quite a few socialists who have held that if one wants to make an omelet one must crack eggs, especially in Stalin's and Mao's days, but gradually more and more socialists have come to profess faith in the power of persuasion and democratic processes. To push the point, some-one may believe that women should graciously submit to their husbands and may believe with all his heart that God created the universe in six days and rested on the seventh, and still not favor forcing others to subscribe to these beliefs. In short, there are millions upon millions who disavow the use of violence in matters of belief and rely on persuasion to advance their ideas, but who simultaneously do not support the values of a liberal-democratic polity.[18]

No place have I found the fault line between coercive and persuasive beliefs more clearly delineated than when I was a guest in 2002 of the reformers in Iran, at an institution that was aptly called the International Center for the Dialogue of Civilizations. Here I found that many of the reformers who strongly opposed the mullahs' theocracy were also not seeking to build a secular civil society or liberal democracy. They favored a Muslim society in which "people will want to pray (as well as observe many of the other tenets of Islam) but nobody will be coerced to do so."

Nematollah Shahrani, Minister of Hajj and Islamic Instruction in Hamid Karzai's government, has similar hopes for Afghanistan. Though he received criticism in the West for his proposal in the summer of 2006 to reinstate the Department for the Prevention of Vice and the Promotion of Virtue—the Taliban's feared moral police force—Shahrani insists that the new department will be different. "Vice and Virtue is one of the principles of Islam," he explained. "This means we lead people to the virtues, and we stop them from committing bad acts in the society. And how we would practice that would be in a very good way, that does not create any resentment from people against that. It would be totally different than the Taliban way. . . . [It] won't use violence, only words."[19]

Why should people of such faith not be included on our side of the civilization fault line? To be courted to be our allies, in opposition to the apostles of violence?

To put it differently, we can dream of a world in which everyone respects all human rights, and we can prefer liberal democracy over all other forms of government. We can try to convince all people to embrace the beliefs and the form of regime which we cherish. However, we should refrain from sending Special Forces or cruise missiles to transform others into supporters of the particular beliefs we champion. And we should limit our desires for now and focus on the more realistic goal of promoting a world in which everyone renounces violence against other peoples and their own, putting security first.

The full importance of this point will come into full relief once the policy implications of these different fault lines are elicited. For now I merely note that it takes much more to foster liberal democracy than to lead people to foreswear violence. And that if we ally ourselves only with the champions of liberalism our lines will be short—and remain short for a long time to come—while if we join with those who favor persuasion, the majority of people in the world will be in our camp, quite naturally.[20] To give a pictorial expression to my point, the following simple chart may serve. The estimates of the size of each camp are merely illustrative although some polling data follow in Chapter D below.

Preachers		Warriors
Liberals 15%	Illiberal Moderates 70%	"Islamists" 15%

Aside from being grossly unfair to tar all true believers as supporters of violence, as holy or secular Warriors, this presumption also severely misguides public policy. It leaves hundreds of millions of people on the wrong side of a line that separates us from our true opponents. It leaves out all the true believers who favor persuasion over violence, those with whom we should ally ourselves in the war on terror.

People of a given faith often argue that although it is true enough that there are some Warriors in their camp, and that beliefs that sanction violence can be found in their texts and exhortations, there are many more in everyone else's camps. This may well be the case, but it should be noted that these proportionalities, the ratios of Warriors as compared to Preachers, have changed throughout history. Thus in recent decades there have been relatively few Christian Warriors, while during the period of the Crusades they were quite common. And there have been more Jewish Warriors since Israel was reestablished than during the centuries in which Jews were stateless and dispersed in the Diaspora, and so on. Moreover, the same group can switch from one camp to the other, as the IRA did in Ireland, and as one hopes Hamas will also do one day in Palestine. The same holds for individual leaders such as Malcolm X, who once advocated violent revenge against whites, but became much less of a Warrior in his later years. More generally, while for first-approximation purposes I divided the belief systems—and their respective champions— into two categories, within each a large variety of gradations can be found. However, when all is said and done, one can distinguish beliefs that systemically sanction violence from those that argue for persuasion. And one can tell quite readily whether or not a given person, political faction, or religious sect is on a war footing, or seeking to win the hearts and minds of others without coercion—within a given period of time.

An Anti-Religion Bias

One reason the fault line is often misplaced is that there are a fair number of contemporary liberals who are suspicious of all religions, and in effect of all strong beliefs, including secular ones. Some are proceduralists; they are willing to endorse almost any position that is the outcome of properly constructed moral dialogues—but not one based directly on an examination of the truth of one's values. Others hold that every belief is always subject to further questioning and deliberation; there are no incontestable truths, although often they consider this claim to be beyond contesting.[21] Still others consider the only sure belief to be belief in the right of people to refuse to submit to shared moral standards, even if they are not en-sconced in the form of positive law but are customary and promoted only socially. All these moderates hence tend to *mis*place the fault line as run-ning between what might be called "weak believers" (like themselves) and both coercers *and* strong believers, whom liberals tend to suspect of being likely to favor the use of force.[22]

The eyes of many liberals are in this respect glued to the rearview mirror, focused on the twentieth century, in which strong belief systems did lead to massive violence, as two totalitarian movements, fascism and communism, slaughtered millions and inflicted untold harm on many millions of others in the name of their ideologies. Several significant liberal thinkers—such as Hannah Arendt, Ernest Gellner, and Isaiah Berlin, all refugees from the Nazis—feared that strong beliefs, especially if introduced into the public realm, might lead to a recurrence of totalitari-anism. Hence, they held that one should not impose one's beliefs on others by the use of force, and that one should refrain from judging others morally (at least in most matters). Since the 1960s various forms of moral and cultural relativism have therefore been accepted and even championed, while arguments that point to the existence of universals have increasingly become an anathema. The aversion such liberals have for religion in particular blinds them to the opportunities to ally with those who are true believers, many of them part of the "religious right" but who are adamantly opposed to violence. If you did a double take here and said, "Wait a moment, allies on the *religious right?*," then the following pages are seeking especially to engage you in a dialogue as to who are our real enemies and who are at least potential allies.

Some weak believers and strong normative privatizers—those who hold that all beliefs should be kept out of the public square[23]—are blinded because they hold on, not always with complete, critical awareness, to the Enlightenment view that religion (like magic) expresses an earlier, more primitive and superstitious stage of human development.[24] They con-tinue to associate progress first of all with secularization. In fact, in this day and age, the moral vacuum generated by people of little or no faith *invites* fundamentalism, including its violent expressions.

Fundamentalism and, much more worryingly, its violent expressions, have tended to rise after those eras in which traditional values and habits were undermined—sometimes for good reasons, as in the United States of the 1950s, '60s, and '70s—but few new shared moral understandings were formulated to replace them. Moreover, rapid modernization often leaves spiritual hunger in its wake—as has recently been the case in places as varied as North Africa, Turkey, Russia, and China. The best antidotes to violent beliefs are strong, persuasive, nonviolent ones, not abject relativism, nihilism, or the liberalism of weak believers and strong normative privatizers.

Are There Good Warriors?

The question may be raised whether the defenders of Stalingrad, the Jews in the Warsaw ghetto uprising, those who violently opposed the apartheid regime in South Africa, and other such fighters—because they employed force—meet my criteria for the definition of Warriors. Were they not good Warriors? As I see it, they were *just* warriors, but as there is no such thing as a war that is good, that is moral in its own right, there are no good warriors. It may seem like hairsplitting to distinguish "good" from "just" in this context. It is not. There are specific, limited, exceptional conditions, spelled out in the literature on just war theory from Augustine to Grotius, which may justify the use of force—for instance, when all other means of resolving a conflict or of protecting the innocent have been exhausted. *However,* just as physicians are sometimes obliged to prescribe highly toxic medications in order to combat an illness, so violence sometimes needs to be employed, but these situations do not make the employment of force morally wholesome. Risky, painful medical procedures and just wars alike serve as tools to be employed to ameliorate an already very poor condition—to heal a man who is deathly ill, or to coerce a man who refuses, say, to be persuaded to live in peace with his neighbor. Morally one ought always to prefer the use of nonviolent methods, as Gandhi did, realizing one must also sometimes accept violent methods as a last resort.

Matters of Focus and Terminology

This book focuses on beliefs, because evidence shows that when they underwrite and legitimate various forms of behavior, those behaviors often become more massive and extreme. This is particularly true for violence, which becomes especially damaging when "blessed," socially celebrated, and institutionalized, as compared to the violent actions of those who are merely psychologically warped or unable to control their impulses. Large scale violence of the kind that Hitler, Stalin, Mao, the Khmer Rouge, and, earlier, the Crusades inflicted, occurs when people believe that killing is what they *ought* to do—that God, the Church, the Fatherland, or the Party commands them to kill. To quote the UNESCO constitution: "Since wars begin in the minds of men, it is in the minds of men that the defenses of peace must be constructed."

I have used the term *civilization* thus far to locate my thesis in the debate that uses this term, especially the one that has followed the publication of Samuel Huntington's *The Clash of Civilizations*. The word has been defined as "a developed or advanced state of human society."[25] It might be interpreted to encompass everything from poetic, religious, and philosophical culture to politics, economics, technology, and artifacts, and is therefore far too broad and vague a notion to be useful for the purposes of this book. Hence from here on I use the term *belief systems*, which refers specifically to the values, doctrines, morals, and mores that groups collectively hold as right.[26]

The frequently cited difference between religious and secular beliefs pales here first of all because bodies of both religious and secular principles qualify as belief systems. Both Hinduism and socialism are included. Reference, it is important to reiterate, is made to the value judgments that justify conduct, help motivate it, defend it from critics, and provide context to the informal social controls that sustain it.

Second, and most important from the viewpoint here laid out, religious *and* secular Warriors belong on one side of the fault line, religious *and* secular Preachers on the other. This fault line is much deeper, for the reasons I already spelled out, than is the religious-secular one. And the often-implied notion that secular is somehow better, more rational, and above all less prone to violence, is belied by the experience of the last century. Coercive secular nationalists and socialists are no better, more rational, or less violent than devout religious Warriors. William Cavanaugh of the University of St. Thomas makes this point and takes it a step further: "My hypothesis is that 'religion and violence' arguments serve a particular need for their consumers in the West. These arguments are a part of a broader Enlightenment narrative that invents a dichotomy between the religious and the secular and constructs the former as an irrational and dangerous impulse that must give way in public to rational, secular forms of power. The danger is that, in establishing an Other which is essentially irrational, fanatical, and violent, we legitimate coercive measures against that Other."[27]

A telling and familiar example of the fault line between coercive and persuasive beliefs is the line that separates two major theories of socialization on the question of how to bring up children to become mature members of the community. On one side are those who hold that corporal punishment is an essential part of raising children to become virtuous and upstanding citizens. They believe that those who "spare the rod, spoil the child."[28] On the other side are those who hold that, in all but extreme situations, children should be given reasons, rewarded for good conduct, and chided when they stray—but not spanked or locked in a room.

True, Warriors are often quite content to use their propaganda machines to try to win people over to their regimes, as Stalin and Hitler did, that is, they persuade, though obviously there is an enormous element of deception and ideological distortion involved in their propaganda. However, Warriors certainly have no qualms about using violence on a massive scale.

Preachers are also found among both religious and secular believers. To gain a sense of their societal role and positions it is best to contrast them with various kinds of relativists, multiculturalists, and some pluralists; some who would make the public sphere as neutral as possible, and others who are simply bereft of any particular strongly held belief. I deliberately use the term *Preacher,* although I realize that it grates on some, especially those who associate preaching with irresponsible exhortations and who hold that everyone should sort out their beliefs on their own, in private, and refrain from promoting—much less imposing—them on others. The trouble with such positions is that people of little belief, or those who oppose engaging their beliefs in the global marketplace of ideas and the public forum, leave a vacuum. Preachers are needed to fill it, lest the Warriors will.

The Normative Importance of the Fault Line

Belief systems and their components can be grouped in an almost endless number of ways. The question hence must be addressed: what is the rationale for focusing on the application of force vs. persuasion? I make this distinction central to this analysis because I hold that, morally, the most important fault line runs between those who seek to change people's behavior, hearts, and minds by force, and those who seek such changes by convincing people to do what Preachers believe people ought to do. I take it for granted that all societies must seek to curb some antisocial behavior coercively in order to maintain social order. The notion that people will live in harmony with one another due to complementary motives of self-interest *may*, possibly, hold true for some economic transactions, but it most assuredly does not apply to political regimes. Belief systems provide a moral justification for self-government and self-control and for political authorities to curb the unfettered expression of human passions, whether it be greed, sexually inappropriate conduct, or violence. In other words, all societies face the challenge of maintaining at least a modicum of order.[29]

If no human order can rely exclusively on persuasion, and if even the most benign regimes employ some coercion—hard power in addition to soft power—there remains a very substantial difference between those regimes which are based largely on persuasion and those which draw extensively on coercion. The *kibbutzim* in their heyday fell at one end of the continuum, the Soviet gulags at the other.

There is a limited set of options available to maintain order. Forcing people to adopt whatever behavior a given belief system extols is—morally speaking—by far the worst option because it degrades their essential human dignity. Coercion (as used here meaning the exercise of physical force) greatly curtails considered choice, if it does not obviate it completely, depriving those subject to it of their due autonomy. Respect for human dignity entails the freedom to deliberate about life's alternatives and to render meaningful choices (within reasonable confines). Coercion essentially nullifies this freedom, transforming people from morally responsible agents into objects.[30] To put it in the most basic terms, people who are jailed have their dignity severely degraded, and those who are shot or hanged are, on the face of it, deprived of nearly all that makes them human.

In all belief systems here examined one finds those who claim that it is morally appropriate to coerce someone in order try to save his or her soul. According to this position it may be justifiable to punish, torture, or threaten people with death—and execute them—if they resist conversion to the "true" faith. It has been argued that such violence is a service to those on whom it is inflicted because it is better for those resisting conversion to suffer some pain in this world than to suffer eternally in hell. As I see it, conversion, and more generally compliance with moral precepts, if coerced, fail by both extrinsic and intrinsic moral criteria. Those coerced will try to circumvent whenever possible that to which they are forced to adhere; and an authority based on brute force conflicts with our deepest perceptions of justice.

In sharp contrast to coercion, persuasion leaves the final say to the actor. Preachers may appeal to people's values, sensibilities, intellect, and interests. The main point is that at the end of the day those subject to persuasion are still fundamentally free to choose to follow a different course, though they may incur some cost, say in terms of social popularity or prestige. Granted, few (if any) choices are entirely free. There is, however, a continuum of restrictions on choice, from minimal to absolute. When these restrictions are relatively limited, we can still speak of a capacity to follow one's own beliefs and that one is treated with basic respect. In contrast, extensive or complete restrictions obviate one's freedom. This level of restrictiveness is as a rule achieved only when violence is employed and is incompatible with respect for human dignity.

There are those who say that extreme forms of persuasion, such as brainwashing, in which bureaucrats and propagandists recast an individual's preferences, leave no room for autonomy, and hence are coercive. However, study upon study has shown that brainwashing does not work well. The experience of the Soviet Union serves as a strong example. The U.S.S.R. had total control over its educational system, media, and culture (including music, books, films, etc.) and greatly limited its people's access to independent voices from other nations. And yet the Soviet government was unable to "brainwash" most of its people most of the time. Communist regimes would not need gulags, and theocracies such as those established by the Taliban, Saudi Arabia, and Iran would not need stonings or moral police squads if persuasion sufficed to convince people to follow the precepts on which their societies are based.

It is true that under special conditions, such as when people's lives have been uprooted after a defeat in war, a deep economic crisis, or a massive terrorist attack, a demagogue may win people over, for a while. However, in the longer run, most people will return to expressing their authentic political beliefs.[31]

Because this distinction between persuasion and coercion is at the heart of much of what follows, it deserves to be highlighted by an example. If the authorities seek to prevent vehicles from parking in the fire lane of a hospital, they can rely on either persuasion, by posting a sign that says, "Please Do Not Park Here—Save Lives: Fire Lane"; or force, by placing a tow truck nearby that immediately removes any offending cars. In the first case, the decision whether or not to park at the forbidden spot is up to the drivers. In the second case, the drivers' capacity to make such a choice is preempted.[32]

Legalized Violence

One may wonder whether my negative view of coercion holds when force is employed to uphold the law. The answer is fairly obvious: only if the law has been issued by a political authority that is not legitimate, for instance, totalitarian governments. However, most laws enacted even by the best of governments also obviously depend for their enforcement, ultimately, on the police and prisons—that is, on coercion. Political theory may have it that "we the people" consent to democratic laws, or even to undemocratic laws which are nevertheless rendered legitimate by public support and customary application. But does it follow that democratic coercion has none of the failings I attribute to coercion in general?

First, note that the law at its best draws on noncoercive means. It defines what is right and persuades citizens to follow it. Thus, the laws that ban drinking and driving, smoking in public spaces, and so on, are first of all expressions of our common good and thus have a normative element that often suffices to ensure a good part, often the major part, of the needed compliance.[33] Second, the law often employs economic sanctions in the form of fines or incentives, appropriation of property, and other economic measures—means that are less coercive than physical force.

To the extent that the law does rely on coercion rather than on persuasion, the practical outcomes of such an approach tend to support the key observation about coercion's grossly negative nature. Good regimes that minimize the use of coercion in law enforcement, that labor to promote compliance with the law through persuasion (and economic incentives), and that limit the application of law to as few areas of conduct as is consistent with the common good, are vastly more effective than opposite regimes. Regimes that apply the law to a broad range of behaviors and that often fail to secure compliance by persuasion are normatively inferior.

When a regime must use coercion on a large scale and on a broad front, this extensive use of force is a sign that the regime, or at least the law at issue, either has lost or has never had legitimacy in the eyes of the citizens. *Extensive use of force to maintain order—however legal the application of force, even if it is applied merely to uphold the law—is a sure sign of regime failure.* The U.S. "war" against controlled substances is a case in point. Well-governed societies rely largely on persuasion and on voluntary compliance. The dream of a society without a state, the dream of a world that will know no coercion,³⁴ may well not be attainable. However, the closer a society moves toward such a regime—that is, to one based primarily on persuasion—the more it meets with our moral approbation.

Are Psychological and Economic Pressures Coercive?

Granted, some who are subjected to psychological or economic pressures may feel they are being coerced; they may believe that they have no choice in the matter before them. Thus a Jew may feel "coerced" because he must pass as a Christian to obtain membership in a country club or admission to an Ivy League university (as was the case in earlier generations). However, in the terms used here, he is not coerced, because the choices are his. He may *feel* he has no choice, but a social science observer will note that there are merely costs attached to his choices, not the kind of voiding of choices that occurs when, say, Jews are exiled or killed not because they have committed a capital crime, but simply because they are Jews—the kind of voiding of choices associated with true coercion.

For purposes of first approximation I draw on a dichotomy of choice (fully coerced vs. free). I grant that that there are various gradations; some people are more coerced than others. However, morally speaking, as long as there is a meaningful "out," a person can be said to have a choice. The situation may be structured in ways that are highly prejudicial, making some choices much less attractive than others. Morally, however, one cannot exempt that person from the responsibility for whatever choice that individual makes just because the other, immoral options appear to be more attractive than the moral one. Thus, one may well hold that a pimp who is poor is less morally abhorrent than a rich pimp; but both have made a moral choice.

One can to a large extent correctly and fairly blame "the system"—socioeconomic and political conditions—as well as early childhood experiences. These factors may indeed severely curb freedom of choice and surely influence perception of available choices. However, as long as some meaningful measure of freedom remains, as long as people *have choices,* though these choices are circumscribed or unattractive, individuals possess moral agency and in a decisive respect are responsible for their choices.

I cannot emphasize sufficiently the preceding point because one of the main, often-repeated arguments of those who engage in and systematically justify violence is that psychological pressures (e.g., humiliation) and economic deprivations (e.g., poverty) are just as coercive as the use of force, and hence justify the killing of those who inflict these injuries. Among those who have made these arguments are figures as different as Osama bin Laden, Malcolm X, Che Guevara, and Frantz Fanon. The moral consequence of this argument is to treat violence, from terrorism to racial or class war, as legitimate, because one can always find some psychological or economic injury to make the claim that counter-coercion is called for. Hence I reiterate that, first of all, those who are humiliated or deprived will typically live to see another day and can work to bring about change, as they have done throughout human history. In contrast, those who are killed have all their options and their future extinguished. One can feed the hungry and nurture malnourished children, and apologize to those who have been humiliated and invite them to one's home. But nothing can restore the lives of those who have been killed.

None of this is to make light of, let alone justify, psychological or economic injury. I merely suggest that coercion (or violence) should be treated as a class by itself; it is a much more severe form of oppression that ought not be lumped together or confused with material or social pressures.[35]

In short, both coercion and economic and psychological pressures may be condemnable, but morally these cannot be equated. Coercion, because it denies people free agency, is a unique and encompassing violation of human dignity. Persuasion may intend to lead people to make undesirable decisions, but it respects to a certain extent the possibility of free agency and some measure of human dignity.

Next

To document my thesis that there are major coercive and persuasive subsystems in all major belief systems, I turn now to examine three religious and two secular ones. The following chapter shows that the *same division* is found in Islam. Some may find the examination of the fault line in various belief systems of considerable interest, especially given the similarities between the arguments made by very different sources. Others may prefer to move along to focus on the discussion of Islam, where I support the claim that there are many more Muslim Preachers than Warriors and examine the implications of this finding for Western foreign policy.

By necessity my study is strictly illustrative. Any attempt to analyze even one major belief system comprehensively would take many hefty volumes. Here I seek simply to demonstrate that coercive and persuasive beliefs exist in all major belief systems.

An historian might point out that in the following study I draw on different historical periods and take texts and statements out of their historical contexts. However, as I see it, historical documents live with us and influence us after their authors are long gone. Thus, those who quote a passage from the Bible to justify their acts may interpret it differently than those who read it when it was first written, but the moral dictates live on in the sense that they influence those who believe in such texts precisely because of their traditional authority—disregarding the historical context in which they were first written or revealed. Whatever their original context, Martin Luther King Jr.'s speeches are still persuasive, and *Mein Kampf* is still a brief for violence. Similarly, the words of the Prophet still carry weight for Muslims. Hence, whenever a text has been composed, it is relevant as long as it is still used to persuade or to try to legitimate violence.

CHAPTER B. VIOLENT VS. PERSUASIVE BELIEFS IN THREE RELIGIOUS BELIEF SYSTEMS

Christianity

Born of a small, nonviolent sect within Judaism that faced hostile, sometimes vicious reactions to its early adherents, Christianity spent three centuries growing in size, ecclesiastical organization, and political power, before it could flex its muscles in potentially violent ways. Its first evangelists sought through persuasion, not warfare, to establish communities of believers in major cities throughout the Roman Empire.[36] As minorities in virtually every city, they lacked the numbers, the internal stability, and the goodwill of the state to coerce either non-Christians or wayward members, even if their early theology had demanded it. As the new religion began to take hold, however, it was transformed from a persecuted sect characterized by nonviolence into a formidable institution able and willing to employ force. Christian persecution of pagans and heretics began during the reign of Emperor Theodosius (c. 346–395 CE), who declared Christianity the official religion of the Roman Empire in 380 and outlawed all other religions but Judaism.[37] From then on, forceful imposition by rulers joined peaceful proselytizing as a means to spread Christianity. Violence in the name of Christianity occurred in different forms and with diverse justifications during the Crusades (from the eleventh to the thirteenth centuries), the Inquisition (especially the Spanish Inquisition, 1478–1834), and the Protestant Reformation (beginning in 1517). Yet each period also saw the revisitation and defense of the nonviolent orientation of early Christianity as a superior alternative to coercion.

To illustrate these separate theological traditions that run through Christian history, this chapter will present a number of theologians who contributed to the development of the two perspectives. The following are intended to be strictly illustrative and will select examples drawn from different historical periods. They center on the religious concepts and justifications that undergird the two different belief subsystems. Numerous factors beyond the scope of this analysis also shaped the decision to use violent or nonviolent means; the focus here is on the level of theological arguments.

One can find in the Scriptures texts that support both pacifistic and violent arguments. St. Augustine (354–430 CE) made sophisticated theological arguments for the limited use of force to compel heretics back into the Church. His rationale largely consisted of interpretation of select biblical passages. For example, Augustine advised that they be brought back through "the stripes of temporal scourging."[38] He also referenced Proverbs 23:14, which says of children that "if you beat them with a rod, you will save their lives from Sheol [here understood as hell]."

From the Gospel, Augustine cited the parable of the feast in which a man decides to hold a great dinner to which he invited a number of guests who decline to attend (Luke 14:16–23).[39] The man then orders his servant to bring in the poor and crippled from the streets to share in the feast.

After discovering that there was still more room at the table, the man commands his servant, "Go out into the roads and lanes, and compel people to come in." Augustine believed that this passage sanctioned coercion in order to bring people back to the table of Catholic communion.

Augustine's theological justification of religious persecution developed out of the Church's struggle with the breakaway Christian sect known as Donatism. At first Augustine had argued against any kind of coercion of the Donatists, familiar as he was with the history of Christian martyrdom at the hands of the pagans. Yet he eventually changed his mind, reasoning that "there is a persecution of unrighteousness, which the impious inflict upon the Church of Christ; and there is a righteous persecution, which the Church of Christ inflicts upon the impious."[40] Augustine still conceded that "it is indeed better (as no one ever could deny) that men should be led to worship God by teaching, than that they should be driven to it by fear of punishment or pain"; but "it does not follow that because the former course produces the better men, therefore those who do not yield to it should be neglected."[41] Physical harm committed in the name of the Church could be excusable, and even sanctioned, Augustine argued, when used to bring the fallen back to Christ.

Augustine also cited St. Paul's theological interpretation of civil obedience as divine obedience: "Let every person be subject to the governing authorities; for there is no authority except from God, and those authorities that exist have been instituted by God. Therefore let whoever resists authority resist what God has appointed, and those who resist will incur judgment" (Romans 13:1–2). Augustine believed this passage gave license to embedding Church doctrine into civil law, thereby granting civil authorities the right to discipline heretics. He cited the Old Testament story of King Nebuchadnezzar, who incorporated the biblical law against blasphemy into the law of his kingdom, as an example all Christian kings should follow.[42] Emperor Theodosius accomplished this wedding of Christian theology with political rule through a series of decrees that officially criminalized pagan worship. He was attempting to move toward a state in which "membership [in] the Catholic Christian church was almost coextensive with Roman citizenship."[43] Heresy and paganism were then not merely religious disorders, but also civil disorders that threatened the integrity of the state. This conjunction of religious and state interests had far-reaching effects for much of Christian history, in-

cluding the persecution of religious dissidents under the auspices of secular political leaders attempting to unify their subjects into a cohesive,
ideological whole.

Augustine believed that violence must be considered only as a final
and desperate solution if persuasion or negotiation failed to produce results. Nevertheless, when Pope Urban II called all of Christendom to
embark on the First Crusade in 1095, he initiated a shift (albeit one that
had been long in the making) in how the Church conceived of the use of
violence. In his speech at the Council of Clermont, Urban II declared
famously that "Christ commands" the Crusade to "expel that wicked race
[Muslims] from our Christian lands."[44] Although the immediate cause of
his call to arms was the persecution of Christians in the Holy Land, Urban
II encouraged far more than merely providing aid to beleaguered pil-
grims. Violence here was no longer merely a reviled means to a desired
end, namely peace. Rather, God willed violence against Muslims as a
positive good. Thomas Asbridge of the University of London wrote of this
theological change: "With the preaching of the First Crusade the Latin
Church went far beyond simply condoning violence; it energetically encouraged military conflict and promoted carnage as an expression of
pious devotion."[45] Asbridge went on to assert that, although Augustine
provided the general framework, Urban II's vision of the Crusades represented a new form of "holy war" that "God actively supported, even demanded, which could be of spiritual benefit to its participants."[46]

Developing alongside this concern about non-Christians was a growing apprehension about heretics. As in Augustine's time, the late medieval period saw a number of popular heretical sects break off from the
Catholic Communion. Their proliferation generated a backlash of intense
persecution, such as the bloody Albigensian Crusade against the Cathars
in southern France (1209–29). These anti-heretical efforts were intended
to contain the spread of heresy, reform those who would repent, and
extirpate those who would not. To accomplish the task, the Church dis-
seminated instructions for local bishops to investigate all charges of
heresy in their parishes. Soon, however, papal delegations of inquisitors
were sent actively to uncover heretics and punish them accordingly, including by prescribing the death penalty.[47] St. Thomas Aquinas developed
the theological rationale behind this enlargement of ecclesiastical power,
writing: "On the part of the Church . . . there is mercy which looks to the

conversion of the wanderer [the heretic], wherefore she condemns not at once, but 'after the first and second admonition,' as the Apostle [Paul] directs [Titus, 3:10–11]: after that, if he is yet stubborn, the Church no longer hoping for his conversion, looks to the salvation of others, by excommunicating him and separating him from the Church, and furthermore delivers him to the secular tribunal to be exterminated thereby from the world by death."[48] It is noteworthy that Aquinas specifies the *secular* authorities as the dispenser of punishment. Church law forbade priests from directly engaging in violence, but not from recommending violence when it seemed to them as warranted.

Yet despite Aquinas's approval of the persecution of heretics, he was in many ways essentially a moderate. He disapproved of persecuting Jews and Muslims. He thought monarchy the best form of government in theory but for practical purposes preferred a "mixed regime," with an important democratic element. Perhaps most remarkable is his high view of the priority of individual conscience: "Absolutely speaking, every will at variance with reason, whether right or erring, is always evil"; that is, a person ought always to do what he thinks is right, even if what he thinks right is mistaken.[49] (That is not by any means the same thing as a right to religious freedom in the sense in which we now understand it, but nevertheless it is a significant step in that direction.) Indeed, writing of Aquinas's understanding of salvation through faith, one scholar said that "within the framework of orthodox Catholic theology this is perhaps the strongest possible expression of the principle of free Christian spirituality."[50] Thomas was resolutely orthodox, but not fundamentalist; often illiberal, sometimes moderate.

The sixteenth century ushered in the Reformation and a whole new wave of systematic violence promoted by religious zeal. Catholics and Protestants across Europe warred for several generations before the Peace of Augsburg (1555) granted the right of existence to Lutherans as well as Catholics under the principle of *cuius regio, eius religio* ("whose rule, his religion"), giving individual sovereigns the right to decide what religion would be practiced in their territories. The Treaty of Westphalia (1648) later extended that privilege to Calvinist rulers as well. At the same time, the violent suppression of heretics continued unabated in both Catholic and now Protestant lands. Martin Luther, for example, recommended the use of force against many Protestant sects such as the Spiritualists, Anabaptists, and Antinomians, although he had earlier argued for tolerance when his own sect was small and overwhelmed by its Catholic enemies.[51]

The next generation's major Protestant leader, John Calvin, contributed even further to the Protestant justification of violent suppression of heresy. Calvin famously presided over the experiment in theocracy at Geneva. For Calvin, "not only does government provide for men's living together," but it "also prevents idolatry, sacrilege against God's name, blasphemies against his truth and other public offences against religion from arising and spreading among the people."[52] This meant that the coercive power of the state could be directed against blasphemers and heretics as well as against murderers and thieves. Just as in Theodosius's Rome, the combination of religious and secular authority made crimes against the ecclesial body crimes against the state also.

Calvin himself was adamant that heretics, blasphemers, and adulterers who refused to repent must be condemned to death. He played a notorious role in the trial and execution of Michael Servetus for heresy in 1553. His stance is uncompromising: "Those who would spare heretics and blasphemers are themselves blasphemers."[53] This clearly enlarges the limited scope of religious coercion for which Augustine had argued. Yet Calvin did not flinch from using Augustine to defend himself; in response to the argument that his persecutory tactics were first used by Catholics seeking to squash the Protestants, he replied, "Because the Papists persecute the truth should we on that account refrain from repressing error? As St. Augustine said, the cause, not the suffering, makes the martyr."[54] Still, the Calvinist justification for religious violence, like those that came before, relied upon an absolute certainty of being on the right side of a battle for control over the Christian faith.

Apologists for the Crusades, the Inquisition, and the Protestant spate of persecutions each reaffirmed Augustine's conclusion that Christian theology could condone acts of violence for a religious purpose. Some Christians today still adhere to this tradition, although in general Christian justifications for violence have fallen out of favor among theologians. Most contemporary Christian thinkers would no doubt place themselves within a separate tradition of Scriptural exegesis and interpretation that emphasizes nonviolence. Many people indeed assume that peaceful Christianity represents its more authentic face. This tradition favors peaceful evangelization, verbal reprimands, and internal ecclesiastical discipline (or, at worst, excommunication), to combat heterodox belief or practice. It holds that true belief results only from a freely made decision. Forcing orthodoxy on the unwilling may obtain outward conformity, but only persuasion can result in true faith. Putting infidels or heretics to death indeed deprives them of the opportunity to repent and be saved. The use of violence to stamp out heterodoxy elevates human judgment to that of God's, judging what only God can determine. It is usually in this context that the parable of the tares (Matthew 13:24–30) is read, in which Jesus portrays sinners as weeds and the virtuous as wheat, and declares that the weeds should not be pulled but left to grow side by side with the wheat until the harvest, that is, Judgment Day. Most ancient and modern commentators think that the passage actually tries to point to the difficulty of identifying true heretics or unbelievers and so argues against persecutory tactics.[55] Such an interpretation fits better with other themes from Jesus's sayings, as in John 8:7, where Jesus tells a group of Pharisees who stone an adulteress, "Let anyone among you who is without sin be the first to throw a stone at her." The New Testament emphasizes humility in trying to judge the moral worth of others.

This may have led to Jesus's apparent belief in nonviolence. The evangelists record a number of arguments for nonviolence in Jesus's sayings. One finds the Beatitudes to be essentially pacifistic (Matthew 5:3–10), as well as several other important exhortations: "You have heard it said, 'An eye for an eye and a tooth for a tooth.' But I say to you, Do not resist an evildoer. If anyone strikes you on the right cheek, turn the other also" (Matthew 5:38–39); and "Put your sword back in its place; for all who take the sword will perish by the sword" (Matthew 26:52). Many evangelists record that Jesus knew in advance of his death by crucifixion but chose not to offer resistance to his persecutors. Many early Christians followed Jesus's example in accepting martyrdom without resistance. The majority of other Christians committed to Jesus's nonviolence by refusing to enter the Roman military or engage in fighting, which Jean-Michel Hornus described as a "spontaneous reaction by the Christians, a virtual state of mind, rather than a dogma or a Church law."[56]

Although later Christians certainly did not think their religious beliefs incompatible with serving in the military, many theologians continued to insist that a Christian must refrain from employing any form of violence. Tertullian (c. 160–230 CE), for example, opposed war as well as capital punishment, abortion, gladiatorial combat, and religious persecution. He wrote eloquently on religious freedom: "It is a fundamental human right, a privilege of nature, that every man should worship according to his own convictions: one man's religion neither harms nor helps another man. It is assuredly no part of religion to compel religion—to which free-will and not force should lead us."[57]

Tertullian's strong belief in religious liberty no doubt sprang, in part, from the persecutory context in which he was writing. In his day, Christians were still a beleaguered minority sect. Yet even after Christianity became the official state religion, many theologians continued to argue against coercion in religion. Lactantius (c. 250–325 CE), tutor to the son of Emperor Constantine and writing at the time of the important transition from a pagan to a Christian Roman empire, advocated freedom of conscience:

"Religion cannot be imposed by force; the matter must be carried on by words rather than by blows. . . . For if you wish to defend religion by bloodshed, and by tortures, and by guilt, it will no longer be defended, but will be polluted and profaned. For nothing is so much a matter of free-will as religion."[58] Lactantius's *Divine Institutes* argues vigorously against the pagans but urges persuasion over force in trying to convert them to Christianity.

Meanwhile, St. Ambrose of Milan (c. 340–397 CE) expressed his intolerance of paganism by urging the removal of the Altar to Victory from the Roman Senate, rebutting the pagan Symmachus's belief that there are many ways to divine truth. Yet Ambrose also recoiled at the use of violence, threatening Theodosius with excommunication until he performed penance for the massacre of political dissidents at Thessalonica. St. John Chrysostom (347–407 CE) also expressed intolerance for non-Christians and heretics, writing and preaching a series of eight homilies "Against the Judaizers." Yet, at the same time he wrote that gentleness must be used in correcting heretics: "If a human being wanders away from the right faith, great exertion, perseverance and patience are required; for he cannot be dragged back by force, nor constrained by fear, but must be led back by persuasion to the truth from which he originally swerved."[59]

The early Augustine also felt the tension between Christian exclusivism and the precept of nonviolence. His literary career produced several thousands of pages of theology, often written in the form of rebuttals of the heretical doctrines of the Manichees, the Donatists, and the Pelagians. These treatises were Augustine's original and only "sword" in combating heresy. He even wrote a refutation, now lost, of the use of coercion. Although he later decided that persuasive tactics were insufficient, thereby changing the course of Christian moral theology permanently, later medieval theologians did return to the nonviolent positions of Augustine's predecessors.

St. Bernard of Clairvaux (1080–1153), although a supporter of the Second Crusade, advocated the use of persuasion rather than coercion in the case of heretics, stating in one of his numerous sermons: "Heretics are to be caught rather than driven away. They are to be caught . . . not by force of arms but by arguments by which their errors may be refuted."[60] Bernard also displayed his abhorrence of violence in preaching against anti-Semitic riots being stirred up by a fellow monk in Mainz. His attitude toward heretics characterized many of the Church's representatives during the first century and a half of widespread popular heresy. As historian Edward Peters noted, medieval historians often ignore attempts by bishops and clerics to restore Catholic unity peacefully; these historians tend to focus on the bloody side of the Church's dealing with heretics. Peters argued that "within this period, the Church looked hard at itself, explored ways of persuading dissidents to return to obedience, and launched a great pastoral effort designed to teach religion effectively."[61]

At the same time, many of the heretical movements, based on the overarching idea of *sola scriptura,* advocated a philosophy of nonviolence in line with the pacifistic character of the New Testament Jesus. Geoffrey Nutall likened the pacifism of the heretical movements to that of the early Christians "in being but part of a wider reaction. Only now, instead of being rebels against a heathen empire, the heretics were rebels against a worldly and secularized Church."[62] He points out that three of the major popular heretical movements of this period rejected war and military service as well as various violent institutions of medieval society. The Waldensians, the Lollards, and the Moravian church all shared a common rejection of the ways of the world in favor of the "law of the gospels" or the "law of Christ." Once again, medieval historians often pass over the pacifism of these movements as a side issue and focus instead on their repudiation of the sacraments or the corruption of the ministry, harbingers of the Reformation. Yet, at least in their theological writings, if not always in practice, the heretics of the medieval period kept alive the doctrine of nonviolence to pass on to later generations of Christian thinkers.

The two strands, violent beliefs and persuasive ones, continued to be extended over the centuries. The first to truly inherit the nonviolent mantle were the Christian humanists of the fifteenth century, many of whom were dedicated to the same theological principle of *sola scriptura*. Chief among them was Erasmus (1466–1536), whose theology of a personal moral relationship with God and whose dislike for the ritualistic aspects of the Catholic liturgy pointed to the coming Reformation. Although he was unreservedly anti-Semitic, Erasmus pushed for greater tolerance for different points of view among Christians as he witnessed the beginning of violent clashes between Catholics and Protestants. He advised the quarrelers to take only what is represented in Scripture to be essential to the Christian faith and to regard the rest as matters of relative indifference: "The sum of our religion is peace and unanimity, but these can scarcely stand unless we define as little as possible, and in many things leave each one to follow his own judgment. . . . When faith is in the mouth rather than the heart, when the solid knowledge of Sacred Scripture fails us, nevertheless by terrorization we drive men to believe what they do not believe. . . . That which is forced cannot be sincere, and that which is not voluntary cannot please Christ."[63]

Despite Erasmus's best pleas for patience and reconciliation, the Reformation opened up a period of religious violence on a scale unseen before in Europe, a violence caused as much by struggles for political primacy among rulers as by differences of religious opinions. The trial and execution of Michael Servetus for his unorthodox religious beliefs thus becomes "the first major controversy in Western history over the question of religious toleration and the killing of heretics."[64] A great storm of pamphlets and treatises in support and in protest of the execution descended upon Europeans.

Significant among them was a pseudonymous tract, *Concerning Heretics*, most likely written by Sebastian Castellio (1515–1563), a French theologian who had worked with John Calvin in Geneva earlier in his career. After the execution of Servetus, Castellio began writing on the subject of religious toleration, repeating many of the same arguments that had been in use for centuries within the Christian tradition against the use of violence. He knew that much of the conflict between Protestants and Catholics was over points of doctrine which were open to doubt (e.g., predestination and free will), and practical abuses (e.g., the sale of indulgences). Castellio reasoned that these extra-biblical theological points must be considered inessential to true faith, "for if these matters were so obvious and evident . . . all Christians would agree among themselves on these points as readily as all nations confess that God is one."[65] He urged therefore that his contemporaries lay aside their arms and try to work at reconciling their theological differences peacefully.

Such a theological reconciliation never did occur, although respect between Protestants and Catholics has risen to the point that almost none of their contemporary religious disputes ends in violence. Yet even as relations between Christians became amicable, Christians began more and more to confront non-Christians as they left Europe to build colonial empires around the globe. Some Europeans traveled to the New World with the putative objective of converting the people of the Americas. But as Bartolome de Las Casas, a Spanish priest who came with the conquistadors, related in his writings, the Spanish "massacred uncounted thousands of persons, burned villages, drove away flocks, destroyed cities, and without cause or pretext of plausible cause did abominable and shameful things to a miserable people."[66] His work *In Defense of the Indians* represents one of the earliest humanitarian objections to colonialism, racism, and genocide. He urged Spain to reconsider its violent policies and attempt to convert the Indians by persuasion or risk divine retribution.

From George Fox (1624–1691), founder of the Quaker movement, down to Martin Luther King Jr., main architect of the nonviolent civil rights movement, nonviolence has often characterized modern Christian religious thinking. In the twentieth century many denominations have made their opposition to coercion official. The Second Vatican Council of the Roman Catholic Church stated in its document on religious freedom, *Dignitatis Humanae,* that "the human person has a right to religious freedom. This freedom means that all men are to be immune from coercion on the part of individuals or of social groups and of any human power, in such wise that no one is to be forced to act in a manner contrary to his own beliefs."[67] Similar commitments to tolerance have been accepted by the councils of most major Protestant denominations. Although individual

Christians in the modern world commit acts of violence, virtually no supporting religious institution sanctions or condones them.

In short, the Christian tradition, as we shortly shall see with all the others here examined, offers numerous thinkers and witnesses to both coercive and persuasive beliefs. This dual legacy has its origins in the New Testament itself, in which Christ is portrayed alternately as a shepherd sacrificing his life for his sheep (John 10:11) and as a wrathful conqueror striking down sinners with his sword and ruling with an iron rod (Revelation 19:15).

Judaism

As in other belief systems, in Judaism the relative weight of the subsystems that justify violence as compared to those that favor persuasion has changed over the centuries. The subsystems legitimating violence were relatively stronger when Judaism was invested in a state—during the periods of the first and second temple, and after 1948—and particularly weak in between, when Jews lived without a state of their own, in the Diaspora.

Both subsystems of belief are reflected in the Old Testament. Violence is legitimated in the decrees that anyone who violates the Sabbath or blasphemes be executed (Exodus 31:14–17; Numbers 15:35–36; Leviticus 24:14), and in God's commands that the people of Israel annihilate the Amalekites (Deuteronomy 25:17–19; 1 Samuel 15:3) and other peoples (Deuteronomy 20:16–18). In Deuteronomy 20:16–18 Moses tells the people of Israel, "As for the towns of these people that the Lord your God is giving you as an inheritance, you must not let anything that breathes remain alive. You must annihilate them . . . just as the Lord your God has commanded, so that they may not teach you to do all the abhorrent things that they do for their gods." In Deuteronomy 25:19, Moses commands, "When the Lord your God has given you rest from all your enemies . . . you shall blot out the remembrance of Amalek from under heaven"; and in 1 Samuel 15:3, God exhorts the Israelites to "go out and attack Amalek, and utterly destroy all that they have; do not spare them, but kill both man and woman, child and infant, ox and sheep."

In contrast, in other passages in the Old Testament various prophets see God as bringing peace to the world. Isaiah famously states, "He [God] shall judge between the nations and shall arbitrate for many peoples; they shall beat their swords into plowshares, and their spears into pruning hooks; nation shall not lift sword against nation, neither shall they learn war anymore" (Isaiah 2:4; cf. Micah 4:3). Moreover, "I will make a covenant of peace with them [the Israelites]; it shall be an everlasting covenant with them: and I will place them, and multiply them, and will set my sanctuary in the midst of them for evermore" (Ezekiel 37: 26). The vision of peace is echoed at the end of the Kaddish, an often-recited prayer: "May there be abundant peace from Heaven, and life upon us and upon all Israel. He who makes peace in His heights, may He make peace, upon us and upon all Israel."

Advocacy for "peace" per se does not necessarily indicate a commitment to persuasion; it could merely mean the desire to avoid violence in favor of a neutral, even non-normative, position—hence the importance of other passages that seek to persuade Jews to do what is right in the eyes of the Lord and avoid what is wrong. Some of these passages involve threats against those who defy the Lord. The persuasion-oriented ones, however, call for doing what ought to be done because the Jews are a holy people (e.g., Deuteronomy 14:2; 14:21). Still others call for special obligations because, as Moses declared to the people of Israel, "The Lord your God has chosen you out of all the people on earth to be his people" (Deuteronomy 7:6).

Warriors, those who hold beliefs that justify violence, and Preachers, those who believe in persuasion, give different interpretations to the same sacred texts. For example, Warriors find in "an eye for an eye, a tooth for a tooth" (Exodus 21:24) a Biblical justification for violent revenge and capital punishment. Preachers embrace the Talmudic interpretation that this passage is meant as a requirement to provide monetary compensation to a victim of violence.[68] (This interpretation has been widely held since the days of the Talmud.) Every Passover, Warriors recite verse 79:6 from Psalms as a part of their Haggadah: "Pour out your anger on the nations that do not know you."[69] Preachers, however, tend to omit these verses from their Haggadah texts. Others have given us a particularly curious interpretation, that the violence involved was the act of God and not of his people, and even that one ought not to follow God's "bad" traits!

Whether developed over the centuries in the Diaspora or interpreted from earlier eras, many Jewish texts do not legitimate the use of violence. Thus only in rare circumstances do several of the rabbis, cited in the

Talmud, allow for capital punishment.[70] Indeed, a court is branded as murderous if it hands down a death sentence more than once in seven, or even seventy, years, and two witnesses must testify against the accused for a death sentence even to be considered.[71]

The coercion-persuasion fault line has emerged with new force since the establishment of the state of Israel in 1948. Extreme religious nationalists arose in the years after 1948 and became more prominent following the 1967 war. Their beliefs differ starkly from those of peaceful Jewish subsystems, such as the Reform Jews, most of whom live in the United States. The contrasting beliefs of these two subsystems readily illustrate the coercion-persuasion fault line within Judaism. (I use the term *extreme religious nationalists* because the actual names of the Jewish groups that advocate violence have changed several times, and not all the members of these groups—such as Gush Emunim and, more recently, the Youth of the Heights—share the same opinions.)

The Jewish Reform movement is composed of approximately 1.5 million members and 900 congregations, most of which are in the United States. Central to Reform Judaism is the belief that religion must evolve and adapt to the modern age. The Union for Reform Judaism, the chief institutional body of the Reform movement in the United States, asserts that "a Judaism frozen in time is an heirloom, not a living fountain. The great contribution of Reform Judaism is that it has enabled the Jewish people to introduce innovation while preserving tradition, to embrace diversity while asserting commonality, to affirm beliefs without rejecting those who doubt, and to bring faith to sacred texts without sacrificing critical scholarship."[72]

This conception of Judaism provides Reform Jews with the space to take an adaptive interpretation of Jewish scripture and traditions, which in turn allows them to emphasize the persuasive elements of both. In 1885, leaders of the Reform Jewish movement formally stated that Jews should "accept as binding only the moral laws, and maintain only such ceremonies, as elevate and sanctify our lives, but reject all such as are not adapted to the views and habits of modern civilization. . . . We hold that all such Mosaic and rabbinical laws as regulate diet, priestly purity and dress originated in ages under the influence of ideas altogether foreign to our present mental and spiritual state."[73]

This emphasis on individual conscience, over and against following the letter of the law, allows Reform Jews to eschew any need for coercion in matters of belief. Reform Jews take radical departures from Orthodox Judaism, especially as concerns questions of inclusion and permissiveness. Examples include ordaining women as rabbis, accepting homosexuals into the community, affirming interfaith marriages, and recognizing patrilineal descent as grounds for being Jewish.

A 1937 document titled "Guiding Principles of Reform Judaism" strongly rejects war and advocates peaceful solutions to conflicts. It provides a clear statement for the persuasive approach: "Judaism . . . advocates the promotion of harmonious relations between warring classes on the basis of equity and justice. . . . Judaism, from the days of the prophets, has proclaimed to mankind the ideal of universal peace. The spiritual and physical disarmament of all nations has been one of its essential teachings. It abhors all violence and relies upon moral education, love, and sympathy to secure human progress."[74]

The leaders of American Reform Jews have actively supported all of the major initiatives for peace with the Palestinians, from the Camp David accords to the "Road Map." A resolution passed by the Union for Reform Judaism in June 2004 illustrates the ways the Reform Jewish position on the Arab-Israeli conflict are justified: "We reaffirm our position from prior resolutions, that the greatest impediment to peace is terrorism. . . . At the same time, we cannot ignore the suffering of the Palestinians. Innocent civilians have been killed regularly as Israel retaliates against terrorist targets purposefully situated in civilian population centers. . . . We reaffirm that the government of Israel has every right to defend and protect her citizens in her ongoing fight against terror, but we respectfully encourage the use of tactics that respect the human rights of Palestinians. [T]he Union for Reform Judaism resolves to . . . [r]eaffirm that the only course that offers hope for long-term peace and the sustainability of a Jewish state is a two-state solution, with security for Israel and independence for the Palestinians."[75]

Reform Jews have publicly protested the administrative demolition of Palestinian homes by the Israeli government and the construction of sections of the security barrier that cut into the West Bank. Although strong supporters of the state of Israel, they favor "land for peace"; Reform Jews are content to cede the West Bank and the Gaza Strip to the Palestinians if this will lead to a lasting peace. These positions do not mean that Reform Jews are pacifistic; they do strongly support the right of Israel to protect itself from terrorism and retaliate against its enemies. However, they do not believe in the use of coercion to expand Israel's borders or enforce Jewish law on secular Jews.

Extreme Religious Nationalists: Jewish Holy Warriors

Gush Emunim (The Bloc of the Faithful), whose followers numbered in the hundreds of thousands from the mid-1970s to the early 1980s, is an umbrella organization encompassing a network of schools, cultural institutions, local councils, and settler organizations. Its members tend to take literally God's promise to the people of Israel in Exodus 21:31: "I will establish your borders from the Red Sea to the Sea of the Philistines [the Mediterranean], and from the desert to the River [the Euphrates]. I will hand over to you the people who live in the land and you will drive them out before you." Hence its members often favored and fought for a "Greater Israel" (including the West Bank, Gaza Strip, and Golan Heights as permanent parts of the Israeli state). They were among those who established settlements throughout the occupied territories in accordance with their belief that this land rightfully belongs to Jews. In the view of the spiritual figureheads of Gush Emunim, Rabbi Abraham Isaac Kook (1865–1935) and his son, Rabbi Tzvi Yehuda Kook (1891–1982), God had worked through secular Zionists to establish the state of Israel. This return of the Jews to their Holy Land marked the beginning of the messianic age, when the Messiah would come to earth and redeem the Jewish people. According to Tzvi Yehuda Kook: "When this State of ours is in full control, both internally and externally, then the fulfillment of this mitzva [commandment] of the Inheritance can be truly revealed—the mitzva that is the basis and essence of all of the mitzvot relating to settlement in the Land. It is these mitzvot that, by means of our rule, can accomplish the act of Redemption, and it is by their means that the vision of Redemption must be progressively fulfilled according to the word of the Universal King."[76] Thus, according to Gush Emunim, the settlement of the occupied territories by Jews is the performance of a divine commandment.

Gush Emunim members were not seditious nor were they opposed to the government of Israel in general (several politicians and political parties have in fact represented their interests); however, they did act extra-legally to establish and protect settlements. In their view they had a sacred duty to contravene the policies of the state if these violated the will of God, although by and large they resorted only to nonviolent means of civil disobedience.

James Hunter of the University of Virginia found, "Within Gush Emunim, war is a central component to the purgative process that will bring about messianic times. Some within the movement quite literally view Arabs (including women and children civilians) as Amalekites or Canaanites that contemporary Jews, in the tradition of Joshua from biblical times, have a duty to destroy."[77]

In 1984 Gush Emunim followers were behind a number of terror attacks against Arabs in the occupied territories, including a 1980 attack on three Arab mayors in the West Bank, a 1983 attack on an Islamic college in Hebron, and a plot to blow up the Muslim Dome of the Rock in Jerusalem.[78] Armed vigilante groups, supported by Gush Emunim, have roamed the occupied territories dispensing justice where they see fit and harshly responding to any perceived threats from Arabs. Gush Emunim has justified these violent, extralegal activities in part on utilitarian, pragmatic grounds, as necessary to defend settlers when the government is not fulfilling its duty. One vigilante member told a *Washington Post* reporter that "the army is not doing its job, so we are helping them. . . . Arabs are afraid of us."[79] Others have justified violence against Arabs by citing the rule from the Talmud: "If a man comes to kill you, rise early and kill him first."[80]

Rabbi Meir Kahane and his followers were even more extreme Warriors. Raised in New York City, where he cofounded and led the militant Jewish Defense League, Kahane stated that "Jewish violence to protect Jewish interests is *never* bad."[81] In 1971 he moved to Israel and advocated the complete eviction of Arabs. In 1984 he was elected to the Knesset, where he proposed laws that would require the separation of Jews from non-Jews in all aspects of Israeli life, including schools, neighborhoods, and marriages.

Kahane warned that there would be great catastrophes and horrors before the age of redemption if Jews did not reclaim Greater Israel and drive the Arab "cancer" from the land.[82] In his books and speeches Kahane developed a philosophy of sacred violence that justified slaughtering Arabs as an expression of God's will.[83] Several of his associates were arrested for plotting terrorist attacks and killing Arabs.[84] In 1988, Kahane and his party Kach were disqualified from running for the Israeli parliament because of his racist and antidemocratic statements. Two years later he was shot dead in New York by an American of Egyptian descent.

On the domestic front, Gush Emunim Warriors, and other extreme religious groups such as Kach, have rarely resorted to outright use of violence against other Jews. There have been incidents of rock-throwing at cars that travel through ultra-Orthodox neighborhoods on the Sabbath and attempts to burn down non-Orthodox synagogues,[85] but such violence has largely been avoided. Death threats against Israeli prime ministers (including Ariel Sharon) were arguably a factor in the only killing of a major Israeli political figure, that of Prime Minister Yitzhak Rabin. However, the point of conflict here was not the prime minister's domestic lack of compliance with what the extremists considered to be Jewish law, but his foreign policy. Rabin's promises to cede parts of the occupied territories gravely threatened the extremists' notion of a Greater Israel and the coming of the Messiah. Prime Minister Sharon's life was also under threat as extreme religious nationalist groups voiced outrage over his decision to cede the Gaza Strip.[86]

There have also been extensive and quite effective drives to use the political power of ultra-Orthodox Jews (a minority in Israel and often different from religious nationalists such as Gush Emunim) to ban public transportation on the Sabbath and Jewish holidays, close businesses and entertainment establishments on these same occasions, prohibit the sale of pork, determine who can marry whom, outlaw abortions, regulate who can be buried where, and much else. These laws may constitute religious coercion, especially to the extent that they are enforced through prison sentences and other means of legalized violence.

One thus finds in Judaism—as a religious belief system—both coercive and persuasive subsystems.[87]

Hinduism

This account of the fault line within Hindu civilization focuses on the modern era. Through much of their history, Hindus have not identified themselves as belonging to a single religion with a common, orthodox set of beliefs and practices, in the manner of Christianity or Islam.[88] No one deity, scripture, saint, or ritual has held sway over all Hindus, and no one central religious authority has existed. In fact, the sheer variety of traditions has led many scholars to question whether it is possible to make any descriptive claims about Hinduism as a whole.[89] Thus, while it is possible to identify a shifting fault line of coercive and persuasive belief subsystems within specific parts of the Hindu tradition (such as between the duties of a warrior and the doctrines of nonviolence in the epic *Mahabharata*), it is untenable to claim that, at certain points in history, Hinduism as a whole has had a greater predilection for coercion or persuasion.

Over the past two centuries, however, several Hindu scholars and religious leaders have sought to define and systematize the central tenets of their faith, often in reaction to Islam and Christianity. Their efforts have contributed to the formation of more uniform, pan-Hindu identities, whereby it has become possible to speak meaningfully of *one* Hindu community and *a* Hindu faith. In the competing assertions that modern exponents of Hinduism have made, fault lines between Hindu belief subsystems have emerged. In particular, a coercion-persuasion fault line has taken shape between what might be called coercive Hindu nationalist beliefs and persuasive Hindu pluralist beliefs.

The following discussion draws on two exponents of Hinduism to illustrate these subsystems; we briefly visit the thoughts of Nathuram Godse, an advocate of the first kind of beliefs, and Mohandas Gandhi, a champion of the second kind. I cannot stress enough that not all Hindu nationalists subscribe to violent beliefs, just as not all Jewish nationalists favor violence and not all conservative Catholics believe in bombing abortion clinics. A central point of this volume is that *fundamentalism and religious nationalism do not invariably overlap with belief in violence.* One should not turn a correlation into a crude, prejudicial stereotype. Those of strong beliefs often have a greater predilection for violence than do pluralists or those who lack compelling convictions, to paraphrase Yeats—but the fault line I highlight finds on one side all those who believe in relying principally on persuasion, whether fundamentalist or not.

Nathuram Godse, the man who murdered Gandhi on January 30, 1948, was a champion of a Brahman-led movement that envisioned India as a nation defined by a militant form of Hinduism and ruled by Hindus alone. At his trial, Godse invoked the *Ramayana* and the *Mahabharata*, texts revered by Hindus, to condemn Gandhi's belief in nonviolence.[90] Godse knew well that these were the same scriptures from which Gandhi derived his justifications for nonviolence as a force against abusive physical power. To Godse, and many like him in India, Gandhi's nonviolent interpretation of Hinduism was an intolerable perversion. He contended that if Hindus continued to follow Gandhi, they would become weak and vulnerable in the face of "aggressive" communities, especially the Muslims. Moreover, Godse believed that Gandhi's composite conception of the Indian nation, in which all religions were to receive equal respect and protection, was traitorous to the majority Hindu population.[91]

The form of Hindu nationalism that Godse represented is based on the notion that India has always been the home of the Hindu people, while Muslims and Christians came as foreign invaders. Only Hindus are therefore truly Indians, and the Muslims and Christians living in India should be subordinate to them or leave; nationality is based strictly on religious identity. Vinayak Savarkar, the father of Hindu nationalism, coined the term *Hindutva*, meaning "Hindu-ness," to point to this form of identity. In his book *Hindutva: Who Is a Hindu?* (1923), Savarkar declared that Hindus alone are the rightful rulers of India and defines a Hindu to be "a person who regards this land . . . from the Indus to the seas as his fatherland as well as his Holy Land, that is, the cradle land of his religion."[92] Of Christians and Muslims, he wrote, "They cannot be recognized as Hindus. For though Hindustan to them is a Fatherland as to any other Hindu, yet it is not to them a Holy Land too. Their Holy Land is far off in Arabia and Palestine. Their mythology and Godmen, ideas and heroes are not the children of this soil. Consequently their names and their outlook smack of a foreign origin. Their love is divided."[93] In 1939 Madhav Sadashiv Golwalkar, a prominent Hindu nationalist leader, offered a solution for the Muslim and Christian "problem": "Germany has . . . shown how well-nigh impossible it is for races and cultures, having differences going to the root, to be assimilated into one united whole, a good lesson for us in Hinduism to learn and profit by . . . the non-Hindu people in Hindustan must either adopt the Hindu culture and language, must learn to respect and revere Hindu religion, must entertain no idea but the glorification of the Hindu nation . . . in one word they must cease to be foreigners or may stay in the country wholly subordinated to the Hindu nation claiming nothing, deserving no privileges, far less any preferential treatment, not even citizen's rights."[94]

When Hindu Warriors translate their antagonistic view of non-Hindus into action, it often takes the form of highly organized and symbolically charged attacks against the Muslim community. On December 6, 1992, two hundred thousand *karsevaks,* or militant Hindu activists, descended on the city of Ayodhya in northern India to destroy a sixteenth-century mosque called the Babri Masjid, the Mosque of Babur. The karsevaks believed that India's Muslim conquerors, the Mughals, had destroyed an ancient Hindu temple commemorating the birthplace of Lord Ram and constructed the Babri Masjid in its place. Rebuilding the temple was the first step, they declared, in restoring Hindu rule in India.[95] The destruction of the mosque had the effect of setting off long and brutal Hindu-Muslim riots as far away as London. Such violence between the communities has continued to occur sporadically in many parts of India.[96]

Another form of violence perpetrated by Hindu Warriors has been the forcible reconversion of Hindu converts to Christianity and Islam. The Vishwa Hindu Parishad (VHP), one of the largest Hindu nationalist organizations, has been especially active in coordinating these reconversions and attacking missionaries. With the help of its militant youth wing, the Bajrang Dal, VHP activists have terrorized Dalits (untouchables) who have converted to Christianity and Islam, Christian charity groups, and others they have suspected of "anti-Hindu" activities.[97] During the Christmas season of 1998, VHP activists went on a ten-day rampage against Christians in the southeastern part of Gujarat. They assaulted parishioners, burned down churches, and forcibly reconverted many Christians to Hinduism. One of the fliers passed out in the region to incite riots proclaimed, "India is a country of Hindus. . . . Our religion of Rama and Krishna is pious. To convert [or] leave it is a sin."[98] The leaders of the attacking Hindu mobs often justify their actions by claiming that conniving Christian missionaries have forcibly converted the lower castes. Because many Indian Christians were once untouchables who converted in an attempt to escape caste prejudices, the attacks on Christian converts by Hindu nationalists express both anti-Christian sentiment and enduring hostility to the lower castes. Their violence was justified by the belief that the lower castes do not possess agency in matters of faith. Moreover, conversion from Hinduism to a nonindigenous religion such as Christianity or Islam represents an affront to the integrity and cohesion of the Hindu nation.

Hindu Warriors therefore often justify violence against non-Hindus in terms of national honor and revenge. They argue that the Muslims ruled illegitimately over the Hindus for centuries, that they destroyed Hindu places of worship and raped Hindu women; in recent decades they were said to ally themselves with Pakistan and threaten India with terrorism. Hindus must now avenge these wrongs and reassert their pride, so their argument goes. Uma Bharati, who was a prominent leader in the movement to destroy the Babri Masjid, once crudely declared, "When ten Bajrang Dalis will sit on the chest of every Ali [any Muslim], then only will one know whether this is the birthplace of Ram or Babri Masjid, then only will one know that this country belongs to Ram."[99] Her message is simultaneously religious and political; religion defines nationality, which in turn shapes the forms of religiosity emphasized.

Hindu nationalists like Bharati draw heavily on the symbols of the Hindu tradition that support an ideal of masculinity as violent and warlike. For instance, the images of Lord Ram that Hindu nationalists have popularized portray him with weapons in hand, poised for battle. A god that had traditionally been depicted standing serenely next to his brother and wife, displaying a beatific smile and with a bow over his shoulder, came to be presented with anger distorting his face and his bow drawn for war.[100] The spiritual and moral aspects of Hinduism are eclipsed in Hindu nationalist discourse by the call to reassert Hindu pride and—in some—in the violent reclaiming of the nation.

In stark contrast with Hindu nationalism, Gandhi's conception of Hinduism focuses overwhelmingly on the spiritual and moral elements of the tradition.[101] He spoke of the same deities that the Hindu nationalist movement invokes, Lord Ram for instance, but instead of the angry and vengeful Ram of Hindu nationalism, Gandhi invoked him as a loyal husband, a pious son, and a just ruler. The scriptural stories of cosmic battles and heroic warriors who fight to restore the order of the universe represented to Gandhi the inner battlefield within us all, where good and evil struggle to gain control over our souls and minds. His accounts of the epic battles in the *Mahabharata* and *Ramayana* emphasized ethical lessons and decision-making. He readily admitted that he doubted whether the account of these wars was historically accurate; in his mind, it was not the historical or literal truth of the Hindu scriptures which constituted their greatest worth.[102]

Gandhi's outlook did not mean, however, that for him Hinduism was meant only to be a private faith with no political or social expression or consequences, and thus with only a limited capacity for persuasion.[103] In his speeches around the country, Gandhi made extensive references to the significance of the Hindu tradition for political and social reform and the quest for independence from Great Britain. He invoked the concept of *Ram Rajya*, the ideal polity in the Hindu tradition, as a vision for the nation that Indians should strive to attain and urged Hindus to become involved in the political life as a form of worship. Yet, unlike the Hindu nationalists, Gandhi never sought to realize his goals through religiously justified coercion. Such uses of religion denied what Gandhi considered to be at the heart of Hinduism and all major faiths: nonviolence.[104]

Satyagraha (*satya* meaning "truth" in Sanskrit, and *agraha* "effort" or "endeavor") was Gandhi's well-known technique of transforming the abstract concept of nonviolence into a potent political tool. At its core is the conviction that persuasion is always superior to coercion. When a person, community, or nation acts immorally toward another, the oppressed has a duty to persuade the perpetrator to atone, by nonviolently refusing to obey or cooperate, and by not responding with violent force.[105] Gandhi considered this nonviolent action to be both a political and a religious duty, enjoined upon everyone facing a tyranny. His conception of the role of religion in politics sought to convince political factions and social antagonists to subordinate their concerns to the common good, rather than to emphasize the irreconcilability of sectarian identities, religious or secular.

One of the most notable particular instances of Gandhi's approach was the 1930 Salt *Satyagraha*, in which he and his followers broke the colonial salt laws (the British had made the production of salt by Indians illegal), and encouraged their countrymen to do the same. Throughout the campaign Gandhi wrote to the British viceroy attempting to convince him to repeal the laws. Hundreds of thousands were arrested, including Gandhi, and thereby demonstrated their belief that it is better to suffer time in jail than to commit or consent to an injustice by obeying an unjust law. When the police attacked a large band of Gandhi's followers at a salt depot north of Bombay, the *satyagrahis* received the blows without retaliating. The Salt *Satyagraha* had the persuasive effect it sought to achieve: the British recognized that Indians would no longer submit to their rule and world opinion shifted in favor of the Indian cause.[106]

Being a Hindu himself, Gandhi used language that was typically grounded or cloaked in Hindu terms, which some argue has limited his appeal among Muslims.[107] However, his idea of the Indian nation, in which all religions would be accorded due respect, was not of service to violent Hindu nationalists.

The final stand Gandhi took on this issue came when the subcontinent's Hindu and Muslim communities were at their most antagonistic: during the partition of India and Pakistan. While Delhi was being consumed in brutal riots, Gandhi resolved to fast until death if the violence did not cease. After six days the rioters gave in to Gandhi's appeals, and the public disorder came to an end.[108] This powerful testament to the possibility of Hindu-Muslim unity posed a grave threat to the cause of Hindu nationalists like Nathuram Godse, who believed Muslims deserved to be punished for dividing the nation; twelve days after the end of the fast, on January 30, 1948, Godse shot Gandhi dead at a prayer meeting in Delhi.

Gandhi's willingness to die for his vision of a nation in which no one religion would dominate the others emerged in part from his belief in nonviolence, as well as from his recognition of India's historic religious diversity. But equally important was his conviction that all religions are in some sense true and thus deserving of respect. In 1907 he wrote, "There may be many religions, but the true aim of all is the same. . . . Hence, if we look at the aim, there is no difference among religions."[109] Gandhi derived this position from Hinduism, as he believed it to be "a faith based on the broadest possible toleration," which "enables the followers of that faith not merely to respect all other religions, but also to admire and assimilate whatever is good in them."[110] For Gandhi, this religious pluralism did not translate into a passive tolerance of religious differences but a highly persuasive, active effort—including fasts to the death—to convince his fellow Hindus to practice respect for all religions, to refrain from coercing their followers to Hinduize.

Gandhi's belief in nonviolence and religious pluralism has earned him the title of traitor among coercive Hindu nationalists. It has become common in some parts of Indian society to pass Gandhi off as a weak and ineffective holy man who pandered excessively to religious minorities. This position, exemplifying the coercive side of Hinduism's fault line, became especially common when Hindu nationalists began to wield more political power in the 1980s and reached its fullest expression in the pogroms against Muslims in cities such as Bombay and Ahmedabad.

However, on the other side of the fault line, Hindu beliefs that preach nonviolence and respect for all religions also remain active in Indian society. Among the most telling examples of Hinduism's continuing affirmation of pluralism are the many shrines and pilgrimage places found throughout India where Hindus pray side by side with Muslims. Of this tradition John S. Hawley of Columbia University wrote, "This unruly mix is one of the glories of India, giving the lie to all those airtight textbook chapters on Hinduism, then Islam. Such a tradition is more than tolerance: it's life together, unbrokered by secularism or any other mediating ideology."[111]

CHAPTER C. VIOLENT AND PERSUASIVE BELIEFS IN SECULAR THEORIES OF SOCIAL CHANGE

The Civil Rights Movement

Among the major leaders and organizations of the American civil rights movement, some held that the use of violence to advance social justice was justified. These included leaders such as Malcolm X, Robert Williams, and Huey P. Newton, and organizations including the Black Panther Party and the Nation of Islam. On the other side of the divide were men such as Martin Luther King Jr., James Farmer, and James Lawson, and organizations that included the Southern Christian Leadership Conference (SCLC), the Student Nonviolent Coordinating Committee (SNCC), and the Congress of Racial Equality (CORE). As in the other cases examined here, it is not suggested that those who favored the persuasive approach never considered striking out in anger, nor that those who held violent beliefs did not also support persuasion. The fundamental differences between the two are clear, however, even dramatic. As in other cases, I merely illustrate the fault line by focusing on a few select figures from each camp.

Malcolm X's famous phrase—"by any means necessary"—provides an initial cue.[112] By this he meant that if nonviolent means were unsuccessful in gaining greater freedom for blacks, then any other means, including violence, could be employed legitimately. More explicitly, he declared, "If the black man doesn't get the ballot, then you're going to be faced with another man who forgets the ballot and starts using the bullet."[113]

Malcolm X invokes the Koran and the Bible to support his positions: "There is nothing in our book, the Koran, which teaches us to suffer peacefully. . . . That's a good religion. In fact, that's the old-time religion. That's the one that Ma and Pa used to talk about: an eye for an eye, and a tooth for a tooth, a head for a head, and a life for a life. That's a good religion."[114]

In a 1963 speech in Detroit he argued against those who believed that a revolution in U.S. race relations could be undertaken through nonviolent action: "You don't have a peaceful revolution. You don't have a turn-the-other-cheek revolution. There is no such thing as a nonviolent revolution. . . . Revolution is bloody, revolution is hostile, revolution knows no compromise, revolution overturns and destroys everything that gets in its way."[115]

Civil rights movement leaders who championed persuasion argued that violence would increase the hatred and hostility between whites and blacks rather than build solidarity. Leaders such as King envisioned their movement as leading to greater integration between the races and full recognition of the rights of all Americans. They were more concerned with persuading whites to change their ways than with punishing them for past and present wrongs. King, for example, wrote in *Stride Toward Freedom* that he "does not seek to defeat or humiliate the opponent, but to win his friendship and understanding. . . . The aftermath of nonviolence is the creation of the beloved community, while the aftermath of violence is tragic bitterness."[116]

James Lawson, in a speech before SNCC, stated, "The Christian favors the breaking down of racial barriers because the redeemed community of which he is already a citizen recognizes no barriers dividing humanity. The Kingdom of God, as in heaven so on earth, is the distant goal of the Christian."[117] Many of the civil rights movement's leaders and organizations provided religious justifications for their faith in nonviolence. In biblical passages such as the Sermon on the Mount and the sayings of the Hebrew Prophets, they found inspiration for their message of suffering nonviolently to transform the hearts of their opponents. SNCC's 1962 Statement of Purpose exemplifies the religious character of the nonviolent civil rights struggle: "We affirm the philosophical or religious ideal of nonviolence as the foundation of our purpose, the presupposition of our faith, and the manner of our action. Nonviolence as it grows from the Judeo-Christian tradition seeks a social order of justice permeated by love. . . . Through nonviolence, courage displaces fear; love transforms hate. . . . By appealing to conscience and standing on the moral nature of human existence, nonviolence nurtures the atmosphere in which reconciliation and justice become actual possibilities."[118]

In addition to religious and moral justifications for nonviolence, persuasive civil rights leaders believed that nonviolent direct action was highly effective in generating social change. King reminded his followers: "Nonviolent resistance is not a method for cowards; it does resist. The phrase 'passive resistance' often gives the false impression that this is a sort of 'do-nothing method' in which the resister quietly and passively accepts evil. But nothing is further from the truth. For while the nonviolent resister is passive in the sense that he is not physically aggressive toward his opponent, his mind and emotions are always active, constantly seeking to persuade his opponent he is wrong."[119]

The students who initiated the first lunch counter sit-in discovered how effective nonviolent direct action could be: "We knew that probably the most powerful and potent weapon that people have literally no defense for is love, kindness. That is, whip the enemy with something that he doesn't understand."[120] While strongly preaching the message of love and community, civil rights leaders maintained that they would hold fast to the goal of social change and employ nonviolent direct action as forcefully as necessary to attain it.

In addition to supporting nonviolence because it tore down racial divisions and appealed to religious values, civil rights leaders recognized that unlike a violent struggle in which only men with guns could participate, anyone could take part in nonviolent resistance. In his book *Why We Can't Wait* King vividly brings out this democratic dimension of the civil rights movement:

A nonviolent army has a magnificent universal quality. To join an army that trains its adherents in the methods of violence, you must be of a certain age. But in Birmingham, some of the most valued foot soldiers were youngsters ranging from elementary pupils to teen-age high school and college students. For acceptance in the armies that maim and kill, one must be physically sound, possessed of straight limbs and accurate vision. But in Birmingham, the lame and the halt and the crippled could and did join up. . . . In the nonviolent army, there is room for everyone who wants to join up. There is no color distinction. . . . Nonviolent soldiers are called upon to examine and burnish their greatest weapons—their heart, their conscience, their courage, and their sense of justice.[121]

Socialism

The line that divides violent from persuasive beliefs is readily discernible in socialist thought. Specifically, the fault line separates revolutionaries, who justify violence as a means to overthrow the capitalist system and erect a new order over its grave, and reformers, who rely on persuasion to gain justice for the working classes by gradual and peaceful change. True, the division is not perfect; some revolutionaries have held that the change from capitalism to socialism will arrive through a natural process of attrition, with more and more members of the bourgeoisie joining the proletariat. And some reformers have supported limited acts of violence. However, by and large, the fault line between socialist revolutionaries and reformers parallels the line that separates the Warriors from the Preachers in our terms—between those who believe in the right to use force and those who seek to avoid it by relying on the persuasive power of their cause.

The following presents key arguments provided by the two sides to justify their positions. As in other belief systems here briefly visited, the following discussion is strictly illustrative and focuses on one key point. There are scores of other comparisons that could be made between different socialist camps and between the numerous differences within each camp.

One of the major justifications for violence that revolutionaries draw upon is the historical inevitability of conflict between the bourgeoisie and the feudal aristocracy, and later between the proletariat and the bourgeoisie. This second conflict rests on Marx's theory that—to put it briefly and in basic terms—profits in a capitalist system are created by ensuring that the price of labor remains below the price of the commodities produced, thus guaranteeing that the laboring classes remain impoverished as the capitalist classes grow richer. Over time the laborers will revolt against the capitalists to capture the means of production and thereby achieve greater material equality. Some socialists have argued that this revolution will come about by a withering away of the bourgeois state, gradually eroding on its own; others—socialist Warriors—have insisted that the conflict between laborers and capitalists can be resolved only through violence. Taking the latter position, the Russian revolutionary Vladimir Lenin wrote: "The theory of Marx and Engels of the inevitability of a violent revolution refers to the bourgeois state. The latter *cannot* be superseded by the proletarian state (the dictatorship of the proletariat) through the process of 'withering away,' but, as a general rule, only through violent revolution. . . . [T]he suppression of the bourgeois state by the proletarian state is impossible without a violent revolution."[122]

Other socialist Warriors argue that the fundamental restructuring of a society's modes of production demands the overwhelming force of a violent revolution. Anything short of this would lead only to halfhearted reforms and weak compromises, which leave power in the hands of the capitalists. William Z. Foster expressed this position in his 1928 speech accepting the presidential nomination of the communist Workers Party of America. He declared, "The capitalist class would never allow the working class peacefully to take control of the state. . . . The working class must shatter the capitalist state. . . . Our Party is a revolutionary Party. It aims not simply to ease conditions a bit under capitalism for the workers but to abolish capitalism altogether."[123] Rosa Luxemburg, the Polish-born Marxist political theorist and revolutionary, argued that without employing devastating force against capitalism any socialist uprising would ultimately fail: "The Russian Revolution has but confirmed the basic lesson of every great revolution, the law of its being, which decrees: either the revolution must advance at a rapid, stormy, and resolute tempo, break down all barriers with an iron hand and place its goals ever farther ahead, or it is quite soon thrown backward behind its feeble point of departure and suppressed by counterrevolution. To stand still, to mark time on one spot . . . is never possible in revolution."[124]

A complementary position has justified revolutionary violence by depicting it as a positive, constructive force that has transformative power. In his "Apology for Violence" Georges Sorel, the French Marxist who urged violent direct action through labor unions or syndicates, wrote, "The social war, for which the proletariat ceaselessly prepares itself in the syndicates, may engender the elements of a new civilization suited to a people of producers."[125]

Moreover, a violent struggle between labor and capital transforms the proletariat from a subordinate, servile class into those strong enough to seize the reins of power. Lenin has argued that revolutionary violence was necessary to forge the proletariat into a ruling class: "We do not expect the proletariat to mature for power in an atmosphere of cajoling and persuasion, in a school of mealy sermons or didactic declamations, but in the school of life and struggle. To become the ruling class and defeat the bourgeoisie for good the proletariat must be *schooled,* because the skill this implies does not come ready-made. The proletariat must do its learning in the struggle, and stubborn, desperate struggle in earnest is the only real teacher."[126]

These positions are reminiscent of Frantz Fanon's theory, laid out in *The Wretched of the Earth,* that "violence is a cleansing force. It frees the native from his inferiority complex and from his despair and inaction; it makes him fearless and restores his self-respect."[127]

Once the dictatorship of the proletariat has been attained, violent socialism maintains that coercion must be a central element of the new regime. In an argument Joseph Stalin would come to rely upon, Leon Trotsky emphasizes that without a policy of terrorism any socialist regime would fail: "The man who repudiates terrorism in principle—i.e., repudiates measures of suppression and intimidation towards determined and armed counter-revolution, must reject all idea of the political supremacy of the working class and its revolutionary dictatorship. The man who repudiates the dictatorship of the proletariat repudiates the Socialist revolution, and digs the grave of Socialism."[128] In sum, violent socialism has maintained that without the use of force, revolution is impossible; the exercise of force by an oppressed class is psychologically liberating and socially transformative. Moreover, force is necessary to protect the socialist regime from any reactionary counterrevolution.

In contrast, persuasive socialists, including Fabian socialists and ideologues of European social democratic parties, have repudiated violence and have instead sought to achieve justice for the working classes through political education and action within the context and confines of the liberal democratic order. Other such reformers have merely considered the use of force a poor tactic.

Karl Kautsky, a Marxist theorist and close friend of Friedrich Engels, laid out a strong case against the use of force by combining arguments as to what is just with concerns for the psychological side effects of using violence. He argued that by using violence in the name of socialism the

Bolsheviks had turned "the cause of humanity into a mere cause of the working-men . . . transforming what should have been the social struggle for liberty, and for the raising the whole of humanity on a higher plane, into an outbreak of bitterness and revenge, which led to the worst abuses and tortures."[129] Kautsky continued that instead of bringing about a more equitable way of life, violent socialism foments "thirst for vengeance on the part of the proletariat. . . . It thinks to gain happiness by being able to trample down those men who, by their destiny, have been in more favorable circumstances."[130]

Several persuasive socialists have also disagreed with their coercive counterparts that conflicts between labor and capital are irreconcilable and inevitable. Democracy in their view provides a means by which the working classes can address their grievances without having to resort to violence. Workers in a democratic system can elect their own governmental representatives, who in turn pass laws to protect their interests and gradually transform the economic structures of society in their favor. Labor can thus reconcile its differences with capital through the give-and-take of democratic politics, rather than by violently replacing the supremacy of the bourgeoisie with a dictatorship of the proletariat.

Many of the late nineteenth- and early twentieth-century socialists believed that this democratic workers' revolution was already under way. Eduard Bernstein, a founder of democratic socialism, wrote in his book *Evolutionary Socialism:* "In all advanced countries we see the privileges of the capitalist bourgeoisie yielding step by step to democratic organizations. Under the influence of this, and driven by the movement of the working classes which is daily becoming stronger, a social reaction has set in against the exploiting tendencies of capital. . . . Factory legislation, the democratizing of local governments . . . the consideration of standards of labor in the work undertaken by public authorities—all these characterize this phase of the evolution."[131]

In *Terrorism and Communism* Kautsky compared social democratic change to that of violent revolution and strongly found favor in the first. He wrote: "[I]n a democracy each party addresses itself to the whole social community. Each party certainly defends definite class interests; but it is compelled to show every side of these interests, which are intimately connected with the general interest of the whole social community. . . . In democracy the horizon of the masses becomes enormously extended by participation in politics. All these possibilities of education of the people become simply shattered if, as the Soviet Republic has done, democracy is set aside in favor of an autocracy."[132]

Kautsky advocated the persuasive course: socialists must demonstrate that the interests of the working classes are closely linked with the interests of society as a whole. This argument stands in sharp contrast to the confrontational Marxist concept that there are no general societal interests, only those of one class or the other, which are in natural conflict and are bound to clash. Violent socialism focuses exclusively on the interests of the working classes (or at least its claims as to what those interests are), and therefore it need not pay much attention to seeking the approval of other classes or to justifying its case in terms of a common good. The nonproletariat is perceived as the enemy, which at best will vanish under the effects of technological and economic progress, but most likely will have to be overthrown and liquidated. The individuals in this group cannot be persuaded to remove themselves from power or even to reform their policies. In contrast, persuasive socialists seek to institute change through the democratic process and therefore must present their case in terms that speak to the members of all classes. Their call for greater material equality and workers' rights is thus framed as an elaboration of democratic principles already agreed upon.

CHAPTER D. VIOLENT AND PERSUASIVE BELIEFS IN ISLAM

Islam has been characterized often in recent years as largely of one kind—one that legitimizes violence and clashes with the peaceful and liberal-democratic West. Hence nowhere is the need to recognize major differences among belief subsystems as immediate and important, indeed vital, as within Islam. And—nowhere has this crucial fault line between violent and persuasive beliefs, between Warriors and Preachers, been so ignored, as in Islam.

On one side of the fault line are those whose interpretations of Islam justify massive violence against nonbelievers *(kuffar)* and apostates (as in Afghanistan's attempt to sentence a Muslim to death for converting to Christianity). In stark contrast to them are Muslim beliefs that condemn coercion in the name of Islam and rely on persuasion to advance their religion. For them *jihad* is meant only to be defensive and must never target innocent people through terrorism. Interpretations focus on the spiritual element of jihad, the internal battle with the passions and vices. Indeed, when a pollster asked 10,004 adults in predominantly Muslim countries "what *jihad* means to you," he found that the majority of responses spoke of jihad as a "duty toward God," a "divine duty," or a "worship of God"—"with no explicit militaristic connotation at all.[133] It is important to remember, though, that this rejection of violence does not necessarily entail acceptance of democratic regimes and human rights.

Too many commentators and leaders in the West have ignored this crucial fact by projecting Islam as a monolithic belief system that legitimizes and even extols the indiscriminate use of violence. Samuel Huntington, in his influential book *The Clash of Civilizations*, famously treated Islam as if it were one coherent, violent civilization, intent on perpetual warfare with the West. Indeed, Huntington scoffed at those who pretend to see differences: "Some Westerners . . . have argued that the West does not have problems with Islam but only with violent Islamist extremists. Fourteen hundred years of history demonstrate otherwise. . . . The underlying problem for the West is not Islamic fundamentalism but Islam, a different civilization whose people are convinced of the superiority of their culture."[134]

It was from historian Bernard Lewis, whose work has influenced U.S. foreign policy, that Huntington borrowed the phrase "clash of civilizations." While in recent years Lewis has emphasized the differences between mainstream and radical Islam,[135] he nevertheless continues to speak of an angry, embittered Muslim world, frustrated by the West's power and bent on fighting against it.[136] And he is unequivocal in his assertion that Islam will clash with the West until Muslim nations secularize and modernize.[137]

Azzam Tamimi, director of the Institute for Islamic Political Thought in London, observed: "There is a deep rooted feeling that Islam and the West contradict each other, that they cannot coexist. . . . Strong lobbies have emerged in several Western capitals prophesying the inevitable clash between the two remaining antagonists, the West and Islam. The mere advocating of Shariah, the law of Islam, is considered by some lobbyists, such as Daniel Pipes, Judith Miller and others, to be a great threat to world peace and stability."[138]

Daniel Pipes, director of the Middle East Forum and a frequent media commentator, wrote, "To me, every fundamentalist Muslim, no matter how peaceable in his own behavior, is part of a murderous movement and is thus, in some fashion, a foot soldier in the war that bin Laden has launched against civilization."[139] He thus equates strong believers with those who advocate violence.

Leon Hadar of the Cato Institute noted in *Foreign Affairs:* "[Journalists] impose the term 'Islamic fundamentalism' to describe diverse and unrelated movements that range from CIA-trained Islamic guerrillas in Afghanistan to the anti-American clerics in Iran, from the Muslim Brotherhood in Egypt, operating in a parliamentary system, to murderous terrorist organizations like the Lebanese Hezbollah, from pro-American Saudi Arabia to anti-American Libya. Think-tank studies, op-ed pieces and congressional hearings add color to this image of a unified and monolithic Islam."[140]

According to many observers and policymakers in the West, a moderate Muslim—and therefore an acceptable U.S. ally—is only one who supports liberal democracy and human rights. These observers fail to recognize that millions of devout Muslims hold to an orthodox interpretation of Islam without seeking to impose it coercively on others. Although it is wrong to claim, as George W. Bush has, that all of Islam is a religion of peace—extensive evidence points to the contrary—it is also a grievous error to argue that a strict believer is invariably a supporter of terror. The following is intended to briefly illustrate the two sides of the central fault line within Islam, and to demonstrate how moderate Muslim beliefs differ from violent ones.

Coercion Within Islam

The subsystems of belief in Islam that have been used to legitimate coercion are well known. From the earliest jurists to today's violent extremists, Muslims seeking to justify coercion have looked to verses in the Koran, such as "Slay the idolaters wheresoever you find them, and take them captive or besiege them" (9:5), and "Fight them till sedition comes to end and the law of God (prevails)" (2:193). Such passages have been widely interpreted as commanding that Muslims battle with unbelievers until all have either been killed or converted to Islam. This position has been supported by select *hadith,* the sayings of the Prophet, in which Muhammad states, "I have been commanded to fight against people so long as they do not declare that there is no god but Allah."[141] Imam Shafi'i (767–820 CE), founder of one of the four schools of Sunni jurisprudence, argued that even if polytheists surrender, Muslims must continue to fight them until they submit to Islam. While most scholars have not extended this "convert or die" rule to the "Peoples of the Book" (i.e., Jews and Christians), the Koran commands Muslims to fight them until they surrender and pay a protective tax (9:29).

During the modern period, Hassan al-Banna (1906–1949), founder of the Muslim Brotherhood, takes this command a step further in his book, writing in *On Jihad:* "There is a clear indication [in the hadith] of the obligation to fight the People of the Book, and of the fact that God doubles the reward of those who fight them. *Jihad* is not against polytheists alone, but against all who do not embrace Islam."[142]

Some of the harshest words and strongest punishments in Islamic law have been reserved for apostasy. The Koran states, "Those who turn back on their faith and die disbelieving will have wasted their deeds in this world and the next. They are inmates of Hell and shall abide there forever" (2:217). A hadith records the Prophet as saying, "Whoever changed his Islamic religion, then kill him."[143] The founders of the four Sunni schools of law agree that an unrepentant apostate must be executed. In the fourteenth century Ibn-Taymiya, a theologian whose thought has inspired extremists such as Osama bin Laden, wrote, "The apostate is more crude in his infidelity than an original unbeliever."[144] Bin Laden himself often invokes the stigma of apostasy when singling out Muslim nations or individuals who conspire with the United States. According to these violent interpretations of Islam, every Muslim must battle unbelievers and apostates until they submit or are killed.

Traditions of Persuasion Within Islam

Such interpretations have been far from universal over the course of Islamic history. Beginning with the Koran, prominent traditions have existed that condemn coercion and favor religious tolerance. Such traditions find much support in an often-cited passage from the Koran that states, "There is no compulsion in matter of faith" (2:256). It is said that when Umar, a companion of the Prophet and second caliph of Islam, asked his slave to convert to Islam and the slave refused, he cited 2:256 and did not persist.[145]

The futility of coercion in matters of faith is expanded upon in Koran 10:99–100: "If your Lord had willed, all the people on the earth would have come to believe, one and all. Are you going to compel the people to believe except by God's dispensation?" The duty of each Muslim is to proclaim the truth of Islam without compulsion or force; no human can force a change of heart over which God alone has control.

In contrast to the passages commanding that all unbelievers be made to submit to Islam, the Koran also contains rather clear affirmations of religious tolerance and diversity: "To each of you We have given a law and a way and a pattern of life. If God had pleased He surely could have made you one people (professing one faith)" (5:48); and "O you unbelievers, I do not worship what you worship, nor do you worship who I worship. . . . To you your way and to me mine" (109:1–6). These verses do not mean that Muslims should not attempt to convert those of other faiths. The Koran exhorts all Muslims to "call them [unbelievers] to the path of your Lord with wisdom and words of good advice; and reason with them in the best way possible." Some may never respond to the call, but force must not be brought to bear against them; when Muhammad exclaims, "Oh Lord, these are certainly a people who do not believe," Allah responds to him, "Turn away from them and say: 'Peace'" (43:88–89).

From the earliest years of Islam many have naturally asked, how can such condemnations of religious coercion be reconciled with the passages of the Koran and hadith that favor coercion? Several classical jurists resolved this matter by reasoning that Koran 9:5, the so-called verse of the sword cited above, supersedes declarations against violence; other scholars have not found jihad and religious freedom inherently contradictory. Some have interpreted the call for jihad in a strict military sense, whereby "religious freedom could be granted to the non-Muslims after their defeat."[146] Several modern commentators interpret the verses of the sword to concern specifically the period of Muhammad's conquests in the Arabian peninsula and therefore as not applicable today.[147] Others set such passages from the Koran alongside those that state, "Permission is granted those (to take up arms) who fight because they are oppressed" (22:39), and "Fight those in the way of God who fight you but do not be aggressive: God does not like aggressors" (2:190). This interpretation of jihad as solely defensive is particularly strongly held among influential modern commentators such as Muhammad Abduh (1849–1905), Rashid Rida (1865–1935), and Jamal al-Din al-Qasimi (1866–1914).

Another interpretation of jihad, associated with the mystics of Islam known as Sufis, is that it refers primarily to the internal spiritual struggle against the ego and lust, rather than the outward battle with one's enemies. An influential saying attributed by some to the Prophet states, "The greater *jihad* is the struggle against the self."[148] The twelfth-century Sufi master Abd al-Qadir al-Jilani explained, "[There are] two types of *jihad:* the outer and the inner. The inner is the *jihad* of the soul, the passion, the nature, and Satan. The outer is the *jihad* of the infidels who resist Him and His Messenger. . . . The inner *jihad* is more difficult than the outer *jihad* because it involves cutting the forbidden customs of the soul, and exiling them."[149] Seyyed Hossein Nasr wrote, "*Jihad* is therefore the inner battle to purify the soul of its imperfections, to empty the vessel of the soul of the pungent water of forgetfulness, negligence, and the tendency of evil and to prepare it for the reception of the Divine Elixir of Remembrance, Light, and Knowledge."[150]

In recent years some of the most revered leaders of Sunni and Shia Islam have denounced coercion in the name of Islam. Sheikh Mohammed Sayed Tantawi, Grand Imam of Egypt's al-Azhar mosque and one of the most authoritative voices of Sunni orthodoxy, has declared, "*Jihad* doesn't mean aggression in Islam, it means defending one's soul, land and nation against those who attack them. . . . Bin Laden expresses his personal point of view of *jihad;* he doesn't represent Islam."[151] After the 9/11 attacks, Sheikh Yusuf al-Qaradawi, a highly influential conservative cleric with a show on the al-Jazeera television network, stated, "Our hearts bleed for the attack that has targeted the World Trade Center. . . . Islam, the religion of tolerance, holds the human soul in high esteem, and considers the attack against innocent human beings a grave sin."[152] The Grand Ayatollah Ali al-Sistani, among the world's most influential Shia religious authorities, has repeatedly condemned assassinations, kidnappings, and other forms of terror.

Yusuf al-Qaradawi observed that the virtue of moderation finds a natural home in Islam: "Moderation, or balance, is not only a general characteristic of Islam, it is a fundamental landmark. The Koran says: 'Thus have we made of you an *umma* [community] justly balanced, that you might be witness over the nations, and the Messenger a witness over yourselves' (2:143). As such, the Muslim *umma* is a nation of justice and moderation. . . . Islamic texts call upon Muslims to exercise moderation and to reject and oppose all kinds of extremism."[153]

To reiterate, the preceding quotations are merely illustrative, and many more could be given, from both sides of the fault line. However, those already provided may suffice to show that as far as the all important distinction between coercive and persuasive beliefs is at issue, Islam is not different from other belief systems. One may argue that the violent interpretations have many more followers in Islam than are found in other belief systems. Even if this were true, one would have to note that the proportion of Warriors over Preachers changed as well in other civilizations; the same holds for Islam during its "golden period" in medieval Spain as compared to more recent developments. Moreover, there is no convincing evidence that there is something inherent in Islam that will prevent the camp of Preachers from growing much larger in the future. Above all, I challenge the claim that the majority of Muslims are Warriors, believing in the virtue of violence. They may be illiberal and may not favor democratic regimes, but this does not make them violent. It is wrong, unfair, and unwise to lump Illiberal Moderate Muslims together with the violent ones.

CHAPTER E. ILLIBERAL MODERATE MUSLIMS: THE GLOBAL SWING VOTE

Several public opinion polls, leading academic studies, and numerous media reports all indicate that the rejection of violence in the name of Islam is not limited to liberal Muslim immigrant groups in the West, to Western Muslim scholars, and to small liberal groups in Muslim countries. As a matter of fact, *only relatively small minorities in numerous Muslim nations hold violent beliefs.*

Before citing public opinion polls to support the preceding statement, I need note that these polls were not designed to answer the questions I raise. Moreover, different polls use different wording, are conducted at different points in time, and use different methodologies. Hence they are bound to come up with different findings—and these in turn are all subject to varying interpretations.

Keeping these qualifications in mind, we learn that polls conducted in 2005 found only 13 percent of Moroccans, and 2006 polls found only 17 percent of Turks and 10 percent of Indonesians, supported suicide bombing.[154] A higher proportion of the citizens of Mali believed in 2002 that suicide bombings in the defense of Islam were justifiable, but still amounted to only one out of three.[155] In Pakistan, support for bombers fell from 41 percent in 2004 to 25 percent in the spring of 2005.[156] Also in 2005 fully 81 percent of Afghans expressed a negative view of al-Qaeda.[157] Seventy-two percent strongly supported disarming fighters under local warlords, and 70 percent didn't believe attacks on U.S. forces in Afghanistan were justifiable.[158] Meanwhile, in 2006 only minorities of 35 percent of Pakistanis and 22 percent of Egyptians showed support for Islamic extremist groups.[159]

Support was higher for suicide attacks on U.S. forces and its allies in Iraq. Still, in 2005 it encompassed only a minority in Pakistan and Turkey at 29 percent and 24 percent, respectively. In Jordan, Lebanon, and Morocco support was exceptionally high at 49 percent, 49 percent, and 56 percent.[160] Still, in those countries nearly half the people were on the nonviolent side of the divide.

A majority of women in eight Muslim nations listed violence not as something they favored—but rather as one of their major concerns.[161] In February 2006, 73 percent of Palestinians favored a peaceful solution to the conflict with Israel, and 62 percent believed that Hamas should change its position on the destruction of the Israeli state.[162] (It is true that close to 45 percent voted for Hamas in parliamentary elections, but many did so because they enjoyed the social services the terrorist organization provides and considered the other main party, Fatah, as too corrupt.)[163] Eighty-six percent of Palestinians believed that public protests were justifiable against Denmark for the allegedly insulting cartoons of Muhammad published in the Danish press—however, only 8 percent held that the reaction should have been violent.[164]

Those who reject violence (under most conditions) include liberal and illiberal. One can gain an indication of the size of the moderates who are not liberals or pro-democracy by examining the proportion of the populations in various Muslim nations that support a stronger role for Islam in their politics (especially as religion already plays a strong role in their public lives, and is used as a key argument to restrict individual rights). For instance, large majorities in Pakistan (86 percent), Indonesia (82 percent), and Bangladesh (74 percent) favored a greater role for Islam in their nation's politics, according to a 2002 poll.[165] Pluralities of those surveyed in Jordan (42 percent), Saudi Arabia (48 percent), and the United Arab Emirates (45 percent) in 2004 believed the clergy should play a greater role in their governments. Egyptians were almost evenly divided on whether clerics should dictate the political system.[166]

In the summer of 2002 fewer than half of Indonesians (42 percent) believed that religion should be kept separate from government, and 92 percent believed that schools should not focus less on religious education. (This is despite the fact that 86 percent of Indonesians said that Islam already plays a large role in their political life.) In Lebanon in 2003, 72 percent of Lebanese Muslims believed that religious leaders should play a larger role in politics; even in secularized Turkey 40 percent thought the same way.[167] Sixty-two percent of Nigerian Muslims believed that Islam plays a large role in politics, but as many as 91 percent still hoped that religious leaders would play even a larger role. In Bangladesh in 2003 there was also wide support, at 76 percent, for religious leaders playing a large role in politics. The proportions were smaller in Uzbekistan, but far from small: 40 percent of the people believed religious leaders should play a larger role in politics, even though 55 percent believed that Islam already plays a large role in their political life.[168]

Of special interest is a study of women's attitudes. Their interests are often trampled over in Muslim countries, and women are often assumed to be a major force for change, favoring a more liberal, and less religious-driven, democratic society. However, at least according to some sources, many Muslim women are not such a force and do not favor such a society: "An overwhelming majority of the women polled in each country cited 'attachment to moral and spiritual values' as the best aspect of their own societies. In Pakistan, 53 percent of the women polled said attachment to their religious beliefs was their country's most admirable trait. Similarly, in Egypt, 59 percent of the women surveyed cited love of their religion as the best aspect."[169] A majority of the women polled in eight predominately Muslim countries cite violent extremism as one aspect of their societies they resent most but make no mention of gender equality, which they associate, negatively, with the West:

When asked what they resented most about their own societies, a majority of Muslim women polled said that a lack of unity among Muslim nations, violent extremism, and political and economic corruption were their main concerns. The *hijab*, or headscarf, and *burqa*, the garment covering face and body, seen by some Westerners as tools of oppression, were never mentioned in the women's answers to the open-ended questions, the poll analysts said.

Concerning women's rights in general, most Muslim women polled associated sex equality with the West. Seventy-eight percent of Moroccan women, 71 percent of Lebanese women and 48 percent of Saudi women polled linked legal equality with the West. Still, a majority of the respondents did not think adopting Western values would help the Muslim world's political and economic progress.[170]

Thus many millions of women in the Islamic world seem also to qualify as Illiberal Moderates.

In short, to the extent that one can draw on the available polls, one must conclude that the overwhelming majority of Muslims in the world do not believe in the justice of violence and do not support acts of violence, and thus are not Warriors.[171] However—and it is here that the intellectual, normative, and political confusion reigns high—many of these non-Warriors, or moderates by my definition, do not support human rights or democratic regimes. Hence, to reiterate, if one approaches the Muslim world with the notion that, if you are not in favor of liberal-democratic regimes, you are opposed to us and support terrorists, such a position (a) will define the majority if not most Muslims as opposed to Western ideas, and (b) will reject hundreds of millions that might be at least neutral if not allies in fighting against terrorism and other forms of violence.

So far we have seen that the proportion of Muslims who favor a greater place for religion in their societies is vastly larger than that of those who support violence. I presume that the difference between these two proportions helps to estimate the size of the "Illiberal Moderate" bloc, although one would prefer to know much more about the attitudes involved. I could rest my case here. However, I take note that there also exists a slew of polls showing very large segments of Muslims favoring democracy and some select individual rights. For instance, in a poll conducted in 2006, Muslims were asked whether they believed that democracy could work well in their countries. Seventy-four percent of Jordanians believed that it could work well, as did 70 percent of Indonesians, 65 percent of Egyptians, 50 percent of Pakistanis, and 44 percent of Turks.[172] And several polls show that many Muslims favor one right or another, such as women having the right to vote, to hold office, to seek education, and to work outside the home.[173] (There are considerable differences on this particular issue among Muslim nations, but these need not detain us here.)[174]

If one interprets the responses to these questions as indications that the majority or at least large segments of Muslims favor democracy and some individual rights, it would seem to follow that liberalism could have a bright future in Islam, and that the ranks of Illiberal Moderates are relatively small. However, three legitimate questions must be raised about these estimates for support for democracy in the Muslim world.

First, the term democracy is not defined in these polls. Democracy means different things to different people. The term was of course adopted by communist police states: East Germany, for example, styled itself the "German Democratic Republic." A leading scholar of Islam writes: "I do not think that 'democracy' as supported by Muslims in the polls is necessarily an anti-human rights, faux democracy. I think that there is such a thing as 'Islamic democracy' that is not simply like the use of the term by communist police states but also is not simply a carbon copy of 'liberal democracy' as defined by the U.S. and Westminster models."[175] I agree that it is relatively easy to make use of Islam for the purpose of promoting social cohesion; but I doubt that Islamic principles translate as easily into a valid form of democracy. Without a constitutional framework to ensure basic individual rights, democracies, whether based on consensus-building or elections, tend to become majoritarian tyrannies.[176]

Second, even in the West "democracy" is often equated with elections, but we have seen that one can hold elections regularly and still maintain an authoritarian regime. This is the case, for instance, in Syria, Egypt, and Iran. All conduct elections but ban most if not all of the opposition from participating, and those in power monopolize the media, prevent civil society from flourishing, and otherwise undermine the elements required by a liberal democracy. To assess how many Muslims support genuine rather than faux democracy, additional study seems badly needed.

Third, speaking generally, social scientists point out that people do not hold fully consistent opinions. Specifically in the case at hand Muslims may think that they favor democratic regimes and at the same time support political systems that are, in effect, theocracies. Indeed because most surveys ask if you favor A (say, democracy) and then if you favor B (say, a greater role for religion in politics), they seem to invite an affirmative response to both. In most surveys there are no questions about the obvious tensions between attitudes, or any "costs" attached to embracing one or the other.

In this context the survey of women is especially revealing. Women were asked to rank their concerns. The majority, we have seen, were much more concerned about law and order (thus opposing violence) than about rights. This survey suggests that, if religion and freedom must be ranked, among the majority of Muslim women freedom comes in second; and that most of those who favor both democracy and theocracy favor theocracy more. They are thus Illiberal.

The same is also revealed in the proportion of those who consider themselves Muslims first and citizens second, an arguably illiberal attribute. When Muslims were asked in 2006 if they considered themselves Muslim ahead of being national citizens, those polled who agreed included 36 percent of Indonesians, 59 percent of Egyptians, 67 percent of Jordanians, and 87 percent of Pakistanis.[177] In 2005, an overwhelming majority of Muslims believed it was wrong to ban head scarves in public—specifically, 59 percent of Lebanese, 64 percent of Turks, 77 percent of Pakistanis, 90 percent of Moroccans, and 97 percent of Jordanians.[178]

All said and done, there is room for considerable difference of opinion on the proportions of Muslims who support a liberal democracy for their respective nations; those who are Illiberal Moderates, opposing violence but not favoring a liberal-democratic regime, either; and those who are neither liberal nor moderate, the Warriors. However, even if the proportion of the Liberals is larger than I suggest, the Illiberal Moderates still crucially constitute the all-important "swing vote." To reiterate, liberals need little courting, while the Warriors cannot for the most part be won over. Courting Illiberal Moderates is much more likely to succeed—that is, this holds as long as one's goal is Security First, and regime change, especially one brought about forcefully by foreign powers, is not considered a prerequisite for acceptable citizenship in the new world order.

Travelers' Notes

In former times much of that which was known about other societies was based on travelers' notes, ranging from those of medieval and Renaissance explorers, to those of Jesuit missionaries, and even to those of the adventurer-journalists of the nineteenth century like Sir Henry Morton Stanley. In this genre of texts one thinks perhaps most famously of the Venetian trader Marco Polo and his *Description of the World*—dictated while he was in prison in Genoa in 1298—and who was satirized by his initially skeptical audience as "Il Milione," for the million marvels, or lies, he was supposed to have told![179] Today academics, diplomats, and reporters assume the role that men like Marco Polo and Stanley once had. Therefore, it might be useful to provide a few reports filed by such contemporary observers on similar points to those found in the public opinion polls just mentioned. They do not constitute a representative sample; on the contrary, they were chosen deliberately to highlight a side of Muslim societies often hidden by the polarized reporting that views these societies as largely torn between Islamists and liberal democrats.

In Malaysia, Islam is the official religion, and *shariah* applies to all Muslims in matters of personal law. However, the central government is also committed to respecting religious freedom, and non-Muslims can worship openly without fear. In fact, Malaysia was proud host in 2004 of a commission meeting of the World Council of Churches, as a testament to the country's diversity. Addressing this meeting, Malaysian prime minister Abdullah Ahmad Badawi stressed the importance of dialogue between faiths and attacked "absolutist" forms of religiosity.[180] Badawi's predecessor, Mahathir bin Mohamad, similarly committed Malaysia to moderate, nonviolent Islam. Speaking at a 2003 regional conference, Mohamad, asked about how to address militant Islam in Malaysia, responded: "It is quite easy for me to answer that because I am a Muslim fundamentalist. If you go back to the actual teachings of Islam, you don't cause problem to yourself and to others because Islam advocates peace and brotherhood not only among Muslims but to others as well. It also advocates nonviolence unless you are attacked by others. These are the fundamentals of Islam."[181]

The nonviolent tradition in Malaysia is not limited to politicians and enjoys considerable mainstream support. Sisters in Islam, a nongovernment organization formed in 1988, for example, strongly opposes violence or coercion while seeking to spread Islam through persuasive measures: "Religion depends upon faith and will, and this would be meaningless if induced by force. Islam itself means submission to the will of God; and the willing submission of the self to faith and belief must be attained through conviction and reason, not through coercion and duress."[182] All this is not to disregard that there has been a slow but noticeable increase in the reports of radicalism seeping into the country's religious dialogue. The United Malays National Organization, the country's largest party, has recently witnessed several delegates calling for a violent rejection of non-Islamic faiths.[183] There has also been a noted rise in the extremist sentiments voiced by the Islamic Party of Malaysia.

Several modern day Marco Polos have made their way to Islamic countries such as Mali and Tunisia, and have brought back reports of tolerant, moderate Islam. On a three-year journey through the Islamic world after September 11, *Wall Street Journal* reporter Yaroslav Trofimov spoke to a number of religious authorities in Mali. Talking to a cleric from the influential Ansar ed-Din sect, Trofimov noted:

> [Cleric Ousmane Madani] Haidara's outfit focused on preaching Islam and good morals at its stadium sermons, while taking care not to undermine the old Africa rituals, still ingrained in Mali's way of life. Despite its militant name, Ansar ed-Din, unlike Islamists in charge of northern Nigerian states, didn't endorse the imposition of Sharia law. "The Sharia cuts off the hands of thieves. But if you preach the right way, the thief will not steal," the cleric laughed. "Here it is a secular country. If you like to drink, you can drink. It doesn't matter to me." Women, he added, do not have to wear the veil as long as they keep their breasts covered: "You have to be worthy—do not steal, do not kill, do not commit adultery. It doesn't matter what you wear."[184]

Later, Trofimov conversed with Mahmoud Dicko, a Wahhabi preacher. Despite Wahhabi's connotations of intolerant Saudi-style repression, the reporter observed that "the last thing" Dicko wants is to mimic the Saudis or Nigerians:

> "Mali was always a particular place. It's for everyone's advantage for the country to stay secular," he told me. "This is our tradition. The religions always coexisted here. When the ancient emperors of Mali held court, they had a Muslim marabout on one hand, and a fetish doctor on the other. . . . If Mali today changes and starts to respect the norms of Islam, this will make me happy. But I'm not for imposing my vision." He reminded me of the bloodshed in places like Nigeria after the introduction of Sharia law: "We have no interest in plunging our country into something like this."[185]

On a journey across Africa's Sahel region another reporter, Jeffrey Tayler, stops in Timbuktu and asks a local businessman about Osama bin Laden:

> "Bin Laden?" Moussa's eyes narrowed. "Bin Laden? We *reject* him. We don't allow *anyone* to come to Timbuktu and preach divisions in Islam. We don't even want to *know* about Wahhabism"—the intolerant, puritanical Islamic sect to which bin Laden adheres. "I know what the Qur'an says: it says *not* to kill, it says to be *peaceful*. If a fundamentalist comes to my house I wouldn't even offer him *tea*. Look, after September 11, Jimmy Carter, a man of peace, came here to this mosque with the American ambassador. They asked the imam to say a prayer for world peace, and that's what he did. This is what we believe in here in Timbuktu—*peace*. The Qur'an orders us not to kill so much as an *ant*." He belched whiskey. "Not even an *ant!*"[186]

Even in Nigeria, which has seen a dramatic rise in Muslim-Christian violence and intolerant imposition of shariah law, Tayler finds more moderate approaches even in some of the northern states, which have been most strongly associated with the rise of intolerant Islam: "The closest thing the northern states have to an Islamic police force, zealous Muslim activists called Hizba, has no legal authority. A scholar at the Aminu Kano College of Islamic Legal Studies in Kano had justified to me the lax enforcement of shari'a in another way: 'The Qur'an says, "There is no compulsion in religion." Our [Islamic] principles are voluntary, and only for those who profess Islam. The Hizba can only persuade Muslims to follow their religion.' "[187]

To the north, in Tunisia, Trofimov found a secular Islamic state, somewhat like Turkey, where the veil and burqa are prohibited and where the state avidly avoids Islamicization. Speaking to Tunisian Religious Affairs Minister Jalloul Jeribi: "He told me that all of the nation's thirteen thousand imams, or prayer leaders, had to be appointed by his ministry, after passing tests of religious and general knowledge—and of political correctness. . . . I asked him whether that was how the suicide bomber in Djerba received his ideas. Taken aback, Jeribi hastened to point out that the bomber had spent several years in the West. 'No, no, here in Tunisia, the entire society completely rejects fundamentalism. What happened in Djerba, this was a Western import,' he said."[188]

At Zeitouna, Tunisia's main university, professor Mohamed Mahjoub staunchly defended Tunisia's nonviolent strain of Islam: " 'We need to reinvent Islam. It's necessary to be receptive to the spirit of other religions, to foster tolerance,' he explained. . . . The challenge of reconciling Islam with modernity could be met, he believed. 'If we marginalize the religion, it will breed fanaticism and extremism. But what we can do is to reunderstand our religion, to bring it alive.' "[189]

In Morocco, an Islamist party is expected to win 2007's parliamentary elections, but the party is fairly moderate in its views and committed to the legitimate political process. Non-Muslims in Morocco can openly practice their faith, and women are not obliged to wear the hijab.[190] A 2001 antiterrorism law forbids preaching support for or solidarity with terrorism, and, despite the emergence of Salafi radicals in scattered towns, nonviolence and tolerance enjoy widespread support. In 2004 the Moroccan government appointed fifty women to be state religious leaders in order to promote moderate Islam and to counter fundamentalist clerics.[191] But as in Malaysia, cracks in the nonviolent façade can be found, a reality underscored by a 2003 multiple suicide bombing in Casablanca carried out by homegrown extremists.

In Indonesia, where the world's largest Muslim population resides, legislators have overwhelmingly opposed incorporating Islamic law into the constitution and there is relatively little (albeit growing) public support for Islamist organizations.[192] Nahdlatul Ulama, the country's largest

Islamic organization (with forty million members), is supportive of indigenous forms of Islam, which are often heterodox, and regularly campaigns against extremism. Abdurrahman Wahid, a former president of Indonesia and leader of Nahdlatul Ulama, is an outspoken critic of radical Islam: "The essence of Islam is encapsulated in the words of the Koran, 'For you, your religion; for me, my religion.' That is the essence of tolerance. Religious fanatics—either purposely or out of ignorance—pervert Islam into a dogma of intolerance, hatred and bloodshed."[193]

In the Hashemite monarchy of Jordan, King Abdullah has long been a leader promoting moderate versions of Islam. He called for "the quiet majority of Muslims to take back our religion from the vocal, violent, and ignorant extremists. . . . Over the past one hundred years, Islam has been hijacked by the fringe Muslim elements. We're trying to galvanize the silent majority to stand up and say, 'Enough is enough.' "[194]

In Bangladesh, the world's fourth-largest Muslim nation, news coverage has largely focused on the sporadic political and religious violence that is often linked to two fringe, radical Islamist parties. While the violence there has increased, it has done so only relatively—the nation as a whole remains known for its brand of Islam that has historically been "tolerant, inflected by Sufism and coexistence with Hinduism."[195]

On the Arabian peninsula, the legal system in Qatar is based on strict Wahhabi Islam, but the state does not allow Saudi-style vice squads to roam the streets, women can go about in public unveiled, and Christians are permitted to build churches and import Bibles. Criticism of the government in Qatar is rare and there are no political parties, but "no one visiting Doha . . . would mistake it for Taliban-era Kabul."[196] Moderate forms of Islam predominate in the kingdoms of Bahrain, the United Arab Emirates, and Kuwait.

In 2006 in Syria during Ramadan, the Muslim holy season, the producer Najdat Anzour ran a popular television series called *Renegades,* which dealt with the story of a religious British Muslim immigrant who returned to Damascus after the attacks on the London Underground. In the series "terrorists are condemned and Westerners are shown in an unflattering light. The only ones generally portrayed as decent and moral are observant Muslims who are tolerant and peaceful."[197] Syrian television has engaged controversies like terrorism, polygamy, and HIV, once considered taboo. Furthermore, the number of religious schools in

Damascus specifically for girls has proliferated. Fatima Ghayeh, sixteen, a pupil at one such school who hopes to become a graphic designer, describes the change in Syrian popular culture this way: "The older girls were told, 'This is Islam, and so you should do this.' They [felt] that they [couldn't] really ask questions. It's because ten years ago Syria was really closed, and there weren't so many Islamic schools. But society has really changed. Today girls are saying, 'We want to do something with Islam, and for Islam.' We're more active, and we ask questions."[198]

Like all such travelers' reports, one can find many different ones; they are strictly illustrative and do not purport to be controlled surveys. However, they provide one more source to show that the Muslim world is hardly monolithically pro-violence.

In Conclusion

The claim that there is a "clash of civilizations," especially that a superior Western culture is clashing with various less worthy cultures, is empirically wrong, morally misguided, and a foundation for a whole slew of misbegotten foreign and domestic policies. It obscures that crucially important differences run *through* each "civilization," between those who believe in the use of violence to advance their cause and those who seek to rely on persuasion, between Warriors and Preachers. The legitimization of violence, found in all major civilizations, is antithetical to our profoundest human dignity, while relying on persuasion—also found in all major civilizations—is respectful of human dignity and of the communal nature of the person.

Those who believe in persuasion and who abhor violence, probably the majority of the world's inhabitants, hail from a large variety of belief systems, Muslims included. They are our potential allies in opposing those who advocate violence. Many of these anti-violence, pro-persuasion supporters are not liberal in the sense that they do not favor some of our key legal-political and socioeconomic rights, and in the sense that they strongly believe in religious or other normative sources of legitimacy, a far cry from democratic forms of governance. Nevertheless, these Illiberal Moderates can be our allies. One may hope to convert them to more liberal positions over time. Meanwhile we share with them the opposition to violence, to terrorism, and to unjust war.

PART IV

The Importance of Moral Culture

CHAPTER A. THE SOFT UNDERBELLY OF SECURITY

Security cannot merely or even mainly be based on military forces, police, and other means of law enforcement. Some might find it odd, but security is based largely on values, on most people most of time doing what must be done because they believe they ought to. True, a brutal regime can terrorize people into submitting to hated, illegitimate laws, the way, for instance, that the Stasi, the communist East German secret police, did for decades. However, even under such regimes, great efforts are made to generate the perception of legitimacy, because otherwise security is precarious. The failure either to respect the citizens' values or to change them in the end undid these regimes.

The role of what might be called the "soft underbelly" of security, the moral culture, can be highlighted if one asks: what do Russia, Afghanistan, and Iraq all have in common? In nations where an authoritarian regime has collapsed, or is failing, or where the regime has been toppled by outside forces—irrespective of whether the regime was militantly secular or theocratic, communist or Islamist—liberation is followed by explosive increases in antisocial behavior. This fact is rarely discussed in the West for reasons that are not fully clear. Many seem to presume that antisocial behaviors will go away on their own; that the perturbed condition of society following liberation will correct itself. The champions of democracy are, understandably, not keen to dwell on the ugly—often very ugly—aspects of the transformation. Still others seem to believe that the pain of transformation is the price we must pay for securing liberty, and that the price is well worth paying.

The fact is that antisocial behaviors (detailed below) do not naturally subside by themselves. Indeed, they have remained at a high and damaging level for years on end in liberated and failing states (in Russia for fifteen years and counting). After surveying some telling details I will ask what it takes to curb such conduct. Law enforcement may keep it in check initially. However, in the longer run—and I refer to months and years, not decades—a rather different kind of authority must become the major source of social order. After introducing this source—moral culture—I explore the ways in which it might be fostered, despite the severe limitations of social engineering in general and those working to foster moral cultures in particular.

Antisocial Behavior and Its Consequences

Russia provides an especially important and troubling example of the social consequences of liberation. In the period immediately following the fall of the communist regime, from 1989 to 1993, the total crime rate in Russia increased by 72 percent, or 1.18 million more reported criminal incidents. The murder rate during the same period rose by 116 percent, and assaults by 81 percent. Especially indicative of the breakdown in the social fabric was that 63 percent of reported physical assaults were committed by a friend or relative of the victim.[1] Eleven years later the situation showed no improvement; nearly 2.9 million crimes were registered in 2004, compared with 2.8 million in 1993. And in 2005 Russia's prosecutor general, Vladimir Ustinov, estimated that the true number of crimes committed—including those that were not registered—was on the order of 9 million.[2]

Russia is rife with organized crime that has infiltrated business, municipal government, police forces, and the judiciary. Murders often remain unsolved because the police are bought off, and judges are intimidated into delivering the "correct" verdicts. In a far from unusual case, a judge who refused to release a mafioso's crony from prison "was savagely beaten with iron bars in the street."[3] The police refused to investigate the attackers, and the judge left the hospital handicapped for life, refusing to hear anything but divorce cases.

The following journalistic account captures the overall condition of postcommunist Russia. "You have no idea of the level of corruption nowadays," says Tanya, the owner of two Moscow supermarkets. "Gangsters in Yeltsin's time didn't even dream of this." Tanya began her business career by leaving her children at home and working long hours at a market where "the rules were the same as inside a prison. Disagreements were resolved at knife-point, extortion was rife, people got beaten up." She moved through the ranks by sleeping with her boss, who was found dead one morning in the market, shot in the head. Tanya continued moving up, paid bribes to the right people, and now enjoys a rich lifestyle as long as she "pays up." "Who don't I give bribes to? The pencil pushers at the police station, the firemen, the hygiene inspectors, the municipal governments. And the gangsters whose land my shops are on. Actually, I bought them from the gangsters." Tanya ended up running for a seat in the municipal *duma*. Her reason? "It's very simple," she explains. "I don't want to pay bribes to our councilor. . . . If I become councilor that will be one 'tax' less."[4]

The number of drug addicts in Russia has skyrocketed. Between 1991 and 1995 the number doubled and then over the next five years quadrupled. In 2003 it was estimated that there were roughly 3 to 4 million drug abusers in Russia.[5] Dramatic increases have also been seen in alcohol consumption and suicide rates.[6] In the first half of 2001 alone 17,000 Russians died as a result of alcohol poisoning.[7] The suicide rate increased from 26.5 per 100,000 people in 1991 to 39.7 per 100,000 people in 2001. This is three times the world average.[8] The situation does not seem much better in many of the other former Soviet republics.[9]

The trends in antisocial behavior manifest in Russia are also evident in China, as the latter country's commitment to communism diminishes. Crime has become rampant throughout the country, and there have been considerable increases in the number of youths joining street gangs.[10] Official statistics indicate that between 1978 and 2001 there was a 300 percent increase in crime.[11] Moreover, drug abuse has sharply escalated; in 2004, Chinese officials put the number of registered drugs addicts at 1.6 million, double what it was in 1995 (some analysts believe the actual number to be anywhere between 7 and 12 million).[12] A majority of registered addicts are heroin users, which has led to an alarming rise in the national HIV infection rate. Though statistics are uncertain, the Chinese government and the Joint U.N. Program on AIDS (UNAIDS) estimated in January 2006 that 650,000 people in China were living with HIV, and that this number is rising quickly. UNAIDS forecasts that by 2010 there will be between 10 and 20 million HIV-positive Chinese.[13]

The authoritarian regimes of Afghanistan and Iraq fell more recently, but their collapse was also followed quickly by sharp increases in anti-social behavior. Since the defeat of the Taliban at the end of 2001, wide-spread pedophilia has resurfaced, especially among the Pashtuns in the south.[14] The Taliban suppressed the practice by imposing the extreme penalty of toppling a wall onto anyone caught committing this offense, a punishment prescribed by shariah law. Since their defeat, however, pedophilia has again become a common practice.[15] All this of course does not suggest a return to the "good old days" of the Taliban (or to the "good old days" of Uncle Joe in Russia and Chairman Mao in China), but indicates *the need for new sources of social order.*

Police forces are not much help in curbing violence because of rampant incompetence and corruption in their ranks. In 2002 only 30 percent of Afghanistan's police were literate, and 80 percent were without needed equipment.[16] Four years later, in 2006, that number had declined only marginally: a joint Pentagon and State Department study found that Afghan police had persistently high rates of absenteeism and only about 50 percent of authorized equipment.[17] Judges are routinely bribed to overturn verdicts and turn a blind eye to bargains in which women and sheep are traded in exchange for dropping murder charges or for other favors. A considerable number of husbands force their wives into prostitution (especially their second and third wives), and those women who complain to the authorities have been jailed for committing adultery.[18]

Under the Taliban the cultivation of poppies for opium and heroin production was forbidden and effectively suppressed. In 2001, before the fall of the Taliban, Afghanistan was responsible for a mere 185-ton output. Just a year later, in 2002, the output was an estimated 3,400 tons, and by 2006 Afghanistan's opium production had risen to 6,100 tons—90 percent of the world's supply.[19] Although most is exported, it sustains a huge criminal substructure of drug lords, couriers, and illegal cash flows, which adds greatly to the corruption of government officials. General James Jones, NATO's top commander in Europe, put it succinctly when he stated that Afghanistan is turning into a "narco-state."[20]

In Iraq, violence associated with the insurgency is often difficult to distinguish from ordinary violent crime and interpersonal score-settling. There is, though, considerable evidence of a sharp increase in the number of unnatural deaths with no connection to the insurgency. For instance, in 2005, "In Baghdad alone, officials at the central morgue counted 8,035 deaths by unnatural causes in 2004, up from 6,012 the previous year. . . . In 2002, the final year of Saddam Hussein's regime, the morgue examined about 1,800 bodies. Of the deaths occurring now, 60 percent are caused by gunshot wounds, officials say, *and most are unrelated to the insurgency.* . . . Much of the violence, officials say, is inspired by the ethnic, tribal and religious rivalries that were held in check by Hussein's brutal rule, and facilitated by a ready supply of firearms. That deadly combination has let loose a wave of vengeance killings, tribal vendettas, mercenary kidnappings and thievery."[21]

"Regular" families earn money by opening up rooms in their homes as holding facilities for kidnapping victims. Moreover, the kidnappings are rarely random; acquaintances of the victims often pass on information that helps kidnappers determine when to strike and how much to ask for ransom.[22] Many women and children are now forced to remain indoors for fear of kidnapping, rape, and murder—and not just those living in the Sunni triangle. A high school principal in Iraq summed up the condition in his country as a place where "if you say anything good about Saddam, you will be killed. If you say anything bad, you will be killed by someone else. We used to be only afraid of Saddam. Now there are many people to fear."[23]

Social scientists raise questions about the prevalence of antisocial behavior in newly liberated and failing states. They point out that what seems antisocial to some is not so to others. For instance, if one included the very considerable increases in divorce rates in Russia since the fall of communism, quite a few social scientists might well point out that higher divorce rates merely reflect the undoing of what they consider an obsolete, patriarchal institution. Few would disagree, however, that the forms of behavior I have chosen to focus on here are truly antisocial. And in any case, the question of what must be done to help newly liberated states to maintain a reasonable level of social order—above and beyond training and arming police forces—cannot be ignored.

To put it succinctly: security is not self-sustaining. Either it is undergirded by a police state, albeit at great human costs and with ongoing instability, or by a firm social fabric, which entails a shared moral culture, supported largely by informal social controls, in which law enforcement authorities are used mainly as a backup and a last resort.

Poor Security—Democratic Reversals

The low level of social order is one major reason there are strong anti-democratic tendencies in most, if not all, of the nations referenced here. These tendencies are most evident in Russia, where, despite the initial euphoria after the collapse of the Soviet Union and the introduction of democratic freedoms, it now seems that most Russian citizens support long-term, strong-armed political leadership. A 2003 survey found that only 22 percent of Russians favored democracy, while 53 percent "positively disliked" it; another poll found that 74 percent of Russians "regretted" the collapse of the U.S.S.R., and nearly one in four would "actively support" a communist coup.[24]

Similarly, a weak social order is a major reason that tribal warlords continue to dominate most of Afghanistan, and the Taliban are making a comeback. It is also a key reason one can predict that if and when the Iraqi government stabilizes, it will be authoritarian, like Putin's regime. Moreover, it is sad but perhaps understandable that millions of citizens in these nations yearn for the old regimes, in which social order was much stronger.[25] Many people in these and other newly liberated societies would rather have their daughters be able to walk safely in the streets than have free speech; they would rather not worry about being kidnapped and sold for ransom than have the right to vote. This is not an argument against individual rights, but for nurturing the moral culture that is an essential basis for sustainable security, including individual rights. (How this might be done follows.)

A female doctor in Mosul reported that "education is really what will improve the place of women, but it's difficult to insist on that when it is difficult to be out safely after 5 o'clock."[26] A preelection conference organized by the Nineveh Women's Center in northern Iraq was supposed to have 250 participants; but only 80 managed to show up due to security concerns, and the chairwoman refused to be shown on camera for fear of experiencing the fate of her predecessor, who was murdered in 2004.[27] In Afghanistan's Helmand province, one tribal leader, skeptical of Karzai's administration, asked in frustration: "Is this a government? Anyone other than me would join the Taliban."[28]

To reiterate: this is not to join those who seek to return to the old regime, but to stress that assuming that democratization or declarations of human rights will restore social order is a grave mistake. Law enforcement authority, backed by a moral culture, is the first step on the road to a stable and free social order.

The Role of Values in Security

In the longer run, measured in months or years, not in decades, as security is established and democratization is pursued by nonlethal means, changes in the moral culture must also be cultivated. A society can function well and remain healthy only as long as most people, most of the time, do what they do *because they believe that it is right and just,* not because they fear the power of the authorities. Hence the pivotal role of the moral culture and the informal social controls that sustain it.

Changes in the moral culture are also called for because the regimes that are being replaced, such as the command-and-control systems of communist societies and Taliban-like theocracies, were based on and fostered beliefs incompatible with a free and stable society. To nurture "freedom" requires much more than free speech, free and fair elections, and the other typical features of liberal democracy. It also requires that the citizenry share a core of basic values, a broad toleration for a variety of different political and religious opinions, an opposition to unwarranted discrimination, and an abhorrence of the speedy resort to violence to solve problems.[29]

One may wonder, given that the preceding discussion repeatedly stressed the limits of social engineering, how one adds "reengineering a moral culture" to the list of what can and must be done? After all, moral cultures are surely less amenable to reengineering than most, if not all other, features of political and social life. Indeed the needed changes in moral culture generally come about gradually, and as the result of changes in the "hearts and minds of the people, not as the result of foreign importation and imposition. Yet there are some useful and concrete steps the West can take to foster the desired changes.[30]

Recruiting new police forces and retraining others, establishing border controls, and introducing customs inspectors are significant ways to begin laying the foundations for security where it is lacking. However, building such forces alone is woefully insufficient. No state can field the number of law enforcement personnel needed to provide even basic security if most of the billions of interactions within the population must be surveyed and policed. And the law enforcement agents are likely themselves to violate the law, if they are not imbued with a sound moral culture.

The American experience with Prohibition and the "war on drugs" has shown that when there is no widespread, voluntary compliance with the law, based on the conviction that the law ought to be observed, effective compliance cannot be engineered. Prohibition of the manufacture, sale, and transport of alcoholic beverages began with the passage of the Eighteenth Amendment in 1920. This expression of the Temperance movement was largely ineffective, as there was a great deal of bootlegging across the borders from Canada and Mexico, and rum-running from the Caribbean to Florida and from Europe to the East Coast. In addition, home brewing of alcohol became popular, as did underground establishments that served liquor. Organized crime and racketeering spread. Politicians and federal agents, who were often poorly trained and underpaid, were especially susceptible to bribery. If these attempts were unsuccessful, members of organized crime would either kill the uncooperative officer or politician or, in the case of politicians, run an opponent in the next election. These organized crime rings often had enough money and power to ensure their corrupt candidate was elected, allowing the continued smuggling of alcohol. Years later, these gangs were still able to blackmail politicians with the illegal deals that had taken place during Prohibition. When, in 1933, it became clear that Prohibition was not working, the Eighteenth Amendment became the only constitutional amendment to be repealed, the ultimate mark of the failure of a compliance regime, due to its lack of legitimacy.

In contrast, the principal reason the American tax system works relatively well, unlike, for example, the Italian one, is because most Americans believe that they should pay what is due to their government, whereas many Italians consider being taxed as being cheated of their birthright. The same holds for speed limits, bans on smoking in public, and so on. If the laws are to be effective in a free society, law enforcement must be the last resort of the moral culture, not the first or even second line of defense.

The second reason a viable moral culture is essential for a free society is that there is a significant set of responsibilities that citizens must assume for their children, parents, community, and nation not specifically enumerated by any law, and undergirded only by ethical precepts and informal social controls. Most of what parents do for their children is not legally required. Similarly, most of what grown children do for their elderly parents reflects their moral sense of obligation. The same holds for charitable giving and contributions to the common good, such as environmental protection.

At stake is nothing less than our basic assumptions about human nature and the sources of political and social order. Some champions of liberty presume that once the yoke of a Taliban-like or communist government is lifted from people's shoulders, their self-interest will naturally lead them to pro-social behavior; a new social order, based on consent, will quickly arise. Many others assume that democratization merely requires a certain set of political institutions such as elections, separation of powers, and so on. Others add the elements of a civil society, including a rich fabric of voluntary associations, a growing middle class, and educational institutions. *All this is of merit but these elements are also insufficient bases for a stable and free social order.* The evidence of common human experience shows that people have a darker, unruly side which must be disciplined and restrained. Hence, as the totalitarian or authoritarian sources of order are removed, new and legitimate sources of order must be put in their place.[31]

In free societies, order relies mainly on a moral culture promoted informally. This is one of those observations that many social scientists will take for granted (what they will call "Socio 101") but that many others are not quick to acknowledge or grasp. They tend to hold that people obey the law out of fear of fines or imprisonment. However, study upon study shows that the main reason most people, most of the time, obey the law, in those societies in which the moral culture is intact, is because they believe that the laws are right and just; that is, that they *ought* to heed them. Thus Alan Lewis in *The Psychology of Taxation*[32] reviewed numerous studies showing that if people believe that the burden of taxation is fairly proportioned and that the revenues collected are spent for worthy purposes and in an efficient manner, they will pay most of what they owe. Paul Stern has shown in his *Improving Energy Demand Analysis*[33] that the number one reason people conserve energy is because they believe it is their civic duty.

Especially relevant are studies of voting. Economists often wonder why people trouble themselves to cast a ballot. According to them no rational person can be expected to gain anything in return for his or her vote, as extremely few elections are determined by one or even a few votes. It turns out that the main factor determining whether people vote is the extent to which they believe that it is their civic duty to do so. This is but one more example that highlights the general observation that, to function well, free societies require many behaviors not mandated by law but supported by the moral culture—as voting is, in most democracies. When these sources of order are absent we talk about "broken windows,"[34] and note an urgent need to restore or reshape the society's moral culture.

In short, *security and, more generally, social order, are paramount, but these rest only in part on law enforcement; they must have the backing of moral culture.* In a highly chaotic situation, such as when looters were emptying Iraq's National Museum and Library in Baghdad shortly after the 2003 invasion, a contingent of American troops or military police could have stopped them. But even if the number of Americans troops sent to Iraq had been greatly increased, as many think should have been done, the streets in the Triangle of Death could not have been secured—unless the majority of the people accepted the occupation as legitimate. There are simply too many street corners, building complexes, dark alleys, groves, holy shrines, and so on to be protected by law enforcement officers in three shifts, twenty-four hours a day, seven days a week. This is especially the case if the authorities are going to refrain from using the methods of a police state.

In speaking of the development of moral culture, I refer most immediately to nations at relative peace—Russia, for example. However, in situations of the kind faced in Baghdad since the occupation, obviously a greater use of force, of the police and military, is unavoidable. Here too, though, the presence or absence of a shared moral culture plays a key role. Sectarian violence would be much lower if the taboo on killing were taken seriously, if there were a societywide core of shared values, and if there were a stronger sense of shared national identity.

What Might Be Done? A Basic Premise

One may well wonder, given the great difficulties involved in changing societies, especially from the outside, whether there is anything that the United States or other Western powers could do to foster moral cultures— and the informal social controls that nurture them—in recently liberated countries and failing states? I should note that the issue cannot be separated from the quest for truly democratic regimes, because without a stronger moral culture, as I have already indicated, neither political stability nor democratic liberalism can be established, surely not securely sustained, and a return to some kind of authoritarian regime be avoided.

The discussion from here on focuses only on Islam and especially on the situation in Afghanistan and Iraq because the problems of social order there are much more acute than in the ex-communist nations. The United States and the West in general have more leverage in these two societies; moreover communism has largely lost its appeal, which can hardly be said about radical Islamism.

The analogue to the way that the United States confronted communism is relevant here. After all, that struggle, too, contained a major "cultural" element, a fundamental disagreement over what is moral, the issue that now troubles our relationship with Islamic societies. And, just as all too many now cannot see important differences among Muslims at the issue at hand, so during the Cold War many refused to recognize important differences between communists and social democrats. Slowly it became clear that one of the best ways to counter the influence of communism, especially as it spread in Italy and France, was to support not only the anticommunist conservative parties (especially the largely Catholic, Christian democratic parties) but also the various social democratic parties, labor unions, and youth movements. In effect, social democrats had a competitive advantage over conservatives because they could speak with legitimacy to many of the same concerns communism addressed in places where workers, students, and other citizens would not have been receptive to more conservative ideas.

To support largely secular forces in order to challenge Islamic radicalism is akin to supporting largely conservative forces during the Cold War. One cannot generally gain traction or start a dialogue with a pious Muslim by quoting Locke, Kant, and the Universal Declaration of Human Rights. However, by pointing to interpretations of Islamic texts and the shariah that oppose the use of violence (as we saw in Part III), one can appeal to *their* basic beliefs.[35] This will work only as long as the West seeks a safe and peaceful world, not one in which all regime types are identical or in which their moral cultures are universally secular. And—the free nations support moderate Muslim groups even if they are Illiberal.

To build on this premise, the United States needs to accept fully that *the Establishment Clause of the First Amendment to the Constitution applies to Americans in the United States, but should not be foisted on the peoples of other nations.* The main reason is that religion is one source, in many cases a main source, and in some cases the major or exclusive source, of moral culture. This is true for Roman Catholicism in Poland; for Eastern Orthodoxy in Russia; for Islam in Afghanistan and Shiism parts of Iraq; and for Confucianism in China (as well as Christianity, currently on the rise in China). One may wonder, given that religion, most recently under the Taliban in Afghanistan, has so often been the source of oppression, and that Islam is considered by many to be the "civilization" most threatening to the West, how the United States could benefit from supporting religion in general, and mullahs and imams in particular? The answer to this question lies in what may be obvious to some but is surely not widely agreed upon and is certainly not a cornerstone of U.S. foreign policy: by actively supporting moderate religious teachings (as well as secular sources of moral culture), and opposing only those that promote violence and persecution. This position stands in sharp contrast to the practice of lumping together all religious leaders, factions, and parties, as if they were basically of one kind, opposed to modernity and enlightenment, and, above all, prone to violence. Reza Aslan, for example, criticizes the Bush administration and others for interpreting Iranian politics as a struggle between "Islamic theocracy" on the one hand and "Western secular democracy" on the other. He writes:

> Over the past two decades academics, reformist theologians and
> liberal clerics in Iran have been struggling to redefine traditional
> Islamic political philosophy in order to bring it in line with mod-
> ern concepts of representative government, popular sovereignty,
> universal suffrage and religious pluralism. What these Iranians
> have been working toward is "Islamic democracy": that is, a lib-
> eral, democratic society founded on an Islamic moral frame-

work. . . . What the United States must learn from the colonialist experience is that *the only way to promote lasting democratic reform in the Middle East is to encourage it to develop according to its own indigenous culture and its own religious identity.*[36]

(I turn below to the issues our positions raise with respect to the Establishment Clause of the Constitution.)

What Is to Be Done? Specific Measures

I am not suggesting that the idea of actively supporting moderate Muslims while opposing violent Islamic beliefs has never occurred to U.S. policymakers. However, U.S. policy on this matter has been confused, inconsistent, and halfhearted at best. Briefly reviewing this policy serves to illustrate what needs to be done.

Change the "Washington-speak": A nation's positions are often communicated through the ways the head of state, especially of the one and only superpower, frames the nation's policies. Thus every pronouncement of the president of the United States reverberates around the world, is quoted and requoted, and is scoured for signals of changes in policy orientation.

President Bush, for understandable reasons, has consistently argued that the United States' war is not with Islam, but with terrorism. On the president's weekly radio address soon after the 9/11 attacks he said, "Our enemy is not Islam, a good and peace-loving faith that brings direction and comfort to over one billion people, including millions of Americans."[37] In remarks to President Megawati Sukarnoputri of Indonesia, President Bush explained, "I've made it clear, Madam President, that the war against terrorism is not a war against Muslims, nor is it a war against Arabs. It's a war against evil people who conduct crimes against innocent people."[38] This point has since often been repeated.

This formulation of the U.S. position ignores the essential difference between Muslims who subscribe to violent beliefs and those who favor a persuasive Islam. One might say it matters not what they believe, but only what they actually do. However, violent beliefs serve to legitimate violence. This does not mean that the United States should send in the Marines to close all mosques worldwide that preach violent Islam and all *madrasas* that teach the same. It does point, however, to the need to counter the arguments of violent Islamic beliefs just as we have needed to do for violent secular belief systems such as fascism and communism. The best way to do so, to reiterate, is to favor moderate Islam. To state that we have no quarrel with "Islam," with any and all of it, is neither to recognize nor to reward moderation, and not to refute those believers who do incite violence.

Moreover, the U.S. government has alienated moderate Muslims by embracing prominent public intellectuals who argue that the West is in a cultural war with Islam in general—rather than with violent Islam. To give but one telling example: the renowned scholar Bernard Lewis—who coined the phrase "clash of civilizations"—has been reported to have had a significant influence on President Bush's policies.[39] Such reports signal that the White House—speaking for the government of the United States —accepts a simplistic, us-against-them division of the world, the mis-begotten notion that our culture is rational and our polity sensible and commendable, while those of all others are passionate and irrational, and their polities oppressive and objectionable.

Although there is no way to control what public intellectuals pro-nounce, nor should there be, the White House can signal that those who lump all of Islam together into one threatening monolith do not have the ear of the president, are not heeded by the government, whereas those who see important cultural differences within Islam are consulted and publicly recognized.

Public diplomacy to fund religion: If the United States is to befriend moderate Muslims, public diplomacy must once again be recast. Public diplomacy is the systematic attempt to use government resources to pro-mote the U.S. positions overseas, to win the "hearts and minds" of the people of other lands, especially Muslim ones.[40] During the Cold War the Voice of America and various American information centers around the world played a significant role in the culture war with communism. These activities were largely curtailed after 1990.

Public diplomacy gained renewed attention after 9/11. Efforts to reach out to Muslims initially focused on providing entertainment, especially Western music (to build audiences) and objective news (to counter the falsehoods spread by al-Jazeera and other media considered hostile to the West).[41] When these programs had little of the desired effect, an Advisory Committee on Public Diplomacy for the Arab and Muslim World was appointed in 2003. The committee's report endorsed the approach of the "Shared Values Initiative," a series of television advertisements conceived shortly after 9/11 that showed Muslims living happily and freely in affluent America.[42] A Defense Department report on strategic communication to Muslims states that the central themes of U.S. outreach should be, "Respect for human dignity and individual rights; Individual education and economic opportunity; Personal freedom, safety, and mobility."[43] Thus, practically all of America's messages to the Muslim world, in content, form, and symbol, are secular. Moreover, the subtext is that we are good and other people need to commit themselves to our conceptions of the good; that we are bringing light to the heathens.

If public diplomacy is to take into account the key thesis outlined here, it will include religious programming—supporting moderate beliefs. It would include regular sermons preached by moderate Muslim preachers; news reports about the leaders and millions of followers of moderate Islamic religious figures; translations into many languages of moderate texts. (This is especially needed because extremist texts are currently the main ones given large-scale support, primarily by the Saudis.)[44]

Such religious programming should not replace, but significantly add to, the secular messages that dominate public diplomacy. Christian groups in predominantly Muslim countries—and possibly some other groups—may well hold that if public funds are to be used to promote moderate Islam, other moderate religious groups should also be entitled to airtime, support for the translation of texts, and so on. These groups could be accommodated by according them the same proportion of resources as the share of the population they are addressing—for instance, roughly 3 percent in the case of Iraq.

One may well wonder whether this plan could be executed in ways that do not undermine the legitimacy of the moderate religious and political leaders who are endorsed by America and who receive American largesse. To proceed, pain must be taken to ensure that the funds be channeled through other parties, such as a pan-Islamic moderate council (yet to be formed) to avoid this serious problem, rather than be controlled by the U.S. government.

Focus on leaders and opinion-makers: Public diplomacy needs to focus on moderate Islamic and secular leaders and opinion-makers, as opposed to focus on the masses. One of the most important findings of sociology is that it is very difficult to reach the masses directly; persuasion flows in two steps, first to leaders—and then to their followers. These leaders may include elected officials, heads of civil society bodies from universities to foundations, community leaders, religious functionaries, and, arguably, celebrities. American policymakers, however, are often influenced by the Madison Avenue approach, in which commercials sell items directly to the people. But Madison Avenue sells products to which people are already accustomed, and to which there is little passionate or ideological resistance. The same methods cannot be used to "sell" attitude changes, say, to reduce anti-Americanism, ethnic tensions, or fanaticism. To the extent that attitudes can be influenced, one must first reach out to those people involved who are already held in high regard and trust, who already lead, who already are established as opinion-makers. Hence public diplomacy must identify moderate mullahs and imams in a given nation as well as import them from other countries where moderate Islam is dominant, to form and spread messages that support the development of a new, prosocial moral culture.

Just as not all of Islam is of one kind, so it is a grave mistake to treat all Islamic religious figures as if they were of one kind, as the United States has often regrettably done in the past. The U.S. tendency to treat all Muslim religious figures alike has been apparent in the way U.S. officials dealt for all too long with Iraq's Grand Ayatollah Sayyid Ali Husaini Sistani. Al-Sistani has played a major role in marginalizing Shia extremists like Muqtada al-Sadr. He has given legitimacy to the new Iraqi government, openly denounced the insurgency, and professed his belief in the separation of mosque and state. Yet, according to Middle East expert Juan Cole, the Bush administration has "underestimated Sistani from the beginning."[45] Leaders in the Coalition Provisional Authority, like Paul Bremer, initially tried to sideline him, only later realizing his very considerable and moderating influence.

Worldwide, there are numerous religious leaders like Mohammad Khan, a village cleric in Afghanistan who supports allowing women to work and girls to attend school, so long as they suitably cover themselves.[46] The United States should embrace such clerics rather than view the *hijab* as a sign of bigotry and a gross violation of human rights. One must accept that moderate Muslim clerics will be just that, moderate and religious. They will not follow the American separation-of-church-and-state script, and they are likely to reject—at least initially—several parts of the liberal-democratic program. Still, they will promote a moral culture that opposes violence, the essential starting point for rebuilding newly liberated societies.

Other elements that can be applied as part of a multifaceted drive for cultural change are new television and radio programs. However, these are best produced locally and by personalities familiar to the people, rather than fashioned and broadcast from overseas. The issue at hand is illustrated by the failings of the al-Iraqiya TV station, the American-produced rival to the al-Jazeera and al-Arabiya networks. In 2003, 63 percent of Iraqis with access to a satellite dish chose to watch al-Jazeera and al-Arabiya, while only 12 percent chose al-Iraqiya. Don North, an adviser to al-Iraqiya who became disenchanted with its journalistic approach, writes that it "has become an irrelevant mouthpiece for [Coalition Provisional Authority] propaganda, managed news and mediocre foreign programs."[47]

Religious exchanges centered overseas: Various exchange programs, such as the Fulbright Scholarship and the International Visitors Program, should be expanded to include religious figures. In the past most of these programs included secular leaders, professionals, business people, students, and so on, but included few religious figures.

Moreover, the dominant model of foreign exchange programs is to bring people from target nations to America and to send Americans to these nations, on the assumption that if foreigners experienced life in the United States or got to know Americans, they would be converted. However, to bring religious figures from Afghanistan to a typical American suburb is unlikely to have the desired effect. It would be much more effective if they were sent to cultural and religious centers in nations where moderate Islam is dominant. The United States could support these centers but not necessarily run them. The United States could also facilitate sending moderate Islamic clerics from other nations to Iraq and Afghanistan.

The use of intermediaries has several precedents. For instance, in Pakistan, the United States is working through private foundations and the Pakistani Ministry of Education to reform the curricula of Pakistani *madrasas;* in the United Kingdom, the United States is supporting a think tank on moderate Islam; and in Morocco, a journal on moderate Islam.[48]

However, the funding for these projects is miniscule. Much more funding (although still only a modest amount) is dedicated to a random mishmash of projects spanning the globe; these are supposed to buy goodwill but do little if anything for the development of a new, moderate moral culture. Key cases in point include the restoration of old mosques in Bulgaria, Benin, and Turkmenistan, and the preservation of old manuscripts in Uzbekistan.[49] In short, such funding is possible, indeed far from un-precedented, yet it must be increased by several orders of magnitude and properly targeted to make headway.

Endowments to support (moderate) religious activities: Congress provides funds for various endowments and other programs to promote liberal democracy abroad. First among them is the National Endowment for Democracy. In 2005 it received an appropriation of $80 million, $40 million of which is dedicated toward democratization programs in the Middle East.[50] The Endowment in turn has four affiliate institutions, which it funds either entirely or in part. These include the American Center for International Labor Solidarity, founded by the AFL-CIO; the Center for International Private Enterprise, affiliated with the U.S. Chamber of Com-merce; the International Republican Institute (IRI); and the National Dem-ocratic Institute for International Affairs (NDI), tied to the U.S. Demo-cratic Party. These organizations dedicate a substantial amount of their resources to programs in the Muslim world. Their missions are of much merit, but they are also almost exclusively secular and so do not address fundamental questions concerning changes in the moral culture in the Muslim world.

The United States Agency for International Development (USAID) and the Bureau of Democracy, Human Rights, and Labor at the U.S. Department of State, with their much larger combined budgets (well over $1 billion), also see their missions as primarily secular. A State Depart-ment official, working in the Office of International Religious Freedom, explained that promoting moderate religion "is not part of the culture [at the State Department]; people are not on that wavelength; it is considered complicated."[51] When a senior State Department official was asked whether the United States could give more support to moderate religious figures, the response was, "We shall not support a theocracy in Iraq," not recognizing the difference between moderate and extreme forms of Is-lam. This official added, "But we are training mullahs in democracy."[52]

To the extent that religion is explored by these endowments, foundations, and governmental bodies, the question in practically all cases is whether Islam can be made to be compatible with democracy, and whether we should work with Islamic groups (the position taken by Noah Feldman of New York University Law School) or avoid these groups (the position taken by Robert Satloff, executive director of the Washington Institute for Near East Policy).[53] Others have taken various intermediary positions (e.g., working with Islamic groups might be possible, but the United States must proceed with great caution). One major concern in the give-and-take among the said positions is whether the followers of Islam are able to put the laws of the land, which will be democratic, above the laws of the Prophet and the Koran. My concern, however, is a different, narrower one: can religion in general, and Islam in particular (specifically moderate Islam), serve as a major source of the moral culture that newly liberated nations require?

The struggle over constitutions: Nowhere is U.S. ambivalence and confusion about the role of religion in development of a new moral culture more evident than in the attempts to help the people of Afghanistan and Iraq draft constitutions. It goes without saying that a constitution is not merely the crowning legal document of a nation, but also a document that embodies its essential beliefs about the nature of the good and the just. Thus the debate over what a constitution ought to contain is in effect a debate over the substance of the evolving moral culture.

Both the Afghan and interim Iraqi constitutions, ratified respectively in January and March 2004, include, on the one hand, a commitment to human rights, pluralism, and democracy (as promoted by U.S. and U.N. emissaries) and, on the other, a commitment to Islam (as demanded by many of their citizenries). In the Afghan constitution, the first three articles are dedicated to establishing the nation as an "Islamic Republic" (Article 1), in which Islam is the official state religion (Article 2), and in which "no law can be contrary to the beliefs and provisions of the sacred religion of Islam" (Article 3). However, Article 2 also specifies, "Followers of other religions are free to exercise their faith and perform their religious rites within the limits of the provisions of law." Articles 6 and 7 go on to declare the nation's commitment to human rights, international treaties, and the U.N. charter. The text explicitly references the Universal Declaration of Human Rights. In the interim Iraqi constitution, Article 7 declares the nation's commitment to Islam as the national religion and as a basis for law, while also asserting the nation's commitment to religious pluralism and democracy: "Islam is the official religion of the State and is to be considered a source of legislation. No law that contradicts the universally agreed tenets of Islam, the principles of democracy, or the rights cited in Chapter Two of this Law may be enacted during the transitional period. This Law respects the Islamic identity of the majority of the Iraqi people and guarantees the full religious rights of all individuals to freedom of religious belief and practice."

Missing in both cases is any guidance as to *what kind of Islam* these constitutions are to follow. (The Iraqi document includes an apparent attempt to address this concern with the clause, "the universally agreed tenets of Islam," but this provides little guidance.) The references to Islam in both documents ignore the fundamental differences between violent and moderate interpretations of Islam. Hence the door is left wide open for violence-conducive interpretations. At best these documents reveal that this issue has not been addressed seriously; at worse, they indicate that the door to the legitimization of violence could not be closed.

How can a commitment to moderate Islam be expressed in a Muslim nation's constitution? This is a question best addressed by Islamic legal scholars and deliberations of the relevant national community. Resolving moderate Islam's proper expression in a constitution through individual pronouncements is insufficient. Places one might look to in determining whether moderation is or is not reflected in an Islamic constitution center on the concepts of *shura* and enforcement.

I pointed out in an earlier publication the importance for moderate Islam of the concept of *shura*,[54] or "consultation," with the community. In essence, a system guided by the concept of *shura* would not allow for one institution, for instance Iran's Guardian Council, to determine what is appropriate religious conduct or to veto laws enacted by the parliament. Instead a moderate Islamic constitution that incorporates shura would leave it to local communities and voluntary associations to work out how closely to adhere to the various "dos and don'ts" of Islam.

Similarly, one would look for modes of enforcement. A constitution that is moderate would ban amputations, floggings, and moral police squads, but instead of basing these bans on references to human rights, they would base them on court-sanctioned interpretations of the Koran. (The Koran holds that such punishments can be meted out only if a series of stringent conditions are met, which in practice rarely are.) Laws regarding the proper treatment of women can be based on supportive texts within Islam, such as the often-cited accounts of the Prophet's respect for women.

One might ask: don't the references in the new Afghan and Iraqi constitutions to human rights accomplish the desired synthesis? Isn't inclusion in these texts of human-rights references a pledge of moderation? As I see it, the two sets of beliefs—those that legitimate violence and those that prohibit it—have been simply thrown together, incoherently, for the sake of short-term political convenience. For a genuine synthesis of Islam and liberal democracy, the constitution would have to establish that *shariah* be followed, in theory and, more importantly, in practice, in a way that does not violate basic human rights. But this is hardly the case here. Indeed rulings by Afghanistan's supreme court, the *Stera Mahkama,* suggest the fragility of the attempted synthesis. Its chief justice, Faisal Ahmad Shinwari, an ultraconservative, has during his term of office attempted to ban from elections a candidate who questioned polygamy; to ban cable television service; to uphold the death penalty for blasphemy and sodomy; and to deny the right of divorce to a girl forced to marry at age nine, even though the current Afghan law stipulates sixteen as the age of consent.

As the United States sends its consultants and diplomats to help draft constitutions in the Muslim world, and brings pressure to bear on those who compose the Muslim constitution writing assemblies, it should not be principally concerned with insisting upon the inclusion of human-rights language in the new constitutional documents. Rather, the United States should explicitly favor one kind of Islam over another. Otherwise, as the courts go to work out the differences between Islam and human rights, as has been the case in Afghanistan, violent Islamist interpretations may well prevail. And if forced to choose, many moderates might well choose a violent interpretation of Islam over no Islam at all. But if moderate interpretations of Islam are clearly established in the new constitutions of Muslim nations from the outset, the documents could serve as important guides in this crucial matter. True, generating a consensus behind such constitutions may be difficult and a lengthy process. However, deliberations about what kind of Islam ought to be in these documents are essential to reforming Muslim moral culture.

In Conclusion

All newly liberated countries, once their authoritarian regimes collapse, suffer from a lack of order, as measured by sharp increases in many forms of antisocial behavior. Social order in turn requires a supportive moral culture; order cannot be shored up merely or even mainly by law enforcement agencies. A major source of the moral culture in Muslim countries is religion; merely advancing secular values will not suffice. Hence moderate religious beliefs should be favored and only violent ones rejected. Several changes need to be made in public diplomacy, foreign aid, and other components of American and Western foreign policy in order to favor moderate religious beliefs while rejecting violent ones. These changes are needed if the new moral culture of recently liberated nations is to be worthy of respect and capable of persuading the citizens of these nations to abide by its tenets.

CHAPTER B. RELIGION'S KEY ROLE IN U.S. FOREIGN POLICY

Few suggestions are more likely to raise the eyebrows—if not the hackles —of many a good American than the suggestion that religion has a key role to play in U.S. foreign policy.[55] Separation of state and church may be so deeply ingrained in the prevailing American national psyche that such a suggestion has difficulty receiving serious consideration. This is especially the case among those suspicious of the influence of religious conservatives in American politics; however, those on the religious right are also likely to question such a policy when they find out that the main religion I suggest the United States needs to promote internationally is not Christianity. Hence it is with considerable trepidation that I argue that the Establishment Clause does not and should not apply beyond America's borders.

I have already demonstrated the role that moderate religion can play in the reformation of moral culture. I note here that the best place to initiate such efforts is with the young, in schools. The fact is that the United States and its allies are already involved in changing schooling in several Islamic countries, especially Iraq and Afghanistan, but also Pakistan and elsewhere. Specifically the United States promotes and provides resources for changes in textbooks, teacher preparation, and selection of school administrators. However, the fact that there are some precedents to parts of what I am suggesting does not answer the question: *what is the appropriate role for the United States as far as the religious content of education overseas is concerned?*

Should the United States insist that only secular school programs receive its funds, in accordance with a very expansive reading of the First Amendment? Or should the United States fund moderate religious education? Similar questions are also faced by many European countries as they move to reexamine the officially Christian education given in their public schools and consider establishing separate, so-called Koran schools, in which Islam is taught and its tenets guide educational policy.

As with many other matters concerning education, the issues involved are much broader than what books children read and what teachers share with them during classes. The key questions are which beliefs ought to be part of education and what kind of society and moral culture educators seek to advance—a secularized one; one in which religion is relegated and confined to the private sphere; one in which moderate religion is promoted but violent beliefs are checked; or one in which the door is kept open to whatever beliefs people happen to favor, even if these are extreme or bigoted.

I proceed first by examining the legal arguments surrounding the application of the First Amendment overseas. I then turn to study the need for core shared values, the sources from which this cure may be derived, and particularly the role public education might play in nurturing it (a role sometimes referred to as "character education"). The chapter concludes by offering a distinct policy that is the outgrowth of the communitarian "Diversity Within Unity" model I have previously advanced.[56]

Does the First Amendment Apply Overseas?

Some American legal experts argue that it is a violation of the First Amendment to use American taxpayers' money to fund religious education in other nations, just as it is in the United States. USAID struck this position when it stated that it will "fund only 'neutral, apolitical and areligious' [educational] materials because the U.S. constitution prohibit[s] proselytizing with U.S. government money."[57] And although in the case of Iraq USAID holds that all education initiatives must be Iraqi-led, it also confirms that "guidelines exist not to fund school materials that violate the first amendment of the U.S. constitution, which prohibits using government funds to promote religion."[58] According to Jessica Jordan, chief of the USAID program in Baghdad, "Before we use taxpayer money to print textbooks we need to ensure that we are not infringing on separation of church and state and the First Amendment."[59] However, Christina Asquith reports in *Education Week,* "While U.S. officials don't want to be seen as meddling in what Iraqis learn, they don't want the possible alternative: funding textbooks that are anti-Semitic, anti-American, or radically religious, particularly given the strict separation of church and state-sponsored schools in the U.S."[60]

Shannon Meehan, of Creative Associates International, Inc., a company retained by USAID to help Iraq reform its educational system, explains, "If there is a sentence such as 'Praise be to God' in a grammar textbook, we will have a discussion about revising or changing that to a different sentence. We do not remove the lesson from the textbook, we simply change the sentence."[61] Frank Method, who directs RTI International, one of Creative Associates' subcontractors in Iraq, is even more open-ended:

"There are questions as to whether you simply permit religion or require it. There are questions about whether it is taught by government-paid religious instructors or religious educators who aren't paid publicly. . . . In some cases, you [may] have religion [in the schools], but it's very ecumenical. It's kind of a values education, in which you are really teaching issues of tolerance and respect, rather than any content of any of the particular religions."[62]

Charles Haynes, a leading legal authority in this area and senior scholar at the Freedom Forum's First Amendment Center, argues that it is a violation of the U.S. Constitution to use federal money to print religious textbooks in Afghanistan. He writes, "It really would not matter where it was in the world because it is a violation of conscience for the United States government to use tax dollars to support religion."[63] Indeed, in the most germane court case to date, the court agreed, a point to which I return later.

In practice, to the extent that one can determine what is happening in Iraq and Afghanistan, the principle that no U.S. taxpayer money will be used for religious education is not being observed closely.[64] U.S. foreign aid workers, for instance, purged all references to rifles and killing from some textbooks in Afghanistan, but they left Koranic verses untouched.[65] USAID officials have explained that they have left some Islamic materials intact in Afghanistan because they feared Afghan educators would reject books "lacking a strong element of Muslim thought."[66] The agency did, however, remove its logo and any mention of the U.S. government support from these religious texts, USAID spokeswoman Kathryn Stratos said—as if that solved the problem.[67]

The issue was somewhat mitigated in 2004 by an in-house USAID rule entitled "Participation by Religious Organizations in USAID."[68] Although the regulations specifically stipulate that any USAID support for faith-based organizations overseas cannot be used for "inherently religious activities," section 7 "permits the Secretary of State to waive all or any part of the rule, on a case-by-case basis, where the Secretary determines that such waiver is necessary to further the national security or foreign policy interests of the United States." Indeed, USAID now provides some modest funding to radio programs on Islamic tolerance in Indonesia, to the construction of Islamic elementary schools in Uganda, and to other "inherently religious activities."[69]

The fact that the Bill of Rights in general is as a rule not considered applicable to U.S. dealings abroad makes one wonder whether the Establishment Clause deserves special standing. The U.S. Supreme Court's most thorough exegesis on the extraterritorial application of the Bill of Rights was delivered in *United States v. Verdugo-Urquidez* (1990), in which the Court held that "the Fourth Amendment does not apply to a search and seizure by United States officials of property that is owned by a nonresident alien and located in a foreign country."[70] Indeed, U.S. forces regularly, and with legal impunity (at least as far as American law is concerned), search the communications and records of many millions of people overseas, under various surveillance programs.[71]

There seems to be only one court case that deals specifically with the application of the Establishment Clause overseas. It is a case Americans for Religious Liberty, Inc., brought against Alan Woods, director of USAID, and David Santos, director of the American Schools and Hospitals Abroad (ASHA) Office, in *Lamont v. Schultz* (1988). The plaintiffs (Americans for Religious Liberty) challenged the defendants' funding of twenty foreign religious schools that had received one or more grants from USAID and ASHA. The defendants in turn argued that the Establishment Clause does not apply to government activities abroad. Judge Leonard B. Sand, of the U.S. District Court for the Southern District of New York, ruled that "domestic Establishment Clause standards are applicable to the ASHA program," but any ruling on the matter would have to be certified by a higher court.[72] In *Lamont v. Woods* (1991), the Court of Appeals for the Second Circuit concurred with the district court's decision that ASHA grants "are not immune from Establishment Clause strictures."[73]

It is important to note that this case deals with grants given to American organizations (for work to be carried out overseas) and not awarded directly to non-Americans working outside the United States. Moreover, the ruling was never tested in the Supreme Court, nor have parallel cases been tried before other courts. Hence, this one ruling is a very slender reed on which to base such a major policy decision, one of considerable importance for U.S. interests overseas, and one that has a large (and might yet have a larger) impact on the people in the many nations to which the United States makes educational grants or otherwise participates in the reformulation of their educational policies.

Although USAID states that it must adhere to the Establishment Clause in its dealings with non-Americans abroad, when dealing with American citizens in the United States, Congress, the courts, and the executive branch have punched several very sizable holes in the wall separating state and religious activities since *Lamont v. Woods* in 1991. Together they amount to such a change that one may well wonder, were another case like *Lamont v. Woods* to come before the Supreme Court today, whether its result might not be the opposite.

The fact is that taxpayer funds have long been used, and are increasingly used, to fund religious activities *within* the United States. Many of these instances concern the allotment of taxpayer money to religious welfare and health care service providers; educational support is less frequent but far from unknown. Taxpayer funds have been used to build Catholic and Jewish hospitals under the Hill-Burton Act of 1946; the federal government has paid for 75 percent of the funding for the Jewish Board of Family and Children;[74] Catholic Charities' programs have received about 66 percent of their funding from government grants and contracts;[75] and Lutheran Services in America has gained more than 33 percent of its annual budget from government funds.[76] Medicare and Medicaid patients take their federal and state dollars to hospitals owned and run by various religious groups. Students take their federal scholarships to religiously affiliated colleges. Religious groups frequently make use of public school facilities.[77]

Another ongoing issue that has gained a fair amount of court attention is that of "school vouchers." The Supreme Court ruled in 2002 that a Cleveland program allowing parents to use publicly funded vouchers to pay tuition at private schools—including religious schools—did not violate the Constitution, and left the issue to the discretion of state legislatures.[78] Moreover, a provision of the 1996 welfare bill, which came to be known as "Charitable Choice," allows state governments to contract with religious social service organizations when these governments use federal welfare funds. Specifically, it allows government funds to be used for social services carried out in places of worship, where religious imagery or iconography is often present, and recognizes the right of religious organizations receiving funds to discriminate in their hiring practices based on religious beliefs. The funds, however, cannot be used directly to support "sectarian worship, instruction, or proselytization."[79] President Bush has expanded Charitable Choice to cover nearly all federal programs and has established a White House Office of Faith-Based and Community Initiatives, as well as similar offices in ten cabinet departments, to facilitate government support for faith-based social services.[80] In the 2004 fiscal year, faith-based organizations received more than $2 billion in federal funds.[81]

The formulas that legalize these transactions vary. They have often been examined,[82] so here I list just a few instances to illustrate the ways in which the courts and other authorities have justified the use of taxpayer funds to support religious organizations. My limited purpose is to point to formulas that can be applied overseas. In some cases, the support for religious organizations is deemed as not violating the First Amendment because it is indirect (as when public funds are allotted to individuals in the form of Medicare reimbursements or school vouchers rather than direct payments to religious institutions). This was the principal argument made by the Supreme Court in its decision to uphold Cleveland's voucher program. Chief Justice Rehnquist, in his majority opinion, wrote that "the Ohio program is entirely neutral with respect to religion" because "it provides benefits directly to a wide spectrum of individuals. . . . It permits such individuals to exercise genuine choice among options public and private, secular and religious."[83] Though public funds are spent for religious activities under the voucher program, the Court argued that government itself does not advance or inhibit religion because it has no direct contact with the religious organizations. The same principle and approach could be followed overseas.

In other instances, the assumption is that government funds can be used for nonreligious social service provisions carried out by religious organizations, such as when churches feed the homeless. This is the reasoning behind the Charitable Choice provision in the 1996 welfare reform bill, President Bush's executive orders on faith-based and community initiatives, and numerous earlier court cases.[84] (Some churches set up separate 501(c)(3)—nonprofit—corporations for these nonreligious activities, and these entities are expected to follow various federal rules. Religious groups, as noted above, are exempt from various employment discrimination regulations, but these entities must adhere to them.) However, it must be obvious to anyone who took Accounting 101 that if the government reimburses an organization for an activity it previously had to pay for (e.g., feeding the poor), this organization will have more funds available for other activities (e.g., proselytizing).

Moreover, in some cases funding is allowed for activities by religious entities because these activities are not "inherently religious" nor "pervasively sectarian,"[85] and, most recently, even if they are religious but are needed for their nonreligious purposes. Major examples of these latter activities include the many drug-treatment programs with a religious component.[86] In his 2003 State of the Union Speech, President Bush announced a new, three-year, $600-million federal drug-treatment initiative, "Access to Recovery." Under this plan people are able to use federal vouchers to obtain help at all effective treatment organizations, including faith-based organizations where religious activities (e.g., prayer) are a part of the treatment.[87] As I have already indicated, there is no need to examine here in detail these very considerable exemptions from the Establishment Clause (or changes in the ways it has been interpreted), and the rationales given for them. Merely listing several of them leaves little doubt that the position that funding overseas religious education violates the Constitution is overblown.

Before I proceed further, I should point out that there is a very important consideration that affects all these deliberations. My main thesis in this section—that the United States should support the teaching of moderate Muslim beliefs, oppose the teaching of violent Muslim beliefs, and accord proportional resources to non-Muslim minority religions in the Middle East—does not in fact constitute discrimination against one religion in favor of another! It discriminates only against those beliefs, *whatever* the religion or, indeed, secular ideology from which they are derived that are inimical to the common good and public safety. This consideration is but an elaboration of the central thesis of the whole book, namely, that the fault line that separates beliefs is not their religious or secular origins, but whether they are moderate or immoderate, whether or not they respect the Primacy of Life. True, in Muslim countries most of the American support for nonviolent teachings will be dedicated to Muslim texts, teachers, and schools. However, though U.S. taxpayer funds should never be allowed to support the teachings of the Christian Positive Violence school, or the relevant works of Meir Kahane or Malcolm X, *they should freely be dedicated to support those beliefs that serve as persuasive and powerful alternatives.* One cannot beat a violent body of beliefs unless one advances another set of beliefs. Beliefs, like other parts of human existence, abhor a vacuum.

The Normative Vacuum

The need for reform: One major reason to consider American support for moderate religious education overseas is that in several Muslim countries, albeit certainly not in all of them, a large number of pupils are enrolled in *madrasas,*[88] many of which are breeding grounds for terrorism.[89] The education given in many of these schools accords with a violent interpretation of Islam.[90] In addition, *madrasas* and many other Islamic schools are often criticized for being counterproductive in their teaching methods, relying heavily on rote memorization and hectoring. Also, religious education in these schools is the main subject; little or no room is provided for subjects such as math and science, computer technology, and civics, not to mention the teaching of English, which is becoming increasingly important. In short, it is an education entirely unsuited to modernity.

In India, for instance, "both the Hindu-dominated Indian government and secular-minded Muslims have pressed for curriculum reform and modernization in an effort to curb the isolation, poverty and social conservatism they believe are bred by the schools. . . . If Muslims are to overcome their social disadvantages, many hold, they will have to move beyond the *madrasa.*"[91] Indian *madrasas'* studies are largely limited to the Koran, the hadith, and to Islamic law and jurisprudence. Past government attempts to incorporate science, math, and English into the schools have essentially failed.[92] The same holds true for *madrasas* in other countries—Pakistan for instance—and is likely to continue to be the case in parts of postliberation Afghanistan.[93] In short, *madrasas* are locking their graduates out of modern economic and political development.

Assuming one grants that *madrasas* often promote undesirable beliefs and behavior, one may still ask whether the United States or other Western nations should be involved in changing these schools and hence the ways many millions of Muslims are educated. Indeed, the argument that such reforms ought to be left to the citizens of the nations involved to select which education they prefer for their children may, at first, seem persuasive. However, the United States, other Western nations, moderate Muslim nations, indeed the entire global community, have a compelling interest that people in all nations are raised to reject violence against other people and at home. This does not necessarily give the United States the license to impose its educational preferences—by sending troops or even imposing economic sanctions—on nations that have other preferences. However, to the extent that these nations are seeking and willing to accept foreign aid, including for education, the United States and other nations are justified in using nonlethal means to promote an educational system that opposes the advocacy of violence.

If one accepts the moral tenet that rich nations ought to provide foreign aid, few would disagree that the nations (or, for that matter, individuals or foundations) that provide grants are entitled to decide what they wish to fund. Many *madrasas,* at least as constituted, are unsuitable beneficiaries of American aid. The question runs much deeper than who receives which funds, or even what the content of textbooks, curricula, and teacher training programs ought to be. The question is, what kind of society should the United States promote in Muslim nations in which violent interpretations of Islam are common and long-held?

As we saw in the preceding chapter, one major reason that replacing *madrasa* education with "value-free" education—one that focuses exclusively on developing skills—is the *wrong* policy, is that the nations involved have been until recently (or still are) highly authoritarian and/or traditionalist regimes. This was the case for Iraqis under Saddam, for Afghans under the Taliban, and remains the case for the Saudis and to a somewhat lesser extent the Tunisians, Egyptians, and Pakistanis. When the United States and its allies remove these regimes (or when they collapse under their own weight, as with the former Soviet Union), there is an explosive growth in practically all forms of antisocial behavior. What these societies need is the moral culture that undergirds prosocial behavior.

One way to proceed—character education: One major way to help a moral culture where it is absent or has been weakened, or must be recast, is through the education of the next generation. Teaching only math, science, English, and other such normatively neutral subjects does not provide the education needed for weaving or restoring a social fabric. This issue is symbolized by the fact that when the pictures of Saddam and the statements that glorify his regime were torn out of Iraq's old textbooks, they were replaced with nothing. U.S. officials recruited Fuad Hussein, a former Iraqi professor and Middle Eastern scholar, to assist with the delicate task of reviewing textbooks. Mr. Hussein visited Baghdad schools and chose sixty-seven teachers to make up a textbook revision team. Meeting at UNESCO and UNICEF offices, they were initially tasked with "de-Ba'athifying" the textbooks, but faced many challenges when teachers, wishing to remove Ba'ath party propaganda, did not know with what to replace it.[94]

In 2006 the *Washington Post* reported:

> The two-year-old modern history textbook used at Baghdad's Mansour High School for Boys doesn't mention the U.S.-led invasion that toppled Saddam Hussein from power in Iraq in 2003.
>
> There's not a word about Iraq's annexation of—and subsequent expulsion from—Kuwait in 1990 and 1991, or its grinding eight-year war with Iran in the 1980's that took the lives of a generation of young men.
>
> Perhaps most conspicuously absent from the book, earlier versions of which were packed with florid praise for Hussein, is any reference to the former dictator. For the purposes of instruction at Mansour High, and most schools across Iraq, history ends in 1968, before the bloodless coup that swept the Ba'ath Party to power.[95]

What is most needed is not simply introducing better ways of teaching math or English, although there surely is ample room for improvement on these fronts. The question is, what values should be promoted through the various tools of education, including the content of textbooks, curricula and the training and selection of teachers?

Many an educator's first response to such an agenda is that character education should take place at home or in places of worship, or should be provided by other private civic entities, and that public schools should not be involved in what is called moral, value, or character education.[96] However, one must take into account that in nations recently subject to authoritarian regimes, these intermediate institutions are often relatively weak. They either never existed (e.g., voluntary associations), have been weakened (e.g., communal bonds), have been mobilized to support the state (e.g., favored ethnic groupings), or themselves support one form of authoritarianism or another (e.g., various warlords or sectarian leaders). Hence, there is a need to assist the development of a new, postauthoritarian core of shared values through public education. Otherwise the normative vacuum will produce anarchy that, in turn, will lead to the selection of another authoritarian leader.

The thesis that these newly liberated societies need reformed morals, and that public education is a major way to promote them, should be less surprising given that, despite frequent claims to the contrary, even in long-established, free societies, public education is far from normatively neutral. It is hard to imagine how, for instance, an American history teacher could discuss the Civil War, the civil rights movement, the Holocaust, and, indeed, most historical topics in a truly normatively neutral way. The same holds true for much of the humanities and social sciences. Moreover, aside from their inclusion in the curricula, specific beliefs and corresponding behaviors are also inculcated in pupils. These include teaching about the ways they ought to treat one another when a difference of opinion arises (e.g., by teaching conflict resolution methods and communication skills), and on ways of dealing with people of different religions, races, socioeconomic backgrounds, and sexual orientations.[97] The same holds true for teaching respect for authority figures and reasonable rules. I shall refer to all these teachings jointly as "civic ethics."

Educational Options

Theoretically, it is conceivable for the United States to try to replace a religious, fundamentalist school system with a fully secular one, albeit one with a rich normative content of the civic ethics variety. However, forming a civic ethics education program entails much more than taking out the parts of textbooks that seek to legitimate violence, and retraining teachers not to follow these lines of propaganda in their teaching. It would require writing new histories, say for Iraq, that would replace the glorification of Saddam Hussein with narratives about courageous Iraqis who died trying to unseat him, and about those public leaders who served the nation well before his rule. It would entail scanning Arabic literature both for its older, classical poetry and for its contemporary novels to provide students with empathy for people of different experiences and opinions. Teachers would have to be taught pedagogical alternatives to rote memorization. Principals and superintendents would also have to be found to support such educational reforms. I am not implying that they would have to start from ground zero or that there is nothing in the current materials that could be salvaged. But while in Iraq some material might be revived from the pre-Saddam era, in Afghanistan, given the poverty of public education there, much of their civic ethics education curriculum would have to be built from scratch. All in all, it is a gigantic task, one that would take many years to advance.

Moreover, while some parents in the Muslim world, especially in the larger cities, might send their children to secular, public schools, in large parts of these countries, in which most everyone is devout or at least practicing, such education would be rejected out of hand. This is true for most Shias in southern Iraq, most Afghans and Saudis, and many Pakistanis. It follows, therefore, that if the goal is to reach most of the population, and especially those now hostile to economic and political development and inclined to embrace violent beliefs, *some kind of religious schooling must be provided.*

This observation should not come as a surprise to Americans, considering that nearly 10 percent of American children attend religiously affiliated schools.[98] True, some parents send their children to these institutions mainly to gain a quality education at a lower cost than that available at secular private schools. However, a significant subset of these parents wants their children's religious upbringing reinforced at school. The only difference between the United States and several Muslim nations in this regard is that large majorities in Muslim nations hold this view while only a minority in the United States do. Hence either most children will be educated in private schools, in which religious education—often of the *madrasa* kind—will prevail, or public schools will have to provide some religious education.

People who study the specific situation in Iraq have made related arguments. "If religion is desirable, which I imagine it is by the parents [in Iraq], it is best controlled in the curriculum in the public school system, rather than to give the freedom to the mosques and different factions," according to Mona Habib, an American educational consultant.[99] An Iraqi scholar, Ali al-Attar, agrees that teaching religion in Iraqi public schools would help control extremist impulses: "To prevent students from getting the wrong source of information from radical people, you should give them the basics in the school, which is under supervision that is acceptable to the community. . . . You will avoid that private clergy type of schooling that is going to produce brainwashed children with certain ideas that are very dangerous to the society."[100] Al-Attar, half Sunni and half Shiite by birth, suggests that every Muslim student in Iraq should take a regular class in Islam, which would focus on ethics while avoiding radicalism.

Residues of the Enlightenment still color the response of many progressive educators to the question of whether religion may be taught in public schools. In the wake of the "Age of Reason," natural science and economic rationality were exalted, and religion with all its metaphysical baggage was relegated to the status of a relic of the "Dark Ages." It was expected that religion would be replaced by secular thinking. And, indeed, for generations it seemed that secularization was spreading over ever-larger parts of the world as people gave up religion altogether or became less devout. Secularization acquired the aura of being on the side of the march of "Progress" or "History"—only the uninformed or the bigoted could resist it. But, ironically, all *that* is history by now. At least, it ought to be. Religion continues to be a major source of moral guidance and authority for billions of people. And hundreds of million others, especially in the former Soviet republics and China but also in relatively secular places like Turkey (and Israel), are returning to embrace traditional religion. A principal reason for this development is to fill the vacuum left when the morals previously promoted—by communism or consumerism, or by some other secular ideology or material pursuit—are found to be unsatisfying, or indeed hollow. The secular ideologies have proved unable to address fundamental questions, such why we are born to die, what is the purpose of life, and other such transcendental questions.

It is here that the theoretical and practical lines of reasoning converge. As already indicated, one must face the fact that it is utterly inconceivable for a majority of Shias in Iraq, or of Afghans, Saudis, and Pakistanis, to send their children to public schools that teach only normatively neutral subjects or provide only secular civic education. Absorbing the views represented by the following statements of Iraqis, one begins to fathom the depth of this fact:

> Sheikh Abdul Settar Jabber, head of the Muslim Awareness Association, a leading Sunni group, feels the entire role of the schools should be changed to one that trains students in Islamic law and in how to be good Muslims. He opposes any American involvement in the schools. "We are in Islamic society and this is part of the attempt by Americans to break Iraqi identity."
>
> There was talk [from Iraqi religious groups] that the Americans are trying to Westernize the curriculum and move it far from Islamic values. . . . One religious leader asked me, "Is it not possible to abolish history class and just teach religion?"[101]

The focus shifts next to examining how to ensure that religious education is of the persuasive and nonviolent kind, and that those parents who do prefer secular education will be able to find it.

Institutionalization of Diversity Within Unity (DWU)

Parallelism: A major European response to the preceding questions has been to continue de facto to teach some form of generic Christian beliefs in their public schools but to provide taxpayer support to segregated private schools specifically for Catholics, Jews, and now increasingly for Muslims—the latter being referred to as "Koran schools."[102] Another option has been to provide public funds for both secular and religious private schools. The Dutch refer to this kind of parallel structure, which long existed in their country, as *zoilen,* or "pillars," a useful image.

A major difference among various parallel approaches is the extent of state supervision over the content of the education and the selection of the teachers. If the supervision is lax and the respective religious communities select the teachers, the state could, in effect, end up supporting *madrasas*. On the other hand, if the supervision is strict and teachers are selected in a highly professional way, the private religious schools may well refrain from promoting violent beliefs.[103]

Indonesia uses a parallel structure, leaning toward the second kind. Indonesians between the ages of seven and twelve are required to attend primary school, and their parents are given a choice between sending them to state-run, nonsectarian public schools supervised by the Department of Education and Culture, or to private or semiprivate religious (usually Islamic) schools, supervised and financed by the Department of Religious Affairs. Although 85 percent of the Indonesian population is registered as Muslim (according to the 1990 census), less than 15 percent choose to send their children to religious schools.[104]

A variant of this approach has been suggested in a study conducted for USAID by Sharon Benoliel.[105] She concludes, "The best educational strategies in Muslim countries encourage both public and moderate Islamic school systems to complement each other to reach all learners with enriched content." She adds that "the Agency should support improvements in both secular and religious institutions—but only those that foster a respect for universal human values of dignity, compassion, and tolerance." That is, support should be given only to some kinds of religious private schools but denied to others. And, she argues, these schools "must provide a quality education with a content similar to what is provided in public schools."[106] The report cites Malaysian educational practices as an example of this approach.

In Malaysia, every Islamic school is registered, regulated, and inspected by government ministries. The Department of Islamic and Moral Education works to ensure that these schools are organized, taught, and assessed according to national standards. In accordance with the president's zero-tolerance policy regarding extremist activities, schools where an extremist element has been observed are often closed.[107]

Recently some *madrasas* have opened as private schools right in the heart of America, with little public oversight. Although there have been a handful of Nation of Islam schools catering to African Americans since the early 1970s, a recent explosion of interest in private education among

Arab, Pakistani, and African immigrant communities has raised the number of Islamic schools in the United States to more than two hundred.[108] These schools differ from those in the Malaysian context, for example, in that there is little state supervision and no intervention concerning curricula and admissions policies or teacher selection and training. Textbooks used in New York Islamic schools have been found to be riddled with anti-Semitic and anti-Christian messages. At the Muslim Center Elementary School in Flushing, Queens, for example, a sixth to eighth grade textbook, *What Islam Is All About,* asserts that Jews and Christians "lead such decadent and immoral lives that lying, alcohol, nudity, pornography, racism, foul language, premarital sex, homosexuality and everything else are accepted in their society, churches and synagogues"; and another book, in use at the Ideal Islamic School in Long Island City, Queens, asserts that "the reasons for Jewish hostility lies [*sic*] in their general characteristics," supporting that statement with excerpts from the Koran, e.g., "You will ever find them deceitful, except for a few of them."[109]

It might be of interest to see the way the same issue arises in a society that does not have an Establishment Clause, on the contrary, in which the church is established, namely the United Kingdom. Britain has long provided government support for religious schools. Out of twenty-two thousand state schools, approximately seven thousand are religious. Of this number, only forty-five are affiliated with a denomination other than a principal Christian one.[110]

The head teacher of Islamia Primary School, a state-funded school in London which offers Muslim religious instruction along with the standard national curriculum, believes that schools such as Islamia can help form a new Muslim identity. It combines being a good Muslim with being a good citizen in a pluralist society. The teachers also believe that developing a strong religious core contributes to the academic success of the graduates of faith schools: over 97 percent of them go on to study in a university.[111]

In contrast, Rabbi Jonathan Romain is a strong critic of faith schools. He states that "whereas most clergy see faith schools as reinforcing values, I see them as dividing different communities."[112] Jay Tolson reported that "while British citizenship is heavily emphasized at schools like Islamia, there is legitimate concern about what goes on in some of the others." Tariq Ramadan, a Swiss-born Muslim scholar who serves on a British task force on religious extremism, reports that he approves of faith schools "in principle, but is disturbed by schools—mainly those for Muslim girls—whose real intention is to isolate the students from the rest of society."[113] And that would not be the worst of it. At least some are reported to serve like extremist *madrasas*, teaching and preaching violent versions of Islam.

Diversity Within Unity (DWU): The approach I favor is founded on the argument that all members of society must be expected to honor a core of shared values (such as human rights, civic duty, and a broad toleration for a variety of political and religious opinions), while on other cultural matters they are free to be diverse (such as to which subcultures they adhere, and the particular observances of the religions they follow). The image of a mosaic illustrates this approach; its beauty is enhanced by its various parts not being all of one color, shape, or texture, but it has a definitive pattern which governs the order of the individual pieces, and it has a shared framework and a glue that keep the pieces together. Applying this image to schooling generates a single-track system containing many suboptions. Basically, all children would be expected to attend public schools and receive the essential elements of both civic ethics and modern education, but they could simultaneously opt to take electives that nurture their particular religious or other subcultural allegiances, as long as these allegiances do not ally them with Warriors or violent beliefs.

Specifically such a program entails:

(a) All pupils should be taught subjects with strong normative content, general literature and history classes for example.

(b) All pupils should attend classes in math and science, as well as other classes that provide them with the skills they need to live in and contribute to modern economies.

(c) While 80 to 85 percent of the total curriculum might be shared by all students (representing unity), the remaining classes could be electives divided according to the religious and cultural heritage of the parents and pupils (representing the diversity element). In a given religious track, Muslim students for instance would spend several hours each week studying the Koran, Muslim literature and history, and other subjects of particular interest to them. All students would mix, not merely in the majority of the curriculum and classes devoted to shared subjects (unity element), but also in assemblies and other such common activities, especially sports and social activities. However, participation in activities that offend religious sensibilities, such as certain gym classes (many Muslims object to girls wearing swimsuits, for example), would not be required.

(d) If, under the DWU plan, the number of students who have a given preference is small and does not justify setting up separate classes, the students involved may have to be bussed to another school in which the preferred classes are offered, or, if the number of students is very small, students may be provided with appropriate tutorials in the school library. When this approach was suggested to Europeans, some of their officials—not keen to allow for Koran schools or tracks— responded that Muslims cannot agree with one another on what to teach their children. If and when this is the case, more than one Muslim (or Christian, or Jewish) tutorial might be made available.

(e) A crucial detail concerns the selection of teachers and teaching materials for the various elective classes. Some have suggested that these should be left to the discretion of the local communities in question, and their functionaries—be they priests, rabbis, or mullahs—could teach the said classes. This might well open the door to teaching of violent beliefs and goes against the public interest and the well-being of students involved. Instead, the selection of teachers of electives should be performed by the same authorities that select all other teachers. This should also hold true to an extent for the selection of textbooks and other teaching materials and the composition of specialized curricula. They could all have rich religious and subcultural content, but it would not be of the violence-exhorting kind.

This position is implied by the following statement made at the second National Seminar on Strategies and Curriculum Reform of the New Education System, hosted by Iraq's Ministry of Education in March 2004. The Ministry cited the following as a primary principle in reviewing and modernizing the curriculum: "All decisions concerning reform of the curriculum must be strictly Iraqi and in line with Iraqi values and culture. . . . This would include *enlightened religious upbringing*, the establishment of and appreciation for the values of democracy, free speech, human rights, justice, equality, and tolerance. It would also discourage sectarianism and racism.[114]

In Conclusion

The question of whether American tax dollars should support religious education overseas is typically framed in an unhelpful manner. First, posing the question in this way implies a constitutional limitation on such teaching to prevent a violation of the Establishment Clause—a violation that either does not exist or can be accommodated. Second, the question ought not to about religious education per se, but rather the distinction should be drawn between the promotion of violent beliefs, as provided by many *madrasas,* and moderate religious education. The first should be discouraged, the second encouraged.

Finally, the question points to ultimately much broader concerns about the nature of politics. What is narrowly at issue is the normative vacuum that is engendered when the regimes of the Taliban, Saddam Hussein, or the communist kind collapse. Explosive increases in antisocial behavior follow. *The broader issue is that preferable sources of social order must be found.* These are best centered on a civic ethics—a sense of responsibility members of communities have for one another, for the common good, and their commitment to a core of shared values. School is one major way to help form and promote such a culture.

In American public schools character education is far from absent, though it is essentially secular. In many parts of the Islamic world, parents would not send their children to public schools that provide secular education only. The options, then, are to:

(a) provide state-funded but private religious schools for those who seek them; or
(b) provide two tracks within public schools—religious and secular. Both of these tracks segregate the religious students from all others; both need close supervision to ensure that they will provide a sufficiently modern and proper moral education.
(c) The preferred option requires that all students attend mainly the same classes, in public schools, but that these schools also set aside about 15 to 20 percent of the class time and curricula for electives on religious subjects. This approach is based on the Diversity Within Unity princi-

ple, which ensures that students of different backgrounds mix socially and learn many of the same core materials and adopt many of the same beliefs, but which also enables them to nurture their unique subcultures and religions. The selection of teachers and teaching materials for the electives must follow the same procedures as those employed for other classes. By promoting such school systems, the United States can, through education, help other nations (that seek assistance) build up the moral foundations of their social order, without violating the U.S. Constitution or offending the strongly held beliefs of the very citizens the United States is seeking to help.

PART V

Grounds for Intervention

CHAPTER A. WHOSE SECURITY?
THE RESPONSIBILITY TO PROTECT

The focus on Security First as the guiding principle of U.S. foreign policy does not refer, as followers of narrow realism might have it, only to the security of the United States and its allies. The Primacy of Life principle places a responsibility on the major powers not only to ensure basic security for their own peoples, but also to contribute to the basic security of other peoples. The legitimacy of the approach relies in part on its consistent application, one that respects life—not American or British or some other Western life—but life simply, indeed all lives. This entails, under limited conditions, interfering in the internal affairs of sovereign nations.

To sort out where Security First takes us when we consider whether a foreign government acting unilaterally, a "coalition of the willing," or for that matter the United Nations, should send troops into a given nation, I proceed first to discuss the profound change in the moral weight attached these days to sovereignty and to a nation's right to be free from interventions. I then explore the implications of this change for armed humanitarian intervention and the quest to stop the proliferation of nuclear weapons. In plain English, this chapter asks: when is it okay to bomb or invade someone else's homeland?

Sovereignty as Responsibility

In 1996 the most important moral principle that had guided international relations for more than three hundred years, since the signing of the Treaty of Westphalia in 1648—namely, that sovereign states are not to interfere in one another's internal affairs[1]—was turned upside down. This radical change was initiated by what was at first a little known book, *Sovereignty as Responsibility,* by the Sudanese diplomat and Brookings Institution senior fellow Francis M. Deng and his associates.[2] They argue in this book that when nations do not conduct their internal affairs in ways that meet certain internationally recognized standards—the Sudanese government's support for marauding militias in Darfur provides a contemporary example—other nations not only have a passive right to intervene, but an active duty to do so. In other words, governments that fail to abide by internationally recognized standards of decency forfeit their sovereign rights. Sovereignty is thus transformed from an absolute claim into a conditional one, revocable in case of bad behavior.

Deng and his co-authors originally may have had a limited purpose in mind, in that they were primarily concerned with the various African nations which were blocking U.N. humanitarian relief to refugees, known in international jargon as "DPs," or displaced persons. (As a former DP myself I have a special interest in the fate of such people.) *Sovereignty as Responsibility* seeks a moral ground to justify sending U.N. troops to clear the way for caravans carrying medical supplies and food. However, in the process of seeking a systematic rationale for such a line of action, the book in effect redefines sovereignty. Deng and his co-authors replace the long-standing definition of sovereignty as "supreme authority within a territory,"[3] with a new definition: "sovereignty as responsibility means that national governments are duty bound to ensure minimum standards of security and social welfare for their citizens and be accountable both to the national body politic and the international community."[4]

Like all groundbreaking books, this one was not without its precursors. These include works by the political philosophers Bertrand de Jouvenel, specifically his *Sovereignty: An Inquiry into the Political Good* (1957), and Jacques Maritain, *Man and the State* (1951). Both call for changing the notion of sovereignty, or, in Maritain's case, eliminating it altogether, and obliging outside governments to intervene in the affairs of those governments that do not uphold or obey the natural or moral law. De Jouvenel writes that much more important than the particular constitutional form a government takes is the "spirit of government and the spirit of citizens," which "consists in awareness that the sovereign, as such, is unfree to do anything not consonant with the performance of its function."[5] Maritain meanwhile speaks caustically of the "false pretense" of the modern state "to be a superhuman person, and to enjoy, as a result, a right of absolute sovereignty."[6] He adds further that internal peace and self-sufficiency, regarded by Aristotle and Thomas Aquinas as the distinguishing characteristic of a complete city or kingdom, could be realized in the present day only in "a pluralist world-wide political society."[7] And long before de Jouvenel and Maritain, the early modern natural lawyers Hugo Grotius, Alberico Gentili, and Francisco Suarez all wrote on similar themes, arguing that a cruel prince could be subject to disciplinary action from his neighbors.[8]

Feminist critiques of the traditional concept of privacy provide a useful analogue to the dramatic shift in perspective for which Deng and his associates called. We used to hold as semisacred the precept that "a man's home is his castle"; that is, it was regarded as a gross violation of basic human rights for the government, indeed for anyone from Peeping Toms to busybody social workers, to intrude into this private space. However, feminists fairly pointed out that when husbands abuse their wives behind closed doors, the public has not merely a right but a duty to intervene. Protecting women and children from violence trumps privacy.[9] And that which holds for households also holds to some extent for the political community, for the nation.

As Deng puts it, if a nation-state fails to fulfill its obligations, the "right to inviolability should be regarded as lost, first voluntarily as the state itself asks for help from its peers, and then involuntarily as it has help imposed on it in response to its own inactivity or incapacity and to the unassuaged needs of its own people."[10] It follows therefore that "the sovereign state's responsibility and accountability to both domestic and external constituencies must be affirmed as interconnected principles of national and international order."[11] The international community expects states to bring their domestic laws and conduct into line with established international standards; if they do not, others have a responsibility to interfere in the offending state's internal affairs. Thus, Deng's justification for armed humanitarian intervention turns what was once a taboo of international relations into an ethical imperative.

Deng wryly notes that "the obligation of the state to preserve life-sustaining standards for its citizens . . . as a necessary precondition of sovereignty . . . is not yet fully or consistently observed in practice."[12] Little wonder. The traditional conception of sovereignty, allowing for complete national autonomy, prescribed for centuries what a legitimate international order entailed. Ever since the Treaty of Westphalia brought into being the sovereign nation-state by placing authority over matters of religion exclusively in the hands of each state's ruler, one ruler could no longer go to war with another in order to protect fellow believers. French and Spanish kings could no longer rush to the aid of beleaguered English and Dutch Catholics, and England could no longer suit up to fight for Protestants on the Continent. This emergent notion of sovereignty was expanded to encompass domestic matters in general. War could be legitimate only if one state violated the territorial integrity of another.

Stephen Krasner powerfully points out in his book, provocatively entitled *Sovereignty: Organized Hypocrisy,* that the principle has often been violated.[13] Nevertheless, the Westphalian ideal of the sovereign nation-state continues to carry considerable moral force. To provide but one significant example: when Saddam Hussein's troops invaded Kuwait in 1990 and the United States led a coalition to force Saddam to retreat, this act of war in defense of Kuwaiti sovereignty was considered fully legitimate, in the sense that the United Nations approved it, numerous scholars of international law regarded it as just, the U.S. allies picked up the lion's share of the cost, and Arab nations joined the coalition and provided bases for the military action. Conversely, when the United States invaded Iraq in 2003 without such justification, this act of war generated a global tsunami of protests, even from many close U.S. allies.

The genocides and other atrocities of the 1990s, however, have led several statesmen and public intellectuals to favor a reassessment of the inviolability of state sovereignty. Their concerns were reinforced and gained more of a public hearing in the wake of the widespread condemnations that followed the U.N. failure to stop the 1994 Rwandan genocide, which left upward of eight hundred thousand dead. The advocates of change found still more support following the outrage over the 1995 massacre at Srebrenica, in which Serbian troops in eastern Bosnia killed approximately seven thousand Bosnian Muslim men—a killing several observers believe was facilitated rather than prevented by U.N. peacekeeping troops.[14]

These events and the growing international reaction to them led U.N. Secretary General Kofi Annan to pose the question, "If humanitarian intervention is, indeed, an unacceptable assault on sovereignty, how should we respond to a Rwanda, to a Srebrenica—to gross and systematic violations of human rights that affect every precept of our common humanity?"[15] To respond to this challenge, the Canadian government established a commission with the kind of title such bodies typically acquire: the International Commission on Intervention and State Sovereignty (ICISS). It was chaired by the former Australian foreign minister Gareth Evans and Mohamed Sahnoun, special adviser to Kofi Annan. The commission put the recharacterization of sovereignty as responsibility at the center of its proposals:

"The Charter of the U.N. is itself an example of an international obligation voluntarily accepted by member states. On the one hand, in granting membership of the U.N., the international community welcomes the signatory state as a responsible member of the community of nations. On the other hand, the state itself, in signing the Charter, accepts the responsibilities of membership flowing from that signature. There is no transfer or dilution of state sovereignty. But there is a necessary recharacterization involved: from *sovereignty as control* to *sovereignty as responsibility* in both internal functions and external duties."[16]

The same recharacterization of sovereignty as responsibility has also been strongly endorsed by another commission, with an even more ponderous title: the High-Level Panel on Threats, Challenges, and Change. The international panel of experts, formed at the behest of Kofi Annan in 2003, released a report the following year entitled "A More Secure World: Our Shared Responsibility." This report, too, reached the same conclusion that the time has come for the global community to mind the basic security of people within nations, not just relations among nations. The report states: "History teaches us all too clearly that it cannot be assumed that every State will always be able, or willing, to meet its responsibilities to protect its own people and avoid harming its neighbors. And in those circumstances, the principles of collective security mean that some portion of those responsibilities should be taken up by the international community, acting . . . to help build the necessary capacity or supply the necessary protection, as the case may be."[17]

Annan warmly received the commission's report—not always the fate of such documents. Indeed he subsequently urged that "the international community should embrace the 'responsibility to protect,' as a basis for collective action against genocide, ethnic cleansing and crimes against humanity."[18] The High-Level Panel's recommendations now rank significantly among the proposals for reform under consideration by the United Nations.

The Commission and the High-Level Panel pointed out that the re-characterization of sovereignty is far from unprecedented. The Universal Declaration of Human Rights has set standards that all governments are expected to follow, and the Security Council has authorized interventions in the internal affairs of nations such as Somalia and Haiti to protect these rights. Such authorizations, however, have been rare and have come on an ad hoc basis. Gareth Evans makes this point well when he stated that "the problem with intervention to deal with purely internal human-rights violations is that there is no real foundation at all in the Charter for such action—with the prohibition against intervention in the internal affairs not really balanced with the desultory references to human rights."[19]

In contrast, the new concept of sovereignty seeks to legitimate a systematic and fundamental shift in the role of the international community in the internal affairs of states. As Deng writes, "On the international level . . . sovereignty becomes a pooled function, to be protected when exercised responsibly, and to be shared when help is needed."[20] Although the new duty to protect hardly favors wanton and reckless intervention, it accords much greater moral weight to the international community. Sovereignty thus changes from being an exclusive right of individual nation-states to an internationally shared responsibility.

I suggested earlier that, in contrast to the position held by narrow realists, "values" broader than short-range national self-interest do matter in international relations.[21] Hence the ways sovereignty—arguably the most important principle in international relations—is defined profoundly impacts the legitimacy of foreign policy decisions. It informs us whether an armed intervention of one or more nations in the internal affairs of another is to be condemned (e.g., as the 2003 invasion of Iraq), to win widespread approval (e.g., Australia in East Timor), or to be criticized for not occurring at all (e.g., Darfur and Rwanda). I turn shortly to the question of whether these interventions ought to be limited merely to providing security or whether they should serve other ends as well. But first I present a discussion of the importance of introducing the concept of *responsibility,* next to that of *rights,* into moral deliberations about international relations.

CHAPTER B. RESPONSIBILITY AS AN INTERNATIONAL COMMUNITARIAN PRINCIPLE

The introduction of responsibility as a central moral principle of international relations is of greater significance than even the specific duty to protect. Exploring the origins, dynamics, and implications of the concept of responsibility in international relations is a vast undertaking that others have already begun.[22] A few points, however, are called for here.

Attempts by the InterAction Council to augment the Universal Declaration of Human Rights (UDHR) with a "Universal Declaration of Responsibilities" have been rebuffed for nearly two decades.[23] In this sense, the U.N. Charter and especially the UDHR tend to reflect an Enlightenment stress on liberty and autonomy—and the historical context in which these principles were formulated, in the early modern West. However, the three great premodern Abrahamic faiths, Judaism, Christianity, and Islam—not to mention the major premodern Asian belief systems—have no essential concept of inalienable human rights. (I say "essential" because worthwhile attempts have been made to interpret various religious and ethical texts to find some measure of support for individual rights.)[24] These belief systems characteristically focus not on the ways people merit being treated, or on that to which they are entitled, but rather on what each person is obligated to do, for others, for the common good, and for God—that is, on their responsibilities.

To provide a brief and very simple example: it is Friday night in a traditional Jewish community in the Diaspora. The congregation has just finished the communal evening prayers and the members are about to retire to their respective homes for a celebratory dinner to welcome "queen" Sabbath. There is one poor person who does not have a home to go to. Members of the congregation have a *responsibility* to see to it that someone takes him to that individual's home, but the poor person does not have a *right* to demand such charity. The community will foster moral precepts and informal social controls to ensure that this responsibility is discharged properly, but the individual is not entitled to sue if he believes, say, that sufficient hospitality was not offered.

Communitarianism is often associated with the same emphasis on the responsibilities that members of a community have to one another and to the common good, without particular attention or commitments to their rights. This kind of communitarianism, called "authoritarian," is held primarily by East Asian communitarians such as former prime minister of Singapore Lee Kuan Yew and former prime minister of Malaysia Mahathir bin Mohamad.[25]

In contrast, in 1990 a group was formed that has defined itself as "responsive" or "neo-communitarian," and has defended the view that a good society is one which strikes a carefully crafted balance between individual rights and social responsibilities, between personal autonomy and the common good.[26] I played some role in putting this group together and authored a text along these lines, *The New Golden Rule*.[27]

Neo-communitarians maintain that the so-called right to be let alone[28] does not necessarily hold for those who violate generally held standards of morality. While neo-communitarians fully respect individual rights, they encourage the recognition that individuals also have responsibilities to their community; the community, in turn, is entrusted with ensuring that both rights and responsibilities are honored.

In effect, the sovereignty-as-responsibility position applies this neo-communitarian insight to the realm of international relations. Just as neo-communitarianism challenges the Enlightenment's conception of autonomous individuals acting as free agents, so too does the notion of sovereignty as responsibility challenge the Westphalian notion of independent, sovereign nation-states. And just as neo-communitarianism balances individuals' rights with their obligations to the community, so does recharacterizing sovereignty as responsibility balance the rights of free nations with the responsibilities they have to the international community. Finally, just as local communities must act when their members fail to live up to their responsibilities, so too must the international community intervene when a nation ceases to fulfill its duties.[29]

One must note, though, that this principle does not *necessarily* justify armed intervention. It points principally to moral expectations, what we ask of one another as individuals or as nations, what is considered good conduct, behavior we cherish or condemn. Violence is justified only as a last resort, for limited purposes.

The Scope of Responsibility: The Primacy of Life

The concept of responsibility has been discussed thus far in general terms. Applying it to specific situations, however, raises a number of subsidiary issues. Only one—albeit a crucial one—needs to be examined here. It concerns the basic question: when is armed intervention legitimate under the new terms of international responsibility? If the threshold for such intervention is set too low, the new concept of sovereignty might end up justifying armed interventions by foreign powers when relatively minor irresponsible acts have occurred—or are feared might occur. For instance, the United States stated that it invaded Grenada in order to save the lives of a handful of American medical students, who many agree were not endangered in the first place, and could have been protected readily enough in other ways.[30] Similarly, in earlier times imperial powers would send a gunboat when some client state was late in paying its bills or was guilty of some other small infraction.[31]

In contrast, if the threshold is set too high, if foreign powers must meet numerous, arduous tests for an intervention to be considered legitimate, genocides may well run their horrible course before the United Nations is ready to authorize action.

Lastly, if the concept is applied inconsistently—one genocide is stopped, while others are ignored—the new concept of sovereignty will lose its legitimacy.

Threshold Too Low?

The danger that the threshold will be set too low arises in two forms. One is that the criteria for determining whether or not a government has failed to live up to its responsibilities are so lax that it is all too easy for foreign powers to justify meddling in the internal affairs of other nations. This is a trap Deng falls into when he and his co-authors define that which is expected from a normal government so widely that any foreign power could readily find fault and failure in another. They write, "Governments, under normal circumstances, strive to ensure for their people effective governance that guarantees a just system of law and order, democratic freedoms, respect for fundamental rights, and general welfare."[32] With the threshold that armed interventions must clear set so low and the specifics left so vague, there are few if any nations in the world today that would not be vulnerable to intervention under some pretext.

In contrast, the ICISS proposes a significantly higher threshold for intervention. It states that for military intervention "to be warranted, there must be a) large scale loss of life, actual or apprehended, with genocidal intent or not, which is the product either of deliberate state action, or state neglect or inability to act, or a failed state situation; or b) large scale 'ethnic cleansing,' actual or apprehended, whether carried out by killing, forced expulsion, acts of terror or rape."[33] This approach is fully compatible with the Primacy of Life principle and the foreign policy based on it, advocated in this volume. According to the Commission, in plain words, security is the first right and must be ensured. Armed interventions for lesser causes should remain a taboo.

The Commission also holds that any intervention must abide by the precautionary just-war principles of 1) right intention (exclusively humanitarian), 2) last resort, 3) proportional means, and 4) reasonable prospects of success. Finally, the Commission seeks to avoid the possibility of interventions led by individual states or ad hoc coalitions with less-than-humanitarian intentions by reforming the Security Council.

As I see it, these additional prerequisites may abstractly be of merit; however, when genocide is taking place it often flares up rapidly and is much easier to stop before it becomes full-blown. Hence one should not rule out the value of intervention by one big power, as for instance Australia did when it stopped the savaging of East Timor's population by militias collaborating with the Indonesian military. Nor should one ban small coalitions of nations from saving the day, of the kind that stopped ethnic cleansing in Kosovo.[34] Above all, the international community should not have to await the reform of the Security Council before national governments are encouraged, and if need be pushed, to live up to their responsibilities to stop and prevent genocides.

A second danger of loosening the international norms barring armed interventions is the "slippery slope" argument. When one sets out to reposition barriers whose positions have long been considered sacrosanct —whether by a body of law, social taboos, or moral norms—one faces the question: how far should we go? To what extent should we loosen the norm? Where do we set down the new markers that separate the "dos" from the "don'ts"? An analogy may help make this point. Traditionalists fight for the preservation of chastity as a social norm because they fear that once this limitation on sexual behavior is lifted, women will become endlessly promiscuous, if not prostitute themselves. What nontraditional-ists can still find interesting is the question—for both men and women—as to whether there should be some limits on when and with whom one has sex? Are even casual sex and "hooking up" to be accepted? If the norm of chastity is abandoned, what is to replace it—if anything?

In the case at hand, the danger is that lowering the threshold for armed intervention runs the risk of leading to yet a further lowering of the threshold. In this way armed interventions could become legitimate on numerous grounds, such as reinstating a deposed head of state or pre-venting a fuel pipeline from being shut down.

My response to this danger is that we must "notch" the slope: when we remove an old barrier we must find another place to erect a new one, set a clear limit as to how far we are willing to go, and no further. The U.N. Convention on the Prevention and Punishment of the Crime of Genocide provides a reliable and defendable "notch" to determine when human-itarian intervention is justifiable. It states:

> Genocide means any of the following acts committed with intent to destroy, in whole or in part, a national, ethnical, racial or re-ligious group, as such:
>
> (a) Killing members of the group;
>
> (b) Causing serious bodily or mental harm to members of the group;
>
> (c) Deliberately inflicting on the group conditions of life cal-culated to bring about its physical destruction in whole or in part;
>
> (d) Imposing measures intended to prevent births within the group;
>
> (e) Forcibly transferring children of the group to another group.[35]

These definitions can easily be understood as reflecting the principle of the Primacy of Life in international relations. Given the gravity of the offenses which the Convention describes, the threshold for intervention in the internal affairs of an independent nation on that basis would not be set too low. Merely self-aggrandizing interventions or frivolous adventures by the major powers could find little justification, while the gravest moral crimes of governments would be punished.

CHAPTER C. A SECOND DUTY: TO PREVENT?

The recasting of international relations in a communitarian direction—rendering responsibility a core element of sovereignty—entered a new phase with the publication in *Foreign Affairs* of a seminal brief by Lee Feinstein and Anne-Marie Slaughter under the title "A Duty to Prevent."[36] The two scholars call for augmenting the obligations of a responsible nation with the commitment to refrain from acquiring or developing weapons of mass destruction (WMD), and they posit a duty on the part of the international community to ensure that nations acting irresponsibly in this regard lose their sovereign privileges and become subject to intervention.

Feinstein and Slaughter fully embrace the responsibility to protect in order to ensure the well-being of a state's population, but they add a duty to prevent, namely to prevent those nations whose rulers "lack internal checks on their power" from developing or acquiring WMD.[37] And they add—to remove WMD in case those nations already command them. Feinstein and Slaughter assert: "Like the responsibility to protect, the duty to prevent begins from the premise that the rules now governing the use of force, devised in 1945 and embedded in the U.N. Charter, are inadequate. Both new principles respond to a growing recognition, born of logic and experience, that in the twenty-first century maintaining global peace and security requires states to be proactive rather than reactive. And both recognize that U.N. members have responsibilities as well as rights."[38]

Like Deng's pivotal work, the Feinstein-Slaughter article articulates recent changes in global sensibilities and seeks to move them in a broadly communitarian direction. Ever since 9/11 there has been a growing concern that terrorists will acquire WMD or learn to make them, or that rogue states will employ them, and that more and more nations will seek to so arm themselves. As a result, there has been a growing, albeit far from advanced, consensus that the international community must act to prevent such developments. The consensus is reflected in several international endeavors, including: U.N. Security Council Resolution 1540 (2004), which calls on all member states to cooperate in preventing non-state actors from developing, acquiring, or transporting WMD; the multilateral negotiations with North Korea and Iran; the Group of Eight's (G-8, leading industrialized nations). Action Plan on Nonproliferation, which seeks to tightly control access to nuclear materials for civilian use and establishes a multipronged effort to prevent proliferation;[39] the commitment expressed by the more than sixty nations in joining the Proliferation Security Initiative (PSI) to prevent trafficking in illicit WMD;[40] and other endeavors that all go beyond the older Treaty on the Non-Proliferation of Nuclear Weapons.

One cannot be surprised that strong advocates of humanitarian intervention—or of deproliferation—favor only one of these two responsibilities. Thus, Gareth Evans, co-chair of the ICISS and head of the International Crisis Group, criticizes the duty to prevent on the grounds that, while humanitarian causes bring the world together, deproliferation divides it.[41] On the other hand, many of the strong advocates of deproliferation are leery of extensive armed humanitarian interventions. They see no vital national interest served, no clear end or exit strategy, and the possibility of large-scale involvement in costly and difficult nation-building projects.

As I see it, the duty to prevent—if properly constructed—finds full support in the Primacy of Life principle. In effect, as I show below, nuclear arms are the major threat to life in the future. They threaten American lives, as well as the citizens of many other nations (e.g., India and Pakistan; Israel and Iran). However, we must return to the question of how to avoid the slippery slope in interfering in nations that are suspected or accused by some authorities of developing nuclear arms or acquiring them, but that adamantly deny such acts and intensions themselves.

Given the loss of credibility of the U.S. and the U.K. intelligence services in the run-up to the 2003 invasion of Iraq—whether due to a genuine intelligence failure or to a deliberate disregard of the evidence, or to some mixture of the two—claims by the U.S. and U.K. governments that a nation is developing nuclear arms will, under present political conditions, hardly suffice. In contrast, when a nation declares that it has acquired such arms, as North Korea has announced, it should be taken at its word. (If a government is faking these claims, it sadly will have to learn that is not a wise policy to follow.) If several intelligence services of nations not involved in the Iraq debacle attest to such concerns, such reports should be given more credibility. Finally, if the International Atomic Energy Agency (IAEA), which has on its board thirty-five nations, many of which are not supportive of U.S. policies, attests to a danger, this should be accorded considerable weight. For instance, it is important that the IAEA—and not merely the United States, Britain, and Israel—has been quite forthcoming in stating that Iran poses a potentially serious nuclear threat.[42]

The next question is whether a government's acquisition of a nuclear weapon suffices to justify declaring that government in defiance of international security and hence subject to legitimate armed intervention. Much depends on the small print, but the essence of the position follows from the overarching principle: nuclear weapons (unlike other WMD, as we shall see in Part VI) are the gravest threat to life the world now faces. The fewer bombs there are and the fewer nations that have them, the safer we all are. When all is said and done, all necessary means should be used to stop nuclear proliferation and reverse it wherever it has taken place. Force should be used only after all other means have been exhausted.

Does that mean that a powerful nation should march tomorrow into India, Pakistan, North Korea, and Israel to remove their nuclear weapons? Hardly. So far, small efforts have been made to encourage these nations to dismantle their nuclear arms and provide them security guarantees by other means. For instance, Israel's suggestion to participate in a WMD-free Middle East has gained next to no attention.[43]

The preceding principle merely provides a general framework and rationale. When these are applied to one state or another, the specific circumstances must be taken into account. These are discussed in the next part. It should be clear, however, that it is a grave mistake to undermine the new taboo against nuclear weapons, the international duty to prevent nuclear proliferation, for example, by encouraging states like India to expand their nuclear programs, as the United States did in 2006, or to be indifferent when a new state embarks on this road because one trusts its current government, such as when the United States was indifferent to Brazil's reignited ambitions in this area, also in 2006.[44]

In the longer run, the issue raised by the new concept of sovereignty, as conditional on good national conduct, concerning our understanding of the way democracies are to function, still needs to be addressed. Democracy (in modern terms at least) assumes that the entire body politic is sovereign and therefore has a right to govern itself. However, the new concept of sovereignty as responsibility would move policymaking in several critical matters, from the governments of "the people" to an unelected or democratically unaccountable international forum, such as the U.N. Security Council, or to the capitals of some group of powerful nations, say the G-8. That is, sovereignty as responsibility may generate a major "democratic deficit." This deficit in turn may be addressed but surely cannot be ignored in the quest for the new principles of a legitimate international order. Indeed, though the United Nations has come to be perceived as a source of legitimacy in Western Europe—in many other nations, above all in America, many entertain grave reservations about its legitimacy and fear that it could grow into some kind of pernicious global government.

To enhance its legitimacy, various U.N. reforms have been suggested. Many of these involve changing the composition of the Security Council in order to make it more representative. It is often pointed out that the Security Council reflects the powers of the world the way they were in 1945; the permanent members are the nations that won World War II, namely Russia, China, France, the United Kingdom, and the United States. Now, it is often argued, other nations should be added, most prominently Germany, Brazil, India, and Japan. The fact is, however, that such reforms are very unlikely to take place in the near future, and even if introduced are still going to leave open many questions about the representative nature of the United Nations. For instance, there will still be other nations that will seek membership in the Security Council, such as Nigeria and South Africa. And if India were included, Indonesia would feel left out, and so on. Moreover, one cannot but wonder whether the representatives of authoritarian governments such as North Korea can legitimately speak for their people; another question is the legitimacy of resolutions by the General Assembly in which tiny nations, such as the likes of Luxembourg and Liechtenstein, have the same vote as China.

Meanwhile, nuclear terrorists may well wipe out a major city any day. Action to promote security cannot await U.N. reforms. Hence, to enhance both the effectiveness and hopefully the legitimacy of armed interventions in the internal affairs of irresponsible nations, the United Nations must be supplemented with another new global architecture that is especially concerned with security. Read on.

PART VI

Security Requires a New Global Architecture

My argument that providing basic security should be our first priority could be misunderstood to imply that there are no critical differences among the various elements of that which makes people secure.[1] The opposite is the case: some elements do indeed matter more than others— by several orders of magnitude. Sorting out which elements of security ought to be accorded the highest priority, and what must be done to advance them, are the subjects I tackle next.

Such a security triage is necessary because, like its various attempts at social engineering overseas, the United States is now following a helter-skelter, scattergun approach to security. America acts as if it had asked itself: why go through the painful process of triage, admitting that attending to some urgent matters may well require the neglect of others? Why inform some interest groups that their ox will be gored? Instead, let's cover the entire waterfront—and, failing that, pretend that we are doing "everything possible."

As a result, the United States vacillates in its dealings with the world between a sense of omnipotence on the one hand ("we have the strongest military in human history, we are the richest nation in the world . . ."), and impotence on the other ("things overseas are a mess; it's time to bring the troops home, and leave these people to fend for themselves"). Even at home the public mood swings back and forth between the mentality of "bring it on," and an increased unease as, years after 9/11, we are still unable to perform many of the most elementary tasks widely understood to be vital to homeland security, for instance securing our borders.

Much of the United States' security apparatus is in a *pre*-Katrina FEMA (Federal Emergency Management Agency) stage: there are strong reasons to expect that a category five terrorist hurricane is going to hit us sooner or later; we know that our protective walls are not strong enough to prevent such an attack; we have purchased some equipment to deal with the storm and have made some vague evacuation plans, but most of what must be done remains undone. Just as many months after Katrina we were still unprepared for the next major hurricane, years after 9/11 we are still unequipped to prevent the next major terrorist attack or to deal with its dire consequences once it occurs.

To proceed, we must recognize that by trying to cover the entire spectrum we squander a good part of those limited resources (they are always limited) that are devoted to security. One may disagree with the exact way I outline the priorities below but hopefully will still find that such a triage is vital. At least the following lineup may serve to feed a much overdue debate: *which fronts must be covered first, and which regrettably must we leave largely uncovered?*

CHAPTER A. THE THIRD OUGHT TO BE FIRST

To proceed, it is best to draw a sharp distinction among the urgency required, the resources allocated, and the attention accorded to the three main frontlines of homeland protection: "hardening" targets, preempting terrorist attacks, and preventing access to nuclear bombs and the materials from which they are made. I report with considerable regret that so far the highest priority has been given to the least promising front, that of hardening the targets, and the lowest to the most essential priority— preventing nuclear terrorism. This is not some far-out conclusion I conjured during a nightmare; there is a considerable consensus among national security experts on many of the following points.

Hardening the Targets

The front that has been given the most extensive attention, and is often the focus of congressional hearings and the media, is the idea that we can protect the nation by reducing the vulnerability of various targets. Such hardening is believed both to deter attacks (because they are less likely to be fatal or devastating) and to greatly reduce the damage (if the attacks occur anyhow). Hardening efforts include making it more difficult to inflict damage on our infrastructure (bridges, trains, electrical and chemical plants, and so on); the populace (especially by preparing and disseminating various vaccines and antidotes to biological attacks), and preventing terrorists from entering the country (through stronger border protection and better intelligence collection and sharing). These measures, most of which involve one or more industries that benefit from the billions spent on them, range from strengthening the domes that cover nuclear reactors and inspecting the cargo containers that enter the United States, to building fences and installing sensors on the borders; from introducing systems to keep track of foreign students visiting the United States, to screening many millions of phone calls.

These measures do have their place. However, the unfortunate but inescapable fact is that one can never sufficiently harden targets to provide basic security from terrorism. This is especially true in a free society. No wonder critics have a field day pointing out the many still-exposed or poorly protected targets; it's like shooting fish in a barrel. I provide here just a small sample of the extensive evidence available. It's difficult to believe that anyone reviewing these materials would persist in treating the hardening of targets as a high priority. Such endeavors serve more to make us feel secure than actually to secure us. It may sound too harsh to say that they provide faux security, but, truth be told, this is about all that they deliver.

- Much has been made recently of protecting the nation's land borders, which are still porous as a sieve. Less attention has been paid to the 12,380 miles of coastlines. To protect these would require a vast increase in the Coast Guard as well as the establishment of onshore observation and patrol posts. Very little has been done along these lines.[2]
- There are also fourteen thousand at best poorly guarded small airports in which terrorists could land, much as drug smugglers often do already with impunity.[3]
- Though Congress has voted to increase funding for port security, in 2006 a mere 6 percent of the approximately eleven million cargo con-

tainers entering U.S. ports every year were examined by the Department of Homeland Security.[4] These containers are sizable and could easily accommodate a nuclear weapon or two (and, if desired, a terrorist SWAT team as well).[5] X-raying these containers is of little use because a terrorist who is sophisticated enough to make or even simply handle such a weapon is very likely aware that shielding a bomb with lead makes it invisible to X rays.

- U.S. borders are notoriously beyond the control of our border patrol. Whole battalions of terrorists could use the same pathways that illegal immigrants follow to enter the country. Some stress that the United States must fortify not only the border with Mexico, but also with Canada, given its lax migration and asylum policies. Terrorists, however, would have to be unusually stupid or poorly financed to choose to wander through the hot desert or northern cold, knowing that there would be at least some probability of arrest by the border patrol—or of an encounter with volunteer Minutemen. Instead they can, like millions of other foreigners, obtain a tourist, student, or business visa, fly to America in the comfort of an airplane (first class if they so desire), and simply remain in the United States once their visa expires. Indeed, by several estimates as many as 40 percent of all the many millions of illegal immigrants in the United States have come and stayed in this way. When these overstayers are caught, they are likely to be released with a request to show up in court one day to face deportation hearings. Many of them simply do not appear and vanish into the huge United States underground society and economy.

- The nation's emergency rooms are "at the breaking point" even if no new pandemic, natural disaster, or terrorist attacks occur, according to a 2006 report by the prestigious Institute of Medicine.[6]

- The nation's information technology infrastructure is "highly vulnerable to terrorist and criminal attacks," a White House–appointed expert panel has concluded.[7] The panel found that "the problems of vulnerable software and easy access from afar are compounded by the lack of security in basic network protocols." Moreover, "hostile activities, such as DDoS (distributed denial of service) attacks, cyber extortion and identity theft on a massive scale have become immensely damaging to personal and economic interests."[8]

Anyone who is still unconvinced that hardening targets is at best an inadequate way to improve homeland security may be won over by a report on water contamination. Evidence has been uncovered suggesting that terrorists may be targeting municipal water systems. This evidence highlights the need for health care providers to be able to recognize unusual disease trends and early warning signs that may result from intentional contamination of water supplies. However, "many of the signs and symptoms of waterborne disease and the health effects of water pollution are nonspecific and often mimic more common medical conditions and disorders."[9] Hence the need to train hospital staff, especially those working in emergency rooms, to recognize the special signatures of terrorist-initiated plagues and to have in place rapid reporting systems. This has basically not been done.

Media reports frequently continue to call attention to lag in the introduction of various security measures in the United States, to the difficulties and costs encountered in implementing them, and so on and on. The clear implication is that, if the authorities just put their mind to it, if Congress provided the needed funds, and if the various agencies were on their toes, these measures could be put in place and we would be secure. A small sample of these headlines follows:

- "Freighted With Worry, Five Years After Sept. 11 Attacks, Jet Cargo Is Mostly Unscreened; New Study Aims to Change That"[10]
- "Screening Tools Slow to Arrive in U.S. Airports, Security Officials Cite Management Lapses"[11]
- "Setbacks Stymie Bid to Stockpile Bioterror Drugs"[12]
- "Debate Over Security for Chemical Plants Focuses on How Strict to Make Rules"[13]

Above all, hardening refers to protection from conventional attacks and not from nuclear ones, which is by far the most serious threat the nation faces. Thus, hardening is akin to locking the windows while leaving the front, back, and side doors wide open.[14]

I could go on until all the cows come home—or, until the next attack—but I hardly believe that this is necessary. Aside from the fact that there are simply too many targets that could be hit—and thus need to be protected—the costs of progressing on this front run into billions of dollars per target. The cost of protecting the airline industry alone from shoe bombs, box cutters, and nail clippers exceeds $5 billion a year.[15] These expenditures serve largely to reassure the public and to keep the airlines in business, but they do not provide safe flights. For instance, airplanes are still fully vulnerable to attacks by mobile, handheld missile launchers.[16] (There are easy-to-operate shoulder-fired Stinger missile launchers that the CIA originally provided the anti-Soviet forces in Afghanistan which have since disappeared. One of them nearly brought down an El Al flight in Kenya. In addition, "there are an estimated 500,000 [antiaircraft missiles] in the world today, many thousands of which are thought to be on the black market and therefore accessible to terrorists and other non-state actors."[17] Our civilian airlines are not protected against these; it costs too much.)[18]

A revealing docudrama entitled *Dirty War* illustrates this issue very well indeed.[19] In the program a drill was conducted in London following the explosion of a staged dirty bomb (a conventional bomb made more vicious by adding radioactive material to the explosives). The chemical hazard suits used by the first responders leaked and were too cumbersome to allow them to discharge their missions. Communication among the police, firefighters, and other government agencies did not work. The public panicked and clogged the roads while privacy laws delayed finding the terrorists still at large. When the person in charge of the British responders wanted to publicize these findings in order to mobilize greater support for preparedness measures, the higher-ranking British minister in charge of homeland security demanded that instead the report about the drill indicate that all went well. Why? She explained—quite correctly— that while this or that aspect of preparedness might be improved upon, there was no way to make London, as a whole, safe from such attacks. The best that could be done was to be sure that the public did not panic. The exchange is reminiscent of the U.S. government's promoting the duck-and-cover method of protection for schoolchildren in case of nuclear attack during the Cold War. Issuing proclamations that safety has been improved does not make the nation any safer than hiding beneath a desk. Aside from leaving us poorly protected, such faux security may make us cynical. As the public finds out that it is—again—being taken for a ride, especially on matters of such import, it becomes even more distrustful of the government and its ability to provide basic security, the first duty of a state.

Many domestic security measures also face the opposition of groups concerned with civil liberties, especially the American Civil Liberties Union (ACLU). Indeed, the concerns that these groups—and others who share their views—raise have already led to the cancellation of several homeland security measures. These include the Terrorism Information and Prevention System (known as TIPS, in which Americans were to report to the authorities about suspicious activities) and the Total Information Awareness Program (known as TIA, in which the government initiated a research project to establish whether data mining was useful for tracking terrorists).

Whether or not one agrees with the objections raised about these specific programs, most everyone would agree that we must constantly be concerned that attempting to protect homeland security by hardening targets on the domestic front will lead to curtailment of civil rights. Or, to put it another way, the more we focus on protecting ourselves by raising barriers at home on travel, communications, disclosure of information, and so on, the closer we move to a garrison state. On these grounds alone, it is best to focus security-building on some other front.

Last but not least, our corrupt political appropriations system further undermines prospects for even a semirational domestic security policy. Homeland security funds are allotted not according to places experts consider them to be most needed, but as if they were regular "pork," which goes to the districts of the most influential members of Congress rather than to those most threatened by terrorists. Thus, in 2006 funds to New York City and Washington, D.C., were cut while those for Omaha and Louisville were increased.[20] One way the political game is played is by skewing the lists of potential targets maintained by the Department of Homeland Security. These include car dealerships, bean festivals, small town parades, and check-cashing stores. At least thirty-two thousand of the seventy-seven thousand targets listed in the National Asset Database have no national significance.[21]

In short, securing the homeland by hardening targets is an inordinately difficult if not impossible task. It also imposes huge political costs and risks all of its own. I am not arguing that protecting the homeland by hardening targets cannot make any contributions to U.S. safety, especially if it leads terrorists to believe that they cannot cause massive damage. Target-hardening could also reduce the scope of the damage resulting from an attack and improve the response after an attack. Nevertheless, this front deserves the lowest priority for reasons already indicated. And it requires the introduction of triage, establishing which targets can be protected with relative ease and which targets simply cannot be protected by hardening (e.g., subways). Failure to prioritize in this manner, and unbounded optimism about one's capabilities, are symptomatic of Multiple Realism Deficiency Disorder. We delude ourselves that we can do all that needs doing and presume that setting priorities is unnecessary. Nothing could be further from the facts on the ground.

Neutralizing Terrorists

Efforts on the second front, which involves capturing or otherwise neutralizing terrorists before they reach U.S. shores or those of other targeted nations, are difficult to assess. We know a considerable amount about what are called "input" measures, but little about outcomes. Thus we know that the budget and staff of the CIA have been much increased,[22] and that Special Forces and FBI agents are now stationed in many parts of the globe.[23]

These preventive efforts are most visible in Afghanistan, but they occur in numerous other places as far apart as the Philippines, Colombia, the Horn of Africa, and Canada. The National Security Agency (NSA) screens phone calls, faxes, and e-mails around the world. The same is true for financial transactions.[24]

However, given the very high level of anti-Americanism in many parts of the world, the pool from which terrorists can be recruited is substantial. The war in Iraq has provided training and recruiting grounds for terrorists vastly superior to anything al-Qaeda had previously set up, and strongly suggests that for every terrorist neutralized, several more are ready to step in.[25] Terrorists are also learning from their experiences, improving the ways they construct bombs (e.g., bombs have become more fatal over time in Iraq), their means of communication (e.g., dispensing with satellite phones and other easily traceable devices), and their modes of organization (e.g., less centralization, which makes them more difficult to detect and neutralize).

Furthermore, one must realize that, given the worldwide increase in the number of people with technical education, there is no shortage of people who command the knowledge needed to make a variety of WMD. Last but not least, statistics favor the terrorists. As one of them put it to those who try to enhance security: "You have to be lucky all the time, we only once."[26] Like the first front, the second needs to be covered, but whatever is done cannot alone provide adequate basic security. Although there have not been attacks on U.S. soil since 9/11, Madrid and London have been hit. And anyone who believes that there will be no more attacks on the American homeland because U.S. forces are hunting down terrorists overseas should send the rest of his wish list to Santa Claus, c/o North Pole.

The Third Front: WMD?

The troubling facts laid out so far lead one to the inevitable but hard-to-accept conclusion that the world will face more terrorist attacks, and indeed these are very likely to be worse than the previous ones. Eight years elapsed between al-Qaeda's first and second attacks on the World Trade Center. The second time the number of casualties was hundreds of times higher than the first. It may well take al-Qaeda or one of its "franchises" sixteen years to strike again, but they are a patient lot. However, if the next attack increases by the same magnitude, it will take out a good part of a city.

Given that terrorist attacks *cannot* be altogether prevented, one must focus on avoiding the worst ones. To prevent the sense that we are powerless or unable to protect ourselves, to focus properly those resources we do command, we must sharply differentiate between *small-scale* terrorism, of the kind the United States and other nations have faced so far, and *massive* terrorism, which involves WMD. Small-scale terrorism, which Britain faced at the hands of the Irish Republican Army, Israel faced during the two *intifadas,* and the United States faced overseas before 9/11, is damaging enough. Its victims include not merely the hundreds of individuals involved but also people's basic sense of safety; these attacks do indeed terrorize. They have often driven governments to curtail individual rights, to everyone's loss, and they have exacted a hefty toll on the victim countries' economies. However, this kind of terrorism is almost trivial compared to the effects of an attack that could obliterate a large city.

I recognize that we are reluctant to "accept" small-scale terrorism and put at the head of our security triage list the prevention of massive attacks. Our natural inclination is to call for doing both, and more. But there are, we have seen, so many dangers posed by terrorism that we must set priorities. And among those, none comes higher than preventing attacks with weapons of mass destruction.

There is more bad news: we cannot even protect ourselves from all or most WMD! Chemical weapons can be readily made from materials found in numerous farms and industries. Timothy McVeigh, who used chemicals to make bombs to blow up the Oklahoma City Federal Building, was neither particularly well trained nor rich, nor did he have the backing of an organization like al-Qaeda. Terrorists apprehended in 2006 in Canada had accumulated three times the chemicals that McVeigh had.[27]

The United States has fifteen thousand chemical plants, most of which produce and store the kind of chemicals from which bombs can be made, such as the kind that destroyed the Oklahoma City federal office building in 1995, as well as bigger ones. There are at least one hundred and twenty-three chemical facilities in the United States that could put a million people at risk if attacked, and more than seven hundred plants that could put at least one hundred thousand people at risk.[28] Safeguarding those would keep a sizable army busy. Though it is true that some plants decreased their risk by switching to less hazardous chemicals, instituting more rigorous inventory and personnel controls, and taking measures to upgrade their security, these steps are at best just a start. The chemical industry has opposed congressional measures to tighten security further. And, of course, chemicals can be and are imported from other nations.

The same holds, only more so, for biological agents, which can be developed in thousands of labs, and possibly in someone's basement or garage. A study conducted by the Defense Threat Reduction Agency found that the equipment required to build a sophisticated biological weapon could be purchased off the Internet for less than $250,000 and would fit inside a standard two-car garage.[29] How can one possibly prevent such an attack?

The radioactive materials needed for making a dirty bomb are found in numerous medical facilities, research institutes, universities, oil wells, and some construction sites.[30]

Fortunately, the potential damage of these weapons of mass destruction is limited, with the possible exception of some biological agents. Most biological agents are difficult to weaponize, stabilize, and distribute in ways that cause massive casualties. Chemical agents are also difficult to weaponize; it is difficult to disperse them effectively in lethal concentrations on a large scale. Damage from chemical and biological weapons used by terrorists so far has been low: the 1984 Oregon Rajneeshee religious group salmonella attack sickened 751 people; the 2001 anthrax attacks sickened 22 and killed 5; the Aum Shinrikyo's 1995 sarin gas attack on the Tokyo subway system killed 12.

Even the casualties from dirty bombs would pale under most conditions in comparison to those of nuclear devices.[31] Some experts hold that such dirty bombs are just as worrisome as nuclear ones because, after all, the purpose of both is to terrorize. First, as I see it, the amount of terror that dirty bombs can generate will depend on how well the public understands their relatively limited effect before an attack. Second, the terrorizing effect of a nuclear bomb—which would kill thousands of times more people than would a dirty bomb—would be much greater. Third, a nuclear bomb would take out many more major resources than a dirty bomb could. Thus, if a nuclear weapon were exploded in Boston it could devastate some of the nation's leading universities, renowned hospitals, major financial institutions, and national monuments—a disaster that no dirty bomb could wreak under most conditions.

The True Culprit

By far the greatest danger is posed from one of kind of WMD: nuclear weapons. Experts including Ashton Carter,[32] Matthew Bunn and his associates,[33] Graham Allison,[34] George Perkovich and his associates,[35] and Charles D. Ferguson and William Potter[36] have all emphasized the danger of a nuclear attack. To gain a sense of the scale of the horror that one could cause, we must recall that the United States incinerated Hiroshima and Nagasaki with the first generation of nuclear-weapons technology available in 1945. Today the number of victims, the human and economic costs, the resulting rage, and the damage to democratic institutions resulting from a mass demand to restore safety whatever the cost—would be of a significantly higher magnitude. Lt. Gen. Robert Gard (Ret.) describes what would happen if al-Qaeda were to detonate a ten-kiloton nuclear weapon in Times Square:

> For a few moments, let's consider the unthinkable, but not un-
> likely, detonation of a ten-kiloton nuclear explosive device in
> Times Square in New York City. Mind you, a ten-kiloton weapon
> is less powerful than the weapon we used to bomb Hiroshima.
> The results in New York City:

- Within a ½ mile radius, half a million people are killed outright.
- Hundreds of thousands of others are killed or injured by collapsing buildings, fire and radioactive fallout.
- Within a ⅓ mile radius, everything is vaporized or flattened.
- Hundreds of buildings are destroyed or hollowed out in a ¾ mile radius.
- Out to 1½ miles, structures are aglow with fires and radiation for many days thereafter.
- The electromagnetic pulse generated by the blast fries all electronic communications and other devices.
- The cost will be in the trillions of dollars.[37]

A few academics have questioned the weight that I and others attach to a nuclear attack, by terrorists or by rogue states. They see no "existential" threat to the United States from such attacks; bin Laden, they say, may make life "unpleasant," but will not finish the United States off the way Hitler tried to finish off Britain,[38] not even cause a regime change, and surely not win the global war of ideas.[39] Some even conclude that terrorists should not be treated differently from garden variety criminals and that providing security should be turned over to the police and the courts. (There terrorists would have the same rights of all U.S. persons, including the right to face their accuser and see all documents relevant to their case.)

Can one count the ways to disagree? Herman Kahn, the "Dr. Strangelove" of the think tanks, argued in his book *On Thermonuclear War* that we should "think" the "unthinkable." What he meant was that Americans naïvely shied away from considering nuclear war an option. He set out to break this taboo, to make nuclear attacks acceptable. His main reason was that even if one hundred million Americans died, America would survive and regenerate.

I argued with him, face to face and in print, that the America rising from the ashes of the nation as we have known it—and rise again it well might—would be a radically different nation, a garrison state. Security would trump all other considerations; civil rights and economic efficiencies would have been cast aside. There thus would have been a real regime change; a change in American culture, morality, and polity. It would also be a nation ready to strike out at true and imagined enemies with little forethought or deliberation. In short, such an attack would have horrible consequences not merely for America but for most if not all other states.

The same holds true if the terrorists took out most of New York, Washington, or even "merely" Chicago. America would survive the same way someone whose eyes have been gouged out and ears severed and leg amputated would continue to exist. But it would be a nation at least as vengeful as Germany was after World War I, and one that would look to strong-armed leaders to take the helm. It would not be the same America. It would continue to exist but would have a radically different existence.

In toto, preventing attacks by WMD is by far the most important front in the war against terrorism. Still, even this front also requires triage. We may have to neglect efforts to prevent attacks from many chemical and even biological and radioactive sources to focus on nuclear (and select biological) ones. Deliberations on the subject would benefit if the phrase "weapons of mass destruction" could be avoided, because it conceals the fact that not all WMD are even nearly of the same caliber. Given that the main danger of a massive and debilitating attack lies in the use of nuclear weapons, not in chemical or most biological weapons, the proper notation for what must be our first priority should be preventing "Nb" attacks—the capital N standing for nuclear, the gravest source of danger, and the lower case b for a smaller subcategory of biological agents that might be used effectively for massive attacks. (Experts hold that some "designer bugs" could plunge a society into an epidemic comparable to the 1918 flu, one for which there would be no cure at the time.)

CHAPTER B. WHO WILL ATTACK?

The Worst Rogues

The White House, Congress, and the media have focused heavily on the so-called Axis of Evil when dealing with WMD in general and nukes in particular. Since the introduction of this term, attention has been focused on three rogue states: North Korea, Iran, and Saddam's Iraq. The 2003 invasion of Iraq, justified initially to prevent Iraq from using or acquiring further WMD, sharpened this focus. As I see it, the combination of terrorism and nuclear weapons poses a graver threat to international security than do the North Korean and Iranian regimes (and than the Iraqi regime did), although these can hardly be ignored. Senator Richard Lugar believes that "the minimum standard for victory in this war is the prevention of any terrorist cell from obtaining weapons or materials of mass destruction."[40] Terrorists—not rogue states.

Terrorists are likely to draw on the failing states (such as Russia, Ukraine, Pakistan, Ghana, and Nigeria), in which nuclear weapons and/or materials are readily available for purchase or can be otherwise acquired. "The prospect that a nuclear-capable state may lose control of some of its weapons to terrorists is one of the greatest dangers the United States and its allies face," warns the Defense Department's Quadrennial Defense Review report. That report states that, at its core, the problem is one of "internal instability."[41]

There are several reasons nuclear terrorism is more challenging than nuclear attacks by rogue states and thus deserves much more attention and a greater dedication of resources than it currently receives. First of all, the list of rogue states is small, well known, and their actions can be monitored. The opposite holds true for terrorists: their number is large, their identity is unknown, and their actions are difficult to track. Second, rogue states are easier to deter from using their nuclear arms than are terrorists, especially those willing to commit suicide, for which more than a few have shown themselves ready. It is true that the leaders of some rogue states could act irrationally or simply miscalculate by believing that their regimes could survive if they hit the United States with nuclear weapons—or if it became known that they provided terrorists with such arms. After all, the Japanese believed when they attacked Pearl Harbor that they could best the United States. However, miscalculations of the magnitude that would lead a Kim Jong Il to use nuclear weapons are exceedingly unlikely.

In contrast, if terrorists acquired the material to make nuclear weapons or the weapons themselves, they would fear neither retaliation nor be deterred by a balance of terror. Indeed, terrorists often hold that if their attacks lead to retaliatory attacks on their homelands, support for their cause will only increase. Moreover, because terrorists are not the army of any one state, it is often difficult to determine which nation to retaliate against. (This was all too evident when the United States learned after 9/11 that most of the terrorists involved in that attack hailed from its ally, Saudi Arabia.)

In short, there are several strong reasons to rank the danger of nuclear terrorism higher than the danger of nuclear strikes by rogue states. Yet since 9/11, U.S. foreign policy, military, and intelligence agencies have focused on dealing with rogue nuclear states, both alleged and real, and specifically with the Axis of Evil, and not on several scores of sites from which terrorists could acquire nuclear materials and arms, mainly in failing states.

Most rogue states are totalitarian; hence, there is only one leader to address and only one party with which to deal and counter. In contrast, failing states are those in which the government is ineffectual, not truly in control. The absence of an effective government allows various governmental agencies (such as the secret services and branches of the armed forces), key individuals (generals, industrialists, scientists), and still others to wheel and deal with nuclear arms and materials on their own. Given the large number and great diversity of these so-called non-state actors, they are more difficult to keep track of—much less to contain—than a rogue state.

What *Can* Be Done

If one accepts that the main threat to our security is on the third front, an attack that unleashes WMD—and among these WMD the greatest danger is posed by nukes possessed by terrorists—*neutralizing this threat ought to be accorded the highest priority.* The good news is that *unlike all the other missions outlined so far, this one is limited and can be accomplished in relatively short order and without huge budgetary outlays.*

Nowhere is this lack of a comprehensive, thought-out security strategy more evident than in the more than $5 billion spent every year on ensuring that no one will carry a pocket knife or a full bottle of shampoo onto an airplane—while keeping the level of funding for neutralizing—blending down—nuclear explosives and securing nuclear arms across the world at more or less the same as it was before 9/11, at *about a fifth* of the airline security budget.[42]

The main reason seems to be psychological, part of faux security. People are concerned about the places the last attacks occurred, rather than where the next ones are most likely to occur; they can see the Transportation Security Administration (TSA) agents at work but not failures to blend down the materials from which bombs are made overseas or failures to guard nuclear bombs. People cannot see how little work has been done to reduce the threat of attacks with nukes in Russia's "closed cities" or in the recesses of the Pakistani army. It is hence easy to see the reasons security priorities are misplaced, but it is unforgivable that there have been few serious attempts to educate the public as to where the true risks lie and what can—and must—be done.

I rush to admit that "educating the public" is one of those statements that rolls easily off the tongue but is hard to accomplish, and that everyone has his own list of what he believes the public "must" know. When I served in the White House, at least once a week some public leader urged the president to give a speech or a Roosevelt-style fireside chat—which they were sure would suffice to teach the people whatever they judged that the people needed to know. To make such an endeavor more plausible, however, public education must be focused sharply; it may well start by stressing that security's highest priority should be the removal of fissile materials and nuclear weapons from failing states—or neutralization by blending them down—and ensuring that no new states obtain them.[43]

Terrorists can gain nuclear weapons from those who have them ready-made, or they can make them out of highly enriched uranium (HEU). HEU fuel enriched to 90 percent or more, which is widely used in nuclear research reactors around the world, should be considered weapons-grade uranium (WGU).[44] In contrast, if only low-enriched uranium (LEU), enriched less than 20 percent, is available, then further enrichment of it would require facilities, resources, and skills of a significant order. Moreover, because such enrichment requires sizable facilities, such activity is more difficult to conceal if conducted by terrorists than by a rogue state.

Hence, to limit the danger of massive terrorism, the focus ought to be on the sources from which terrorists can obtain nuclear arms or WGU, which they are more likely to procure in failing states than from rogue states.

In short, failing states are more dangerous and deserve higher priority than rogue states, which—to reiterate—are currently the center of attention to the extent that attention is paid to nuclear terrorism at all.

The Leading Failure: Russia

I have already pointed out that the United States has used much of whatever leverage it had over Russia to encourage it to continue to democratize rather than to contribute to global security. Russia continues to be the country in which thousands of small, tactical nuclear arms are insufficiently guarded and in which very large amounts of WGU is readily available from both military and civilian sources. Experts estimate that "95% of all nuclear weapons and materials outside the U.S. are in Russia."[45]

Small nukes: In 1997 President Boris Yeltsin's former national security adviser, Alexander Lebed, reported that eighty-four suitcase-sized nuclear weapons went missing in the U.S.S.R., causing worldwide consternation. These reports were never verified, and in 2002 Lebed was killed in an airplane crash. Russian officials denied Lebed's claims of missing nuclear weapons and even the existence of such miniaturized nukes, and the U.S. State Department said that it accepted these assurances as valid, noting that there was "no cause for concern."[46] There is, however, no doubt that the Russian army has many thousands of small, tactical nuclear bombs and that these are deployed under the control of local commanders in areas close to Russia's borders, including borders with unstable republics in the south.[47] Unlike strategic nuclear arms concentrated in the center of Russia, tactical ones are much less securely guarded. This is of particular concern because Russian commanders include quite a few who, in seeking to enrich themselves, are not above making side deals with criminals.

Russia's interests, and those of the United States and the rest of the world, would be well served if the number of tactical nuclear arms could be reduced significantly. Hence they should be included in the U.S.-Russian Strategic Arms Reduction Treaty (START). This treaty has been successful in curtailing the number of long-range missiles and heavy-duty nuclear warheads but does not encompass the "small" stuff—the kind that terrorists seek.

In addition, these small nukes should be subject to the same control systems that cover strategic weapons, i.e., they should be equipped with locks that prevent their use without authorization from the highest civilian authorities.

Loose WGU: There is many times more loose WGU, plutonium, and spent fuel in Russia than in all the other failing states combined: "Russia has declared 500 metric tons of highly enriched uranium in excess to its national security needs. By December 31, 2004, 231.5 metric tons of Russian weapons-grade uranium, the equivalent of 9,261 nuclear warheads, has been recycled into fuel or use in commercial U.S. nuclear power plants under an ongoing U.S.-Russian deal.[48] Even after being fully implemented by 2013 the deal will cover less than 40 percent of existing Russian HEU stocks. Additional HEU elimination efforts to speed up the destruction of this highly proliferation attractive material are thus highly desirable and urgently needed."[49]

Unfortunately, concerns about the security of Russian nuclear materials and facilities are far from theoretical. Out of 660 illicit trafficking incidents recorded in the Stanford Database on Nuclear Smuggling, Theft and Orphan Radiation Sources (DSTO), at least 370 either took place in the former Soviet Union or involved material that had reportedly originated from those parts.[50]

In *Securing the Bomb 2006* Matthew Bunn and Anthony Wier comprehensively address current nuclear materials security issues; they highlight several examples. They record an incident in Russia in the mid-1990s in which an unknown outsider walked through a large hole in a fence, broke a padlock on a shed, removed a quantity of HEU, and left the facility, all without detection. In another instance they note how "a single insider with no particular plan" was successful in "repeatedly removing small amounts of HEU and walking out without detection."[51] Examples in this vein are legion:

> According to the IAEA [International Atomic Energy Agency], 18 cases involving the theft of plutonium and uranium have occurred over the last decade, many of which originated from the former Soviet Union. The vast majority of incidents confirmed by states involve plutonium or HEU in far too limited quantities to produce a nuclear explosive device. However, it is possible that terrorist groups have accumulated some small quantities of fissile material, and it is also possible that black market HEU that has been intercepted may represent only a small portion of larger quantities that are still available for sale.
>
> In December 1998 the Russian Federal Security Services intercepted an attempt to divert 18.5 kg of "radioactive materials that might have been used in the production of nuclear weapons."[52] Russian officials, stating that the perpetrators "could have done serious damage to the Russian state," later confirmed

this attempt, and made it the first confirmed case that apparently involved a conspiracy to steal enough materials for a bomb in a single act. The material involved was fresh HEU.[53]

Instead of transporting from a number of other nations to Russia the material from which nuclear bombs can be made, they should be transported to the West. Ukraine and Belarus were among the sites from which nuclear bombs were moved to Russia. Among the sites from which WGU and plutonium were shipped to Russia were Serbia, Romania, and Bulgaria. I realize that transferring them to Russia has been one of the second-worst scenarios; the worst alternative would have been to leave them in even less stable states. And it is true that Russia is blending down a good part of these materials and selling the resulting fuel to the United States, which uses it in American power plants. However, given the conditions in Russia and the deterioration of its relationship with the United States, whenever possible blending down facilities should be developed in the West, and, above all, nukes should be destroyed rather than shipped to Russia.

During the 2006 G-8 meeting in St. Petersburg, President Bush and President Putin jointly announced a plan for civilian nuclear cooperation. The plan unwisely grants permission for Russia to receive still *more* radioactive materials by allowing it to reprocess U.S.-controlled spent fuel.[54] U.S. policy should be oriented toward removing spent fuel and other radioactive material from Russia, not placing more in Russia's failing care.

Strong negative social trends in Russia compound the risks already laid out. The United Nations Development Program's Human Development Index (HDI) ranks Russia low indeed among developed nations. The deterioration of Russia is evident in areas including infectious disease, homicide rates, suicide rates, dietary- and lifestyle-related illness, and, perhaps most importantly as far as the issues at hand are concerned, "a breakdown in state institutions dealing with law, order, and security."[55]

The budget for the Nunn-Lugar Cooperative Threat Reduction Program, which Congress approved to secure nuclear arms and materials in the former Soviet Union, hence needs to be considerably increased and refocused. The funds are still hovering just over the $1-billion mark, the same amount that was earmarked before the 2001 attack on American soil; moreover, the mission of the program has since been expanded.

Initially it was limited to Russia and the former republics of the Soviet Union. Congress has since allowed the agencies involved (Defense, State, and the Department of Energy) also to spend funds in other nations. Funds were used, for instance, to secure chemical arms in Albania. To expand a mission but not the requisite funds is not exactly the best way to ensure progress.

The Nunn-Lugar program was initially dedicated to reducing the dangers left over from the Cold War, especially the dismantling of long-range intercontinental ballistic missiles and submarine launchers. Over the years, a good part of the funding was redirected to the new antiterrorism goals, but roughly a third is still dedicated to the old ones. Dismantling Cold War arms is a good idea, but the low priority accorded to fighting nuclear terrorism is a grave and serious error. Ergo, unless the budget of the Nunn-Lugar program is significantly increased, it would make a great deal of sense to dedicate all of its resources to the prevention of nuclear terrorism.

Over the course of Putin's administration the Russian state has become more authoritarian and less democratic. This development would at first seem to be a security gain, because authoritarian governments are typically better able to make security arrangements stick than failing ones, at least in the short run. However, this is not what is actually happening in Russia.

A major difficulty is that the Russian government does not see a problem where Americans and others do. Russians who deal with security are repeatedly reported as scoffing at the idea that terrorists—even those in Chechnya—could acquire nuclear weapons.[56] They hence oppose many of the security measures the United States has suggested. For instance, there are about sixty nuclear reactors in Russia that use WGU for civilian purposes.[57] Russia explicitly excluded them from an agreement to convert reactors to LEU or some other fuel, to take place in other nations that Russia (and the United States) previously supplied with WGU.

Russia under Putin has also increased the difficulties faced by Americans who work on nuclear security as part of the Nunn-Lugar program—by limiting the number of Americans who can gain access to sensitive sites (or so-called closed cities), the times they can visit, and the number of places they are allowed to visit.[58]

Worse still, Russia is experiencing a shortage of people willing to work and live in the often remote closed cities, in which many of the relevant facilities are located. Russia hence makes use of immigrants, including many from the former Soviet republics to the south—Kazakhstan, Uzbekistan, Turkmenistan, and Kyrgyzstan—which have large Muslim populations. The fact that many Russians are often contemptuous of these immigrants (the way many Europeans are) is one reason these workers are often alienated and hence hardly reliable personnel to work in such sensitive places. In addition, U.S. funds to build more secure facilities typically end up in the pockets of some of the most corrupt industries in Russia, such as construction. There can be little confidence, then, that work is properly completed.

Robert Orttung and Louise Shelley maintain a center at American University that collects data on corruption, crime, and drug abuse among the Russian personnel assigned to the protection of nuclear arms and fissile materials from which they can be made. These researchers are paying special attention to the closed cities in which many of these facilities are housed. The following draws directly on their findings about one province, the Chelyabinsk oblast,[59] where the Mayak plant is located. Large numbers of former convicts from the Caucasus and Central Asia are now located in this region. (In Soviet times such people were banned from the closed cities.) Most criminals care little what they trade in, and hence they could readily trade in nuclear materials. The researchers also found that drug addiction has increased significantly since it first spread in the closed cities on a massive scale in the late 1990s. By 1999, Ozersk had the most drug users per capita in Russia, including many employees of the Mayak plant. It goes without saying that addicts and their dealers constitute a security risk.

As of the beginning of 2005, Islamist extremists were active among "the Muslim Tatar and Bashkir populations that surround the closed cities of Snezhinsk and Ozersk. Among the ethnic groups from which military conscripts guarding the closed cities are drawn, the second and third largest are Tatars and Bashkirs, the groups targeted by extremist recruiters."[60] Not all the news is disheartening—in recent years the Russians have been utilizing vehicles given to them by the United States for transportation of nuclear arms; these vehicles are more secure than those they relied on previously.

In sum, there is little reason to doubt that Russia is very much a failing state as far as effective control of nuclear arms and materials is concerned, that the conditions are deteriorating, and that the Nunn-Lugar program has not been accorded the resources or priority called for if this major—potentially leading—source for nuclear terrorism is to be shut down.

Pakistan

Among failing states other than Russia, Pakistan ranks high as a state from which terrorists are likely to be able to obtain ready-made nuclear weapons—either by toppling the government, by cooperating with certain elements inside the government, or by corrupting those who guard the bombs.[61] Indeed, the poor security of its nuclear weapons—and the fact that Pakistanis have been selling nuclear designs and technologies to other countries—is largely ignored, presumably because of Pakistan's help in dealing with conventional terrorism. This was highlighted in 2003 when the United States basically ignored the fact that the Pakistani government did little to curb its top nuclear scientist, A. Q. Khan, from serving as the central figure of a very extensive transnational black market of nuclear materials and parts. And when the United States exposed the "nuclear Wal-Mart" Khan was running, the Pakistani government claimed that his actions were illicit but did little to punish Khan. Moreover, the Pakistani government has steadfastly refused to grant the United States access to Khan. The United States has not pressed the issue because of Pakistani cooperation in the "war on terror."[62]

In assessing the situation in Pakistan I am drawing on a report by Thomas Donnelly, a resident fellow at the American Enterprise Institute.[63] He reports:

> Kahuta [a major weapon facility] is a massive complex east of Islamabad, with dozens of buildings reportedly housing 3,000 centrifuges. It is said to produce enough material to make three to six warheads per year. While estimates vary, Pakistan's total inventory of highly enriched uranium is something on the order of 1,000 kilograms, enough material for approximately sixty fission devices. In addition, during the 1990's, Pakistan began construction of a research reactor at Khushab that was capable of producing plutonium and perhaps tritium—key ingredients in the production of smaller nuclear devices. Overall, the Carnegie

Endowment for International Peace has estimated that Pakistan's nuclear weapons, nuclear testing, and civilian nuclear and related facilities extend to nearly two dozen sites clustered in the Punjab and centered in Islamabad. These sites may also be as far away as Karachi, where the Canadian-supplied KANUPP reactor provides power to the city.[64]

Donnelly further observes:

All in all, Pakistan maintains a relatively small amount of nuclear material, which it guards closely; under U.S. pressure, formal command and control mechanisms have been improved. Still, the possibilities of an "insider job" from those in the Pakistani nuclear establishment with radical Islamic sympathies can no longer be dismissed out of hand. For that, thank A. Q. Khan.

   . . . Experts differ as to how complicit the Pakistani military may have been in the creation and running of the networks that included North Korea, Libya, and Iran, but in many ways the more disturbing interpretation would be that Khan operated without the army's knowledge. The civilian prime ministers of the era, Benazir Bhutto and Nawaz Sharif, were both extraordinarily weak, though in different ways. Although Khan's nuclear programs were nominally under civilian control, Khan enjoyed a large degree of autonomy during times of military rule.

   While Khan's clients and potential clients were states— possibly including the Taliban's Afghanistan[65]—the nature of his networks and motivations remains as opaque as Pakistan itself. Khan had an undeniable profit motive, but there was more: he was "also motivated by pan-Islamism and hostility to Western controls on nuclear technology."[66] These two traits—pan-Islamism and resentment of Western constraints on Pakistani strength—are part of what make Khan a figure of Pakistani pride.[67]

All this goes to show the danger of nuclear arms and material in failing states, in which entrepreneurs like Khan can act both on their own and in cooperation with elements of the government, in disregard of national policy. "By turning the bomb into a marketable commodity, Mr. Khan and his network helped sweep away the barriers to entry into the nuclear business. Parts of the network have been shut down. Others are still operating. And, as with any profitable venture, there will be imitators."[68]

The United States chose to ignore this danger because it was instead focused on capturing bin Laden, and Pakistan had just launched a new drive to help find the terrorist leader President Bush had promised to capture "dead or alive" as early as 2001. This is like letting a serial killer go because he promised to help catch a drunk driver.

Taken together, all this evidence points to the need for a radical shift in priorities from small-scale to massive terrorism and from rogue states to the sources from which terrorists might readily acquire nuclear materials or ready-made bombs.

And Many More

In addition to Pakistan and Russia, there are a considerable number of other failing states, such as Nigeria, Ghana, Ukraine, and Kyrgyzstan, in addition to countries that might conceivably turn into failing states in short order, such as Egypt or Thailand. These nations have scores of sites from which terrorists can purchase or steal WGU, because nuclear reactors were set up in these countries for the purposes of producing energy, conducting medical treatments, and research. For example, four metric tons of spent HEU of Russian origin are found in twenty reactors in seventeen different countries, and forty metric tons of HEU of U.S. origin are in more than forty locations around the world. In addition, one hundred and five civilian research reactors all over the world are using HEU.[69] Still other countries, including China and France, have provided various nations with reactors and HEU.

It is an irony of history that many of the nuclear reactors that now need to be defanged were built by the U.S. government under President Eisenhower. After the United States used nuclear bombs to end World War II in Japan, Eisenhower was under public pressure to show that the United States was not a malevolent force.[70] His administration therefore offered to help various nations set up nuclear reactors for civilian purposes by means of a plan called Atoms for Peace. The U.S.S.R. also provided a considerable number of reactors to countries across the globe, as it was competing with the United States for influence. Over the past sixty years a total of 655 such reactors were built for research alone. True, many of these have been decommissioned or hold only small amounts of HEU. Nonetheless there were about 247 "hot spots" as of October 2006.[71] Most of these sites are poorly guarded.[72]

All this was supposed to be "history"; the nuclear-weapon states supposedly learned from their past mistakes. They would no longer provide the potentially dangerous combination of new reactors and HEU, particularly in failing states. However, in 2004 China aided Nigeria in the construction of a nuclear research reactor fueled by HEU in the city of Zaria.[73]

Experts have suggested various remedies to deal with the problems at hand. Mainly these involve (a) converting the reactors to types that function using LEU that cannot be used to make nuclear arms;[74] (b) replacing them with heavy water reactors that usually do not make use of highly enriched uranium;[75] (c) providing the nations involved with other sources of energy; (d) or compensating the nations and entities involved for the losses of giving up the dangerous plants and materials.

More than five years after 9/11, rather little has been done to deal with nuclear reactors in failing states other than Russia. An initiative to speed up efforts to remove HEU from these reactors around the world and replace the fuel with non-weapons-grade uranium was announced by the U.S. Department of Energy in 2004. However, only $20 million was allocated for these deproliferation programs in their first year, arguably enough to convert *one* of the more than two hundred sites that require conversion.

In short, the United States and its allies continue to adhere to a failing policy for failing states. The preceding would be just one more narrative about government incompetence, lack of focus, and prioritization—if the consequences did not entail leaving the door wide open to nuclear terrorism. Meanwhile, at airport security lines we carefully screen and search handicapped people and senior citizens making their way with walkers.

There Are No "Good" Governments

To foster the deproliferation norm it is essential to discourage nations that do not command nuclear arms, or the material from which they can be made, from acquiring them. Because this security goal has the highest priority, it should not be sacrificed to advance other, less pressing policy goals. Moreover, the notion that there are "good" governments that can be trusted with nuclear bombs and fissile materials is illusory. True, some governments are very unlikely to employ these means of war, but governments come and go; the next government may be much more aggressive than the last one. It is easy to imagine a much more nationalistic government gaining power in India, for example. And revolutions do occur that bring about sudden regime changes, the result of which might bring to power a Hugo Chavez–like anti-American head of state in Brazil.

In 2004 Brazil and the IAEA disagreed for six months over inspectors' access to Brazil's uranium enrichment program. This occurred following reports that Brazil was renewing its interest in nuclear arms. During the course of the standoff, Secretary of State Colin Powell said, "The United States understands that Brazil has no interest in a nuclear weapon, no desire and no plans, no programs, no intention of moving toward a nuclear weapon."[76] The disagreements were resolved amicably, but the American position implied that governments seen as trustworthy by the United States could ignore the deproliferation norms without repercussions.

Particularly troubling from the viewpoint of establishing a deproliferation norm was the deal made with India in 2006 (by the Bush administration and approved by Congress) that would provide India with more nuclear fuels and technology. India promises to use these materials exclusively for civilian reactors. However, by utilizing these nuclear assets India can use its existing, limited stockpiles of uranium for military purposes without depriving the civilian sector. The deal also rewards a nation that refused to submit even to the limited controls the Nuclear Non-Proliferation Treaty stipulates. The fact that India promised it would place a majority (fourteen out of twenty-two) of its existing and planned power reactors under permanent IAEA safeguards by 2014 is akin to providing a child with dessert before he eats his spinach. India is going to benefit from U.S. civilian nuclear assistance in the near future, but there is ample time between the current agreement and 2014 to renegotiate what India must do.[77]

The Center for Arms Control and Non-Proliferation put it well: "The agreement rewards bad behavior and fails to devalue nuclear weapons. . . . The agreement creates a double standard in the international community. . . . The agreement undermines the Nuclear Non-Proliferation Treaty."[78] Senator Joseph Biden nailed it: "We must not assist [India]'s nuclear weapons program . . . not because India is an adversary, which it is not, but because nuclear non-proliferation is a vital U.S. national interest, as well as a formal treaty obligation."[79] But it was left to Mohamed ElBaradei, director general of the IAEA, to put it best: "For an international atomic super-power to tell other nations not to develop nuclear weapons is like dangling a cigarette from your mouth and telling everybody to stop smoking."[80]

As expected, other nations responded to the expanding Indian pro-gram by expanding their own nuclear programs. Pakistan in particular extended both the civilian and military components of its nuclear pro-gram. Currently it can make several nuclear weapons per year; but some experts estimate that Pakistan's new Khushab II plutonium reactor will be capable of producing twenty to fifty nuclear weapons per year.[81] While there is no date certain for the completion of the new reactor, it has already raised concerns about a potential arms race in South Asia. Thus the claim that the United States-India nuclear deal undermines the al-ready weak norm favoring deproliferation has been substantiated.

CHAPTER C. A STRATEGIC SHIFT:
FROM CONTROLLED MAINTENANCE TO DEPROLIFERATION

I cannot repeat it often enough: preventing a massive nuclear terrorist attack ought to be our first priority in the war against terrorism, and in advancing the Security First strategy. To be successful in preventing such a catastrophic attack, we must adopt a radical change in our approach to proliferation.[82] The sources from which terrorists could gain nuclear ma-terial or bombs should be *eliminated* rather than kept under one form of *control* or another, because such controls are inherently unreliable. Con-trols, which rely on inspections to ensure that nuclear facilities and mate-rials are used merely for nonmilitary purposes (and are kept on site but are better guarded), have repeatedly failed. Again and again inspectors have failed to discover clandestine use of civilian nuclear facilities for bomb making and diversion of fissile material.

Those who might think that my thesis—a shift from control to re-moval of bombs and blending down of fissionable materials—is a vision-ary idea should note that such policy has been followed in dealing with nuclear bombs in Ukraine and Belarus, among others, and with the nu-clear materials that were removed from Serbia. As already reported, one of the few silver linings of the nuclear mess in Russia is the "Megatons to

Megawatts" project, which does blend down fissile material. Mohamed ElBaradei suggests, "Either we begin finding creative, outside-the-box solutions or the international nuclear safeguards regime will become obsolete."[83]

I refer to the preferred new approach as "deproliferation," which contrasts with "controlled maintenance," a form of arms control. In the latter case nations are allowed to keep nuclear reactors that use weapons-grade fissile material but are expected to guard them well against terrorists and unauthorized use, and have the nonmilitary usages of these facilities and material verified by inspections.

In contrast, deproliferation entails replacing fissile material with other resources that cannot be used for bomb making and moving plutonium from failing states to safe havens and blending it down. Similarly, spent fuel must also be disposed of. Deproliferation also entails preventing new nations from obtaining nuclear bombs and the materials from which they can be made, and using all means available to dislodge them from those who have them, especially failing states. The main issue is not whether one adds to the policy mix this or that item, but whether one accepts that one needs to *change the overarching norm that guides policy from controlled maintenance to deproliferation.*

We should rely ever more on deproliferation policies and foster the norms that support them, leading to the formation of a new international regime in all matters nuclear, to the extent that this is practical. I add the last phrase acknowledging that in several situations continued reliance on controlled maintenance may well be the best that can be achieved; that a mixture of policies and norms of both kinds is likely to persist in the foreseeable future; and that the best one can aspire to is to shift to an ever greater reliance on deproliferation. Still, there is merit in having a clearer vision of the desired end state, even if it cannot be realized in the foreseeable future.

I turn next to spell out this approach to what is the greatest security risk.

The Current Approach: Controlled Maintenance

Many of the best policymakers and analysts still strongly support the Nuclear Non-Proliferation Treaty (NPT), and their hopes for a safer world rely on it. They labor to entice or pressure nations such as Iran and North

Korea to join the treaty or abide by its terms. Generally the supporters of the NPT are considered the good citizens of the international community, and those who evade it the aberrant ones. Although the supporters of the NPT recognize its limitations, they favor improving it rather than shifting however gradually to a different strategy. When the NPT's basic concept is questioned—given that it was conceived in a world in which states were the main actors, not terrorists—they tend to bristle.

The NPT is basically based on the controlled maintenance idea, although it has elements of deproliferation that are not always evident. The NPT divides countries into nuclear-weapon states (NWS) and non-nuclear-weapon states (NNWS), and places specific restraints on each type. The NWS, identified as the United States, Russia, China, France and the United Kingdom, must agree to pursue disarmament, while the NNWS must agree not to develop or attempt to acquire nuclear weapons. The IAEA is entrusted with inspections to verify that "safeguarded nuclear material and activities are not used for military purposes."[84]

In the terms used here, the NPT did and does apply a deproliferation strategy *as far as nuclear arms are concerned,* prohibiting states that did not possess nuclear arms from acquiring them, and requiring the five that did to give them up gradually. At the same time, the NPT applies the controlled maintenance strategy to nuclear *assets* (reactors, centrifuges, fissile material, and so on). The treaty assumes that the governments signing it are responsible actors who will live up to their international obligations and behave as good citizens of the world community, and that limited inspections will therefore suffice to verify that they are trustworthy.

Since the inception of the NPT, the deproliferation part of the treaty, as applied to nuclear arms, has been quite successful. Few formerly non-nuclear nations acquired nuclear weapons, and those that did were mainly the small number that never subscribed to the treaty in the first place (India, Pakistan, and Israel). Several states that began weapon programs were discouraged from advancing them, including Argentina, Brazil, South Korea, and Taiwan. Other nations concluded on their own that their interests were best served by not acquiring nuclear arms. The five NWS (sometimes referred to as the members of the nuclear club) reduced their arsenals, thus arguably living up to the letter of the treaty but not, many observers hold, to its spirit, which called for full elimination.

As far as dual-use nuclear assets—those that can be used for both

civilian and military purposes—are concerned, where controlled maintenance was practiced, inspection turned out to be inadequate to ensure
that these assets were used only for nonmilitary purposes. In several key
instances activities banned under the NPT took place on a small scale
despite inspections in South Korea and Egypt, and on a larger scale in Iraq
(prior to 1991), Libya, Iran, and North Korea.[85]

One must note that any system that relies on inspections, however
fortified with new technologies, gives a strategic advantage to those who
are inspected over those who rely on the validity of the inspections. Indeed, inspections clearly constitute a case of information asymmetry. This
is the case because those who conceal the production of arms or the arms
themselves have an almost unlimited number of sites to place or disperse
their wares and a great variety of methods and ways to conceal them, often
in very sizable territories, including high mountain ranges and extensive
natural caves. Arms-producing nations also enjoy a wide variety of ways to
lead inspectors to pursue misleading and diverting clues. In contrast, the
inspectors, mostly from other nations and cultures, are limited in numbers, resources, capacity, and access. In short, the odds are stacked against
inspectors in favor of those who violate the letter and spirit of the NPT.

Moreover, for inspectors to have a better idea of the nuclear activities
of each of the seventy-one states with significant nuclear programs, these
states have to establish an additional protocol with the IAEA. Forty-seven
states do not yet have these protocols in force, and nineteen have not even
signed such a protocol.[86] Absurdly, even today nations can still establish
nuclear facilities using HEU with the full blessing of the United Nations,
as Nigeria—a failing state—did. This last fact, which received practically
no attention from policymakers, analysts, or the media, is a prime example of the misfocused nature of the war against terrorism.

Most importantly, international conditions have gradually changed,
especially following the end of the Cold War. These changes include (a)
the rise of non-state actors, especially terrorists who actively seek to acquire nuclear arms or the material from which they can be made;[87] (b) the
emergence of a "nuclear Wal-Mart," in which private parties as well as
some governments illicitly trade in dual-use nuclear assets materials,
exemplified by A. Q. Khan's dealings with North Korea, Iran, and Libya;
and (c) a substantial increase in the number of failed and failing states
that are unable to control effectively the nuclear assets and arms in their

territories, especially most of the fifteen former Soviet republics. Unstable governments also gained power in states that have HEU and other nuclear assets, including Pakistan, Ghana, the Congo, and Nigeria.[88]

These developments have led major scholars[89] to call for various policies that, if combined, would amount to deproliferation, not just for nuclear arms—but also for dual-use nuclear assets. In short, the NPT was meant to regulate states—assuming that they had effective governments that could control their own territories. To deal with terrorists and failing states, a new approach is needed. The pre-9/11 conception of controlled maintenance must be replaced by one of deproliferation.

A Distinct Approach: Deproliferation

Deproliferation ultimately aims to:

a) Upgrade security at facilities that store nuclear arms and fissile materials but only as a temporary measure, rather than as part of a lasting solution. The reason I say "temporary," and in general emphasize upgraded security much less than do other analysts (although I recognize its importance), is because the best security is that which removes these items once and for all from the reach of terrorists and other security threats. Rather than upgrading security in facilities in failing states, fissile material, and when possible, nuclear arms, should be blended down or dismantled.

b) Expropriate fissile materials to safe havens and blend them down in such havens rather than doing so on location.

c) Replace all HEU with LEU, which in effect cannot be used in making bombs.

d) Prevent transnational trade and transportation of nuclear bombs and the materials from which they can be made.

e) Prevent the construction of new facilities that use HEU, rather than condone such construction as legal and legitimate (as it currently is under the NPT).

f) Offer rogue states to "trade" nonaggression treaties and arrangements for giving up their nuclear arms programs, an approach discussed in detail in Part I.

It is best to think about controlled maintenance and deproliferation as pure concepts, what social scientists refer to as "ideal types." In reality, these two approaches are mixed in the sense that even under the NPT, which is largely based on the controlled maintenance approach, some deproliferation took place (for instance in South Africa and Brazil). Also, as more nations shifted to deproliferation, some controlled maintenance is likely to prove unavoidable. *Hence, the argument that a major strategic shift ought to occur from controlled maintenance to deproliferation refers to a shift in the prevailing norm, economic resources, and political capital, recognizing that such a shift will inevitably be gradual.*

Can Deterrence Suffice?

Some advocates of the obsolete NPT approach fear, not without reason, that deproliferation may lead to confrontations between the major powers and those nations that refuse to give up their nuclear arms or dual-use nuclear assets. These advocates suggest that it is sufficient to rely on deterrence in the future, even when dealing with new nuclear powers and with non-state actors, terrorists included.[90] After all, it is argued that the United States and the U.S.S.R. kept each other at bay in this fashion for several decades. Pakistan and India may well deter each other; North Korea might be deterred by a nuclear Japan; and Iran will be deterred by Israel and Saudi Arabia. These countries should hence be admitted into the nuclear club so long as they assume the same commitments as other NWS states under the NPT.

This approach has several serious flaws. First, it invites more nations to build the facilities they need to make or purchase nuclear arms and their means of delivery. The larger the number of these states, the greater the probability that sooner or later one of them will use these weapons, due to miscalculations, instability, or unauthorized use.[91] The United States and the U.S.S.R. came close to nuclear blows several times, as did India and Pakistan, and Israel came dangerously close to using missiles armed with nuclear warheads during the Six Day War.[92]

Moreover, this approach reinforces the notion that nations must have nuclear arms to be serious powers, as exemplified by the 2004 temptation of Brazil to violate its commitments to the NPT regime. (Its president complained that Brazil is armed with slingshots while other nations are armed with cannons.)[93] Egypt, Indonesia, and Vietnam are also itching to join the nuclear club.[94] Above all, the more nations that are in this dangerous business, the more sources there are for terrorists to gain nuclear weapons. After all, terrorists cannot obtain nuclear arms or materials from countries that do not have any. Hence, trying to bring more nations into compliance with the NPT—the current governing strategy—is of limited value. Trying to monitor dangerous materials is vastly more dangerous than preventing access to them in the first place.

As a matter of fact, deproliferation is quite possible; indeed, it is increasingly practiced! However, it is not yet viewed as a distinctly new strategy. Deproliferation programs, such as they are, are largely run by the U.S. Energy Department, which has much less clout than the Department of Defense, or even the State Department. The programs are further hobbled by a conflict between House GOP members who distrust the Nunn-Lugar programs (which they see as a boondoggle, because they believe that Russian scientists and the arms industry are taking the United States for a ride), and key senators who support the programs, especially Richard Lugar (R-IN), Pete Domenici (R-NM), and Carl Levin (D-MI).

In May 2004, U.S. Secretary of Energy Spencer Abraham announced the Global Threat Reduction Initiative (GTRI); this program seeks to retrieve fresh fuel of Russian origin and spent fuel of U.S. and Russian origin from research reactors around the world and to convert civilian reactors that use deflectable WGU to safe LEU.[95] The media characterized this announcement as a significant deproliferation step. This drive is best assessed by contrasting it with the overall United States defense budget, which was $419 billion for fiscal year 2006; the amount allocated to the GTRI, $20 million over eighteen months, is small potatoes.[96] It could have been paid for from the petty cash box at the Pentagon.

The effort to deproliferate is further hampered by the fact that the location of all dangerous fissile material is not known. Some believe that merely generating a full list would be a significant step in the right direction: "Neither the United States government nor any other government or organization has a comprehensive picture of nuclear security around the world, or what work would have to be done, at which sites, to improve nuclear security enough to reduce the risk of nuclear theft and terrorism to a minimal level. Since the size of the job is not yet well defined, it is difficult to assess what fraction of the job is done."[97]

Bunn and Wier estimate that around sixty metric tons of HEU is in civilian use or storage in the world, half outside the United States and

Russia. They further estimate that the task of repatriating all of the HEU to either the United States or Russia is 30 percent complete. However, they admit that this is only an estimate,[98] because there is no reliable record of how much HEU is at research reactors worldwide.[99]

The task of collecting the HEU is further complicated by two rather different tasks that must be completed. One task is to collect fuel from reactors that are no longer operating. Many research reactors have been closed down, but the vast majority of these reactors have not yet been decommissioned. According to the IAEA, 405 reactors have been shut down; of these, only 167 have been decommissioned.[100] Of the 106 reactors identified to undergo conversion by 2014, over 60 continue to use HEU fuel. Ergo, there are significantly more reactors that need to be altered than there are those that have been altered.[101] Progress has been slow in China, where only one reactor has so far been converted, and it has been even slower in Russia, India, Pakistan, Israel, and North Korea—where no reactor has been converted.[102]

Several of my colleagues have produced outstanding works containing rich details that, in effect, describe the next steps that must be taken if deproliferation were to become the order of the day.[103] Senator Lugar suggested in 2004 what must be done next; several of the measures he mentioned fit well into a deproliferation strategy.[104] All these measures, if taken together (or even just a considerable number of them), would amount to a major shift in priority and strategy of the kind here favored. Instead of repeating these numerous and detailed recommendations here, I focus next on several points that, in my judgment, deserve special additional attention.

Rogue States: Iran and North Korea, Different Treatments

As far as rogue states are concerned, it is common to treat Iran and North Korea as if they were basically of one kind. As I see it, while maximum efforts should be made to encourage, incentivize, and pressure North Korea to give up its nuclear arms program, it might be too late to prevent it from joining the nuclear club. Not only does it already possess several nuclear arms, but it has artillery equipped with chemical shells that could kill hundreds of thousands of South Koreans. Thus, it will have to be deterred from using its arms via the old-fashioned, Cold War method of threatening nuclear retaliation for any nuclear attack. True, with every new member of the club other nations will seek to join. Hence, an unambiguous declaration by all the nuclear powers must be made that North Korea is the *last* new member. No more such powers will be tolerated.

In contrast, it may well be the case that Iran can yet be defanged. It still possesses no nuclear weapons and has limited conventional capabilities. I assume no one at this point is seriously considering an Iraqi-style "regime change" there. Occupying this large country, whose citizens— even the reformers (as I learned when visiting them)—are fiercely patriotic, would be even more challenging than the occupation of Iraq. The notion that one could find opposition groups in Iran that would topple its government is at best a very long shot. And if they did, they might well continue the nuclear arms program.

However, this does not mean that Iran's nuclear facilities cannot be neutralized. Because Iran situated them in populated areas, people who live there should be given warning to leave the areas before these facilities are attacked. Because these targets have been hardened, special bombs might be needed to neutralize these sites. Special Forces have a much larger role to play here than the air force and the long-range missile command. In short, while a nuclear North Korea might have to be tolerated, it does not follow that Iran cannot forcibly be deproliferated.

HEU, Plutonium, and Spent Fuel

Odd as it may seem, triage must be applied even to the fuels involved; they are not all equally dangerous. Hence, controlling the use of some is much more urgent than that of others. In deliberating what must be done first, second and so on, plutonium and spent fuels are very often thrown together with highly enriched uranium. For instance, in his recommendations on how to strengthen the NPT, Ashton Carter pointed to the simultaneous need to prevent new countries from building uranium enrichment and plutonium reprocessing facilities.[105] Similarly, Secretary Abraham's GTRI treats HEU and spent fuel as if they were basically of equal danger, and hence to that organization it matters not which is treated first.[106] *As I see it, as far as terrorism is concerned, plutonium poses less of a threat than HEU, and spent fuel poses less of a threat than either.*

Plutonium is often referred to as the most hazardous material known. True, it is often used for nuclear arms production by states, hence its removal to safe havens is highly desirable. However, precisely because it is so much more hazardous than HEU, transporting and processing it requires special equipment and skills, it is a much less attractive material for terrorists (than HEU). Moreover, even for established states, it is significantly easier to make nuclear bombs out of HEU than out of plutonium. Hence, removal of HEU should typically be given priority over removal or blending down of plutonium. (There are exceptions to the rule. For instance, a plant in Aktau, Kazakhstan, contains a large amount of plutonium. Its closeness to Iran suggests that, in this case, removing plutonium should be given a high priority.)

Spent fuel is particularly difficult to handle, and it is extremely unlikely that it could be used to make nuclear bombs.[107] Because spent fuel is substantially more radioactive than either fresh fuel or plutonium, it is "self-protecting" in the sense that the radiation is sufficient to make working with spent fuel dangerous and complicated. Spent fuel can be employed to fashion dirty bombs, but these are much less worrisome than nukes. Hence, if choose we must, neutralizing the material needed to make nuclear arms should gain much higher priority than spent fuel.

Opinions may differ about the priorities I have outlined here. However, I believe that no reasonable person will disagree that triage is needed here, too. Responsible policymakers must determine which fuels can be used to make bombs that are significantly more dangerous than others and should therefore be blended down, removed, at least much better guarded, given that there is no way that all nuclear threats will be deproliferated at the same time.

CHAPTER D. MUSCULAR, MORAL POWER

Soft *and* Hard Power

Although the IAEA clearly has a role to play in enhancing nuclear security, one ought best keep in mind that it is dedicated to the norms of "yesterday," to the enforcement of the obsolescent NPT. Moreover, it has a board of thirty-five member nations, including Russia and China. Solid decisions are difficult to come by. Once every five years all of the 187 signatories of the NPT meet to explore whether or not changes ought to be made in the treaty. In their last meeting in New York in 2005, the members spent most of the two weeks squabbling about the agenda. They returned to their respective capitals for another five years with few new agreements, despite all the burning issues of the day. Chief among them was the issue that the treaty allows a nation to build nuclear reactors and enrich uranium—and then announce that it is leaving the treaty and keep the reactors and the enriched uranium to make nuclear bombs at will. This is what North Korea did in 2003, and such action is 100 percent legal as the treaty is worded.[108]

This flaw alone of the NPT is so severe that it makes a compelling case to switch to deproliferation, whether it is achieved by a radical recasting of the NPT or by proceeding along a wholly different avenue. It reminds me of the line *"Otherwise, Mrs. Lincoln, how did you like the play?"* It is a killer flaw.

Deproliferation is best carried out by a new, more muscular, yet legitimate global architecture that is developing, whose first priority is to protect life. Before I briefly depict the ways this architecture is in effect being constructed, and the place deproliferation has in it, a few words about the need to use both "soft" *and* "hard" power. The new international architecture cannot grow as long as it is supplied only with one of the two kinds.

In reaction to the Bush administration's 2003 invasion of Iraq, without the full blessing of the United Nations and without the support of many of the United States' traditional allies, much has been made of the merit of soft power, a term associated with Joe Nye's writings on the subject.[109] The term is now widely used to argue that a superpower (or, for that matter, any power) should obey international law and work with allies, especially through established international institutions; proponents of this approach further argue that conflicts should be resolved through negotiations—rather than through the use of hard power, i.e., military force.

Unfortunately, there is a tendency, especially in public dialogues in the mass media, to oversimplify the debate, to treat such issues as if they were a matter of black and white, with those favoring soft power on the side of the angels. Too often disregarded in this context is the need to undergird soft power with hard power.[110] After all, even most moralists who oppose most wars tend to define conditions under which they can be waged justly.

Those who view the United Nations as a key legitimator and hence a major source of soft power often overlook the fact that the U.N. on its own does not and cannot command the hard power required to back up its resolutions and declarations. It must draw on the armies of this or that nation, or on those of several nations acting in concert. Thus if the United States (in Haiti, Somalia, and Liberia), France (in the Ivory Coast), Britain (in Sierra Leone), Russia and NATO (in Kosovo), or Australia (in East Timor) had not provided the muscle, then the U.N. resolutions would have been of limited consequence at best. Soft power is preferable in general, but in several critical circumstances the application of hard power regrettably cannot be avoided. If deproliferation is to become an integral part of a more secure new global architecture, then sadly both soft and hard power must be exercised.

The Proliferation Security Initiative (PSI):
A New Model for Transactional Relations and Global Architecture

The PSI members include, in addition to the United States, ten "core participants," Australia, France, Japan, Portugal, and Spain among them. These nations—and many others who are members of this coalition of the willing—agreed to share intelligence and to stop all nuclear arms and materials shipments that pass through their territory, ports, airspace, or on ships flying their flags,[111] as well as to stop and board ships on the high seas that are suspected of carrying WMD-related materials.[112]

During the summer of 2003, the countries involved began joint military exercises to prepare for a wider implementation of these robust deproliferation steps. Some interceptions have already occurred, including the boarding of a ship deployed from a North Korean port and the seizure of a cargo ship traveling to Sudan.[113] The Bush administration has credited the PSI for Libya's decision to abandon its nuclear ambitions, after a ship loaded with nuclear components headed its way was intercepted.[114] The State Department is careful to refer to the PSI as an "activity" and not as an organization, which would imply creating a new security architecture outside the United Nations and the NPT. Whatever it is called, this is exactly what it amounts to.

By 2006 the nations participating in the PSI halted more than thirty illicit transfers of nuclear material. China denied Iran the right to fly over its territory to pick up missile parts in North Korea. Additional details on the cases are unavailable because member countries involved prefer not to be identified.[115]

By the end of 2006 the number of nations that participate in the PSI increased to include more than seventy nations. Among the most important new members is Russia. Most significant, the PSI mission was significantly expanded during a Bush-Putin meeting in July 2006. The new mission goes beyond interdiction on the high seas and in airspace—which had been the main goal of PSI—to include operations *inside* countries with nuclear arms and material. The PSI's greatest test will come as it is used to implement sanctions against North Korea, authorized by the United Nations in 2006, following nuclear tests by this rogue nation.

The PSI is a key example of the ways the building of new transnational institutions and enhancing security contribute to one another. The more that nations find that deproliferation serves their interest and the more that they view such action as legitimate, the stronger the transnational institutions these nations are constructing will become—as measured in budgets, command of military resources, and intelligence priorities—and the more these institutions will be able to contribute to deproliferation.

The authority to board ships in international waters (and to inspect other modes of transnational shipments of nuclear arms and materials) is essential for deproliferation. It is incompatible with existing international law, however, at least as it is widely understood. As one expert put it—referring to two international treaties that previously did allow nations to board ships on the high seas—in order to combat slavery and piracy, transport of nuclear materials falls under neither of these two headings. As I see it, the United States, its allies, and other parties that have a vital interest in deproliferation should inspire changes in international law so that nuclear shipments can be treated as piracy (or worse).

Fortunately, the United Nations seems to be moving in the needed direction. Security Council Resolution 1540 of 2004 calls for member states to criminalize WMD proliferation, secure sensitive materials in their own borders, and enact export controls. There are at least some hints that nations are considering deproliferating, instead of just continuing controlled maintenance, and legitimizing the muscular enforcement of this new deproliferation norm. Thus, in this vital area, hard and soft power may be converging and reinforce one another.

In the Longer Run

Historically, nation-states were formed to provide security, then expanded to tackle other objectives. One can envision the same scenario unfolding on the global level: the PSI (working with the United Nations) would expand its missions of dealing with terrorism and nuclear arms to attending to other life-saving missions. These would include stopping genocides and fighting pandemics. Subsequently, other transnational problems such as poverty and illiteracy become candidates for global action.

Similarly, in just the way that national governments born out of force (such as those of the United Kingdom, France, and Spain, and later of Germany and Italy) were gradually democratized and made accountable to their electorates, so too can one envision a PSI that could gradually become more democratically accountable, following a staggered progression of political development.

It might well be a better world if the formation of a world government were democratic from the get-go and served additional interests other than security. The fact is, however, that 9/11 generated a new global architecture focused on security. There is no way to roll this film back and ask the directors to compose a preferable scenario. We can, though, edit the next scenes. But why would the major powers behind the PSI, especially the United States, submit—even in the long run—to a global parliament, say in the form of a much-restructured United Nations, or a new Global Council composed of representatives of democratic governments? "Submit" is a strong term. However, seeking approval and taking into account the views of such a body is far from a visionary notion. In a world where an increasing number of people follow the news and are politically active, the perceived legitimacy of one's actions has become surprisingly important. As the U.S. experience in Iraq in 2003–2004 has demonstrated, acting without United Nations approval cost the United States dearly in "real" terms such as military support from allies, sharing of financial burdens, and public support at home. In one year, the Bush administration was forced to move from declaring that the United Nations was on the verge of irrelevancy to seeking, repeatedly, United Nations endorsements for its presence in Iraq and its help in the transition to a self-governing Iraqi regime.

True, one cannot expect in the near future that the world will be run democratically. However, as more of the governments of U.N. member states are democratized, the voice of the General Assembly will become more democratically compelling. And if the Security Council were to become more representative of today's global power structure, its resolutions would carry more weight. Thus, the United Nations may well become an even more important source for legitimacy than it currently is.

The net result might be nothing more than an antagonistic partnership. The United Nations would continue to chastise various powers for not following its lead closely enough, and continue also to be criticized for being relatively inefficient and ineffective. However, at the same time, both the United Nations and the expanded PSI would recognize that they complement one another. Without the hard power vested in the PSI, the United Nations would be toothless. And without U.N. soft power blessings, the PSI's uses of force would be considered illegitimate. That is, both sides may well take each other into greater account while still trying to follow their own lights, thus jointly fashioning a better world government than each would be able to construct separately. Such a government would focus first on security, but then expand to attend to other human needs.

NOTES

PREFACE

1. For the text of President Kennedy's remarks announcing the "Alliance for Progress" program, delivered at the White House on 13 March 1961, see Department of State Bulletin XLIV, no. 1136 (3 April 1961), 471–74. See also Peter Beinart, *The Good Fight: Why Liberals—And Only Liberals—Can Win the War on Terror and Make America Great Again* (New York: HarperCollins, 2006), 28–29.

2. David E. Sanger, "Bush's Shift of Tone on Iraq: The Grim Cost of Losing," *New York Times,* 2 September 2006, A8.

3. Jim Rutenberg and Helene Cooper, "Presidents Spar Over Iran's Aims and U.S. Power," *New York Times,* 20 September 2006, A1.

4. Peter Baker and Robin Wright, "Bush Appears Cool to Key Points of Report," *Washington Post,* 8 December 2006, A1.

5. Daniel J. Mahoney, "Conservatism, Democracy, and Foreign Policy," *The Intercollegiate Review* 41, no. 2 (Fall 2006): 8.

6. John F. Kerry, "Two Deadlines and an Exit," *New York Times,* 5 April 2006, A23.

7. See Francis Fukuyama, *America at the Crossroads: Democracy, Power, and the Neoconservative Legacy* (New Haven: Yale University Press, 2006), esp. 9–10, 186.

8. For a short discussion of a similar basis for foreign policy, see Robert Wright, "An American Foreign Policy That Both Realists and Idealists Should Fall in Love With," *New York Times,* 16 July 2006: "It's now possible to build a foreign policy paradigm that comes close to squaring the circle—reconciling the humanitarian aims of idealists with the powerful logic of realists." This pro-

posed synthesis Wright labels "progressive realism." See also Anthony Lieven and John Hulsman, *Ethical Realism: A Vision for America's Role in the World* (Pantheon, 2006). See also Jim Hoagland, "Realism, and Values, in Lebanon," *Washington Post,* 16 November 2006.

9. See the Institute for American Values, "What We're Fighting For: A Letter from America," February 2002, <http://www.americanvalues.org/html/wwff.html>. For the German response, see Timothy Slater, trans., "A World of Justice and Peace Would Be Different," *Frankfurter Allgemeine,* 2 May 2002, <http://www.americanvalues.org/html/german_statement.html>. For the Saudi response, see "How We Can Coexist," <http://www.american values.org/html/saudi_statement.html>.

10. Charles Krauthammer, "Democratic Realism," speech given at the American Enterprise Institute, Washington, D.C., 10 February 2004.

11. For a recent discussion, see Henry R. Nau, *At Home Abroad: Identity and Power in American Foreign Policy* (Ithaca, N.Y.: Cornell University Press, 2002).

12. Qtd. in Winston Churchill, *The Gathering Storm* (Boston: Houghton Mifflin, 1948), chap. 8.

13. See Joseph Nye, Jr., *Soft Power: The Means to Success in World Politics* (New York: Public Affairs, 2004).

14. See John M. Owen IV, "Democracy, Realistically," *The National Interest* 83 (Spring 2006): 35.

PART I. SECURITY FIRST: FOR US, THEM, AND THE WORLD

1. An expansive definition of security, especially human security, could be stated to include freedom from hunger, from pandemics, and from "want." However, such an expansive definition hinders analysis by including too much in a single concept. If it were to be used, we would need to refer to human security I (say, what most people mean by security, as mentioned earlier—physical safety, freedom from deadly violence, maiming, and torture); human security II (say, economic security); human security III (such as health); and so on. For an exploration of human security expansively defined, see the United Nations Development Programme, *Human Development Report 1994* (New York: Oxford University Press, 1994); and for a critique of and constructive suggestions regarding human security, see Roland Paris, "Human Security: Paradigm Shift or Hot Air?" *International Security* 26, no. 2 (Fall 2001): 87–102.

2. See Etzioni, *How Patriotic Is the Patriot Act?* (New York: Routledge, 2004).

3. I acknowledge some would make this list longer. But the reasoning behind my focus on these key, inseparable elements of basic security becomes clearer when I discuss their role in foreign policy.

4. See Kurt M. Campbell and Michael E. O'Hanlon, *Hard Power: The New Politics of International Security* (New York: Basic Books, 2006), 238–46.

5. For a concise treatment of the organic nature of democracy (and adapting de-

mocracy to the African context), see Claude Ake, "The Unique Case of African Democracy," *International Affairs* 69, no. 2 (April 1993): 239–44; for general analysis of the variable nature and conditions of democracies, see Fareed
Zakaria, *The Future of Freedom: Illiberal Democracy at Home and Abroad* (New
York: W. W. Norton, 2003).

6. For more on this perspective as related to Iran, see Scott D. Sagan, "How to
Keep the Bomb from Iran," *Foreign Affairs* 85, no. 5 (September/October
2006): 45.

7. See Michael Lind, *The American Way of Strategy: U.S. Foreign Policy and the
American Way of Life* (New York: Oxford University Press, 2006), esp. chap.
1.

8. Unfortunately I must leave to another day the very important discussion of
the relationship between perceived legitimacy, on the one hand, and true legitimacy, regardless of how it is perceived, on the other. A clearly legitimate
policy—e.g., President Franklin Roosevelt's decision to aid Great Britain before our own entry into World War II—can nevertheless be unpopular; while
a policy that is accepted—e.g., the internment of Japanese Americans during
the war—can lack real legitimacy. I just note here that in a liberal political
order the consent of the people is an essential component of governmental
legitimacy, and that there is more of a connection between perceived legitimacy and true legitimacy than one may at first presume. For more discussion, see Ian Clark, *Legitimacy in International Society* (New York: Oxford
University Press, 2005); and Don Browning, ed., *Universalism vs. Relativism:
Making Moral Judgments in a Changing, Pluralistic, and Threatening World*
(Lanham, Md.: Rowman & Littlefield, 2006).

9. See the discussion of the duty to prevent in Part V, "Grounds for Intervention," below.

10. Etzioni, *How Patriotic*, 14–22.

11. Rich Connell and Richard A. Serrano, "L.A. Is Warned of New Unrest," *Los
Angeles Times*, 22 October 1992, A1.

12. Etzioni, *How Patriotic*, 12–14.

13. For a presentation of both sides of the deproliferation debate, see Scott Sagan
and Kenneth Waltz, *The Spread of Nuclear Weapons: A Debate* (New York: Norton, 1995). Both intentional and unintentional confrontations are of concern;
for a critical look at nuclear bureaucracy and the potential for accidents, see
Sagan, *The Limits of Safety: Organizations, Accidents, and Nuclear Weapons*
(Princeton: Princeton University Press, 1993).

14. Several essays have been written about Libya's 2003 renunciation of
WMDs—its causes, implications for nonproliferation and security policy, and
applicability to other nations. An overview of the analyses that Libya's move
has sparked can be found in Ray Takeyh, "The Rogue Who Came In from the
Cold," *Foreign Affairs* (May/June 2001): 62–72; Chester A. Crocker et al.,
"U.S.-Libyan Relations: Toward Cautious Reengagement," The Atlantic
Council of the United States (April 2003); Yahia H. Zoubir, "The United

States and Libya: From Confrontation to Normalization," *Middle East Policy* (Summer 2006): 48–70; Gawdat Bahgat, "Nonproliferation Success: The Libyan Model," *World Affairs* (Summer 2005): 3–12; and Dafna Hochman, "Rehabilitating a Rogue: Libya's WMD Reversal and Lessons for US Policy," *Parameters* (Spring 2006): 63–78.

15. For further information on human-rights abuses, attempts at democratization, and the response of human-rights groups, see "Libya: Time to Make Human Rights a Reality," Amnesty International, <http://web.amnesty.org/library/Index/ENGMDE190022004?open&of=ENG-LBY>. Although the verdict was originally overturned by the Libyan Supreme Court, a separate trial was called to reconsider the death sentence. As of January 2007, a verdict had not yet been finalized.

16. When the United States restored diplomatic relations with Tripoli, the Geneva-based Libyan League for Human Rights complained that the "democracy drive is being undermined," and insisted that Libya's actions on WMD and terrorism were not "pertinent." See Daniel Williams, "Lack of Surprise Greets Word of U.S.-Libya Ties," *Washington Post*, 16 May 2006, A12. Writing in 2004, Michele Dunne specifically argued that Libya's failure to democratize and address human-rights concerns warranted an ongoing U.S. involvement in the country. See Dunne, "Libya: Security Is Not Enough," Carnegie Endowment for International Peace Policy Brief, October 2004.

17. See *From Empire to Community: A New Approach to International Relations* (New York: Palgrave Macmillan, 2004), 83, 122.

18. "Libya Important Model for Regime Behavior Change, Rice Says," 15 May 2006, <http://usinfo.state. gov/is/Archive/2006/May/19–212673.html>.

19. Judith Miller, "How Gadhafi Lost His Groove," *Wall Street Journal*, 16 May 2006, A14.

20. Ibid.

21. Jay Solomon, "U.S. to Restore Full Diplomatic Ties with Libya," *Wall Street Journal*, 16 May 2006, A6.

22. Joel Brinkley, "U.S. Will Restore Diplomatic Links with the Libyans," *New York Times*, 16 May 2006, A1.

23. For a Neo-Con view, see, e.g., Amir Taheri, "Getting Serious About Iran: For Regime Change," *Commentary* (November 2006): 21–27.

24. Selig Harrison, "It Is Time to Put Security Issues on the Table with Iran," *Financial Times* (London), 18 January 2006, 19.

25. Iran had previously sought U.S. security guarantees in 2002, when it requested them from Zalmay Khalilzad in exchange for cooperation with the U.S. war in Iraq. See Gareth Porter, "Burnt Offering," *The American Prospect*, 6 June 2006, 20. In 2003 it sent, unprompted, a proposal to the United States in which it offered to exchange deproliferation and halting of support for terrorism for security guarantees and lifting of sanctions. See also Glenn Kessler, "In 2003, U.S. Spurned Iran's Offer of Dialogue," *Washington Post*,

18 June 2006, A16. In North Korea, meanwhile, Selig Harrison maintains that U.S. demands and intransigence on the question of security guarantees was a major factor in North Korea's withdrawal from the 1994 Agreed Framework. See Selig Harrison, "Time to Leave Korea?," *Foreign Affairs* 80, no. 2 (March/April 2001): 62–78.

26. For North Korea, see Robert L. Gallucci, Daniel B. Poneman, and Joel S. Wit, *Going Critical: The First North Korean Nuclear Crisis* (Washington, D.C.: Brookings Institution Press, 2004), 389, 392–408.

27. For harbingers of change in Iran, see, e.g., Nazila Fathi, "Iranian Cleric Turns Blogger in Campaign for Reform," *New York Times*, 16 January 2005, A4; and Bagher Asadi, "The Battle for Iran's Future," *New York Times*, 7 January 2004, A21.

28. Steven R. Weisman, "Rice Is Seeking $85 Million to Prod Changes in Iran," *New York Times*, 16 February 2006, A14.

29. Akbar Ganji, "Money Can't Buy Us Democracy," *New York Times*, 1 August 2006, A19.

30. Antony Barnett and Patrick Smith, "U.S. Accused of Covert Operations in Somalia," *The Observer* (U.K.), 10 September 2006.

31. See Bruce Ackerman, *Before the Next Attack: Preserving Civil Liberties in an Age of Terrorism* (New Haven: Yale University Press, 2006), 13–15.

32. See Etzioni, *How Patriotic*, chaps. 3–5.

33. For more on Russia as a failing state, see "The Failed States Index," *Foreign Policy* (July/August 2005): 56–65, and (May/June 2006): 50–58; and Kevin Watkins, ed., *Human Development Report 2005* (New York: United Nations Development Programme, 2005), 21–24.

34. Not only are many of Russia's nuclear resources precariously placed and questionably guarded, but there have also been reports that nuclear material has already been misplaced, lost, or stolen. See Pierre Claude Nolin, "178 STC 05 E: The Security of WMD Related Material in Russia," NATO Parliamentary Assembly, 2005 Annual Session; and David Filipov, "Russia's Scattered Tactical Arms a Temptation to Terrorists," *Boston Globe*, 18 June 2002, A1.

35. "Vice President's Remarks at the 2006 Vilnius Conference," Reval Hotel Lietuva, Vilnius, 4 May 2006, <http://www.whitehouse.gov/news/releases/2006/05/20060504-1.html>. See also Steven Lee Myers, "Strong Rebuke for the Kremlin from Cheney," *New York Times*, 5 May 2006, A1: his speech was "the Bush administration's strongest rebuke of Russia to date," and "officials in Washington said [Cheney's remarks] had been heavily vetted and therefore reflected the administration's current thinking on Russia."

36. "Bush Criticizes Russia's 'Diminishing Commitment' to Democracy," Associated Press Worldstream, 16 March 2006.

37. Terence Hunt, "Bush Says U.S. Has Not Given Up on Russia Despite Kremlin Crackdowns," Associated Press Worldstream, 29 March 2006, in a question-and-answer session after a speech to Freedom House.

38. Douglas K. Daniel, "Rice Skeptical of Future of Democracy in Russia," Associated Press Worldstream, 12 February 2006.

39. U.S. Helsinki Commission hearing, 14 April 2005, <http://usinfo.state.gov/dhr/Archive/2005/Apr/20-249720.html>.

40. Commission on Security and Cooperation in Europe hearing, 8 February 2006, <http://www.state.gov/g/drl/rls/rm2/2006/68669.htm>.

41. U.S. Department of State, "Country Reports on Human Rights Practices," 28 February 2005, <http://www.state.gov/g/drl/rls/hrrpt/2004/>.

42. U.S. Senate Committee on Foreign Relations, hearing on Democracy in Retreat in Russia, 17 February 2005, <http://lugar.senate.gov/pressapp/record.cfm?id=232250>.

43. Sen. Sam Brownback and Rep. Christopher H. Smith, "Resolute with Russia," *Washington Times,* 25 February 2005, A19.

44. Greg Webb, "Nigeria Commissions Research Reactor," Nuclear Threat Initiative Global Security Newswire, 1 October 2004, <http://www.nti.org/d_new swire/issues/2004/10/1/255a6161-b010-4711-a111-b12697bedd56.html>.

45. There is a considerable political science literature on the extent to which this observation is valid. For an overview, see Bruce Russett, *Grasping the Democratic Peace* (Princeton: Princeton University Press, 1993); and Spencer R. Weart, *Never at War* (New Haven: Yale University Press, 1998). For the oldest roots of democratic-peace theory, see Immanuel Kant, *To Perpetual Peace: A Philosophical Sketch,* trans. Ted Humphrey (Hackett Publishing, 2003).

46. See Edward D. Mansfield and Jack Snyder, *Electing to Fight: Why Emerging Democracies Go to War* (Cambridge, Mass.: Massachusetts Institute of Technology Press, 2005).

47. For an overview of the literature on Afghanistan, see Sarah Chayes, *The Punishment of Virtue: Inside Afghanistan After the Taliban* (New York: Penguin, 2006); Marina Ottaway and Anatol Lieven, "Rebuilding Afghanistan: Fantasy Versus Reality," Carnegie Endowment for International Peace Policy Brief, January 2002; Kathy Gannon, "Afghanistan Unbound," *Foreign Affairs* 83, no. 3 (May/June 2004): 35; and Ann Jones, *Kabul in Winter: Life Without Peace in Afghanistan* (New York: Metropolitan, 2006). For an overview of the literature on Iraq, see David Phillips, *Losing Iraq: Inside the Postwar Reconstruction Fiasco* (New York: Westview Press, 2005); Larry Diamond, *Squandered Victory: The American Occupation and the Bungled Effort to Bring Democracy to Iraq* (New York: Times Books, 2005); Thomas Ricks, *Fiasco: The American Military Adventure in Iraq* (New York: Penguin Press, 2006); Michael O'Hanlon and Andrew Kamons, "Iraq Index: Tracking Variables of Reconstruction and Security in Post-Saddam Iraq," The Brookings Institution, July 2006; and George Packer, *The Assassins' Gate: America in Iraq* (New York: Farrar, Straus, & Giroux, 2005).

48. The CPA initially focused heavily not just on the civil service, but especially on the financial sector. Bathsheba Crocker describes CPA efforts to create a "business-friendly investment climate" as well as drafting modern banking

laws and reopening the Central Bank of Iraq. See Crocker, "Reconstructing Iraq's Economy," *The Washington Quarterly* (Autumn 2004): 27.

49. Phillips, *Losing Iraq*, 145.

50. Eric Schmitt, "U.S. Generals Fault Ban on Hussein's Party," *New York Times*, 21 April 2004, A11.

51. Sabrina Tavernise, "As Death Stalks Iraq, Middle-Class Exodus Begins," *New York Times*, 19 May 2006, A1.

52. Vance Serchuk, "Cop Out: Why Afghanistan Has No Police," *The Weekly Standard*, 17 July 2006, 21–23.

53. James Glanz and David Rohde, "The Reach of War: U.S. Report Finds Dismal Training of Afghan Police," *New York Times*, 4 December 2006, A1.

54. Swaminathan S. Anklesaria Aiyar, "Karzai Takes on the Warlords," *Economic Times* (India), 28 May 2003.

55. Ibid.

56. "A Fragile Corner of Order," *The Economist*, 18 March 2006, 46.

57. Yochi J. Dreazen, "Tough Love in Baghdad," *Wall Street Journal*, 1 April 2006, A4.

58. Carlotta Gall, "Afghan Lawmakers Review Court Nominees," *New York Times*, 17 May 2006, A10.

59. Larry Diamond, as qtd. in Mark Leonard, "Drinking the Kool-Aid: An Anatomy of the Iraq Debacle," *The Chronicle of Higher Education* 52 (January 13, 2006): 19.

60. Phillips, *Losing Iraq*, 186.

61. Edward Wong, "Beleaguered Premier Warns U.S. to Stop Interfering in Iraq's Politics," *New York Times*, 30 March 2006, A14.

62. Phillips, *Losing Iraq*, 187.

63. Sabrina Tavernise and Qais Mizher, "In Iraq's Mayhem, Town Finds Calm Through Its Tribal Links," *New York Times*, 10 July 2006, A1. In May 2005, for example, militants in the Mahdi Army, the Shia militia loyal to the firebrand Moqtada al-Sadr, bombed an Amara engineering company owned by the Kaabi tribe. The Kaabi held a traditional tribal trial in response, banished the two bombers, and secured a compensatory $18,000 payment from the bombers' families. Several other tribes then banded together, in the Arab equivalent of a town hall meeting, and agreed to punish any militia member that attacked any of the tribes or its property. Since that time the crime rate in Amara has plummeted. The British political adviser in Amara has since admitted that the Coalition's failure to "encourage the tribes to participate" in establishing security had been a "mistake."

64. Carlotta Gall and Abdul Wafa, "Taliban Truce in Afghan Region Sets Off Debate," *New York Times*, 2 December 2006, A1 (emphasis added).

65. See also Sen. Joseph Biden and Leslie Gelb, "Unity Through Autonomy in Iraq," *New York Times*, 1 May 2006, A19.

66. "Declassified Key Judgments of the National Intelligence Estimate on Global Terrorism," *New York Times*, 27 September 2006.

67. The only weapons of mass destruction found in Iraq as of 2003 are highly degraded nerve agents from the 1980s. During testimony before the House Armed Services Committee on 29 June 2006, Dr. David Kay, formerly the chief U.S. weapons inspector in Iraq, admitted that "there were no weapons of mass destruction as described in the [National Intelligence Estimate] in Iraq. I thought Iraq was actually a more dangerous place than we assumed in the NIE. Iraq was a vortex of corruption filled with people who were capable to make WMD, who knew all the secrets, who were in that vortex of corruption willing to sell their skills to the highest bidder. And given the degraded state of American intelligence, quite frankly, if a willing buyer had come with a willing seller, I don't think we would have known. . . . I in fact think the threat in Iraq was terrorism. It was not state possession of large weapons of mass destruction as described in the NIE." See <http://www.rawstory.com/news/2006/Inspector_Kay_testifies_that_degraded_chemical_0630.html>.

68. Walter Pincus and Dana Milbank, "Al Qaeda-Hussein Link Is Dismissed," *Washington Post,* 17 June 2004, A1.

69. See Andrew Kohut and Bruce Stokes, *America Against the World: How We Are Different and Why We Are Disliked* (New York: Times Books, 2006); "America's Image Further Erodes, Europeans Want Weaker Ties: But Post-War Iraq Will Be Better Off, Most Say," Pew Global Attitudes Project, 18 March 2003; "A Year After Iraq War: Mistrust of America in Europe Ever Higher, Muslim Anger Persists," Pew Global Attitudes Project, 16 March 2004; "U.S. Image Up Slightly, But Still Negative: American Character Gets Mixed Reviews," Pew Global Attitudes Project, 23 June 2005; and "America's Image Slips, but Allies Share U.S. Concerns Over Iran, Hamas: No Global Warming Alarm in the U.S., China," Pew Global Attitudes Project, 13 June 2006.

70. A 2006 Asia Foundation survey found that 44 percent of Afghans felt Afghanistan was headed in the right direction, 21 percent in the wrong direction, and 29 percent in mixed directions. This represented a dramatic decline from an identical 2004 poll, which put the numbers, respectively, at 64 percent, 11 percent, and 8 percent. Carlotta Gall, "Afghans Losing Faith in Nation's Path, Poll Shows," *New York Times,* 9 November 2006, A6.

71. See Joseph S. Nye, Jr., *Soft Power: The Means to Success in World Politics* (New York: Public Affairs, 2004).

72. See John Newhouse, "The Diplomatic Round," *The New Yorker,* 24 August 1992, 60.

73. "The warnings of catastrophe were many and convincing," notes Alison Desforges of Human Rights Watch. Desforges, "Leave None to Tell the Story: Genocide in Rwanda," *Human Rights Watch Report,* March 1999, 114.

74. Ibid., 129.

75. Ibid., 130.

76. Ibid., 132.

77. For more discussion see Part V, "Grounds for Intervention," below.

PART II. THE LIMITS OF SOCIAL ENGINEERING

1. Dana Milbank, "Upbeat Tone Ended with War," *Washington Post*, 29 March 2003, A1.
2. Ari Fleischer, White House Press Briefing, James S. Brady Briefing Room, 18 February 2003, <http://www.whitehouse.gov/news/releases/2003/02/20030218-4.html>.
3. House Committee on Appropriations Hearing on a Supplemental War Regulation, 27 March 2003.
4. Ibid.
5. Dana Milbank and Robin Wright, "Off the Mark on Cost of War, Reception by Iraqis," *Washington Post*, 19 March 2004, A1.
6. "Bush on Democracy in the Middle East," remarks delivered at the National Endowment for Democracy, Washington, D.C., 6 November 2003, transcribed by FDCH E-Media, <http://www.washingtonpost.com/ac2/wp-dyn/A8260-2003Nov6?>.
7. Joshua Muravchik, "Democracy's Quiet Victory," *New York Times*, 19 August 2002.
8. Francis Fukuyama, "The End of History?," *The National Interest* 16 (Summer 1989): 4.
9. Ibid., 5; Fukuyama has since put some distance between himself and prominent Neo-Cons with his book *America at the Crossroads: Democracy, Power, and the Neoconservative Legacy* (New Haven: Yale University Press, 2006).
10. Michael Kelly, "An End to Pretending," *Washington Post*, 26 June 2002, A25.
11. Jeffrey D. Sachs, *Poland's Jump to the Market Economy* (Cambridge, Mass.: Massachusetts Institute of Technology Press, 1993).
12. Parts of this chapter have been adapted from my article "A Self-Restrained Approach to Nation-Building by Foreign Powers," *International Affairs* 80, no. 1 (January 2004): 1–17.
13. Archie Brown, "Russia and Democratization," *Problems of Post-Communism* 46, no. 5 (1999): 5–6.
14. Thomas Carothers, *Critical Mission: Essays on Democracy Promotion* (Washington, D.C.: Carnegie Endowment for International Peace, 2004).
15. Robert A. Dahl, *Polyarchy: Participation and Opposition* (New Haven: Yale University Press, 1971), 3.
16. Adeed and Karen Dawisha, "How to Build a Democratic Iraq," *Foreign Affairs* 82, no. 3 (2003): 47.
17. S. M. Lipset and Jason M. Lakin, *The Democratic Century* (Norman, Okla.: Oklahoma University Press, 2004); and Lipset, *Political Man: The Social Bases of Politics* (Garden City, N.Y.: Doubleday, 1963).
18. Minxin Pei and Sara Kasper, "Lessons from the Past: The American Record on Nation Building," Carnegie Endowment Policy Brief No. 24, April 2003.
19. As qtd. in George Packer, "Dreaming of Democracy," *New York Times Magazine*, 2 March 2003, 60.

20. F. Gregory Gause III, "Can Democracy Stop Terrorism?," *Foreign Affairs* 84, no. 5 (September/October 2005): 62.

21. Marina Ottaway, "Nation Building," *Foreign Policy* 132 (September/October 2002): 17.

22. Robert A. Packenham, *Liberal America and the Third World* (Princeton: Princeton University Press, 1973), 34–35.

23. As qtd. in Packer, "Dreaming of Democracy," 60.

24. Karin von Hippel, *Democracy by Force: U.S. Military Intervention in the Post-Cold War World* (New York: Cambridge University Press, 2000), 187.

25. See, e.g., Kevin Phillips, *American Theocracy: The Peril and Politics of Radical Religion, Oil, and Borrowed Money in the 21st Century* (New York: Viking, 2006).

26. <http://www.freedomhouse.org>.

27. On the profound differences between political orders which are truly liberal and those which are merely democratic, see Fareed Zakaria, *The Future of Freedom: Illiberal Democracy at Home and Abroad* (New York: W.W. Norton, 2003).

28. Thomas Carothers, "The End of the Transition Paradigm," *Journal of Democracy* 13, no. 1 (January 2002): 5.

29. Jonathan Hartlyn and Arturo Valenzuela, "Democracy in Latin America since 1930," in Leslie Bethell, ed., *The Cambridge History of Latin America*, Vol. 6 (Cambridge: Cambridge University Press, 1994), 99; and Carlos H. Waisman, "Argentina: Autarkic Industrialization and Illegitimacy," in *Democracy in Developing Countries: Latin America*, ed. Larry Diamond, Juan J. Linz, and Seymour Martin Lipset (Boulder, Colo.: Lynne Rienner, 1989), 69.

30. James Q. Wilson, "American Exceptionalism," American Enterprise Institute, 29 August 2006, <http://www.aei.org/include/pub_print.asp?pubID=24842>.

31. Charles King, "Potemkin Democracy: Four Myths About Post-Soviet Georgia," *The National Interest* 64 (Summer 2001): 93.

32. Cf. Lilia Shevtsova, "Imitation Russia," *The American Interest* 2, no. 2 (November/December 2006): 69. "Many who once saw Russia as a 'democracy with adjectives,'" she writes, ". . . who believed that 'immature' democracies evolve ineluctably into the full-fledged variety, have now been compelled to define Russia as an autocracy. . . . Russia's experience has clearly undermined a basic assumption of the transition paradigm: the determinative importance of elections."

33. Iraq is a case in point. In the wake of the Iraq Study Group's report, Roger Cohen says of Iraq, "But it's hard to escape the conclusion that the report treats Iraq as an existing country needing a quick fix in the name of resurgent American realism, rather than a still-to-be-born country that needs to be ushered into being in the name of American idealism. Iraq, in short, needs Iraqis—citizens of a nation rather than a tribe—and that, after decades of disorienting dictatorship, is a generational undertaking scarcely amenable

to American electoral timetables." Roger Cohen, "Iraq's Biggest Failing: There Is No Iraq," *New York Times*, 10 December 2006, W4.

34. George W. Bush, "Remarks by the President at Summit of Americas Working Session," delivered at the Hilton Hotel, Quebec City, Quebec, Canada, 21 April 2001, <http://www.whitehouse.gov/news/releases/ 2001/04/print/ 20010423-9.html>.

35. Chris Zambelis, "The Strategic Implications of Political Liberalization and Democratization in the Middle East," *Parameters* 35, no. 3 (Autumn 2005): 94.

36. Shibley Telhami, "The Return of the State," *The National Interest* 84 (Summer 2006): 113.

37. Editorial, "The Case for Democracy," *Washington Post*, 5 March 2006, B6.

38. Madeleine K. Albright, "A Realistic Idealism: There's a Right Way to Support Democracy in the Mideast," *Washington Post*, 8 May 2006, A19.

39. Editorial, "The Case for Democracy."

40. Francis Fukuyama and Nadav Samin, "Destructive Creation: Can Any Good Come of Radical Islam?," *Wall Street Journal*, 12 September 2002.

41. Gause, "Can Democracy Stop Terrorism?"

42. Walt Whitman Rostow, *The Stages of Economic Growth: A Non-Communist Manifesto* (Cambridge: Cambridge University Press, 1960).

43. Charles Krauthammer, "Setting Limits on Tolerance," *Washington Post*, 12 August 2005, A19.

44. "Just a First Step: Kuwait and Democracy in the Gulf," *The Economist*, 8 July 2006, 57.

45. "Should the West Always Be Worried if Islamists Win Elections?," *The Economist*, 30 April 2005, 56.

46. David Brooks, "Democracy's Long Haul," *New York Times*, 13 July 2006, A23.

47. Oxfam Briefing Note, "The view from the summit—Gleneagles G8 one year on," 9 June 2006, <http://www.oxfam.org.uk/what_we_do/issues/debt_ aid/downloads/g8_gleneagles_oneyear.pdf>.

48. Of the approximately $318.5 billion spent to date on the war in Iraq, Congress estimates that $24.7 billion has been allocated directly to reconstruction and embassy operations. This figure probably falls short of the "real" reconstruction amount, however, because it takes into account only non–Department of Defense allocations. Since a portion of the DOD's $290 billion has also been spent on reconstruction, the actual total amount spent is probably much higher. Amy Belasco, "The Cost of Iraq, Afghanistan and Other Global War on Terror Operations Since 9/11," *Congressional Research Service*, 22 September 2006.

49. David M. Walker, "Rebuilding Iraq: More Comprehensive Strategy Needed to Help Achieve U.S. Goals and Overcome Challenges," U.S. Government Accountability Office Testimony before the U.S. House Subcommittee on National Security, Emerging Threats, and International Relations, and Committee on Government Reform, 11 July 2006, <http://www.gao.gov/ new.items/d06885t.pdf>.

50. John W. Anderson and Bassam Sebti, "Billion-Dollar Start Falls Short in Iraq," *Washington Post,* 16 April 2006, A11.

51. "Without Peace, Reconstruction Stalls," *The Economist,* 15 May 2004.

52. Andrew Natsios, "American Fortresses," *The Weekly Standard,* 22 May 2006, 28.

53. Stuart W. Bowen, Jr., "Hearing to Examine Iraq Stabilization and Reconstruction," testimony before the U.S. Senate Committee on Foreign Relations, 8 February 2006, <http://www.sigir.mil/reports/pdf/testimony/SIGIR_Testimony_06-002t.pdf>.

54. Joel Brinkley, "Give Rebuilding Lower Priority in Future Wars, State Dept. Says, Spurning Iraq Strategy," *New York Times,* 8 April 2006, A7.

55. Ibid.

56. Ibid.

57. David S. Cloud, "Top General in Iraq Aims to Shoot Less, Rebuild More," *New York Times,* 1 April 2006, A8.

58. Ibid.

59. Robin Wright and Ann Scott Tyson, "U.S. Military Chiefs Urge Shift in Iraq War: Report," *Washington Post,* 14 December 2006, A1.

60. Carl Conetta, "Reconstructing Iraq: Costs and Possible Income Sources," Project on Defense Alternatives Briefing Memo No. 28, 25 April 2003.

61. Zalmay Khalilzad, "The Future of Iraq: U.S. Policy," speech delivered at the Weinberg Founders Conference, The Washington Institute for Near East Policy, 4–6 October 2002, <http://www.ciaonet.org/wps/winep02/winep02_c.pdf>.

62. As qtd. in B. Crocker, "Reconstructing Iraq's Economy," *The Washington Quarterly* 27, no. 4 (Autumn 2004): 73–93.

63. Ibid.

64. S. Barakat et al., "Attributing Value: Evaluating Success and Failure in Post-War Reconstruction," *Third World Quarterly* 26 (2005): 831–52.

65. Joseph A. D'Agostino, "Plans Taking Shape for Reconstruction of Iraq," *Human Events,* 24 March 2003, 6.

66. Stephen D. Krasner and Carlos Pascual, "Addressing State Failure," *Foreign Affairs* 84, no. 4 (July/August 2005): 153–63.

67. Stuart Eizenstat et al., "Rebuilding Weak States," *Foreign Affairs* 84, no. 1 (January/February 2005): 134 (emphasis mine).

68. *Oxford English Dictionary,* 2nd ed., s.v. "Reconstruction and Development."

69. As qtd. in E. Kuhonta, "On Social and Economic Rights," *Human Rights Dialogue* 2 (September 1995): 3.

70. Noah Feldman, *What We Owe Iraq: War and the Ethics of Nation Building* (Princeton: Princeton University Press, 2004), 80.

71. Ibid., 81 (emphasis mine).

72. Bill Wineke, "Whatever Happened to Freedom Fries," *Wisconsin State Journal,* 12 June 2005.

73. Gerard F. Powers, "The Dilemma in Iraq," *America,* 6 March 2006, 19–26.

74. Naomi Klein, "You Break It, You Pay for It," *The Nation*, 10 January 2005, 12.

75. Ibid.

76. Gause, "Can Democracy Stop Terrorism?"

77. Ibid.

78. Alan B. Krueger and Jitka Maleckova, "Education, Poverty, Political Violence and Terrorism: Is There a Causal Connection?," National Bureau of Economic Research Working Paper 9074, July 2002, 1–36.

79. Peter Singer, "Outsiders: Our Obligations to Those Beyond Our Borders," in *The Ethics of Assistance*, ed. D. K. Chatterjee (Cambridge: Cambridge University Press, 2004), 11.

80. For a further discussion of this position, see Etzioni, "Are Particularistic Obligations Justified? A Communitarian Examination," *The Review of Politics* 64, no. 4 (Fall 2002): 573–600.

81. See also Erin Kelly, "Human Rights as Foreign Policy Imperatives," in *The Ethics of Assistance*, ed. D. K. Chatterjee (Cambridge: Cambridge University Press, 2004), 180: "Decent societies would agree that wealthier societies are under a moral obligation to aid those in need, when providing aid would further the cause of human rights. The inequalities between societies are tremendous and there is much that wealthy states could do to bring poor states up to a minimally decent level of well-being, without incurring unreasonable costs."

82. Denis Goulet, *Development Ethics* (New York: Apex Press, 1995), 153.

83. Ibid.

84. In his book *The White Man's Burden*, William Easterly systematically debunks the idea that increased aid expenditures in and of themselves can alleviate poverty or modernize failed or failing states, and points in part to the effects of bad government and corruption in making this so. Despite vast amounts of foreign aid, in his analysis of data from the Polity IV research project Easterly found that long-term growth "turns negative once you control for quality of government" (p. 44). Steve Knack of the World Bank found that "huge aid revenues may even spur further bureaucratization and worsen corruption" (p. 136). See Easterly, *The White Man's Burden* (New York: Penguin, 2006).

85. Eyal Benvenisti, *The International Law of Occupation* (Princeton: Princeton University Press, 1993), 11.

86. David Scheffer, "Beyond Occupation Law," *The American Journal of International Law* 97, no. 4 (4 October 2003): 842–61.

87. Grant T. Harris, "The Era of Multilateral Occupation," *The Berkeley Journal of International Law* 24, no. 1 (2006): 1–78.

88. Gary J. Bass, "Jus Post Bellum," *Philosophy and Public Affairs* 32, no. 4 (2004): 384–412.

89. Ibid.

90. USAID, "Private Sector Development," 13 July 2006.

91. Paul Blustein, "World Bank Considers Sending Staff Back to Baghdad," *Washington Post*, 18 September 2005, A23.

92. Natsios, "American Fortresses."

93. U.S. Army Corp of Engineers Gulf Region Division and Project and Contracting Office, "The Mission of the Project and Contracting Office," 31 July 2006, <http://www.rebuildingiraq.net/portal/page?_pageid= 95,77425&_dad=portal&_schema=PORTAL>.

94. U.S. Army Corps of Engineers Gulf Region Division and Project and Contracting Office, "Facilities and Transportation," 31 July 2006, <http://www.rebuildingiraq.net/portal/page?_pageid=95,77620&_dad=portal&_schema=PORTAL>.

95. Craig S. Smith, "Even in Iraqi City Cited as Model, Rebuilding Efforts Are Hobbled," *New York Times,* 18 September 2005, A1.

96. USAID, "Iraq Update: Revitalizing Education," September 2003; and Peter Grier, "Funds for Iraq Run Low," *Christian Science Monitor,* 15 June 2006, 1.

97. David M. Walker, "Rebuilding Iraq," U.S. Government Accountability Office, 25 April 2006.

98. M. E. O'Hanlon and A. Kamons, "Iraq Index," The Brookings Institution, 31 July 2006, <http://www.brookings.edu/iraqindex>.

99. Ellen Knickmeyer, "U.S. Plan to Build Iraq Clinics Falters," *Washington Post,* 3 April 2006, A1; and Stuart W. Bowen, Jr., "Management of the Primary Healthcare Centers Construction Projects," Special Inspector General for Iraq Reconstruction-06–011, 29 April 2006.

100. Stuart W. Bowen, Jr., testimony before the U.S. House of Representatives Committee on Government Reform, Subcommittee on National Security, Emerging Threats, and International Relations, 18 October 2005.

101. Walker, "Rebuilding Iraq."

102. George Fella, "Security Strategy for Postwar Iraq," Carlisle Barracks, Penn., U.S. Army War College, 19 March 2004.

103. Peter Galbraith, a leading advocate of partition, argues, "The case for the partition of Iraq is straightforward: It has already happened. The Kurds, a non-Arab people who live in the country's north, enjoy the independence they long dreamed about. The Iraqi flag does not fly in Kurdistan, which has a democratically elected government and its own army. In southern Iraq, Shi'ite religious parties have carved out theocratic fiefdoms, using militias that now number in the tens of thousands to enforce an Iranian-style Islamic rule. To the west, Iraq's Sunni provinces have become chaotic no-go zones, with Islamic insurgents controlling Anbar province while Baathists and Islamic radicals operate barely below the surface in Salahaddin and Nineveh. And Baghdad, the heart of Iraq, is now partitioned between the Shi'ite east and the Sunni west." Peter W. Galbraith, "The Case for Dividing Iraq," *Time,* 5 November 2006. See also Peter W. Galbraith, *The End of Iraq: How American Incompetence Created a War Without End* (New York: Simon & Schuster, 2006).

104. Senator Joseph Biden and Leslie Gelb have advocated a similar plan. See,

e.g., Joseph R. Biden, Jr., and Leslie H. Gelb, "Unity Through Autonomy in Iraq," *New York Times,* 1 May 2006, A19. Ralph Peters, a former army lieutenant colonel, has also supported this approach. He supports allowing true self-determination in the autonomous zones, even if the populace supports illiberal changes: "Stop worrying about Shi'ite extremism. If we mean what we say about democracy, the Shi'ites should be free to choose whomever they want as their leaders—even fundamentalists." Ralph Peters, "Break Up Iraq Now," *New York Post,* 10 July 2003.

105. The Iraq Study Group report itself suggests that the actual preferences of many of Iraq's most important political figures do not include a unity government. The report states, "Iraq's leaders often claim that they do not want a division of the country, but we found that key Shia and Kurdish leaders have little commitment to national reconciliation. Many of Iraq's most powerful and well-positioned leaders are not working towards a united Iraq." Kirk Semple and Edward Wong, "Can They All Get Along in Iraq? Despite the Report, Maybe They Can't," *New York Times,* 8 December 2006, A16.

106. For studies of foreign forces' role in Kosovo and the history of Serbian-Albanian coexistence and tensions in Kosovo up to and since the 1999 war, see Iain King and Whit Mason, *Peace at Any Price: How the World Failed Kosovo* (Ithaca, N.Y.: Cornell University Press, 2006); Edward Joseph, "Back to the Balkans," *Foreign Affairs* 84, no. 1 (January/February 2005): 111–22; Steve Woehrel, "Kosovo's Future Status and U.S. Policy," CRS Report for Congress, 9 January 2006; and Noel Malcolm, *Kosovo: A Short History* (New York: New York University Press, 1998).

107. Vladimir Matic, "Unbreakable Bond: Serbs and Kosovo: A Field Report," Public International Law and Policy Group, December 2003, <http://www .publicinternationallaw.org/publications/reports/UnbreakableBondSerb sandKosovo1203.pdf>.

108. Charles Kupchan, "Independence for Kosovo," *Foreign Affairs* 84, no. 6 (November/December 2005): 13.

109. "Coordination Centre Chief Tells US Diplomat Multiethnic Kosovo 'Illusion,'" BBC News, 30 March 2004.

110. "Special Representative for Kosovo Briefs Security Council," SC/8640, 14 February 2006, <http://www.un.org/News/Press/docs/2006/sc8640.doc.htm>.

111. R. Nicholas Burns, "Briefing on U.S. Strategy for Kosovo," U.S. Department of State, Washington, D.C., 9 November 2005, <http://www.state.gov/p/us/ rm/2005/56651.htm>.

112. Michael Ignatieff, *Empire Lite: Nation-Building in Bosnia, Kosovo, Afghanistan* (Vintage, 2003), 59.

113. International Crisis Group, "Kosovo: The Challenge of Transition," Europe Report No. 170, 17 February 2006, 30 (emphasis mine).

114. Ignatieff, *Empire Lite,* 72.

115. Ibid., 68.

116. Ibid., 37–38.

PART III. THE TRUE FAULT LINE: WARRIORS VS. PREACHERS

1. Address to a joint session of Congress nine days after 9/11, and at a White House news conference on 6 November 2001 with President Jacques Chirac. See <http://www.whitehouse.gov/news/releases/2001/09/ 20010920-8.html>, and <http://www.whitehouse.gov/news/releases/2001/11/20011106-4.html>.

2. David Brooks, "Keeping the Faith in Democracy," *New York Times*, 26 February 2006, WK13 (my emphasis).

3. Samuel Huntington, *The Clash of Civilizations and the Remaking of the World Order* (New York: Touchstone Books, 1996), 209. See also Lee Harris, *Civilization and Its Enemies: The Next Stage of History* (New York: Free Press, 2004); Tony Blankley, *The West's Last Chance* (Washington, D.C.: Regnery Publishing, 2005).

4. Anthony Shadid, "Remarks by Pope Prompt Muslim Outrage, Protests," *Washington Post*, 16 September 2006, A1.

5. " 'Islam Is Peace,' Says President," remarks delivered at the Islamic Center of Washington, D.C., 17 September 2001, <http://www.whitehouse.gov/news/ releases/2001/09/20010917–11.html>.

6. "Europe: A Beautiful Idea?," remarks delivered at the Politics of European Values Conference, Knightshall, The Hague, The Netherlands, 7 September 2004.

7. For more discussion of my intellectual journey, see *My Brother's Keeper: A Memoir and a Message* (New York: Rowman & Littlefield Publishers, 2003). For my views on global community-building, see *From Empire to Community* (New York: Palgrave Macmillan, 2004), and *Winning Without War* (Garden City, N.Y.: Doubleday, 1964).

8. In recent years, however, Lewis has taken a different position. See "Freedom and Justice in the Modern Middle East," *Foreign Affairs* 84, no. 3 (May/June 2005): 36–51.

9. See, e.g., Ali, *The Caged Virgin: An Emancipation Proclamation for Women and Islam* (Free Press, 2006).

10. Fallaci, *The Force of Reason* (New York: Rizzoli International, 2006).

11. Said, "The Clash of Ignorance," *The Nation*, 22 October 2001, 11–13.

12. Esposito and John O. Voll, *Islam and Democracy* (New York: Oxford University Press, 1996).

13. Bulliet, *The Case for Islamo-Christian Civilization* (New York: Columbia University Press, 2004).

14. For a study of the relationship between Catholicism and modernity and a defense of the Catholic contribution to political liberalism, see especially John Courtney Murray, *We Hold These Truths: Catholic Reflections on the American Proposition* (New York: Sheed and Ward, 1960).

15. Manji, *The Trouble with Islam: A Muslim's Call for Reform in Her Faith* (New York: St. Martin's Press, 2004).

16. Khan, *American Muslims: Bridging Faith and Freedom* (Beltsville, Md.: Amana Publications, 2002).

17. El-Fadl, *The Great Theft: Wrestling Islam from the Extremists* (New York:

Harper San Francisco, 2005); and *Islam and the Challenge of Democracy* (Princeton: Princeton University Press, 2004).

18. Cf. William Galston, "Jews, Muslims and the Prospects for Pluralism," *Daedalus* 132, no. 3 (Summer 2003): 73. Galston echoes my identification of the fault line as running between Preachers' persuasion and Warriors' coercion, with his own distinction between religious movements which are essentially "defensive" and those which are "offensive" in nature. Both may be fundamentalist; but whereas defensive movements "participate in [the arena of power] on equal terms with others, so long as they are free to practice their faith," offensive movements "seek power to impose their way on others." Only the latter "are the movements that pluralist societies and those seeking to build such societies (as in Iraq) have to fear, and must resist."

19. As qtd. in J. J. Sutherland, "Afghans Wary of Returning Virtue Police," National Public Radio Morning Edition, 10 July 2006, <http://www.npr.org/te mplates/story/story.php?storyId=5545139>.

20. For more on the reasons I hold that democratization cannot be rushed, see Part II, Chapter B.

21. See, e.g., Simon Blackburn, *Truth: A Guide* (New York: Oxford University Press, 2005). See also Don S. Browning, *Universalism vs. Relativism: Making Moral Judgments in a Changing, Pluralistic, and Threatening World* (Lanham, Md.: Rowman & Littlefield, 2006).

22. See, e.g., Bruce Ackerman, *Social Justice in the Liberal State* (New Haven: Yale University Press, 1980).

23. Ibid.

24. For criticism of this Enlightenment legacy in the field of international relations, see Jonathan Fox and Shmuel Sandler, *Bringing Religion into International Relations* (New York: Palgrave Macmillan, 2004).

25. "Civilization," *The Oxford English Dictionary*, 2nd ed. (Oxford: Oxford University Press, 1989).

26. For a significant critique of Huntington's use of the term *civilization,* see Richard E. Rubenstein and Jarle Crocker, "Challenging Huntington," *Foreign Policy* 96 (1994): 113–28.

27. William T. Cavanaugh, "Sins of Omission: What 'Religion and Violence' Arguments Ignore," *The Hedgehog Review* 6, no. 1 (2004): 35.

28. See, e.g., James Dobson, *The New Dare to Discipline* (Carol Stream, Ill.: Tyndale House, 1996).

29. Dennis Wrong, *The Problem of Order: What Unites and Divides Society* (New York: The Free Press, 1994).

30. Cf. Joan McCord's definition of coercion, in "Introduction: Coercion and Punishment in the Fabric of Social Relations," *Coercion and Punishment in Long-term Perspectives,* ed. McCord (New York: Cambridge University Press, 1995), 1. In a related conversation, Fr. Richard John Neuhaus once told me that true liberty is the freedom to do what the Lord commands. While this

theological-confessional understanding is worthy of all honor and respect, it is not frequently encountered among contemporary thinkers and scholars, and so is not presumed or strictly required by this text.

31. For further discussion, see Etzioni, *The Active Society: A Theory of Societal and Political Processes* (New York: The Free Press, 1968).

32. A philosophy professor might argue that one can choose to park even in the second case, though one's truck will immediately be towed away. Ergo, one's free will is not destroyed: "One always has a choice," he might say. But to choose to think or do something inherently includes the concept of seeing it through to its intended end; thus while technically force cannot be used to deprive a person of the free-will characteristic of his human nature, it most certainly can be and often is used to deprive him of the substance and purpose of his freedom.

33. See, e.g., Alan Lewis, *The Psychology of Taxation* (New York: St. Martin's Press, 1982).

34. See Etzioni, *The New Golden Rule: Community and Morality in a Democratic Society* (New York: Basic Books, 1996), 12.

35. I concede that under some extreme, limited conditions, economic deprivation can become so severe that it ends lives in short order, when hunger persists or medical treatment is denied. However, from these exceptions one cannot draw general conclusions for most other conditions. The exception should not constitute the rule.

36. For example, St. Paul writes in 2 Corinthians 10:3–5: "Indeed, we live as human beings, but we do not wage war according to human standards; for the weapons of our warfare are not merely human, but they have divine power to destroy strongholds. We destroy arguments and every proud obstacle raised against the knowledge of God, and we take every thought captive to obey Christ." St. Luke also attributes the rapid spread of Christianity to the early persecution of Christians in Jerusalem which forced them to flee elsewhere; cf. Acts 8:1–8, 11:19–20.

37. E. Glenn Hinson, *The Early Church* (Nashville, Tenn.: Abingdon Press, 1996), 215.

38. Philip Schaff, ed., *A Select Library of the Nicene and Post-Nicene Fathers of the Christian Church* [First Series], Vol. 1 (Buffalo, N.Y.: Christian Literature Co., 1886–89), 816.

39. Ibid., Letter 93.

40. Ibid., 810.

41. Ibid., 816.

42. Schaff, ed., *A Select Library*, Vol. 4, 810.

43. Steven Williams and Gerard Friell, *Theodosius: Empire at Bay* (New Haven: Yale University Press, 1994), 125.

44. Foucher de Chartres, *Chronicle of the First Crusade*, trans. Martha Evelyn McGinty (Philadelphia: University of Pennsylvania Press, 1978), 16.

45. Thomas Asbridge, *The First Crusade: A New History* (New York: Oxford University Press, 2004), 21.

46. Ibid., 25.

47. Edward Peters, *Inquisition* (Berkeley, Calif.: University of California Press, 1989), 55–56.

48. *Summa Theologiae* IIa IIae, q. 11, a. 3.

49. *Summa Theologiae* Ia IIae, q. 19, a. 5.

50. Eric Voegelin, *The Collected Works of Eric Voegelin*, Vol. 20, *The History of Political Ideas: The Middle Ages to Aquinas*, ed. Peter von Sivers (Columbia: University of Missouri Press, 1997), 230.

51. Martin Luther, "Of Secular Authority and How Far It Should Be Obeyed," in *Martin Luther: Selections from His Writings*, trans. and ed. John Dillenberger (Garden City, N.Y.: Anchor Books, 1961).

52. Harro Höpfl, *The Christian Polity of John Calvin* (New York: Cambridge University Press, 1982), 45.

53. Roland Bainton, *Hunted Heretic: The Life and Death of Michael Servetus* (Boston: The Beacon Press, 1953), 170.

54. Ibid., 169–70.

55. See, e.g., the views of Augustine's contemporary St. John Chrysostom in "Homilies on the Gospel of St. Matthew," *A Select Library*, ed. Schaff, Vol. 10, 393–95.

56. Jean-Michel Hornus, *It Is Not Lawful for Me to Fight: Early Christian Attitudes Toward War, Violence, and the State* (Scottdale, Penn.: Herald Press, 1980), 159.

57. Alexander Roberts and James Donaldson, eds., *The Ante-Nicene Fathers: Translations of the Writings of the Fathers Down to A.D. 325*, Vol. 3 (Buffalo, N.Y.: Christian Literature Co., 1885), "To Scapula."

58. Ibid., Vol. 7, *Divine Institutes*, v.20.

59. Schaff, ed., *A Select Library*, Vol. 9, "On the Priesthood," 41–42.

60. St. Bernard of Clairvaux, *On the Song of Songs*, Pt. 3, trans. Killian Walsh and Irene Edmonds (Kalamazoo, Mich.: Cistercian Publications, 1979), 175.

61. Edward Peters, ed., *Heresy and Authority in Medieval Europe* (Philadelphia: University of Pennsylvania Press, 1980), 166.

62. Geoffrey Nutall, *Christian Pacifism in History* (Berkeley, Calif.: Basil Blackwell & Mott, 1958).

63. Roland Bainton, "Introduction," in Sebastian Castellio, *Concerning Heretics*, trans. Bainton (New York: Octagon Books, 1965), 34.

64. Perez Zagorin, *How the Idea of Religious Toleration Came to the West* (Princeton: Princeton University Press, 2003), 96. Zagorin may be thinking only of the modern West and disregarding the controversy over religious toleration caused by the Donatists in the early fifth century.

65. Sebastian Castellio, *Concerning Heretics*, trans. Roland Bainton (New York: Octagon Books, 1965), 132.

66. Bartolome de Las Casas, *In Defense of the Indians,* trans. and ed. Stafford Poole (DeKalb, Ill.: Northern Illinois University Press, 1992), 255.

67. See <http://www.vatican.va/archive/hist_councils/ii_vatican_council/ documents/vatii_decl_19651207_ dignitatis-humanae_en.html>.

68. See the Babylonian Talmud, Baba Kam 83b: "Does the Divine Law not say *'Eye for eye'*? Why not take this literally to mean [putting out] the eye [of the offender]?—Let not this enter your mind, since it has been taught: You might think that where he put out his eye, the offender's eye should be put out, or where he cut off his arm, the offender's arm should be cut off, or again where he broke his leg, the offender's leg should be broken. [Not so; for] it is laid down, *'He that smiteth any man . . .' 'And he that smiteth a beast . . .'* just as in the case of smiting a beast compensation is to be paid, so also in the case of smiting a man compensation is to be paid."

69. See, e.g., Menachem M. Kasher, ed. *Israel Passover Haggadah* (New York: American Biblical Encyclopedia Society, 1950), 94.

70. Mishnah, Tractate Makkot, 1:10.

71. Ibid.

72. The Union for Reform Judaism, "What Is Reform Judaism?," <http://www .rj.org/whatisrj.shtml>.

73. Michael Meyer, *Response to Modernity: A History of the Reform Jewish Movement* (New York: Oxford University Press, 1998), 387.

74. Ibid., 390.

75. Union for Reform Jews Board of Trustees, "Resolution on Unilateral Withdrawals, Security Barriers, and Home Demolitions: Striving for Security and Peace for Israel and the Middle East," Denver, Colo., June 2004, <http://urj .org/Articles/index.cfm?id=8527>.

76. Ian Lustick, *For the Land and the Lord: Jewish Fundamentalism in Israel* (New York: The Council on Foreign Relations, 1988).

77. James Davidson Hunter, "Fundamentalism: An Introduction to a General Theory," in *Jewish Fundamentalism in Comparative Perspective,* ed. Laurence J. Silberstein (New York: New York University Press, 1993), 33.

78. Ehud Sprinzak, *The Ascendance of Israel's Radical Right* (New York: Oxford University Press, 1991), 3.

79. Ehud Sprinzak, "The Politics, Institutions, and Culture of Gush Emunim," in *Jewish Fundamentalism in Comparative Perspective,* ed. Laurence J. Silberstein (New York: New York University Press, 1993), 143.

80. Babylonian Talmud, Tractate Berakoth 58a, as qtd. in Ehud Sprinzak, "Extremism and Violence in Israel: The Crisis of Messianic Politics," *Annals of the American Academy of Political and Social Science* 555 (1998): 120.

81. Sprinzak, *The Ascendance,* 53.

82. Ibid.

83. Sprinzak, "Extremism and Violence in Israel," 120.

84. Ibid. In February 1994 one of Kahane's disciples, Baruch Goldstein, broke

into the Cave of the Patriarchs, a sacred shrine in Hebron, and murdered twenty-nine Muslims.

85. Larry Derfner, "Unheavenly Flames," *Jerusalem Post,* 30 June 2000, 1B.

86. "Rabbi Says God Will Punish Sharon," *BBC NEWS, U.K. Edition Online,* 9 March 2005, <http://news.bbc.co.uk/1/hi/world/middle_east/4333099 .stm>; and Ken Ellingwood, "Israeli Police Head Off Small Rally by Jewish Group at Temple Mount," *Los Angeles Times,* 11 April 2005, 3.

87. In the state of Israel much more violence has been and is committed in the name of secular nationalism, as is often the case elsewhere; but the present analysis is focused on the study of religious beliefs.

88. Ainslee Embree has written that the term *Hindu* itself "was applied by outsiders—Greeks and Persians—to the people who inhabited the land beyond the river Indus; it was not used until modern times by Hindus to differentiate themselves from other groups." See Embree, *Sources of Indian Tradition,* Vol. 1 (New York: Columbia University Press, 1988), 203. Scholars of Hinduism continue to debate whether, prior to the nineteenth century, Hindus shared a common religious identity. See, e.g., David N. Lorenzen, "Muslims and Hindus in India: Who Invented Hinduism?," *Comparative Studies in Society and History* 41, no. 4 (1999): 630–59; and John S. Hawley, "Naming Hinduism," *The Wilson Quarterly* (Summer 1991): 20–34.

89. Vasudha Narayanan, "Rituals and Story Telling: Child and Family in Hinduism," in *Religious Dimensions of Child and Family Life: Reflections on the U.N. Convention on the Rights of the Child,* ed. Harold Coward and Phillip Cook (Victoria, British Columbia: University of Victoria Press, 1996), 56: "One would have to take into account over 3,500 years of literature and practice in a wide geographic area and materials from over 15 major languages of the last 1,000 years to make even tentative descriptive claims [about Hinduism]."

90. Godse said during a speech at his trial, "[In the *Ramayana*] Rama killed Ravana in a tumultuous fight and relieved Sita. [In the *Mahabharata*], Krishna killed Kansa to end his wickedness; and Arjuna had to fight and slay quite a number of his friends and relations including the revered Bhishma because the latter was on the side of the aggressor. It is my firm belief that in dubbing Rama, Krishna and Arjuna as guilty of violence, the Mahatma betrayed a total ignorance of the springs of human action." For details on Godse's trial, see Tapan Ghosh, *The Gandhi Murder Trial* (New York: Asia Publishing House, 1975).

91. For more on the relationship between Godse and Gandhi, see Ashis Nandy, "The Politics of the Assassination of Gandhi," *At the Edge of Psychology: Essays in Politics and Culture* (New Delhi: Oxford University Press, 1980), 83.

92. Vinayak D. Savarkar, *Hindutva: Who Is a Hindu?,* 6th ed. (Bombay: Veer Savarkar Prakashan, 1989), title page.

93. Ibid., 113.

94. Tapan Raychaudhuri, "Shadows of the Swastika: Historical Reflections on the Politics of Hindu Communalism," *Contention* 4, no. 2 (1995): 145. This explicit expression of support for the approaches and attitudes of the Nazis is by no means universal among Hindu nationalists.

95. This account of the events of 6 December is drawn primarily from Ashis Nandy et al., "Creating a Nationality: The Ramjanmbhumi Movement and Fear of the Self," in *Exiled at Home* (New Delhi: Oxford University Press, 2002), 193. See also Peter van der Veer, *Religious Nationalism: Hindus and Muslims in India* (Berkeley: University of California Press, 1994).

96. The largest outbreak of such violence since the destruction of the Babri Masjid occurred in the state of Gujarat in March 2002, albeit for reasons very different from those that caused the Ayodhya riots. After a train carrying sixty *karsevaks* was reportedly set on fire by Muslims, Hindu militants throughout the state went on a massive rampage, killing, raping, and burning. Upward of two thousand Muslims were massacred, while Hindus suffered few losses. The state government, under the control of the Hindu nationalist party, is widely believed to have been complicit in coordinating the violence and protecting the perpetrators. See "We Have No Orders to Save You: State Participation and Complicity in Communal Violence in Gujarat," *Human Rights Watch Report* 14, no. 3 (2002).

97. Among the most notorious of recent attacks on missionaries was the murder of Graham Staines, an Australian missionary, and his two sons by Bajrang Dal activists in Orissa. On 23 January 1999, Hindu militants poured petroleum on the car in which the three were sleeping and burned them alive. See "Politics by Other Means: Attacks Against Christians in India," *Human Rights Watch Report* 11, no. 6 (1999).

98. Ibid., 18.

99. Nandy et al., "Creating a Nationality," 53.

100. For the Hindu nationalists' transformation of Ram, see Anuradha Kapur, "Deity to Crusader: Changing Iconography of Ram," in *Hindus and Others: The Question of Identity in India Today*, ed. Gyanendra Pandey (New Delhi: Viking, 1993), 74–109.

101. While we recognize that the examples offered below of Gandhi's thoughts and actions occurred over fifty years before much of what has been presented thus far on Hindu nationalism, we find that because of the Gandhian position's continuing presence in India, a comparison remains relevant.

102. Gandhi wrote, e.g., "[The *Bhagavad Gita*] is not an historical work, it is a great religious book, summing up the teachings of all religions. The poet has seized the occasion of the war between the Pandavas and Kauravas . . . for drawing attention to the war going on in our bodies between the forces of Good and the forces of Evil." See *Collected Works of Mahatma Gandhi* (hereafter *CWMG*), Vol. 15 (New Delhi: Publication Division, Government of India), 288; as qtd. in J. T. F. Jordens, *Gandhi's Religion: A Homespun Shawl* (New York: St. Martin's Press, 1998), 130.

103. For more on Gandhi's religious beliefs, see Margaret Chatterjee, *Gandhi's Religious Thought* (Notre Dame, Ind.: University of Notre Dame Press, 1983).

104. See Raghavan Iyer, ed., *The Essential Writings of Mahatma Gandhi* (Delhi: Oxford University Press, 1991), 239, 240–41: "My life is dedicated to the service of India through the religion of non-violence which I believe to be the root of Hinduism." "Non-violence is the greatest force man has been endowed with. Truth is the only goal he has. For God is none other than Truth. But Truth cannot be, never will be, reached except through non-violence. That which distinguishes man from all other animals is his capacity to be non-violent. And he fulfills his mission only to the extent that he is non-violent and no more. He has no doubt many other gifts. But if they do not subserve the main purpose—the development of the spirit of non-violence in him—they but drag him down lower than the brute, a status from which he has only just emerged."

105. For more on Gandhi's ideology of nonviolent resistance, see Joan Bondurant, *Conquest of Violence: The Gandhian Philosophy of Conflict* (Princeton: Princeton University Press, 1988); and Mark Juergensmeyer, *Fighting with Gandhi* (San Francisco: Harper and Row, 1984).

106. For a thorough account of the Salt *Satyagraha*, see Dennis Dalton, *Mahatma Gandhi: Nonviolent Power in Action* (New York: Columbia University Press, 2000).

107. See Roland Miller, "Indian Muslim Critiques of Gandhi," in *Indian Critiques of Gandhi*, ed. Harold Coward (Albany, N.Y.: State University of New York Press, 2003), 205.

108. Gandhi described fasting for the *satyagrahi* as "the last resort in the place of the sword—his or others," in *CWMG*, Vol. 98, 219. To those who argued that Gandhi's fast amounted to a form of coercion, he wrote, "Critics have regarded some of my previous fasts as coercive and held that on merits the verdict would have gone against my stand but for the pressure exercised by the fasts. What value can an adverse verdict have when the purpose is demonstrably sound? A pure fast, like duty, is its own reward. I do not embark upon it for the sake of the result it may bring. I do so because I must. Hence, I urge everybody dispassionately to examine the purpose and let me die, if I must, in peace which I hope is ensured."

109. *CWMG*, Vol. 7, 338, as qtd. in Jordens, *Gandhi's Religion*, 150.

110. *CWMG*, Vol. 35, 255 and 166, as qtd. in Jordens, *Gandhi's Religion*, 151.

111. John S. Hawley, "Ayodhya and the Rubble of Religion," *SIPA News* 6, no. 2 (1993): 3.

112. "After the Bombing," *Malcolm X Speaks: Selected Speeches and Statements*, ed. George Breitman (New York: Merit Publishers, 1965), 165.

113. Breitman, ed., "The Black Revolution," in *Malcolm X Speaks*, 57.

114. Breitman, ed., "Message to the Grass Roots," in *Malcolm X Speaks*, 12.

115. Ibid., 9.

116. Martin Luther King, Jr., "Pilgrimage to Nonviolence," *Stride Towards Freedom* (New York: Harper, 1958).

117. James M. Lawson, Jr., "We Are Trying to Raise the Moral Issue," in *Negro Protest Thought in the Twentieth Century,* ed. Francis L. Broderick and August Meier (Indianapolis: Bobbs-Merrill, 1965), 278.

118. Student Nonviolent Coordinating Committee's Statement of Purpose, in *Nonviolence in America: A Documentary History* (Indianapolis: Bobbs-Merrill, 1966), 399.

119. King, "Pilgrimage to Nonviolence."

120. Howell Raines, *My Soul Is Rested: Movement Days in the Deep South Remembered* (New York: Penguin Books, 1983), 79.

121. Martin Luther King, Jr., *Why We Can't Wait* (New York: Harper & Row, 1964), 29.

122. Vladimir Ilyich Lenin, "The State and Revolution," in *The Lenin Anthology,* ed. Robert C. Tucker (New York: Norton, 1975), 324–25.

123. William Z. Foster, "Acceptance Speech at the National Nominating Convention of the Workers Party of America," in *The Radical Reader: A Documentary History of the American Radical Tradition,* ed. Timothy Patrick McCarthy and John McMillian (New York: New Press, 2003), 321–22.

124. Rosa Luxemburg, "The Russian Revolution," in *Rosa Luxemburg Speaks,* ed. Mary-Alice Waters (New York: Pathfinder Press, 1970), 372–73.

125. Georges Sorel, "Apology for Violence," in *Reflections on Violence,* trans. T. E. Hulme (New York: P. Smith, 1941), 275.

126. Lenin, "On Revolutionary Violence and Terror," in *The Lenin Anthology,* ed. Robert C. Tucker (New York: Norton, 1975), 426.

127. Frantz Fanon, *The Wretched of the Earth,* trans. Constance Farrington (New York: Grove Press, 1963), 94.

128. Leon Trotsky, *Terrorism and Communism: A Reply to Karl Kautsky* (Ann Arbor, Mich.: University of Michigan Press, 1961), 23.

129. Karl Kautsky, *Terrorism and Communism: A Contribution to the Natural History of Revolution,* trans. and ed. W. H. Kerridge (Westport, Conn.: Hyperion Press, 1973), 180.

130. Ibid., 171.

131. Eduard Bernstein, *Evolutionary Socialism,* trans. and ed. Edith C. Harvey (New York: Schocken Books, 1961), xxv–xxvi.

132. Kautsky, *Terrorism and Communism,* 175.

133. Richard Burkholder, "*Jihad,* 'Holy War,' Or Internal Spiritual Struggle," Gallup Poll, 3 December 2002, <http://poll.gallup.com/content/default.aspx?ci=7333>. The surveyed countries included Lebanon, Kuwait, Jordan, Morocco, Pakistan, Iran, Turkey, and Indonesia.

134. Huntington, *Clash of Civilizations,* 209, 217.

135. See, again, "Freedom and Justice in the Modern Middle East," *Foreign Affairs* 84, no. 3 (2005): 36–51.

136. Peter Waldman, "A Historian's Take on Islam Steers U.S. in Terrorism Fight," *Wall Street Journal,* 3 February 2004, A1.

137. Bernard Lewis, *What Went Wrong? The Clash Between Islam and Modernity in the Middle East* (New York: Perennial, 2002).

138. Azzam Tamimi, "Perceptions of Islam in the BBC and Other Western Media," lecture for BBC World Service Training, London, 3 April 1995.

139. Daniel Pipes, "Bin Laden Is a Fundamentalist," *National Review Online*, 22 October 2001, <http://www.nationalreview.com/comment/comment-pipes 102201.shtml>.

140. Leon Hadar, "What Green Peril?," *Foreign Affairs* 72, no. 2 (1993): 27.

141. Muslim, 1.9.30.

142. Hassan al-Banna, "On *Jihad*," in *Five Tracts of Hasan al-Banna,* trans. and ed. Charles Wendell (Berkeley, Calif.: University of California Press, 1978), 142.

143. Bukhari, 9.84.57.

144. As qtd. in Yohanan Friedmann, *Tolerance and Coercion in Islam: Interfaith Relations in the Muslim Tradition* (Cambridge: Cambridge University Press, 2003), 123.

145. Friedmann, *Tolerance and Coercion*, 101.

146. Ibid., 103.

147. See, e.g., the work of Sheikh Muhammad al-Tahir Ibn Ashur (1879–1979), cited in Friedmann, *Tolerance and Coercion*, 103.

148. As qtd. in Reuven Firestone, *Jihad: The Origin of Holy War in Islam* (New York: Oxford University Press, 1999), 139 n. 19.

149. As qtd. in David Cook, *Understanding Jihad* (Berkeley, Calif.: University of California Press, 2005), 45.

150. Seyyed Hossein Nasr, *The Heart of Islam: Enduring Values for Humanity* (New York: HarperSanFrancisco, 2002), 260.

151. Caryle Murphy, "Muslim Leaders Speak Out," *Washington Post*, 13 October 2001, B9.

152. Ibid.

153. Yusuf al-Qaradawi, *Islamic Awakening Between Rejection and Extremism*, ed. A. S. Al Shaikh-Ali and Mohamed B. E. Wafsy (Herndon, Va.: American Trust Publications and the International Institute of Islamic Thought, 1991), 21.

154. Pew Global Attitudes Survey, "Islamic Extremism: Common Concern for Muslim and Western Publics," 14 July 2005, <http://pewglobal.org/reports/display.php?ReportID=248>; and Pew, "The Great Divide: How Westerners and Muslims View Each Other," 22 June 2006, <http://pewglobal.org/reports/display.php?ReportID=253>. These polls were based on samples of around one thousand people in each country.

155. Pew Global Attitudes Survey, "What the World Thinks in 2002," 4 December 2002, <http://pewglobal.org/reports/display.php?ReportID=165>.

156. Pew, "Islamic Extremism."

157. WorldPublicOpinion.org Poll of Afghanistan, 27 November–4 December 2005, <http://65.109.167.118/pipa/pdf/jan06/Afghanistan_Jan06_quaire.pdf>.

158. ABC News Poll, "Four Years After the Fall of the Taliban, Afghans Optimistic About the Future," 7 December 2005.

159. Pew, "The Great Divide."

160. Pew, "Islamic Extremism."

161. Helena Andrews, "Muslim Women Don't See Themselves as Oppressed, Survey Finds," *New York Times*, 8 June 2006, A5.

162. Near East Consulting Group Poll, February 2006, <http://www.neareastcon sulting.com/ppp/p02.html>.

163. Steven Hill, "Palestinian Elections: It's the Voting System, Stupid!," *The Humanist*, New America Foundation, June 2006.

164. Poll conducted by the Near East Consulting Group in February 2006, <http://www.neareastconsulting.com/cartoons/files/nec-pr-en.pdf>.

165. Pew, "Islamic Extremism."

166. F. Gregory Gause III, "Can Democracy Stop Terrorism?," *Foreign Affairs* 84, no. 5 (September/October 2005).

167. Pew Global Attitudes Project, "Views of a Changing World 2003: War with Iraq Further Divides Global Publics," 3 June 2003, <http://people-press.org/reports/display.php3?ReportID=185>.

168. Ibid.

169. Andrews, "Muslim Women."

170. Ibid.

171. I previously noted that often Preachers and their followers will support some violence. In the case at hand, many of those opposed to violence as a rule favor the use of force against Israel.

172. Pew, "The Great Divide."

173. D3 Systems, Inc., "Role of Women in Afghanistan, Iraq and Saudi Arabia," 2004.

174. Ibid.

175. Private communication with Jon Voll.

176. I note in passing that the term *constitutional democracy* is preferable to *liberal democracy* because the term *liberal* connotes to many readers a left-leaning social philosophy.

177. Pew Global Attitudes Survey, "Muslims in Europe: Economic Worries Top Concerns About Religious and Cultural Identity," 6 July 2006, <http://pew global.org/reports/display.php?ReportID=254>.

178. Pew, "Islamic Extremism."

179. See Ronald Latham, "Introduction," *The Travels of Marco Polo* (Baltimore: Penguin, 1958).

180. S. Mark Hein, "A Different Kind of Islamic State: Malaysian Model," *Christian Century* 121, no. 20 (2004): 30–33.

181. Ahmad Talib, "I Am a Muslim Fundamentalist but Not a Terrorist, Says Dr. Mahathir Mohamad," *New Straits Times* (Malaysia), 6 June 2003, 2.

182. Sisters in Islam, "Do Not Legislate on Faith," 29 September 2000, www.sis tersinislam.org.my/lte/29092000.htm.

183. Joe Cochrane and Jonathan Kent, "Drifting Towards Extremism," *Newsweek*, 4 December 2006.

184. Yaroslav Trofimov, *Faith at War* (New York: Henry Holt, 2005), 256.

185. Ibid., 257.

186. Jeffrey Tayler, *Angry Wind* (Boston: Houghton Mifflin, 2005), 204.

187. Ibid.

188. Trofimov, *Faith at War,* 52.

189. Ibid., 50.

190. Max Boot, "Islam's Tolerant Face," *Los Angeles Times,* 8 March 2006, B13.

191. Scheherezade Faramarzi, "Morocco Graduates First Group of Female Muslim Preachers to Promote Moderate Islam," The Associated Press, 4 May 2006.

192. "A Model of Tolerance," *The Economist,* 11 December 2004, 11.

193. Abdurrahman Wahid, "Right Islam vs. Wrong Islam," *Wall Street Journal,* 30 December 2005, A16.

194. Alan Cooperman, "Jordan's King Abdullah Pushes for Moderation," *Washington Post,* 14 September 2005, A14.

195. Jeremy Seabrook, "At the Crossroads of Secular Tolerance and Militant Islam," *Guardian* (UK), 7 November 2006.

196. Boot, "Islam's Tolerant Face."

197. Michael Slackman, "For Ramadan Viewing: A TV Drama Against Extremism," *New York Times,* 6 July 2006, A4.

198. Katherine Zoepf, "Women Lead Islamic Revival in Syria," *New York Times,* 29 August 2006, A1.

PART IV. THE IMPORTANCE OF MORAL CULTURE

1. U.S. Department of Justice Bureau of Justice Statistics, *The World Factbook of Criminal Justice Systems,* 1993, <http://www.ojp.usdoj.gov/bjs/pub/ascii/wfbcjrus.txt>.

2. "Russia's Crime Rate Dropping Because Crimes Aren't Registered," Mosnews.com, 9 March 2005, <http://www.mosnews.com/news/2005/03/09/ustinov.shtml>.

3. Anna Politkovskaya, *Putin's Russia: Life in a Failing Democracy,* trans. Arch Tait (New York: Henry Holt, 2004), 147.

4. Ibid., 90–95.

5. The United Nations Office on Drugs and Crime, *World Drug Report 2004,* Vol. 1 (New York: United Nations Publications, 2004), 85, <http://www.unodc.org/unodc/world_drug_report_2004.html>.

6. The number of alcoholics registered in Russia in 2004 was 2.5 million. See Scott Peterson, "Where Russians Go to Dry Out," *The Christian Science Monitor,* 2 May 2005, 6.

7. "Russia Drink Death Toll Soars," BBC News, 17 August 2001, <http://news.bbc.co.uk/2/hi/europe/1497300.stm>.

8. Rebecca Reich, "Suicide Stats Have Jumped for Russians," *St. Petersburg Times* (Russia), 11 July 2003.

9. In 2004 Georgia's interior ministry, for example, registered nearly twenty-five thousand crimes, an increase of 42.9 percent from the year before. See "Georgian Crime Rate Soars," Global News Wire-Asia Africa Intelligence Wire, 22 February 2005. Between 1999 and 2001, the average number of murders for every 100,000 people was about 1.6 in the European Union. For Russia it was 22.1, and for Estonia and Lithuania both it was 10.6. See Gordon Barclay and Cynthia Tavares, "International Comparisons of Criminal Justice Statistics 2001," no. 12/03 (London: Home Office Research, Development, and Statistics Directorate, 24 October 2003).

10. Paul Mooney, "The Kids Are Not Alright," *Newsweek*, 3 December 2001, 52.

11. Richard Madsen, "Crime and Social Control in a Changing China," *Contemporary Sociology* 32, no. 2 (2003): 239.

12. U.S. Department of State Bureau for International Narcotics and Law Enforcement Affairs, "International Narcotics Control Strategy Report 2005," March 2005, <http://www.state.gov/p/inl/rls/nrcrpt/2005/>.

13. Chinese Ministry of Health, UNAIDS, and the World Health Organization, "2005 Update on the HIV/AIDS Epidemic and Response in China," 24 January 2006, <http://hivaidsclearinghouse.unesco.org/ev_en.php?ID=5854_201&ID2=DO_TOPIC>. See also Louis Sullivan and J. Stapleton Roy, "Averting a Full-blown HIV/AIDS Epidemic in China: A Report of the CSIS HIV/AIDS Delegation to China," ed. J. Stephen Morrison and Bates Gill (Washington, D.C.: Center for Strategic and International Studies Press, 2003).

14. Craig S. Smith, "Shh, It's an Open Secret: Warlords and Pedophilia," *New York Times*, 21 February 2002, A4; and Maura Reynolds, "Kandahar's Lightly Veiled Homosexual Habits," *Los Angeles Times*, 2 April 2003.

15. Ibid.

16. David Rohde, "Afghan Symbol for Change Becomes a Symbol of Failure," *New York Times*, 5 September 2006, A1.

17. James Glanz and David Rohde, "U.S. Report Finds Dismal Training of Afghan Police," *New York Times*, 4 December 2006, A1.

18. Ann Jones, *Kabul in Winter: Life Without Peace in Afghanistan* (New York: Henry Holt, 2006); for more on the status of women in Afghanistan, see the U.S. State Department Bureau of Democracy, Human Rights, and Labor, "Afghanistan: Country Reports on Human Rights Practices 2005," 8 March 2006, <http://www.state.gov/g/drl/rls/hrrpt/2005/61704.htm>; and Human Rights Watch, "Overview of Human Rights Issues in Afghanistan," 12 December 2005, <http://hrw.org/english/docs/2006/01/18/afghan12266.htm>.

19. Jason Straziuso, "Report: Afghan Officials Aid Traffickers," *Boston Globe*, 28 November 2006.

20. Judy Dempsey, "General Calls Drugs Biggest Test for Afghans," *The International Herald Tribune*, 20 May 2006, 1.

21. Monte Morin, "The Conflict in Iraq: Crime as Lethal as Warfare in Iraq," *Los Angeles Times*, 20 March 2005, A1 (my emphasis).

22. James Glanz, "Rings That Kidnap Iraqis Thrive on Big Threats and Bigger Profits," *New York Times*, 28 March 2005, A1.

23. Jonathan Finer, "For Iraqi Students, Hussein's Arrival Is End of History," *Washington Post*, 15 April 2006, A1.

24. Richard Pipes, "Flight from Freedom: What Russians Think and Want," *Foreign Affairs* 83, no. 3 (May/June 2004).

25. Aizenman, "Afghan Crime Wave."

26. Howard LaFranchi, "In Iraq, Security Trumps Women's Rights," *The Christian Science Monitor*, 12 December 2005, 7.

27. Ibid.

28. David Rohde, "Afghan Symbol for Change Becomes a Symbol of Failure," *New York Times*, 5 September 2006, A1.

29. For more discussion see Etzioni, *The New Golden Rule: Community and Morality in a Democratic Society* (New York: Basic, 1996).

30. For further discussion of the role of politics and government policies on moral culture, see Lawrence E. Harrison, "Hearts, Minds and Schools," *Washington Post*, 17 December 2006, B3.

31. It is mistaken to assume that merely increasing the level of income, job security, and other such economic factors will create social order. Social order is grossly deficient in many nations whose annual income per capita is relatively high.

32. Alan Lewis, *The Psychology of Taxation* (New York: St. Martin's Press, 1982).

33. Paul C. Stern, ed., *Improving Energy Demand Analysis* (Washington, D.C.: National Academy Press, 1984).

34. George L. Kelling and Catherine M. Coles, *Fixing Broken Windows: Restoring Order and Reducing Crime in Our Communities* (New York: Martin Kessler, 1996). The authors' central thesis is that when broken windows in urban neighborhoods (and other visible signs of social and economic decay) go unrepaired, criminals feel freer to perpetrate their offenses, secure in the knowledge that the community does not care enough to maintain itself in good order or to prevent crime.

35. In her book *The Mighty and the Almighty*, former Secretary of State Madeleine Albright made a similar point, in the context of the improvement of the state of women in the Middle East. Their "cause is not helped," she wrote, "by ill-informed, smug, or simplistic criticism of Islam. . . . It is a mistake to disparage Islam or to assume that all is lost under sharia law; a better approach is to fight for the prerogatives that women should have under such law and to focus on the rights of women everywhere to define their roles for themselves" (276). This suggestion is in keeping with one of the central theses of her book: "As I travel around the world, I am often asked, 'Why can't we just keep religion out of foreign policy?' My answer is that we can't and shouldn't. Religion is a large part of what motivates people and shapes their views of justice and right behavior. It must be taken into account" (285). See

Madeleine K. Albright with Bill Woodward, *The Mighty and the Almighty: Reflections on America, God, and World Affairs* (New York: HarperCollins, 2006).

36. Reza Aslan, "Can Democracy Take Root in the Islamic World? Why Religion Must Play a Role in Iran," *New York Times*, 18 July 2003, A17 (my emphasis).

37. "The President's Radio Address: October 15, 2001," *Weekly Compilation of Presidential Documents* 37, no. 41 (2001): 1429.

38. "President Building Worldwide Campaign Against Terrorism," The White House, Washington, D.C., 19 September 2001, <http://www.whitehouse .gov/news/releases/2001/09/20010919-1.html>.

39. Carla Anne Robbins and Jeanne Cummings, "New Doctrine: How Bush Decided That Iraq's Hussein Must Be Ousted," *Wall Street Journal*, 14 June 2002, A1; and Jay Tolson, "Portrait: Bernard Lewis," *U.S. News & World Report*, 3 December 2001, 40.

40. Richard Holbrooke has written about such programs. See, e.g., "Get the Message Out," *Washington Post*, 28 October 2001, B7: "Call it diplomacy, or public affairs, or psychological warfare, or—if you really want to be blunt— propaganda. But whatever it is called, defining what this war [on terror] is really about in the minds of the 1 billion Muslims in the world will be of decisive and historic importance."

41. Alexandra Starr, "Charlotte Beers' Toughest Sell: Can She Market America to Hostile Muslims Abroad?," *Business Week*, 17 December 2001, 56; and Dan Gilgoff and Jay Tolson, "Losing Friends? The Departure of a Top U.S. Diplomat Renews Questions About How to Fight Anti-Americanism," *U.S. News & World Report*, 17 March 2003, 40.

42. Advisory Group on Public Diplomacy for the Arab and Muslim World, "Changing Minds, Winning Peace: A New Direction for U.S. Public Diplomacy in the Arab and Muslim World," 1 October 2003, <http://www.public diplomacy.org/23.htm>.

43. U.S. Department of Defense, "Report of the Defense Science Board Task Force on Strategic Communication" (Washington, D.C.: Office of the Undersecretary of Defense for Acquisition, Technology, and Logistics, 2004), 56.

44. Freedom House Center for Religious Freedom, "Saudi Publications on Hate Ideology Invade American Mosques" (Washington, D.C.: Center for Religious Freedom, 2005). Anne Applebaum makes a similar point about public diplomacy. "To fight [extremism], friendly state visits from Laura Bush will not suffice. Neither will more Britney Spears songs for Muslim teenagers, which is what we play on U.S.-funded Farsi and Arabic radio in the Middle East. Instead, we need to monitor the intellectual and theological struggle for the soul of Islam, and we need to help the moderates." See Applebaum, "Think Again, Karen Hughes," *Washington Post*, 27 July 2005, A21.

45. Corine Hegland, "In Iraq, Sistani Is the Chess Master," *National Journal* 36, no. 16 (2004): 1200.

46. "Asia: Here's Your New Constitution; Afghanistan's Political Transition," *The Economist*, 6 November 2003, 66.

47. "U.S.-funded Iraqi Network Challenges Arab Stations," CNN, 28 November 2003, <http://www.cnn.com/2003/ WORLD/meast/11/28/tv.war.ap/>.

48. David Kaplan, Aamar Latif, Kevin Whitelaw, and Julian Barnes, "Hearts, Minds, and Dollars," *U.S. News & World Report,* 25 April 2005, 22.

49. Ibid.

50. Peter Baker, "Funding Scarce for Export of Democracy," *Washington Post,* 18 March 2005, A1.

51. Private communication, September 2005.

52. Private communication, January 2005.

53. Noah Feldman, *After Jihad: America and the Struggle for Islamic Democracy* (New York: Farrar, Straus and Giroux, 2003); and Robert Saltoff, "Memo to: Karen P. Hughes," *The Weekly Standard,* 28 March 2005, 11.

54. Amitai Etzioni, *From Empire to Community* (New York: Palgrave, 2004).

55. Parts of this chapter are adapted from my articles "Should the United States Support Religious Education in the Islamic World?," *The Journal of Church and State* 48 (Spring 2006): 279–81; and "Religion and the State: Why Moderate Religious Teaching Should Be Promoted," *Harvard International Review* 28, no. 1 (Spring 2006): 14–17.

56. See Etzioni, "The Rights and Responsibilities of Immigrants," *Quadrant,* June 2006, 9–13. For a shorter version published in Europe, see "A Different Approach Towards Immigration," *European Voice,* 27 April 2006; in German translation, see "Das Prinzip des Mosaiks: Fur eine gerechte und praktikable Einwanderungspolitik," *Suddeutsche Zeitung,* 8 April 2006; in Dutch, "Recept voor geslaagde immigratie: Verschneidenheid binnen eenheid," *NRC Handelsblad,* 21 May 2006, 15; and in French: "Droits et devoirs de l'immigré," *Courrier International,* 14 June 2006, 50–51.

57. Charles Clover, "Education Minister Hits at USAID over Textbook Policy," *Financial Times* (London), 24 November 2003, 8.

58. Ibid.

59. Ibid.

60. Christina Asquith, "A New History of Iraq," *The Guardian* (London), 25 November 2003, 8.

61. Clover, "Education Minister Hits at USAID."

62. Mary Ann Zehr, "Religious Study Confronts U.S. in Iraq," *Education Week,* 11 June 2003, 1.

63. Ibid.

64. According to Charles Brown, head of book revision for USAID's Central Asia Task Force, eighteen of the two hundred titles the United States is republishing are primarily introductory Islamic textbooks, used in what agency officials refer to as civics courses. These include teachings on how to live and "be a good Muslim." See Joe Stephens and David B. Ottoway, "From U.S., the ABC's of Jihad: Violent Soviet-Era Textbooks Complicate Afghan Education Efforts," *Washington Post,* 23 March 2002, A1.

65. Ibid.

66. Ibid.

67. Ibid.

68. For the complete text, see USAID Center for Faith-Based and Community Initiatives, "Final Rule: Participation by Religious Organizations in USAID," 20 October 2004, <http://www.usaid.gov/our_work/global_partnerships/fbci/fbocomments_101304.doc>.

69. Kaplan et al., "Hearts, Minds, and Dollars."

70. *United States v. Verdugo-Urquidez*, 494 U.S. 259 (1990).

71. For further discussion see Part VI, "Security Requires a New Global Architecture," below.

72. *Lamont v. Schultz*, No. 88 CIV 0684, 1990 U.S. Dist. LEXIS 12956 (S.D.N.Y. 2 October 1990).

73. *Lamont v. Woods*, No. 90–6311, 1991 U.S. App. LEXIS 22998 (2d Cir. 26 September 1991).

74. Michael Tanner, "Corrupting Charity," Cato Briefing Paper 62, 1 March 2001.

75. Catholic Charities, Frequently Asked Questions, <http://www.catholicchariti esinfo.org/faqs/general.htm>.

76. Joseph R. Hagal, "Faith-Based Community Development: Past, Present, Future," *America*, 23 April 2001, 15.

77. In an often-cited case on the issue of religious organizations' access to public facilities, *Good News Club v. Milford Central School* (2001), the Supreme Court ruled that a community religious club offering prayer and Bible instruction could not be prevented from holding after-school meetings when other community organizations were permitted access to school grounds. See *Good News Club v. Milford Central High School* 533 U.S. 98 (2001).

78. *Zelman v. Simmons-Harris*, 536 U.S. 639 (2002).

79. Personal Responsibility and Work Opportunity Reconciliation Act of 1996, Public Law 104–93, 104th Cong., 2nd sess. (22 August 1996).

80. See Ex. Or. No. 13199 of 29 January 2001, 66 Fed. Reg. 8499; Ex. Or. No. 13279 of 12 December 2002, 67 Fed. Reg. 77141; Ex. Or. No. 13280 of 12 December 2002, 67 Fed. Reg. 77145; and Ex. Or. No. 13342 of 1 June 2004, 69 Fed. Reg. 31509. For details, see <http://www.whitehouse.gov/government/fbci/mission.html>.

81. Michael Fletcher, "Two Fronts in the War on Poverty," *Washington Post*, 17 May 2005, A1.

82. See Laura Mutterperl, "Employment at (God's) Will: The Constitutionality of Anti-Discrimination Exemptions in Charitable Choice Legislation," *Harvard C.R.-C.L. Law Review* 37 (2002): 389; Carl H. Esbeck, "Charitable Choice and the Critics," *N.Y.U. Ann. Surv. Am. L.* 57 (2000): 17; Kent Greenawalt, "Religion and the Rehnquist Court," *Nw. U.L. Rev.* 99 (2004): 145; Michael Kavey, "Private Voucher Schools and the First Amendment Right to Discriminate," *Yale L. J.* 113 (2003): 743; and Carmen M. Guerricagoitia, "Innovation Does

Not Cure Constitutional Violation: Charitable Choice and the Establishment Clause," *Geo. J. Poverty Law & Pol'y* 8 (2001): 447.

83. *Zelman v. Simmons-Harris.*

84. See, e.g., *Roemer v. Maryland Public Works Board,* 426 U.S. 736 (1976); *Bowen v. Kendrick,* 487 U.S. 589 (1988); *Zobrest v. Catalina Foothills School District,* 509 U.S. 1 (1993); and *Witters v. Washington Department of Services for the Blind,* 474 U.S. 481 (1986).

85. "Inherently religious" is the terminology used by the White House Office of Faith-Based and Community Initiatives for activities that the government is barred from supporting. See Ex. Or. No. 13279 of 12 December 2002, 67 Fed. Reg. 77141. "Pervasively sectarian" has, until recently, been the test by which to judge whether or not a faith-based institution is eligible for government support. See *Hunt v. McNair,* 413 U.S. 734 (1973); *Roemer v. Maryland Public Works Board;* and *Lemon v. Kurtzman,* 403 U.S. 602 (1971). Since 2000, however, the Court has significantly diluted the applicability of the "pervasively sectarian" test in favor of judgments based on government neutrality in the distribution of funds and the private choice rationale, by which individual aid recipients may choose to use public funds at religious or secular institutions. See *Mitchell v. Helms,* 530 U.S. 793 (2000).

86. Teen Challenge, for example, is a national, faith-based drug-treatment program that has been praised by President Bush. For more information see <http://www.teenchallengeusa.com>.

87. For more information see <http://www.whitehousedrugpolicy.gov/treat/initiative.html>.

88. The Arabic word *madrasa* literally means "school." Its secondary meaning is an educational institution offering instruction in Islamic subjects. See also Febe Armanios, "Islamic Religious Schools, Madrasas: Background," CRS Report for Congress RS21654 (2003); and Zehr, "Religious Study Confronts U.S. in Iraq."

89. A USAID study found links between *madrasas* and extremist Islamic groups to be "rare but worrisome." See USAID Bureau for Policy and Program Coordination, "Strengthening Education in the Muslim World," Issue Paper No. 2, June 2003, <http://www.dec.org/pdf_docs/PNACW877.pdf>.

90. Some writers have implied that all *madrasas* are harbors of militancy. See, e.g., Jessica Stern, "Preparing for a War on Terrorism," *Current History* 100 (2001): 355–57; and Alan Richards, "At War with Utopian Fanatics," *Middle East Policy* 8 (2001).

91. Miranda Kennedy, "Rumors of Jihad," *Boston Globe,* 4 April 2004, D2.

92. Ibid.

93. Husain Haqqani, "Islam's Medieval Outposts," *Foreign Policy* 133 (November/December 2002): 58; and Valerie Strauss and Emily Wax, "Where Two Worlds Collide: Muslim Schools Face Tension of Islamic, U.S. Views," *Washington Post,* 25 February 2002, A1.

94. Christina Asquith, "The Tricky Business of Rewriting History," *The Teacher*, 4 May 2004.
95. Jonathan Finer, "For Iraqi Students."
96. For more see Thomas Lickona, *Educating for Character: How Our Schools Can Teach Responsibility and Respect* (New York: Bantam, 1992).
97. A report by the Center on Education Policy highlights the role of public schools in teaching children about democratic responsibilities. See Diane Starke Rentner, "Public Schools and Citizenship," July 1998, <http://www.cep-dc.org/democracypublicschools/pubschool_citizen.pdf>.
98. Council for American Private Education, "Facts and Studies," <http://www.capenet.org/facts.html>.
99. Zehr, "Religious Study Confronts U.S. in Iraq."
100. Ibid.
101. Asquith, "A New History of Iraq."
102. World Council of Churches, "Religious Education in Plural Societies: An Inter-religious Curriculum Development Project," 22 November 2000, <http://www.wcc-coe.org/wcc/what/education/project.html>.
103. "Asia: Here's Your New Constitution."
104. Federal Research Division of the Library of Congress and the U.S. Department of the Army, "Indonesia Country Study," 1986–1998, <http://countrystudies.us/indonesia/56.htm>.
105. USAID Bureau for Policy and Program Coordination, "Strengthening Education in the Muslim World," PPC Issue Working Paper No. 1, April 2004, <http://pdf.usaid.gov/pdf_docs/PNACW877.pdf>.
106. Ibid.
107. Ibid.
108. Susan Sachs, "Muslim Schools in U.S. a Voice for Identity," *New York Times*, 10 November 1998, A1.
109. Larry Cohler-Esses, "Sowing Seeds of Hatred: Islamic Textbooks Scapegoat Jews, Christians," *New York Daily News*, 30 March 2003.
110. Jay Tolson, "An Education in Muslim Integration," *U.S. News & World Report*, 21 November 2005, 37–40.
111. Ibid.
112. Ibid.
113. Ibid.
114. "Baghdad Educational Symposium Begins," Press Release, Coalition Provisional Authority, 30 March 2004, <http://www.cpa-iraq.org/pressreleases/20040330_ed_symposium.html> (my emphasis).

PART V. GROUNDS FOR INTERVENTION

1. For the development of the Westphalian notion of sovereignty, see Jens Bartelson, *A Genealogy of Sovereignty* (Cambridge: Cambridge University Press, 1995); F. H. Hinsley, *Sovereignty*, 2nd ed. (Cambridge: Cambridge University

Press, 1986); and Leo Gross, "The Peace of Westphalia, 1648–1948," *The American Journal of International Law* 42, no. 1 (1948): 20–41.

2. Francis M. Deng, Sadikiel Kimaro, Terrence Lyons, Donald Rothchild, and I. William Zartman, *Sovereignty as Responsibility: Conflict Management in Africa* (Washington, D.C.: The Brookings Institution, 1996).

3. Dan Philpott, "Sovereignty," *The Stanford Encyclopedia of Philosophy,* ed. Edward N. Zalta (Stanford: The Metaphysics Research Lab, Stanford University, 2006), <http://plato.stanford.edu/archives/sum2003/entries/sovereignty/>.

4. Deng et al., *Sovereignty as Responsibility,* 211.

5. Bertrand de Jouvenel, *Sovereignty: An Inquiry into the Political Good,* trans. J. F. Huntington (Chicago: The University of Chicago Press, 1957), 303.

6. Jacques Maritain, *Man and the State* (Chicago: University of Chicago Press, 1951), 191.

7. Ibid., 197.

8. Philpott, "Sovereignty."

9. See, e.g., Catharine MacKinnon, *Toward a Feminist Theory of the State* (Cambridge, Mass.: Harvard University Press, 1989).

10. Deng et al., *Sovereignty as Responsibility,* xviii.

11. Ibid., xvii.

12. Ibid., xviii.

13. Stephen Krasner, *Sovereignty: Organized Hypocrisy* (Princeton: Princeton University Press, 2001).

14. See David Rohde, *Endgame: The Betrayal and Fall of Srebrenica, Europe's Worst Massacre Since World War II* (New York: Farrar, Straus and Giroux, 1997). Still other instances prior to the 1990s in which the international community failed to act in the face of genocide and ethnic cleansing have been chronicled in Samantha Power, *A Problem from Hell: America and the Age of Genocide* (New York: Basic Books, 2002); Adam LeBor, *Complicity with Evil* (New Haven: Yale University Press, 2006).

15. As qtd. in the International Commission on Intervention and State Sovereignty (ICISS), *The Responsibility to Protect* (Ottawa: The International Development Research Centre, December 2001), 2; James Traub, *The Best Intentions* (New York: Farrar, Straus and Giroux, 2006).

16. Ibid., 13.

17. High-Level Panel on Threats, Challenges, and Change, "A More Secure World: Our Shared Responsibility," 2 December 2004, <http://www.un.org/secureworld/>.

18. Kofi Annan, "In Larger Freedom: Towards Development, Security and Human Rights for All," March 2005, <http://www.un.org/largerfreedom>.

19. Gareth Evans, "Uneasy Bedfellows: 'The Responsibility to Protect' and Feinstein-Slaughter's 'Duty to Prevent,'" speech delivered at the American Society of International Law Conference, Washington, D.C., 1 April 2004, <http://www.crisisgroup.org/home/index.cfm?id=2560&l=1>.

20. Deng et al., *Sovereignty as Responsibility*, xviii.

21. For further context, see Alexander Wendt, *Social Theory of International Politics* (New York: Cambridge University Press, 1999).

22. See Mark Blitz, *Duty Bound: Responsibility and American Public Life* (Lanham, Md.: Rowman and Littlefield, 2005); Susan Sauvé, *Aristotle on Moral Responsibility* (Cambridge, Mass.: Blackwell, 1993); J. R. Lucas, *Responsibility* (New York: Oxford University Press, 1993); John Martin Fischer, *Moral Responsibility* (Ithaca, N.Y.: Cornell University Press, 1986); and Herbert Fingarette, *On Responsibility* (New York: Basic, 1967).

23. See "A Universal Declaration of Human Responsibilities," *The Responsive Community* 8, no. 2 (1998).

24. See, e.g., Amartya Sen, *The Argumentative Indian: Writings on Indian History, Culture, and Identity* (New York: Farrar, Straus and Giroux, 2005). In this book Sen argues that numerous Asian thinkers and statesmen have championed political beliefs analogous to human rights for centuries. See also Daniel Bell, *East Meets West: Human Rights and Democracy in East Asia* (Princeton: Princeton University Press, 2000); and Joseph Runzo, Nancy Martin, and Arvind Sharma, ed., *Human Rights and Responsibilities in the World Religions* (Oxford: One World, 2003). For a contemporary Roman Catholic perspective on human rights, see Mary Ann Glendon, *Catholicism and Human Rights* (Dayton, Ohio: University of Dayton Press, 2001).

25. See Daniel Bell and Joanne Bauer, eds., *East Asian Challenge for Human Rights* (New York: Cambridge University Press, 1999).

26. See "The Responsive Communitarian Platform," 1991, <http://www.gwu.edu/ccps/platformtext.html>.

27. Etzioni, *The New Golden Rule: Community and Morality in a Democratic Society* (New York: Basic Books, 1996).

28. Samuel Warren and Louis Brandeis, "The Right to Privacy," *Harvard Law Review* 4 (1890): 289–320.

29. See also Nikolas K. Gvosdev, "Achieving a Global Community, Realistically," *The Good Society* 14, no. 3 (2005): 10–14.

30. For an overview, see Ronald H. Cole, "Operation Urgent Fury: The Planning and Execution of Joint Operations in Grenada, 12 October–2 November 1983," Joint History Office, Office of the Chairman of the Joint Chiefs of Staff, Washington, D.C., 1997; for the British criticism of the invasion, see Margaret Thatcher, *The Downing Street Years* (New York: HarperCollins, 1993), 331.

31. The "Don Pacifico Incident" of 1850 was a notorious example, in which the British foreign secretary, Lord Palmerston, dispatched a naval squadron to blockade the Greek port of Piraeus, in order to coerce the Greek government into compensating the British-born Portuguese Don Pacifico for an ethnically inspired attack he suffered in Athens. See Norman Dennis, "The Private of the Buffs: Earning Honour," *The Civitas Review* 2, no. 1 (March 2005): 1–8.

32. Deng et al., *Sovereignty as Responsibility*, 223.

33. ICISS, *Responsibility to Protect*, xii.

34. For the implications of the interventions in Kosovo and Timor, and the failure in Rwanda, see Kofi Annan, "Two Concepts of Sovereignty," *The Economist*, 18 September 1999, 49–50: "In cases where forceful intervention does become necessary, the Security Council—the body charged with authorising the use of force under international law—must be able to rise to the challenge. *The choice must not be between council unity and inaction in the face of genocide—as in the case of Rwanda—and council division, but regional action, as in the case of Kosovo.* In both cases, the U.N. should have been able to find common ground in upholding the principles of the charter, and acting in defence of our common humanity" (my emphasis).

35. Office of the High Commissioner for Human Rights, "Convention on the Prevention and Punishment of the Crime of Genocide," 9 December 1948, <http://www.unhchr.ch/html/menu3/b/p_genoci.htm>.

36. Lee Feinstein and Anne-Marie Slaughter, "A Duty to Prevent," *Foreign Affairs* 83, no. 1 (2004): 136–51.

37. Ibid.

38. Ibid.

39. For details, see the Office of the Press Secretary, "G-8 Action Plan on Nonproliferation," 9 July 2004, <http://www.whitehouse.gov/news/releases/2004/06/20040609-28.html>.

40. For more on PSI, see the U.S. Department of State, "Proliferation Security Initiative," 26 May 2005, <http://www.state.gov/t/np/rls/other/46858.htm>.

41. Evans, "Uneasy Bedfellows."

42. See, e.g., Mohamed ElBaradei, "Implementation of the NPT Safeguards Agreement in the Islamic Republic of Iran," report to the IAEA Board of Governors, 31 August 2006, <http://www.iaea.org/ Publications/Documents/Board/2006/gov2006–53.pdf>: "Iran has not addressed the long outstanding verification issues or provided the necessary transparency to remove uncertainties associated with some of its activities. Iran has not suspended its enrichment related activities; nor has Iran acted in accordance with the provisions of the Additional Protocol."

43. See Walter Pincus, "Push for Nuclear-Free Middle East Resurfaces: Arab Nations Seek Answers About Israel," *Washington Post*, 6 March 2005, A24: "Israeli Ambassador Daniel Ayalon said last week that the idea of a nuclear-free zone is something to be discussed. But he described his country as being small and surrounded by 22 Arab countries, 'many of them hostile.' Therefore, he added during an appearance on John McLaughlin's 'One on One' program, a Middle East nuclear-free zone 'will be viewed very favorably by Israel once we have a comprehensive peace in the area and there are no dangers of attacks or delegitimization by any other country.'"

44. George Perkovich, " 'Democratic Bomb': Failed Strategy," Carnegie Endow-

ment, November 2006; Ashley J. Tellis, "Atoms for War? U.S.-Indian Civilian Nuclear Cooperation and India's Nuclear Arsenal," Carnegie Endowment, 2006; George Perkovich, "Faulty Promises: The U.S.-India Nuclear Deal," Carnegie Endowment, September 2005.

PART VI. SECURITY REQUIRES A NEW GLOBAL ARCHITECTURE

1. Some sections of this part are adapted from my article "Pre-empting Nuclear Terrorism in a New Global Order," Foreign Policy Centre, London, October 2004.
2. See, e.g., Margaret T. Wrightson, "Maritime Security: Enhancements Made, But Implementation and Sustainability Remain Key Challenges," testimony before the U.S. Senate Committee on Commerce, Science, and Transportation, U.S. Government Accountability Office, 17 May 2005, <http://www.global security.org/security/library/report/gao/d05448t.pdf>.
3. Matthew Brzezinski, *Fortress America: On the Frontlines of Homeland Security—An Inside Look at the Coming Surveillance State* (New York: Bantam, 2004), 8.
4. Jonathan Weisman, "House Passes $7.4 Billion Port Security Bill," *Washington Post*, 5 May 2006, A4.
5. See Stephen Flynn, *America the Vulnerable* (New York: HarperCollins, 2005); and Clark Kent Ervin, *Open Target* (New York: Palgrave Macmillan, 2006).
6. Committee on the Future of Emergency Care in the United States Health System, "Hospital-based Emergency Care: At the Breaking Point" (Washington, D.C.: National Academies Press, 2006), <http://www.nap.edu/cata log/11621.html>.
7. Barton Reppert, "United States Facing Cyber Security Crisis, Experts Tell Capitol Hill Briefing, as IEEE-USA Prepares New Position Statement," *IEEE-USA Today's Engineer Online*, August 2005, <http://www.todaysengineer.org/2005/Aug/cybersecurity.asp>.
8. Ibid.
9. "Health System Unprepared for Water Terrorism," BORR News Center for the Study of Terrorism and Political Violence, 19 June 2003, <http://www.borrull.org/e/noticia.php?id=18572&PHPSESSID= dbaf2116d3c265aa 6b62f01cee8d5f90>.
10. Andy Pasztor, "Freighted with Worry," *Wall Street Journal*, 15 August 2006, B1.
11. Eric Lipton, "Screening Tools Slow to Arrive in U.S. Airports," *New York Times*, 3 September 2006, A1.
12. Eric Lipton, "Setbacks Stymie Bid to Stockpile Bioterror Drugs," *New York Times*, 18 September 2006, A1.
13. Eric Lipton, "Debate over Security for Chemical Plants Focuses on How Strict to Make Rules," *New York Times*, 21 September 2006, A29.
14. See Ervin, *Open Target*.

15. The budget for the Transportation Security Administration in fiscal year 2006 was $5 billion. See Greta Wodele, "Senate Panel Passes $30.8 Billion Homeland Security Bill," *Government Executive,* 17 July 2005.

16. See Brzezinski, *Fortress America.*

17. "Man-portable Air Defense Systems (MANPADS) Proliferation: Understanding the Problem," Federation of American Scientists, Arms Sales Monitoring Project, <http://www.fas.org/asmp/campaigns/MANPADS/MANPADS.html>.

18. A 2003 RAND estimate put the total cost of installation, operation, upkeep, and associated costs at $38.2 billion. See James Chow et al., "Protecting Commercial Aviation Against Shoulder-Fired Missile Threat," Rand Corporation, 2005.

19. *Dirty War* (HBO Television), 24 January 2005.

20. Eric Lipton, "Security Cuts for New York and Washington," *New York Times,* 1 June 2006, A18.

21. Spencer S. Hsu, "U.S. Struggles to Rank Potential Terror Targets," *Washington Post,* 16 July 2006.

22. Katherine Shrader, "Hayden Would Inherit a CIA in Transition, Agency to Triple Number of Spies Worldwide by '07," *Boston Globe,* 20 May 2006, A2.

23. Federal Bureau of Investigation, "Strategic Plan 2004–2009," <http://www.fbi.gov/publications/ strategicplan/strategicplanfull.pdf>; see also John D. Banusiewicz, "Bush Announces Global Posture Changes over Next Decade," American Forces Press Service, 16 August 2004.

24. Stuart Levey, Under Secretary for Terrorism and Financial Intelligence, testimony before the House Financial Services Subcommittee on Oversight and Investigations, 11 July 2006.

25. See Fawaz Gerges, *The Far Enemy: Why Jihad Went Global* (New York: Cambridge University Press, 2005), 251–76.

26. Michael T. Osterholm and John Schwartz, *Living Terrors* (New York: Delacorte Press, 2000).

27. Sasha Nagy, "Massive Terror Attack Averted," *Globe and Mail* (Toronto), 3 June 2006.

28. James Belke, "Chemical Accident Risks in U.S. Industry—A Preliminary Analysis of Accident Risk Data from U.S. Hazardous Chemical Facilities," in *Proceedings of the Tenth International Symposium on Loss Prevention and Safety Promotion in the Process Industries,* ed. O. Fredholm, A. Jacobsson, and H. J. Pasman (Elsevier Science and Technology: Stockholm, 2001).

29. Randall Larsen, "70–20–10," *Wall Street Journal,* 25 May 2006, A14.

30. "Tens of thousands" of locations around the world make use of commercial radiation sources, and in places like the former Soviet Union regulatory controls are "urgently needed" to secure these sources. See Charles Ferguson et al., "Commercial Radioactive Sources: Surveying the Security Risks," Monterey Institute of International Studies Occasional Paper 11, January 2003.

31. For varied perspectives on nuclear terrorism, see Graham Allison, "How to

Stop Nuclear Terror," *Foreign Affairs* 83, no. 1 (January/February 2004): 64–74; Graham Allison and Andrei Kokoshin, "The New Containment," *The National Interest* 69 (2002): 35–43; Richard L. Garwin, "The Technology of Mega Terror," *Technology Review* 105, no. 7 (2002): 64–68; and William C. Potter and Jonathan B. Tucker, "Weapons Spreading," *Washington Post,* 28 May 1999, A35. For an analysis of the effects of dirty bombs, see Kishore Kuchibhotla and Matthew McKinzie, "Nuclear Terrorism and Nuclear Accidents in South Asia," in *Reducing Nuclear Dangers in South Asia,* ed. Michael Krepon and Ziad Haider (Washington, D.C.: Henry L. Stimson Center, 2004).

32. Ashton B. Carter, "How to Counter WMD," *Foreign Affairs* 83, no. 5 (September/October 2004): 72–87.

33. Matthew Bunn, Anthony Wier, and John P. Holdren, *Controlling Nuclear Warheads and Materials: A Report Card and Action Plan* (Belfer Center for Science and International Affairs and The Nuclear Threat Initiative, March 2003).

34. Graham Allison, *Nuclear Terrorism: The Ultimate Preventable Catastrophe* (New York: Owl Books, 2004).

35. George Perkovich et al., *Universal Compliance: A Strategy for Nuclear Security* (Washington, D.C.: Carnegie Endowment for International Peace, 2004).

36. Charles D. Ferguson and William Potter, *The Four Faces of Nuclear Terrorism* (New York: Routledge, 2005).

37. Remarks delivered by Lt. Gen. Robert Gard, Detroit, Mich., 9 August 2005, <http://www.armscontrolcenter.org/archives/002029.php>; see also Allison, *Nuclear Terrorism,* 3–4. The Harvard terrorism expert, describing what would happen upon detonation of a ten-kiloton nuclear weapon in Times Square, wrote, "Times Square would vanish in the twinkling of an eye. The blast would generate temperatures reaching into the tens of millions of degrees Fahrenheit. The resulting fireball and blast wave would destroy instantaneously the theater district, the New York Times building, Grand Central Terminal, and every other structure within a third of a mile of the point of detonation. The ensuing firestorm would engulf Rockefeller Center, Carnegie Hall, the Empire State Building, and Madison Square Garden, leaving a landscape resembling the World Trade Center site. . . . On a normal workday, more than half a million people crowd the area within a half-mile radius of Times Square. A noon detonation in midtown could kill them all."

38. Robert S. Boynton, "The Neocon Who Isn't," *American Prospect Online,* 5 October 2005, <http://www.prospect.org/web/page.ww?section=root&name=ViewPrint&articleId=10304>.

39. Francis Fukuyama, "The Neoconservative Moment," *The National Interest* 76 (Summer 2004): 57–68.

40. Sen. Richard G. Lugar, remarks to the National Press Club, Washington, D.C., 11 August 2004.

41. Thomas Donnelly, "Choosing Among Bad Options: The Pakistani 'Loose Nukes' Conundrum," *National Security Outlook* (Washington, D.C.: American Enterprise Institute, May 2006), 1.

42. In 2005 combined Nunn-Lugar appropriations, over all of the involved departments, amounted to slightly over $1 billion. See Amy Woolf, "Nonproliferation and Threat Reduction Assistance: U.S. Programs in the Former Soviet Union," CRS Report for Congress, 19 April 2005.

43. See Allison, *Nuclear Terrorism*, chap. 7.

44. Personal communication with Marvin Miller, formerly a senior research scientist in the Department of Nuclear Engineering at the Massachusetts Institute of Technology, 6 August 2004.

45. Remarks by Lt. Gen. Robert Gard.

46. Craig Cerniello, "Russian Officials Deny Claims of Missing Nuclear Weapons," *Arms Control Today* 27, no. 6 (September 1997): 30; and James B. Foley, "U.S. Department of State Daily Press Briefing," 5 September 1997, <http://secretary.state.gov/www/briefings/9709/970905db.html>.

47. Gunnar Arbman and Charles Thornton, "Russia's Tactical Nuclear Weapons, Part I: Background and Policy Issues" (Stockholm: Swedish Defence Research Agency, 2003), 35–37.

48. See the "Megatons to Megawatt" program, at <http://www.usec.com/v2001_02/HTML/megatons.asp>.

49. Morten Bremer Maerli and Lars van Dassen, "Nuclear Terrorism: Eliminating Excessive Stocks of Highly Enriched Uranium," *Pugwash Issue Brief* 3, no. 1 (April 2005): 3.

50. Database on Nuclear Smuggling, Theft and Orphan Radiation Sources (DSTO), Center for International Security and Cooperation, Institute of International Studies, Stanford University, 2002 (restricted access).

51. Matthew Bunn and Anthony Wier, *Securing the Bomb 2006* (Cambridge, Mass.: Project on Managing the Atom, Harvard University, and Nuclear Threat Initiative, July 2006), 11–13.

52. Scott Parrish and Tamara Robinson, "Efforts to Strengthen the Export Controls and Combat Illicit Trafficking and Brain Drain," *Nonproliferation Review* (Spring 2000); and Matthew Bunn, *The Next Wave: Urgently Needed Steps to Control Warheads and Fissile Materials* (Cambridge, Mass.: Carnegie Endowment for International Peace, March 2000).

53. Maerli and van Dassen, "Nuclear Terrorism," 4.

54. Peter Baker, "U.S. and Russia to Enter Civilian Nuclear Pact," *Washington Post*, 8 July 2006, A1.

55. Kevin Watkins, ed., "Human Development Report 2005" (New York: United Nations Development Programme, 2005), 21–24. See also "Putin's Methods Counterproductive in Russian Fight on Corruption and Terrorism," Radio Free Europe/Radio Liberty, 19 December 2004, <http://www.rferl.org/releases/2004 /12/289-191204.asp>.

56. Private communication with Laura Holgate, Vice President for Russia/New Independent States Programs at the Nuclear Threat Initiative.

57. Union of Concerned Scientists, "Research Reactors Fueled by Highly Enriched Uranium," 10 August 2005, <http://www.ucsusa.org/global_securi

ty/nuclear_terrorism/research-reactors-fueled-by-highly-enriched-urani
um-heu.html>.

58. Private communication with Laura Holgate.

59. Robert Orttung and Louise Shelley, "Linkages Between Terrorist and Organized Crime Groups in Eurasian Nuclear Smuggling," remarks delivered at
the Woodrow Wilson International Center for Scholars, Washington, D.C., 12
December 2005.

60. Considerable additional evidence is posted at Orttung and Shelley's Transnational Crime and Corruption Center Web site, <http://www.american.edu/
traccc/>; evidence is available from other sources such as Foreign Policy's
Failed State Index and Transparency International's Corruption Perceptions
Index.

61. Cf. Robert J. Einhorn, "Dangerous States: North Korea, Iran and Pakistan,"
Center for Strategic and International Studies (unpublished manuscript).

62. See, e.g., Joel Brinkley and Steven R. Weisman, "Rice Seeks Details on
Pakistan's Nuclear Help to Iran," New York Times, 16 March 2005, A8.

63. Thomas Donnelly, "Choosing Among Bad Options," AEI Online National
Security Outlook, 17 May 2006, <http://www.aei.org/publications/
pubID.24416/pub_detail.asp>. His findings are here reported with
his permission. See also U.S. Department of Defense, Report of the Quadrennial Defense Review (Arlington, Va.: Department of Defense, 6 February
2006), 32.

64. Joseph Cirincione, Jon Wolfsthal, and Miriam Rajkumar, Deadly Arsenals:
Nuclear, Biological, and Chemical Threats, 2nd ed. (Washington D.C.: Carnegie
Endowment for International Peace, 2005), 239–58 passim.

65. See David Albright and Corey Hinderstein, "Unraveling the A. Q. Khan and
Future Proliferation Networks," The Washington Quarterly (Spring 2005):
111–28.

66. Ibid., 112.

67. Donnelly, "Choosing Among Bad Options."

68. "Books and Arts: Opening the Door; Nuclear Proliferation," The Economist,
29 July 2006, 83.

69. Spencer Abraham, "How to Stop Nuclear Terror," Washington Post, 17 July
2004, A19.

70. Susan Eisenhower, presentation to the board of the Nuclear Threat Initiative,
Washington, D.C., 18 May 2004.

71. According to the IAEA, as of 1 October 2006, 247 research reactors are oper-
ational worldwide. Two-hundred and thirty-nine have been shut down, and
169 have been decommissioned. An additional 10 are under construction,
and 4 more are planned. In a private communication with Benn Tannenbaum, project director, Center for Science, Technology & Security Policy,
American Association for the Advancement of Science.

72. Private communication with Benn Tannenbaum.

73. Greg Webb, "Nigeria Commissions Research Reactor, HEU-Fueled Facility

Goes Against U.S.-led Nonproliferation Effort," Nuclear Threat Initiative Global Security Newswire, 1 October 2004, <http://www.nti.org/d_news wire/issues/2004/10/1/255a6161-b010-4711-a111-b12697bedd56.html>.

74. See Alexander Glaser and Frank von Hippel, "On the Importance of Ending the Use of HEU in the Nuclear Fuel Cycle: An Updated Assessment," 2002 International Meeting on Reduced Enrichment for Research and Test Reactors, 3–8 November 2002.

75. See Jeremy Whitlock, "The Evolution of CANDU Fuel Cycles and Their Potential Contribution to World Peace," International Youth Nuclear Congress 2000, 9–14 April 2000.

76. Steven R. Weisman, "Warming to Brazil, Powell Says Its Nuclear Program Isn't a Concern," New York Times, 6 October 2004, A5.

77. "Remarks of Secretary of State Condoleezza Rice at the House International Relations Committee on the U.S.-India Civil Nuclear Cooperation Initiative," U.S. House Committee on International Relations, 5 April 2006, <http://state.gov/secretary/rm/2006/64146.htm>.

78. Leonor Tomero, "U.S.-Indian Nuclear Deal: Proliferation Risks and Costs," Center for Arms Control and Non-Proliferation, 2 March 2006, <http://www.armscontrolcenter.org/archives/002248.php>.

79. Sen. Joseph R. Biden, Jr., "U.S.-India Atomic Energy Cooperation," hearing before the U.S. Senate Committee on Foreign Relations, 5 April 2006.

80. Kevin Howe, "Nobel Winner Sees Nuclear 'Hypocrisy,'" Monterey County Herald, 31 May 2006.

81. David Albright and Paul Brannan, "Commercial Satellite Imagery Suggests Pakistan Is Building a Second, Much Larger Plutonium Production Reactor: Is South Asia Headed for a Dramatic Buildup in Nuclear Arsenals?," Institute for Science and International Security, 24 July 2006, <http://www.isis-online.org/publications/southasia/newkhushab.pdf>; see also Joby Warrick, "Pakistan Expanding Nuclear Program," Washington Post, 24 July 2006, A1. Some experts, such as the Natural Resources Defense Council's Thomas Cochran, have contested the forty–fifty nuke assertion. What is not contested, however, is that the new reactor will augment Pakistan's ability to produce nuclear weapons.

82. For a related set of ideas, see Ashton Carter, "Overhauling Counterproliferation," Technology in Society 26 (2004): 257–69.

83. Similar to the approach I outline here, ElBaradei aims at eliminating potential sources of materials for nuclear weapons with steps moving beyond controlled maintenance. ElBaradei places disarmament at a high priority; he urges nations to "move away from national security strategies that rely on nuclear weapons, which serve as a constant stimulus for other nations to acquire them." Then he urges "tightened controls on the proliferation-sensitive parts of the nuclear fuel cycle." See Mohamed ElBaradei, "Rethinking Nuclear Safeguards," Washington Post, 14 June 2006, A23.

84. The inspections role for the IAEA is somewhat new, having taken on this role

in a detailed manner after the first Gulf War. Its original and, some would argue, still primary, mission was to promote the use of nuclear power worldwide. See "Pillars of Nuclear Cooperation: Promoting Safeguards & Verification," <http://www.iaea.org/OurWork/SV/index.html>.

85. Mohamed ElBaradai, interview with Lally Weymouth, "Q&A: ElBaradai, Feeling the Nuclear Heat," *Washington Post*, 30 January 2005, B1; and Carl E. Behrens, *CRS Issue Brief for Congress: Nuclear Nonproliferation Issues,* Congressional Research Service, 3 June 2005.

86. Pierre Goldschmidt, "Future Challenges for Nuclear Non-proliferation Instruments," presented at a conference of the NATO Defense College and the Senior Politico-Military Group on Proliferation, Rome, March 2004.

87. Allison, *Nuclear Terrorism,* 19–42.

88. Perkovich et al., *Universal Compliance,* 87.

89. Allison, *Nuclear Terrorism,* 141–42; Carter, "How to Counter WMD," 79–80. See also Perkovich et al., *Universal Compliance,* chap. 1; and Ferguson and Potter, *Four Faces of Nuclear Terrorism,* chap. 7.

90. See David Glenn, "A Bomb in Every Backyard," *Chronicle of Higher Education* 51, no. 2 (September 2004): A16.

91. See Etzioni, *Winning Without War* (Garden City, N.Y.: Doubleday, 1964); and *The Hard Way to Peace: A New Strategy* (New York: Collier, 1962).

92. On the United States and the U.S.S.R., see Fred Kaplan, "JFK's First Strike Plan," *The Atlantic Monthly,* October 2001, 81; on Pakistan and India see Scott D. Sagan, "The Perils of Proliferation in South Asia," *Asian Survey* 41 (2001): 1064–86; and on Israel see Benny Morris, *Righteous Victims* (New York: Alfred A. Knopf, 1999), 404.

93. Larry Rohter, "Brazil Pressing for Favorable Treatment on Nuclear Fuel," *New York Times,* 25 September 2004, A3.

94. Gordon Fairclough, "Nuclear Testing Triggers Calls for More Control," *Wall Street Journal,* 16 September 2004, A16.

95. See <http://www.energy.gov/news/1359.htm>. See also, e.g., Matthew L. Wald and Judith Miller, "Energy Department Plans a Push to Retrieve Nuclear Materials," *New York Times,* 26 May 2004, A16; and Carola Hoyos, "U.S. and Russia to Sign Enriched Uranium Retrieval Accord," *Financial Times* (London), 26 May 2004, 12.

96. Peter Slevin, "Plan Launched to Reclaim Nuclear Fuel," *Washington Post,* 26 May 2004, A21.

97. Bunn and Wier, *Securing the Bomb 2006,* 59.

98. Private communication, 13 July 2006.

99. The IAEA database does not include any data on how much HEU or LEU was ever at a reactor.

100. See <http://www.iaea.org/worldatom/rrdb/>.

101. Bunn and Wier, *Securing the Bomb 2006,* 64.

102. Ibid.

103. See Graham Allison, ed., *Confronting the Specter of Nuclear Terrorism* (Thousand Oaks, Calif.: SAGE, 2006).

104. Sen. Richard G. Lugar, remarks to the National Press Club, Washington, D.C., 11 August 2004.

105. Carter, "How to Counter WMD," 80.

106. Abraham, "How to Stop Nuclear Terror."

107. U.S. Department of Energy Office of Civilian Radioactive Waste Management, "Factsheet: What Are Spent Nuclear Fuel and High-Level Radioactive Waste?," <http://www.ocrwm.doe.gov/factsheets/ doeympo338.shtml>.

108. Observers do contend that North Korea's actions violated the spirit of the 1994 Agreed Framework.

109. A national policy that combines both soft and hard power has been coined "smart power" by Joseph Nye. See Joseph Nye, Jr., *Soft Power: The Means to Success in World Politics* (New York: Public Affairs, 2004).

110. See also Joseph Nye, Jr., "Redefining the National Interest," *Foreign Affairs* 78, no. 4 (July/August 1999): 22–36.

111. Carla Anne Robbins, "Why U.S. Gave U.N. No Role in Plan To Halt Arms Ships," *Wall Street Journal*, 21 October 2003, A1.

112. The White House, Office of the Press Secretary, "Fact Sheet: Proliferation Security Initiative: Statement of Interdiction Principles," 4 September 2003, <http://www.state.gov/t/np/rls/fs/23764.htm>.

113. Mark Valencia, "Pressing for Sea Change," *Washington Times*, 25 August 2003, A15.

114. John Bolton, "The Bush Administration's Forward Strategy for Nonproliferation," address given at the American Enterprise Institute, Washington, D.C., 24 June 2004.

115. David Sanger, "U.S. and Russia Will Police Potential Nuclear Targets," *New York Times*, 15 July 2006, A9.

ACKNOWLEDGMENTS

I am indebted to Derek Mitchell, who worked with me as a research assistant on this book from inception to completion, making numerous editorial and substantive suggestions. Kristin Bell served as an outstanding research assistant on the same project. Jon Ehrenfeld, Ean Fullerton, and Nicholas Wheeler helped greatly in the last stage of developing this manuscript. Kyle Burgess helped to put the book to bed and prepared the index. Kelly Makowiecki herded the many pieces until they became one.

I am indebted to numerous colleagues for comments. William Friedland and Michael Horowitz on the role of Warriors. The case studies included in Part III benefited greatly from comments by Vasudha Dalmia, John S. Hawley, Vinay Lal, and John Nemec on the Hinduism section; by Stephen M. Fields, SJ, Alan Mitchell, Kip C. Richardson, Patrick Provost-Smith, Christopher W. Steck, SJ, and Robert Wilken on the Christianity section; by John O. Voll on the Islam section; and by Robert Eisen, Eva Etzioni-Halevy, Elanit Rothschild, and Marc Saperstein on Judaism. Michael Kazin supervised the research and Kevin Noble Powers served as research assistant on the study of socialism and the civil rights movement. Benn Tannenbaum, Laura Holgate, and Mary Beth Nikitin guided me through Part VI. Gary E. Langer and Juliana Menasce Horowitz helped me a great deal in the use of public opinion polls in Part III.

I greatly benefited from comments about the development in Kosovo by Nida Gelazis and Marty Sletzinger; in Iraq and Afghanistan by James Hershberg and Frederick Starr; in Libya by Bruce Jentleson; and in Iran and North Korea by Selig Harrison and Michael Levi.

I would especially like to thank Clifford Bob and Henry Nau for their comments on the book as a whole.

My book agent, Fredrica Friedman, served as an invaluable guide in bringing this book to publication.

Parts of following sections of this book have been adapted from previous publications:

Part I—Segments are included in "Security First: Ours, Theirs, and the Global Order's," *The National Interest* 88 (March/April 2007).

Part II—"A Self-restrained Approach to Nation-building by Foreign Powers," *International Affairs* 80, no. 1 (January 2004): 1–17.

Part II—"Reconstruction: An Agenda," *Journal of Intervention and Statebuilding* 1, no. 1 (2006).

Part III, Chapter F—"The Global Importance of Illiberal Moderates," *Cambridge Review of International Affairs* 19, no. 3 (September 2006): 369–85.

Part IV, Chapter A—"Stati in crisi, cultura morale e politica estera," *Quaderni di scienza politica* (April 2006): 7–16.

Part IV, Chapter B—"Religion and the State: Why Moderate Religious Teaching Should Be Promoted," *Harvard International Review* (March 7, 2006): 7–16.

Part IV, Chapter B—"Should the United States Support Religious Education in the Islamic World?" *Journal of Church and State* (Spring 2006): 369–85.

Part V—"From Right to Responsibility, the Definition of Sovereignty Is Changing," *Interdependent* (Winter 2005/2006): 35.

Part VI—*Pre-Empting Nuclear Terrorism in a New Global Order*, Foreign Policy Center, October 2004.

INDEX

Abduh, Muhammad, 139
Abraham, Spencer, 231n69, 240, 242
Ackerman, Bruce, 14n31, 94n22
Afghanistan, 2–3, 14–15, 19–29, 45–46,
    134, 141, 213; antisocial behavior in, xvii,
    91–92, 152, 155, 157–58; constitution of,
    26, 170–72; and democratization, xiii,
    xv, xvi, 2–3, 19, 25–26, 32, 44–46, 49–
    50; education in, 173, 175, 181, 184; and
    Hi-Devolution, 30, 78–79, 168; moral
    culture in, 91–92, 152, 163, 167–68,
    172; and nation-building, 45, 77–78;
    and reconstruction, xviii, 41, 64–66;
    and social engineering, 41, 45, 65–66;
    supreme court of, 26, 172; and women,
    21, 26, 155. See also Taliban
Aizenman, N. C., 157n25
Ake, Claude, 3n5
al-Attar, Ali, 185
al-Banna, Hassan, 137
Albright, David, 230n65, 234n81
Albright, Madeleine, 51, 163n35
Ali, Ayaan Hirsi, 90
al-Jaafari, Ibrahim, 20
al-Jilani, Abd al-Qadir, 139
Allawi, Iyad, 20
Allison, Graham, 218, 219n37, 223n43,
    237n87, 238n89, 241n103

al-Maliki, Nouri, 26, 27
al-Qaradawi, Yusuf, 139–40n153
al-Qasimi, Jamal al-Din, 139
al-Sadr, Muqtada, 27, 60
al-Sistani, Grand Ayatalloh Ali, xiv, 26,
    139, 167
Ambrose of Milan, Saint, 110
American Center for International Labor
    Solidarity, 169
American Civil Liberties Union (ACLU),
    214
Americans for Religious Liberty, 176
Anderson, John W., 60n50
Anderson, Joseph, 75
Anklesaria Aiyar, Swaminathan S., 24n54
Annan, Kofi, 197, 198, 202n34
anti-aircraft missiles, 213
antisocial behavior, xvii, 98, 152–57, 173,
    181–82, 191; in Afghanistan, xvii, 91–
    92, 152, 155, 157–58, 182, 191; in China,
    154–55; in Iraq, xvii, 30, 152, 156, 181–
    82, 191; in Russia, xvii, 15, 98, 153–54,
    156, 182; in the United States, 159; cf.
    moral culture
Applebaum, Anne, 166n44
Aquinas, Thomas, Saint, 106–7, 195
Arbman, Gunnar, 224n47
Arendt, Hannah, 94

Aristide, Jean-Bertrand, 31
Asadi, Bagher, 13n27
Asbridge, Thomas, 106
Aslan, Reza, 164n36
Asquith, Christina, 175, 182n94, 186n101
Atoms for Peace, 231
Augustine of Hippo, Saint, 95, 109n55
Aum Shinrikyo, 218

Badawi, Abdullah Ahmad, 146
Bahgat, Gawdat, 9n14
Bainton, Roland, 108n53, 112n63, 113n65
Bajrang Dal, 123–24
Baker, Peter, xv n.4, 169n50, 226n54
Bangladesh, 77, 89, 142, 150
Banusiewicz, John D., 215n23
Barakat, Sultan, 63
Barclay, Gordon, 154n9
Barnes, Julian, 168n48
Barnett, Anthony, 14n30
basic security, def. 2; xiii–xv, 8, 30–33,
    59–61, 76, 159, 208. See also human
    security; responsibility to protect;
    Security First
Bass, Gary, 69–70
Bauer, Joanne, 200n25
Beinart, Peter, xiv n.1
Belke, James, 217n28
Bell, Daniel, 199n24, 200n25
Ben-Gurion, David, 22–23
Benoliel, Sharon, 187
Benvenisti, Eyal, 69
Berlin, Isaiah, 94
Bernard of Clairvaux, Saint, 111
Bernstein, Eduard, 133
Bethell, Leslie, 48n29
Bharati, Uma, 124
Biden, Joseph, 29n65, 78n104, 233–34
bin Laden, Osama, 102, 136–37, 139, 148,
    219, 231
bin Mohamed, Mahathir, 146, 200
Blackburn, Simon, 93n21
Blitz, Mark, 215n22
Blustein, P., 71n91
Bolton, John, 245n114
Bondurant, Joan, 125n104
Boot, Max, 149n190, 150n196
border control, 14; in Afghanistan, 25, 29;
    in Iraq, 62, 72, 74; in Russia, 15, 16,

224; in the United States, 158–59, 209,
    210–11
Bowen, Stuart, Jr., 60, 73–74
Boynton, Robert S., 219n38
Brandeis, Louis, 200n25
Brannan, Paul, 234n81
Brazil, 233; and deproliferation, 206, 233,
    236, 239; and reform of the U.N., 207
Bremer, L. Paul, 20, 23, 26–28, 167
Brinkley, Joel, 13n22, 60n54, 229n62
Brooks, David, 58, 87
Brown, Archie, 42
Brown, Charles, 175n64
Brown, Gordon, 59
Brownback, Sam, 18
Browning, Don, 5n8, 93n21
Brzezinski, Matthew, 210n3, 213n16
Buber, Martin, 89
Bulliet, Richard, 90
Bunn, Matthew, 218, 225, 240, 241n101
Burkholder, Richard, 135n133
Burns, R. Nicholas, 81
Bush, George W., xv, 16, 21, 26, 49, 70, 85,
    88, 136, 164, 178–79, 226, 231

Calvin, John, 108, 112
Campbell, Kurt M., 3n4
Carothers, Thomas, 42, 45, 48n28
Carter, Ashton, 218, 234n82, 238n89, 242
Castellio, Sebastian, 112–13
Catholics, xix, 90, 91, 105–7, 111–13, 121,
    162–63, 177, 186, 196; and Eastern
    Orthodox, 84, 163; and education, 174,
    186, 188; and human rights, 199; and
    moral culture, 163; and Protestants,
    104, 107–8, 112–13, 196; and relations
    with Civil Rights Movement, 113, 128;
    and relations with Hinduism, 120–23;
    and relations with Islam, 88, 134, 137,
    148, 150, 166, 173, 188; for persuasion
    in Christianity, see Preachers; for coer-
    cion in Christianity, see Warriors
Cavanaugh, William, 96
Center for International Private Enter-
    prise, 169
Cerniello, Craig, 224n46
Chalabi, Ahmad, 25
Chatterjee, Margaret, 125n103
Chavez, Hugo, 47, 233

Chayes, Sarah, 20n47
Cheney, Dick, 16
Chiarelli, Peter, 61
China, xiii–xiv, 64, 95; antisocial behavior in, 154–55; and deproliferation, 19, 231–32, 236, 241, 243, 245; moral culture in, 163, 185
Christian Positive Violence School, 180
Christianity, 103–14
Chrysostom, John, Saint, 109n55, 110
Cirincione, Joseph, 230n64
Civil Rights Movement, 113, 127–30, 183; for coercion in Civil Rights Movement, see Warriors; for persuasion in Civil Rights Movement, see Preachers
Clark, Ian, 5n8
Clinton, Bill, 31, 88
Cloud, David S., 61n57
Clover, Charles, 174n57, 175n61
Coalition Provisional Authority, 20, 167, 168
Cochrane, Joe, 147n183
coercion (coercers), 94, 95, 98
coercive (forced) regime change or democratization, 2, 3, 31, 42, 44; and minimal use of coercion by good regimes, 98, 99–101; and psychological and economic pressures, 101–2; and religious fundamentalism, 86, 90–91, 93; and secular fundamentalism, 96–97; for coercion in different belief systems, see Warriors. See also persuasion
Cohen, Roger, 49n33
Cohler-Esses, Larry, 188n109
Cole, Juan, 167
Cole, Ronald H., 201n30
Coles, Katherine M., 161n34
communitarianism, 64, 199–200, 204
Conetta, Carl, 62
Connell, Rich, 7n11
controlled maintenance, def. 235; 235–39; cf. deproliferation. See also weapons of mass destruction
Cook, David, 139n149
Cooper, Helene, xv n.3
Cooperman, Alan, 150n194
Crocker, Bathsheba, 21n48, 62–63
Crocker, Chester A., 9n14
Crocker, Jarle, 96n26

Crusades, 93, 96, 104, 106
Cummings, Jeanne, 165n39

D'Agostino, J., 63n65
Dahl, Robert A., 42
Dalits, 123
Dalton, Dennis, 125n106
Daniel, Douglas K., 16n38
Dawisha, Adeed, 42
Dawisha, Karen, 42
de Jouvenel, Bertrand, 194–95
de Las Casa, Bartolome, 113
democratic peace theory, 19. See also democratization
democratization, xiii–xvi, xxii, 1–3, 37–39, 42–58, 61, 76, 80; as driving security, or security-driven, xiii, xvi, 2, 7, 10, 22, 25, 32, 158, 247; and elections, 50–54, 56–58; and faux democracies, 46–50; in Iraq, 20–23; as leitmotif of U.S. foreign policy, xiv, 1, 11, 35, 46; and noncoercive (nonlethal) forms, 10, 12, 34–36, 55–58, 158, 169–72; in Russia, xxi, 16–19, 223–24. See also nation-building
Dempsey, Judy, 155n20
Deng, Francis M., 194–96, 198, 201, 204
Dennis, Norman, 201n31
deproliferation, def. 238; 8–14, 205, 234–46; in India, 205–6, 233–34, 236, 239, 241; in Iran, 11–14, 206, 230, 235–45 passim; in Libya, 8–11, 245; in North Korea, 11–14, 205, 239, 241–42; in Serbia, 226, 234; cf. controlled maintenance. See also Global Threat Reduction Initiative; Nunn-Lugar programs; Proliferation Security Initiative; weapons of mass destruction
Derfner, Larry, 120n85
development, economic. See economic development
development, political. See political development
development, social. See social development
Diamond, Larry, 20n47, 26n59, 42, 48n29
Dignitatis Humanae, 113
Diversity Within Unity (DWU), 174, 186–87, 189–91. See also education

Djindjic, Zoran, 79
Dobson, James, 97n28
Domenici, Pete, 240
Donaldson, James, 110n57
Donnelly, Thomas, 221n41, 229–30
Dreazen, Yochi J., 26n57
dual-use nuclear assets, *def.* 237; 237–39
Dunne, Michele, 10n16
duty to prevent, *def.* 204; 204–7; *cf.*
    responsibility to protect

East Timor, 199, 202, 245
Easterly, William, 68n84
economic development, 39, 41, 53, 58, 61–
    67, 76, 84
education, 57, 78, 157, 168, 175–82; and
    "character education," *def.* 174; 182–83,
    191; public, 174, 183–84, 223; religious,
    142, 168–69, 173–74, 180–92. *See also*
    Diversity Within Unity; madrasas
Einhorn, Robert J., 175n61
Eisenhower, Dwight, 231
Eisenhower, Susan, 213n70
Eizenstat, Stuart, 63
ElBaradei, Mohamed, 222n42, 234–35
El-Fadl, Kahled Abou, 90
Ellingwood, Ken, 120n86
Embree, Ainslee, 120n88
Engels, Friedrich, 131–32
Erasmus, 112
Ervin, Clark Kent, 211n5, 212n14
Esbeck, Carl H., 178n82
Esposito, John, 90
Establishment Clause, 163, 173–77. *See
    also* First Amendment
ethnic cleansing. *See* genocide and ethnic
    cleansing
Etzioni, Amitai, 2n2, 7n10, 8n12, 15n32,
    67n80, 99n31, 101n34, 158n29, 171n54,
    174n56, 200n27, 239n91
Evans, Gareth, 197–98, 205

failing states, xvi, xxi, 2, 6, 14–19, 36, 47,
    63–64, 152–62 passim, 202, 221–38
    passim
Fairclough, Gordon, 239n94
Fallaci, Oriana, 90
Fanon, Frantz, 102, 132
Faramarzi, Scheherezade, 149n191

Farmer, James, 127
Fatah, 55, 57, 141
Fathi, Nazila, 13n27
Feinstein, Lee, 198n19, 204
Feldman, Noah, 65, 170
Fella, George, 75n102
Ferguson, Charles D., 218, 238n89
Filipov, David, 16n34
Finer, Jonathon, 156n23, 182n95
Fingarette, Herbert, 199n22
Firestone, Reuven, 139n148
First Amendment, 163, 174–80. *See also*
    Establishment Clause
Fischer, John Martin, 199n22
Fleischer, Ari, 38
Fletcher, Michael, 178n81
Flynn, Stephen, 211n5
Foley, James B., 224n46
Foster, William Z., 131
Foucher de Chartres, 106n44
Fox, George, 113
Fox, Jonathan, 94n24
Friedmann, Yohanan, 137nn144–45,
    138n147
Friell, Gerard, 105n43
Fukuyama, Francis, xv, 38–39, 52, 219n39

Gall, Carlotta, 26n58, 28n64, 29n70
Galston, William, 91n18
Gandhi, Mohandas, 95, 121–26
Gannon, Kathy, 20n47
Gard, Robert, 218, 224n45
Garwin, Richard L., 218n31
Gates, Daryl, 7
Gause, F. Gregory, III, 45, 52, 66,
    142n166
Gelb, Leslie, 29n65, 78n104
Gellner, Ernest, 94
genocide and ethnic cleansing, xx, xxii, 3,
    6–7, 31–33, 113, 196–97, 201–4, 247.
    See also responsibility to protect
Gentili, Alberico, 195
Gerges, Fawaz, 215n25
Germany, 34, 55, 77, 247; and Weimar
    Republic, 8, 53–54, 220; and postwar
    West Germany, 19, 30, 44–46, 64; and
    postwar East Germany, 144; and reform
    of the U.N., 207
Ghosh, Tapan, 121n90

Gilgoff, Dan, 165n41
Glanz, James, 24n53, 155n17, 156n22
Glaser, Alexander, 232n74
Glendon, Mary Ann, 199n24
Glenn, David, 239n90
global public opinion. *See* public opinion
Global Threat Reduction Initiative (GTRI), 240, 242
Godse, Nathuram, 121–22, 126
Goldschmidt, Pierre, 237n86
Goldstein, Baruch, 119n84
Golwalkar, Madhav Sadashiv, 122
Gorbachev, Mikhail, 8, 54
Goulet, Denis, 67n82
Greenawalt, Kent, 178n82
Gross, Leo, 194n1
Grossman, Marc, 63, 80
Grotius, Hugo, 95, 195
Guerricagoitia, Carmen M., 178n82
Guevara, Che, 102
Gvosdev, Nikolas K., 200n29

Habib, Mona, 185
Hadar, Leon, 136n140
Hagal, Joseph R., 177n76
Hamas, 50, 51, 55, 87, 93, 141
Hanford, John V., III, 16
Haqqani, Husain, 181n93
hard power, 98, 243–45; *cf*. soft power. *See also* smart power
Harris, Grant, 69
Harrison, Lawrence E., 158n30
Harrison, Selig, 12, 296
Hartlyn, Jonathan, 48n29
Hawley, John S., 120n88, 127, 295
Haynes, Charles, 175
Hegland, Corine, 168n45
Hein, S. Mark, 146n180
Hezbollah, 50, 136
Hi-Devolution, *def*. 78; 78–79; in Iraq, 28–29, 78nn103–4; in Kosovo, 79–89
Hill, Steven, 141n163
Hinderstein, Corey, 230n65
Hinduism, 120–27; and relations with Islam, 120–24, 126–27, 180–81; for persuasion in Hinduism, *see* Preachers; for coercion in Hinduism, *see* Warriors
Hindutva, 122
Hinsley, F. H., 194n1

Hinson, E. Glenn, 104n37
Hochman, Dafna, 9n14
Holbrooke, Richard, 165n40
Holdren, John P., 218n33
Holgate, Laura, 227nn56–58, 295
Hopfl, Harro, 108n52
Hornus, Jean-Michel, 109
Howe, Kevin, 234n80
Hoyos, Carola, 240n95
Hsu, Spencer S., 214n21
Hulsman, John, xvii n.8
Human Development Index (HDI), 226
human rights, 5, 67, 110, 199–204; in Afghanistan, 26, 170; and Illiberal Moderates, 86, 89, 90, 135; and Islam, 135–36, 143–44, 158, 167, 170–72; in Libya, 9–11; in North Korea, 12; and Palestinians, 117; and premodern belief systems, 199; in Russia, 16–18; and U.S. promotion of, xix, 16, 33. *See also* U.N. Universal Declaration of Human Rights
human security, 1n1; *cf*. basic security. *See also* Security First
humanitarian interventions, xvii n.5, 31–35, 69, 202, 205; in Bosnia, 197; and criteria for, xx, 31–35, 195–97, 203; in East Timor, 202; in Haiti, 34, 198, 245; in Kosovo, 32, 79–84, 202; in Rwanda, xiv, 32, 197, 199
Hunt, Terrence, 16n37
Hunter, James Davidson, 119
Huntington, Samuel, xix, 88, 90, 96, 135
Hussein, Fuad, 182
Hussein, Saddam, 5, 14, 20, 23, 25–26, 29, 56, 59, 62, 65, 73, 156, 181–82, 184, 191, 196, 220

Ibn Ashur, Muhammad al-Tahir, 138n147
Ibn Taymiya, 137
Ignatieff, Michael, 82n112, 83
Illiberal Moderates, *def*. xiv, 86–87; estimates of, 92, 143; as global swing-vote, xxii, 86, 145; importance, 85–103; among Muslims, 140–51; and women, 57, 91, 117, 141–43, 145
India, 77, 121–27, 180–81; and deproliferation, 205–6, 233–34, 236, 239, 241
Indonesia, 14, 89, 141–42, 144–45, 149–50, 202, 207, 239

informal social controls, 96, 157, 158, 160, 162, 200
International Atomic Energy Agency (IAEA), 206, 225, 233–34, 236–37, 241, 243
International Center for the Dialogue of Civilizations, 91
International Commission on Intervention and State Sovereignty (ICISS), 197, 202, 205
International Crisis Group, 82, 205
International Republican Institute, 35, 169
Iran: and democratization, 52, 91, 144, 163–64; and deproliferation, 11–14, 205–6, 230, 235–45 passim; and Iraq, 27, 29, 182; and North Korea, 8–10, 29, 205, 220, 241–42; and regime change, xiii, xvi, 11; theocracy in, 56, 99, 136, 171
Iraq, 2–3, 15, 19, 45–46, 215; 2003 invasion of, 5, 38–39, 46, 196, 198, 205, 220–21, 244, 247; antisocial behavior in, 152, 155–57, 161; constitution of, 20, 26–27, 170–72; and democratization, 19–24, 42, 50–51; education in, 174–75, 181–82, 184–86, 190; as a failing state, 29; and Hi-Devolution, 30–31, 77–79; and reconstruction, 59–60, 62–66, 70–74; and social engineering, 27–28, 41, 59; and tribal roles, 30, 56, 77. See also Coalition Provisional Authority
Irgun, 22–23
Islam, 91–92, 103, 134–51, 162–69, 172, 199, 230; and clash of civilizations, xix, xxii, 87–90, 134–36; and democracy, 21, 27, 38, 52, 144, 162–63, 170–72; and education, 173–76, 180–81, 185–89, 191; and relations with Christianity, 88, 134, 137, 148, 150, 166, 173, 188; and relations with Hinduism, 120–24, 126–27, 180–81; and Shias, 20, 25, 27–28, 30, 56, 77–78, 139, 163, 167, 184, 186; and Sufis, 139, 150; and Sunnis, 20, 25, 27, 30–31, 77–78, 137, 139, 156, 185–86; for persuasion in Islam, see Preachers; for coercion in Islam, see Warriors. See also Islamism
Islamism (Islamists), xix, 14, 18, 27–28, 35, 88, 92, 135, 146–47, 152, 172, 228; and participation in elections, 50–52,

54–57, 149–50. See also Hamas; Hezbollah
Israel, 4, 56, 93, 114–15, 117, 120, 141, 185, 216, 239; and 1948 war of independence, 22–23, 116; and deproliferation, 206, 236, 241
Iyer, Raghavan, 125n104

Jabber, Abdul Settar, 186
Jewish Defense League, 119
jihad (jihadism, jihadists), 55, 87, 134–35, 137–39; and polls, 135
Jones, Ann, 20n47, 155n18
Jones, James, 155
Jordan, Jessica, 174
Jordens, J. T. F., 124n102
Joseph, Edward, 79n106
Judaism, 103–4, 114–20, 199; and Orthodox Jews, 91, 117, 120; and Reform Jews, 116–18; for persuasion in Judaism, see Preachers; for coercion in Judaism, see Warriors
Juergensmeyer, Mark, 125n105
just war, 70, 95, 202

Kahane, Meir, 119–20, 180
Kahn, Herman, 219
Kahn, Ismael, 20, 25
Kamons, Andrew, 20n47, 73n98
Kant, Immanuel, 19n45, 162
Kaplan, David, 168n48, 176n69
Kaplan, Fred, 239n92
Kapur, Anuradha, 124n100
karsevaks, 123
Karzai, Hamid, 20, 24, 26, 91, 157–58
Kasher, Menachem, 115n69
Kasper, Sara, 44
Kautsky, Karl, 132–34
Kavey, Michael, 178n82
Kay, David, 29n67
Kelling, George L., 161n34
Kelly, Erin, 67n81
Kelly, Michael, 39n10
Kennedy, John F., xiv, 40
Kennedy, Miranda, 181n91
Kenney, Jeff, 61
Kent, Jonathan, 147n183
Kerry, John, xv, 66
Kessler, Glen, 12n25

Khalilzad, Zalmay, 26–27, 62
Khan, A. Q., 9, 11
Khan, Mohammad, 167
Khan, Muqtedar, 90, 229–31, 237
Kimaro, Sadikiel, 194n2
King, Charles, 48
King, Iain, 79n106
King, Martin Luther, Jr., 103, 113, 127–29
King, Rodney, 7
Klein, N., 66n74
Knickmeyer, E., 73n99
Kohut, Andrew, 29n69
Kokoshin, Andrei, 218n31
Kook, Abraham Isaac, 118
Kook, Tzvi Yehuda, 118
Kosovo-Metohija, 32, 41, 77–84, 202, 245;
    and Kosovo Liberation Army, 80; and
    social engineering, 41; and United
    Nations, 80–84
Krasner, Stephen 63, 196
Krauthammer, Charles, xviii, 54
Krueger, Alan, 66
Kuchibhotla, Kishore, 160n31
Kuhonta, E., 65n69
Kupchan, Charles, 79n108
Kurds (Kurdistan), 20, 27–28, 30, 77–78
Kuwait, 50, 56, 150; and 1990–91 war, x, 5,
    196

Lactantius, 110
LaFranchi, Howard, 157n26
Lakin, Jason M., 42n17
Lamont v. Schultz, 176
Lamont v. Woods, 177
Larsen, Randall, 217n29
Latham, Ronald, 146n179
Latif, Aamar, 168n48
Laval, Pierre, xix
Lawson, James, 127–28
Lebed, Alexander, 224
LeBor, Adam, 197n14
Lenin, Vladimir Il'ich, 131–32
Leonard, Mark, 26n59
Levey, Stuart, 215n24
Levin, Carl, 240
Lewis, Alan, 100n33, 160
Lewis, Bernard, xix, 90, 135, 165
liberalism (liberals), xiv, xvii, 2–3, 21,
    40, 89–90; and anti-religious bias, 93–

95; cf. neo-conservatism; cf.
    communitarianism
Libya, 136, 230, 237, 245; as deprolifera-
    tion model, 9–11, 13; human rights
    abuses in, 9–10
Lickona, Thomas, 183n96
Lieven, Anatol, xvii n.8, 20n47
Lind, Michael, 4n7
Linz, Juan J., 48n29
Lipset, Seymour Martin, 42
Lipton, Eric, 212nn11–13, 214n20
Lorenzen, David, 120n88
Lowenkron, Barry F., 17
Lucas, J. R., 199n22
Lugar, Richard, 221, 240–41
Lustick, Ian, 118n76
Luther, Martin, 107
Luxemburg, Rosa, 131
Lyons, Terrence, 194n2

MacKinnon, Catherine, 195n9
madrasas, 168, 180–81, 185–91 passim.
    See also education
Madsen, Richard, 154n11
Maerli, Morten Bremer, 225n49, 226n53
Mahoney, Daniel J., xv
Malaysia, 89, 146–47, 149, 200; educa-
    tion in, 187
Malcolm, Noel, 79n106
Malcolm X, 93, 102, 127, 180
Maleckova, Jitka, 66
Mali, 19, 141, 147–48
Manji, Irshad, 90
Mansfield, Edward D., 19n46
Maritain, Jacques, 194–95
Martin, Nancy, 199n24
Mason, Whit, 79n106
Matic, Vladimir, 79n107
McCord, Joan, 98n30
McVeigh, Timothy, 217
Meehan, Shannon, 175
Megatons to Megawatts, 234–35
Meier, Golda, 22
Method, Frank, 175
Meyer, Michael, 116n73
Milbank, Dana, 29n68, 37n1, 38n5
Miller, Judith, 11n19, 135, 240n95
Miller, Marvin, 223n44
Miller, Roland, 126n107

Mooney, Paul, 154n10
moral and muscular. *See* principled and pragmatic
moral culture, xvii–xix, 152–53, 157–61; fostering of, 153, 162–72; religious source of, 163. *See also* informal social controls
Morin, Monte, 156n21
Mormons, 86, 91
Morocco, 50, 89, 141, 149, 168
Morris, Benny, 239n92
Moynihan, Daniel Patrick, 47
Multiple Realism Deficiency Disorder (MRDD), xviii–xix, xxi, 215
Muravchik, Joshua, 38
Murphy, Caryle, 139n151
Murray, John Courtney, 90n14
Muslim Brotherhood, 50, 56, 136, 137
Mutterperl, Laura, 178n82
Myers, Steven Lee, 16n35

Nagy, Sasha, 217n27
Nandy, Ashis, 122n91, 123n95, 124n99
Narayanan, Vasudha, 121n89
Nasr, Seyyed Hossein, 139
Nation of Islam, 127, 187
nation-building, xxi, 15, 22–23, 31, 44–46, 76–84, 205. *See also* democratization
National Democratic Institute for International Affairs, 35, 169
National Endowment for Democracy, 35, 169
Natsios, Andrew S., 38, 60, 71
Nau, Henry R., xix n.11
"Nb weapons," 220
neo-communitarianism. *See* communitarianism
neo-conservatism (neo-conservatives), xviii; and democratization, xiv, 10, 21, 37–38, 46, 90; and social engineering, 2–3, 40–41; *cf.* liberalism; *cf.* communitarianism
Neuhaus, Richard John, 98n30
Newhouse, John, 34n72
Newton, Huey P., 127
Nigeria, 47, 142, 147–48; and deproliferation, 19, 231–32
Nolin, Pierre Claude, 16n34
non-governmental organizations (NGOs), xxi, 5, 17, 21, 147

non-state actors, *def.* 14, 14–15, 213, 222, 237
non-violence. *See* persuasion
North, Don, 168
North Korea, 29, 220; and deproliferation, 11–14, 205, 239, 241–42; and regime change, xiii, xvi
Nuclear Non-proliferation Treaty (NPT), 235–40, 242–45
Nunn-Lugar programs, 18, 226–29, 240
Nutall, Geoffrey, 111
Nye, Joseph S., Jr., xx n.13, 33n71, 244

O'Hanlon, Michael E., 3n4, 20n47, 73n98
Orttung, Robert, 228
Osterholm, Michael T., 216n26
Ottaway, Marina, 20n47, 45n21
Owen, John M., IV, xxi n.14

Packenham, Robert A., 45n22
Packer, George, 20n47, 45n19, 46n23
Palmach, 22–23
Pakistan, xx, 126, 141–45, 168, 181, 206, 234, 239; as a failing state, 18–19, 48, 221, 229–31
Paris, Roland, 1n1
Parrish, Scott, 225n52
Pascual, C., 60, 63
Pasztor, Andy, 212n10
Paul, Saint, 103n36
Pei, Minxin, 44
Perkovich, George, 218
persuasion, 86–95 passim, 103, 106, 109, 111, 114–16, 121, 125, 127–32, 134, 137; and Martin Buber, 89; and maximal use by good regimes, 98–102; *cf.* coercion. *See also* Preachers
peshmerga, 28
Peters, Edward, 111
Phillips, David, 20n47, 23n49, 27n60, 28n62
Phillips, Kevin, 46n25
Philpott, Dan, 194n3, 195n8
Pincus, Walter, 29n68, 206n43
Pipes, Daniel, 135
Pipes, Richard, 157n24
Plattner, Marc F., 42
plutonium, 19, 224–26, 229, 234–35, 242–43. *See also* uranium

political development, 19, 25, 30, 43, 52–53, 76, 79, 82, 84, 181, 247. *See also* democratization; nation-building

Politkovskaya, Anna, 153n3

polls (polling), 140–46; on church-state relations, 142–43; on democracy, 144–45, 157; on jihad, 135; on support for violence, 141, 143; on United States civil liberties, 7

Poneman, Daniel B., 12n26

Porter, Gareth, 12n25

Potter, William C., 218

Powell, Colin, 66, 233

Power, Samantha, 197n14

Powers, Gerard F., 65

Preachers, *def.* 86; 88–89, 92–93, 96–99; in Christianity, 103, 107, 108–14; in Civil Rights Movement, 128–30; in Hinduism, 124–27; in Islam, 137–40; in Judaism, 114–15, 115–18; in socialism, 132–34; *cf.* Warriors. *See also* persuasion

Primacy of Life, xvi, 1–2, 31–36 passim, 180, 193, 201–5 passim

principled and pragmatic, xiii, xvii, xx–xxi, 1, 5–6, 33–34, 36; *cf.* idealism and realism, xix, 4–5, 33, 193

Prohibition, 159

Proliferation Security Initiative (PSI), 245–48

public opinion, 4–5; in the Middle East, 140–51; and opinion-makers, 166–68; in Russia, 157. *See also* polls

Putin, Vladimir, 8, 16–18, 157, 226–27, 246

Qaddafi, Muammar, 9–11

Qatar, 150

Rabin, Yitzhak, 120

Raines, Howell, 129n20

Rajkumar, Miriam, 230n64

Rajneeshee, 217–18

Ram Rajya, 125

Ramadan, Tariq, 189

Raychaudhuri, Tapan, 122n94

realism deficiency. *See* Multiple Realism Deficiency Disorder

reconstruction, *def.* 61–62, 64; 38, 41, 58–

76, 83; and legal obligation, 68–70; and moral/ethical obligation, 65–68; and postwar Germany and Japan, 45–46;

regime change, xxi, 7–8, 13, 15, 18, 29, 37, 41, 84, 146, 219, 233, 242; and coerced (forced), 2, 3, 31, 42, 44; and Iran and North Korea, xiii, xvi, 11. *See also* democratization

Reich, Rebecca, 154n8

Rentner, Diane Starke, 183n97

responsibility to protect, *def.* 198; 193–99; as communitarian principle, 199–204. *See also* duty to prevent

Reynolds, Maura, 155n14

Rice, Condoleezza, 10, 16

Richards, Alan, 180n90

Ricks, Thomas, 20n47

Rida, Rashid, 139

Robbins, Carla Anne, 165n39, 245n111

Roberts, Alexander, 110n57

Robinson, Tamara, 225n52

rogue states, xiii, xvi, 2, 6, 9–11, 36, 85, 204, 219–23, 231, 238, 241–42, 246

Rohde, David, 24n53, 155n16, 158n28, 197n14

Rohter, Larry, 239n93

Romain, Jonathon, 188

Rothchild, Donald, 194n2

Roy, J. Stapleton, 155n13

Rubenstein, Richard E., 96n26

Runzo, Joseph, 199n24

Russet, Bruce, 19n45

Russia/U.S.S.R., 15nn33–34, 54, 131, 161, 223–26, 228, 240–41; antisocial behavior in, xvii, 15, 98, 153–54, 156, 182; and closed cities, 223, 227–28; and democratization, 15–19, 16n35, 46; as a failing state, xvi, 2, 8, 48, 152, 232; public opinion in, 157

Rutenberg, Jim, xv n.3

Rwanda, 196

Sachs, Jeffrey, 39

Sachs, Susan, 188n108

Sagan, Scott D., 3n6, 8n13, 239n92

Sahnoun, Mohamed, 197

Said, Edward, 90

Samin, Nadav, 52n40

Sand, Leonard B., 176
Sandler, Shmuel, 94n24
Sanger, David E., xv n.2, 245n115
Santos, David, 176
Satyagraha, 125
Sauve, Susan, 199n22
Savarkar, Vinayak, 122
Schaff, Philip, 104nn38–39, 105nn40–42, 110n59
Schmitt, Eric, 23n50
Schwartz, John, 216n26
Seabrook, Jeremy, 150n195
Sebti, Bassam, 60n50
Security First, xiv, xvi, xxi, 1–2, 6, 10, 12, 15, 92, 146; and basic security, 29–30; and democratization, 21, 34–35, 37, 39; and Hi-Devolution, 31, 79; and humanitarian intervention, 31, 193; and moral criterion, 32; and nuclear terrorism, 234; and practicality, 33, 53; and reconstruction, 59, 61
Sen, Amartya, 199n24
Serbia/Yugoslavia, 34, 77–84 passim; and deproliferation, 226, 234. *See also* Kosovo-Metohija
Serchuk, Vance, 24n52
Serrano, Richard A., 7n11
Servetus, Michael, 108, 112
Shadid, Anthony, 88n4
Shafi'i, Imam, 137
Shahrani, Nematollah, 91–92
shariah, 30, 47, 135, 146–48, 155, 162–63, 163n35, 172; and apostasy from Islam, 134, 137
Sharma, Arvind, 199n24
Shelley, Louis, 228
Shevtsova, Lilia, 48n32
Shinwari, Faisal Ahmad, 26, 172
Shrader, Katherine, 215n22
shura, 171
Singer, Peter, 67
Slackman, Michael, 150n197
Slaughter, Anne-Marie, 204
smart power, 293n109
Smith, Christopher H., 18
Smith, Craig S., 72n95, 155n14
Smith, Patrick, 14n30, 295
Snyder, Jack, 19n46
social development, 43, 79, 82, 84, 161,

167, 169, 170, 183. *See also* social engineering
social engineering, xxi, 3, 27, 39–42, 76–79, 153, 158, 208; in Iraq, 59–63, 71–76; in Kosovo, 79–84; and neoconservatism, 40–41; in postwar Germany and Japan, 45–46
socialism, 130–34; for persuasion in socialism, *see* Preachers; for coercion in socialism, *see* Warriors
soft power, xx, 33, 244–46, 248; *cf.* hard power. *See also* smart power
Solomon, Jay, 11n22
Somalia, 2006 intervention in, 14, 32, 198, 245
Sorel, Georges, 131
sovereignty, xx, 163; and humanitarian intervention, 69, 193–201; as responsibility, *def.* 194; 194–200, 204, 207. *See also* responsibility to protect
Sprinzak, Ehud, 119nn78–84
Srebrenica, 3, 197
Stalin, Joseph, xix, 91, 96–97, 132
Starr, Alexandra, 165n41
Stern, Jessica, 180n90
Stern, Paul C., 161n33
Stokes, Bruce, 29n69
Strategic Arms Reduction Treaty (START), 224
Student Nonviolent Coordinating Committee (SNCC), 127–28
Suarez, Francisco, 195
Sukarnoputri, Megawati, 164
Sullivan, Louis, 155n13
Sutherland, J. J., 92n19
Syria, 35, 144, 150–51

Taheri, Amir, 11n23
Takeyh, Ray, 9n14
Taliban, 25, 28–29, 92, 155
Tamimi, Azzam, 135
Tannenbaum, Benn, 232nn71–72, 295
Tanner, Michael, 177n74
Tantawi, Mohammed Sayed, 139
Tavernise, Sabrina, 24n51, 28n63
Taylor, John B., 62
Telhami, Shibley, 50n36
Terrorism Information and Prevention System (TIPS), 214

Tertullian, 109–10
Thatcher, Margaret, 201n30
Theodosius, 104, 105, 108, 110
Thornton, Charles, 224n47
Tito, Marshal, 77
Tolson, Jay, 188, 165nn39–41, 188n110
Tomero, Leonor, 233n78
Total Informational Awareness Program
    (TIA), 214
triage: *def.* 75; and reconstruction, 71–76;
    and terrorism, 208–9, 215–16, 220,
    242–43
Trofimov, Yaroslav, 147
Trotsky, Leon, 132
Tucker, Jonathan B., 218n31
Tunisia, 149, 182

U.N. High-Level Panel on Threats, Chal-
    lenges, and Change, 197–98
U.N. Mission in Kosovo (UNMIK),
    81–82
U.N. Universal Declaration of Human
    Rights (UDHR), 26, 90, 162, 170, 198,
    199
United Kingdom, 54, 79, 238; education
    in, 187–88
United Nations, 9, 14, 20, 31, 193, 201,
    237, 244–48; and legitimacy, 9, 196,
    207, 244; and genocide and ethnic
    cleansing, 31, 34; and Kosovo, 80–84;
    reform of, 198, 207
United States v. Verdugo-Urquidez, 176
uranium, 9, 18–19, 223–25, 229, 232–33,
    242, 244. *See also* plutonium
U.S. Agency for International Develop-
    ment (USAID), 35, 38, 60, 71, 80, 174–
    77, 175n64, 187
U.S. Department of Homeland Security,
    211, 214
U.S. State Department Bureau for Inter-
    national Narcotics and Law Enforce-
    ment Affairs (INL), 24

Valencia, Mark, 245n113
Valenzuela, Arturo, 48n29
van Dassen, Lars, 225n49, 226n53
van der Veer, Peter, 123n95
violence. *See* antisocial behavior; coercion
Vishwa Hindu Parishad (VHP), 123

Voegelin, Eric, 107n50
Voll, John O., 90n12, 144n175
von Hippel, Frank, 232n74
von Hippel, Karin, 46n24

Wahid, Abdurrahman, 150
Waisman, Carlos H., 48n29
Wald, Matthew L., 240n95
Waldman, Peter, 135n136
Walker, David M., 59n49, 73n97, 74
Waltz, Kenneth, 8n13
Warren, Samuel, 200n28
Warriors, *def.* 86; 92–97 passim, 189; in
    Christianity, 104–7, 108; in Civil Rights
    Movement, 127–28; in Hinduism, 121–
    24; in Judaism, 114, 115, 118–20; in
    socialism, 130–31; *cf.* Preachers. *See also*
    coercion
Watkins, Kevin, 15n33, 226n55
weapons of mass destruction (WMDs),
    215, 216–20; and deterrence, 239–41;
    and duty to prevent, 204–7; in Iraq,
    29n67; in Libya, 9, 10–11; in rogue
    states, 220–22; and triage, 216, 220,
    222–23. *See also* controlled mainte-
    nance; deproliferation; Global Threat
    Reduction Initiative; "Nb weapons";
    Nunn-Lugar programs; Proliferation
    Security Initiative
Weart, Spencer R., 19n45
Webb, Greg, 19n44, 232n73
Weisman, Jonathan, 211n4
Weisman, Steven R., 13n28, 229n62,
    233n76
Wendt, Alexander, 198n21
Westphalia, Treaty of, 107, 194, 196,
    200
Weymouth, Lally, 237n85
Whitelaw, Kevin, 168n48
Whitlock, Jeremy, 232n75
Wier, Anthony, 218n33, 225n51, 227, 240,
    240n97, 241n101
Williams, Daniel, 10n16
Williams, Robert, 127
Williams, Steven, 105n43
Wilson, James Q., 48
Wilson, Woodrow, xiv
Wineke, Bill, 65
Wit, Joel S., 12n26

Woehrel, Steve, 79n106
Wolfowitz, Paul, 37, 38
Wolfsthal, Jon, 230n64
women: in Afghanistan, 21, 26, 155; dress of, 28, 31, 147, 149, 150, 167; Illiberal Moderates and, 57, 91, 117, 141–43, 145; in Iraq, 156–57; and political participation, 26, 57, 144, 149, 157
Wong, Edward, 27n61, 79n105
Woods, Alan, 176
Woodward, Bob, 66
Woolf, Amy, 166n42
Wright, Robert, xvii n.8

Wrightson, Margaret T., 210n2
Wrong, Dennis, 98n29

Yeltsin, Boris, 8, 54, 154, 224
Yew, Lee Kuan, 65, 200

Zagorin, Perez, 112n64
Zakaria, Fareed, 3n5, 47n27
Zambelis, Chris, 50
Zartman, I. William, 194n2
Zehr, Mary Ann, 175n62, 180n88, 185n99
Zoepf, Katherine, 151n198
Zoubir, Yahia H., 9n14